"Janis Kent has done it again! The WorksTutorial - A hop, skip, and jump into VectorWorks provides users with a concise, easy to follow, quick start introduction into the MiniCAD VectorWorks environment. An invaluable resource for both professional users and classroom environment."

Richard Diehl
President & CEO of Diehl Graphsoft Inc.

"Your books have been superior support! Actually they have taught me the program, given me guidance and even kept me company. THANK YOU SO MUCH!!"

G. Dombek
Pro Design Graphics
Phoenix, AZ

"Just wanted to comment on the high quality of the MiniTutorial. I was able to read it from cover to cover in one session. The book answered all of my basic technique questions and allowed me to see the 'big picture' of how one sets up an efficient drawing. Many thanks for letting me look at Mini-CAD from your level of expertise."

C. Tietjen
Island Builders
Guilford, CT

"This is to CONGRATULATE you on the excellent work you have compiled. I believe the MiniManual, not so mini with so many pages and such an amount of information, put forward in a friendly understandable language, is a very important milestone in the evolution of MiniCAD. Your manual is the second most important thing to have at hand after the application itself!"

S.M. Jonsson
Interior Designer
Seltjarnarnes, Iceland

"I'm very pleased with your product. It certainly has given me a good grasp of the potentials of the system, and has introduced me to many tools and shortcuts that I would never have found on my own."

R. Struzyna Architects
Philadelphia, PA

"...extremely well written and provides the novice MiniCAD user a wealth of information not easily found. Thanks again for the wonderful book. It has truly made a difference in my understanding of and ability to use MiniCAD."

R. Petersen, AIA
Sacramento, CA

"Your book is great! Thank you...nice format, easy to read."

C. Whitaker
Cambridge, MA

"I have learned a lot from the MiniManual and the MiniTutorial. I was up and running in a short period of time and still continue to learn valuable information from them."

K. Morgan
Barrett & Corner Architects
Ardmore, OK

"I want to tell you just how much value your tutorial was to me. I really feel like a single black diamond pro and am looking forward to mastering the more advanced features."

B. Brown
Reno, NV

"Already these books have proven to be indispensable resources for novices like myself."

D. Catchpaugh
Automated Systems Inc
Bromont, QU Canada

"They are great! Thanks for making the effort to prepare such an intelligent tutorial and manual."

H. Grody
Pegasus Design Group
Evergreen, CO

"They are marvelous. I can SEE them, they ANSWER questions, I can FOLLOW them. Just great!"

J. Roth, Architect
New York, NY

"Your manuals are so much easier to use I've become addicted."

E. Quenneville Architect
Tampa, FL

"Your MiniTutorial was such a great help for me when I first began trying to use MiniCAD. It was logical, intuitive, and well arranged."

J. Russell
Jackson, MI

"...your book is outstanding, and you do wonders for MiniCAD users."

G. Woodzell
Schenectady, NY

"As soon as I received the MiniTutorial, I realized that it is exactly what is needed to introduce the neophyte to MiniCAD. I learned a lot from it myself! Besides, it look great, it is very well organized, and the cover is stunning."

E. Mahfuz Arquitetos
Porto Alegre, Brazil

"Your book is a masterpiece of forethought and organization. What a pleasure to look at such a well constructed document ."

L. Case
A Dull Type
Concord, MA

"Great Book!"

B. D. Judd, FAIA
Architectural Resources Group
San Francisco, CA

"How would you like to have a resident MiniCAD consultant right in your own office? There is a way. Janis Kent's new book the MiniManual...is a marvelous collection of well organized information about using all of MiniCAD's features. It is presented in a way to save you hours of groping and searching for the way to do things."

J. Bruce
Santa Ana, CA

"...I am thoroughly impressed! You did an absolutely super job. Your prior manual was great, but this one is a quantum leap ahead. I hope that others like me appreciate the amount of time that you must have spent updating your manual...keep up the good work. What you do is going to make my job not only easier to do, but certainly more enjoyable."

J. Gasho
ETC GraphX
Reno, NV

"Fantastic book! Your personal insights are a big help...I learned more the first afternoon with the MiniManual than the previous 8 months of trial and error and user manual. Thank you, thank you, thank you!"

T. Pardun
N. Brunswick, NJ

"A great book. Succinct, insightful, and useful. Even the most seasoned MiniCAD users will discover new (or rediscover forgotten) solutions to everyday CAD problems."

D. Bornstein Audio
New York, NY

Version 8

the WorksTutorial

A hop, skip, and jump into VectorWorks

Janis Kent, AIA

Third Edition

the WorksTutorial

A hop, skip, and jump into VectorWorks

by Janis Kent, AIA

Published by :

improbability press
369 South Doheny Drive Ste. 189
Beverly Hills, CA 90211 USA

Third Printing October, 2000
Printed and bound in Canada
Published in the United States of America

ISBN 0-9651981-6-2 : $49.00

This book is dedicated to the memory of Gene Moss
whose foresight and assistance enabled
this continuing journey into the computer world

Acknowledgements
I wish to thank all those people who generously offered their support and encouragement through out this whole process; the people at Diehl Graphsoft for making VectorWorks in the first place; Ted Mader Associates who provided a wonderful design and went above and beyond; all those who beta-tested the book and gave invaluable feedback; and then there was The Furf who made sure I was not asleep at the computer.

Colophon
This book was created in PageMaker 6.5 along with some old fashioned pen and paper. The screen shots obviously came from VectorWorks 8.5, using Captivate Select 4.6 to capture them, and Adobe PhotoDeluxe 2.0 for editing. The fonts used are Universe, Bell Gothic, and Graphite all by Adobe.

CONTENTS

CHAPTER 1

CHAPTER 2

CHAPTER 3

CHAPTER 4

CHAPTER 5

CHAPTER 6

CHAPTER 7

CHAPTER 8

CHAPTER 9

CHAPTER 10

Chapter 1

WHAT THIS IS ALL ABOUT

INTRODUCTION

This tutorial was initially requested by many instructors of VectorWorks, previously known as MiniCAD, to assist them in teaching people how to use the program as well as learning it themselves. After many years of training new and intermediate users, I have developed a methodology that is geared towards how the user actually learns and absorbs information. This book has now been completely updated for version 8.5 and while the majority of the software has remained the same, you will find some new and exciting changes that have greatly expanded the program's capabilities and ease of use once again.

Our objective of what we are specifically trying to accomplish with this tutorial, is to build your vocabulary in VectorWorks as quickly as possible so that you can jump in and actually start drawing both in 2D and 3D. While you may not be using Vector-Works for architecture or other directly related fields, going through these step-by-step lessons does develop your vocabulary and understanding of the program. If you find difficulty in accomplishing one of the lessons, do go back and review the preceding chapter, since each chapter is based on the preceding one - a building block approach.

There are many new features in VectorWorks that automate the process of drawing objects and creating files, which greatly enhance the program's ease of use. While many of these features quickly create objects and set up the files so that you can start drawing right away, if you totally rely on them, you will be somewhat limited in what you can accomplish with the program. The intent of *THE WORKSTUTORIAL* is to teach you how to create your own specific objects and file setups so that you know how and understand the process, thereby allowing you as much flexibility as possible. This way, you will be able to customize the program to create objects and files meeting your own criteria. Some of the new timesaving plug-ins and scripts are touched upon, but do spend time and explore the others on your own.

It is assumed that you already know how to use the computer, whether Macintosh or Windows, but are not necessarily familiar with CAD programs. You will need to familiarize yourself with the Macintosh or Windows environment first, if it is indeed new to you.

" THE WORKSTUTORIAL - A HOP, SKIP, AND JUMP INTO VECTORWORKS" by no means answers all questions or brings you through the use of all tools and commands in VectorWorks, but it does provide you with a quick start to working in the VectorWorks world. For more in-depth explanations you would need to reference *" THE WORKS-MANUAL - AN INTRODUCTION AND BEYOND TO VECTORWORKS."*

Terminology

Some of the basic terminology used throughout this tutorial are;

- **3D solids object** - a 3D object made with the *SPHERE, HEMISPHERE,* or *CONE* 3D tools
- **axis line** - temporary line some tools use either as a pivot, rotation, cutting, or other demarcation depending on the tool
- **boolean object** - a 3D object created with the *ADD SOLIDS, SUBTRACT SOLIDS,* or the *INTERSECT SOLIDS* command

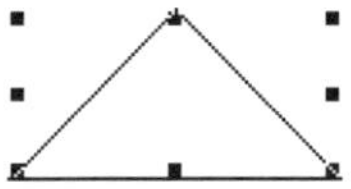

- **bounding box** - the rectangular area designated by an object's selection handles which may or may not be directly on the edge of the object
- **click** - quickly push and release the mouse button
- **click/click** - click the mouse button, drag the mouse and then click the mouse again

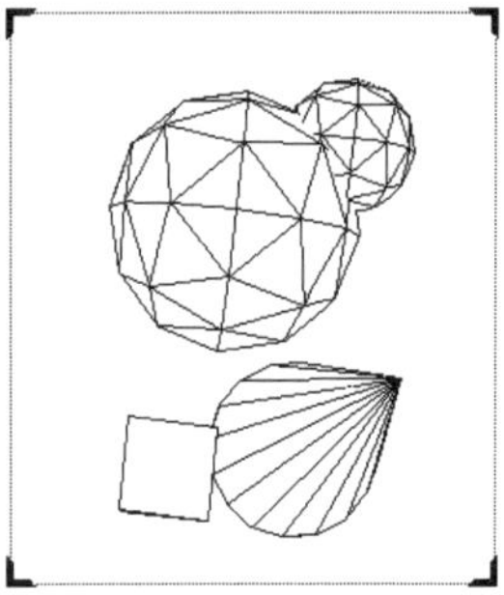

- **clipping frame** - bounding region of the perspective view which can be resized by press/dragging the corners; picture frame
- **double-click** - quickly clicking the mouse twice
- **drag** - moving the mouse while the button is pressed (usually part of **press/drag**)
- **drawing area** or **drawing window** - the white area in a file that can be used for drawing
- **edit window** - white area in a file similar to the drawing window but used when editing symbols, groups, meshes, or VectorWorks native objects

• **global** - affects everything, even existing items
• **ground plane** - the horizontal plane in a 3D drawing where the ground is at a 0 elevation; there is one ground plane per file
• **hit** - pressing and releasing a key
• **hold** - pressing a key and releasing it when task is done
• **hybrid** - an object having both a 2D and a 3D component
• **marquee** - a dashed non-printable rectangle that appears as a guide when press/dragging with the *selection* cursor

• **mesh object** - a 3D object made with the *EXTRUDED RECTANGLE*, or *EXTRUDED POLYGON* tools, or the *CONVERT TO MESH* command
• **navigate** - using a pop-up menu to locate items in files or folders
• **origin point** - point where X and Y or I and J equal 0
• **out of bounds** - the gray area surrounding the white drawing area sometimes visible when zoomed out
• **page** - measurement for an object that does adjust for scale; used in hatches; vs **world**
• **plug-in object** - a new type of complex hybrid object created by setting the parameters with a plug-in tool and can only be modified with the *OBJECT INFO* palette; it can be ungrouped as well
• **press** - push the mouse button and hold it down; pressing a key and releasing it once the task is complete
• **press/drag** - press the mouse button, drag the mouse and then release the mouse button
• **printable area** - space in **drawing area** outlined by a gray rectangle (**printable boundary**) showing the area that actually gets printed

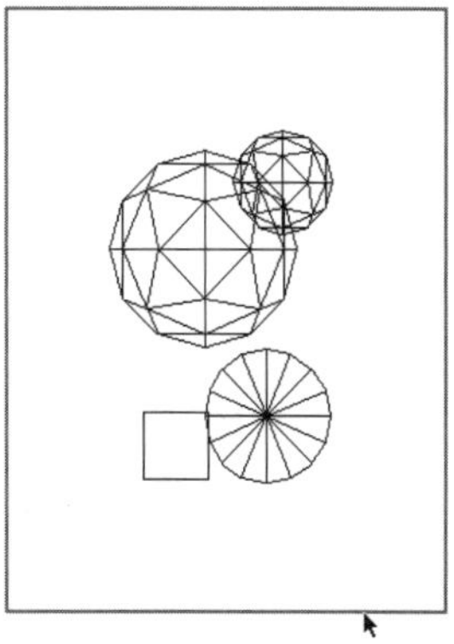

• **release** - releasing the pressed mouse button
• **script** - a custom command created within VectorWorks either by writing from scratch or using one of the commands that automatically create the script; previously known as macro or parametric
• **select** - click an object to get the selection handles; press/drag a **marquee** totally around an object(s); press the *Option [Control]* key and press/drag a **marquee**

partially around an object(s); click a tool or icon to highlight; press/drag to a hidden tool to highlight; press/drag to a command; click a box or button in a dialog box

• **shift-select** - select an object, press the *Shift* key, and click other objects to select
• **snapping dot** - dot appearing to the lower right of the cursor showing that you are within snapping distance to an object
• **VectorWorks native** - a 3D object made by either sweeping or extruding a 2D object
• **working plane** - plane(s) in a 3D drawing that can be horizontal or at any slope; initially it is set to match the **ground plane**
• **world** - measurement for an object that does not adjust for scale; used in hatches; vs **page**

MACINTOSH AND WINDOWS

This is the third version of VectorWorks that has been available as a cross platform program. Whether you are working in the Macintosh operating system or Windows, the program interface is the same, although there are several differences to note.

There are several different keys to use, since the keyboards in both systems are not identical. The keys shown will be Macintosh with Windows keys following in brackets; ie. *Option* + a command *[Control* + a command*]*, *Option + Command [Control + Shift]*, *Command* + a key *[Control* + a key*]*, *Return* or *Enter [Enter]*, and *Delete [Delete* or *Backspace* in text*]*. *Command*-selecting in a scrolling list for out-of-order multiples in Macintosh is *Control*-selecting in Windows. *Control* pressing on the Mac to access the *object edit mode* is right-click with the mouse for Windows.

Several command names not identical for both systems are the *PAGE SETUP* command in Macintosh which is *PRINT SETUP* in Windows and *QUIT* in Mac, *EXIT* in Win. Also note, that name lengths in Macintosh are not as limited as some of the versions in Windows, so adjust file names accordingly. For Windows under the *command menu title* of *WINDOW*, there are a series of commands visible in Windows only (these are controlled by the operating system in Macintosh). Windows also has two more options for importing and exporting than Mac. And the last item has to do with saving. For Windows users, you would need to append .MCD to a file name or .STA if it is a template file. If you forget this in Windows, it will be done automatically. For Mac users, do remember to append these letters if you want a Mac file to be read in Win. Just as a note, screen shots used in this tutorial are all Macintosh.

CONVENTIONS USED IN THIS TUTORIAL

Both *"The WorksTutorial"* and *"The WorksManual"* are set up in the same manner. Many of the items discussed in the text are illustrated directly below or in the side column. You will also periodically find icons in the side margins to call out a new version 8 feature, a hot tip, or an alert you should be aware of.

At this point, if VectorWorks is not opened, you should click the VectorWorks icon and then select the *Open* command under *FILE* so that the program opens along with a blank unformatted sheet. Several items for understanding the organization are outlined as follows.

Command Menu Title And Pull-Down Menu

There are ±11 *command menu titles* (depending on the *WorkSpaces* selected) across the top in the menu bar, and each has *menu item names* found within their pull-down menus. The *command menu titles* will always be shown with caps and italics. For example, *FILE, EDIT, TOOL, ORGANIZE...*

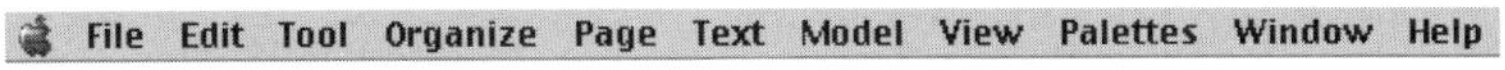

Submenus, Dialog Boxes, And Other Stuff

Some of the *menu item names* in the pull-down menus have an arrow or an ellipsis (**...**) to the right.

Menu items with a triangular arrow are known as hierarchical menus. The arrow indicates a submenu with more choices.

ie. *Set Attribute Defaults* under *PAGE* has a submenu or pop-out menu with several selections *Arrow Heads...*, *Color Palette...*, *Dash Styles...*, etc.

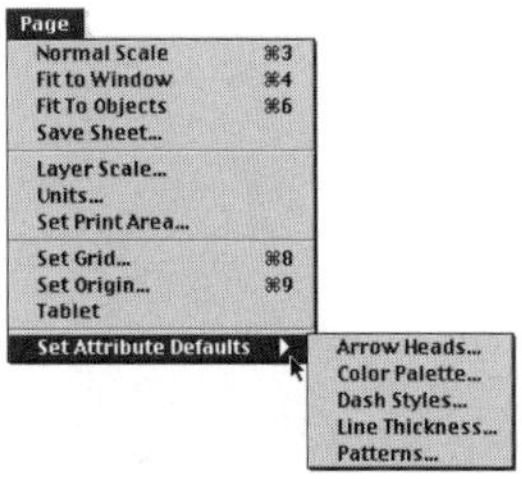

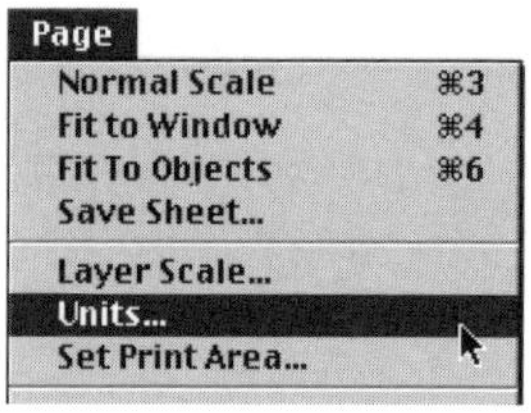

Menu items with an ellipsis (...) indicates a command needing more input and a dialog box will open when selected.
ie. *Units...* under *PAGE* opens a dialog box called *Set Units.*

Some of the tool icons in the various *Tools* palettes also have a small triangular arrow in the lower right corner indicating a pop-out menu with more choices. When you press/drag the cursor and release on one of these hidden tools, it will replace the existing tool in the palette. So be aware and look for the hidden tools.

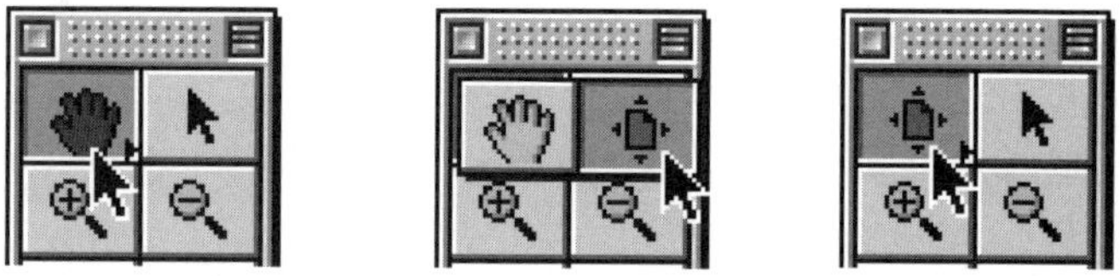

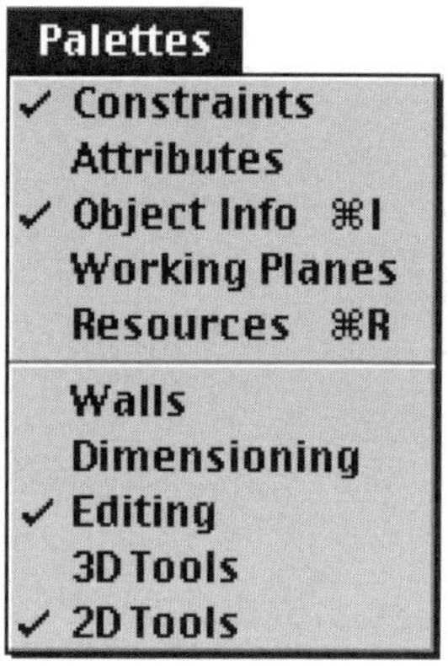

The *menu item names*, the commands within submenus, and titles of dialog boxes will be shown with upper/lower case caps and italics. The various floating palettes opened under the *PALETTE command menu title*, as well as the various tools and icons within each palette, will also be shown with upper/lower case caps and italics.

The various modifier icons for the tools in the mode bar as well as all of the boxes and buttons within dialog boxes will be shown in lower case caps and italics. Keys will be shown in upper/lower case italics (no caps). Other identifiers and labels will be shown in just lower case italics.

Convention Example

An example of the shorthand used in this book to get rid of all the pop-up, pull-down, submenus, edit fields, dialog boxes, and buttons and still allow you to see where the command is located would be; select the *1/8"* button under *ORGANIZE>Layers>Layers Setup>Scale>layer scale.* It's still a mouthful, but...

THE ENVIRONMENT

So that everything appears the same on your computer as in the examples in "*The WorksTutorial,*" it will be necessary first to make sure the environments match each other. Why one selection might be better or more useful is not addressed here, but if you do need more information, "*The WorksManual*" does go more in depth.

The selections below are not necessarily the best choices for you once you become more fluent in VectorWorks, since it really does depend on how you actually use the program. What we are doing here is just making sure your environment matches "*The WorksTutorial*" so that everything works the same!

Preferences

Open the *VectorWorks Preferences* dialog box under *FILE> Preferences> VectorWorks Preferences* and make the selections so that they match the dialog boxes as shown on the following pages.

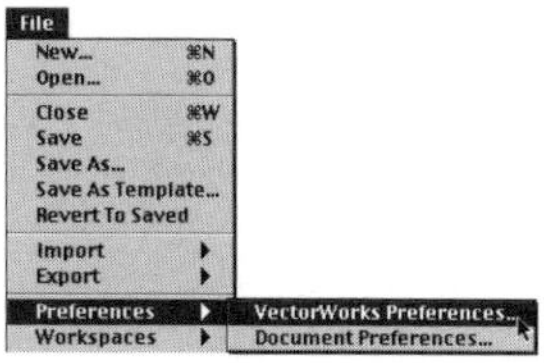

The *edit* tab is the active pane when the dialog box opens. Click to select or deselect the boxes on the left, highlight the edit boxes and type in the appropriate numbers on the upper right, and use the pop-out menu to select the choice on the center right.

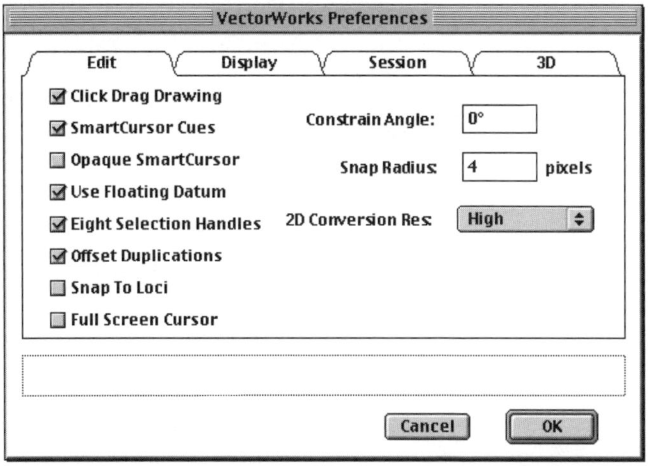

Click the *DISPLAY* tab and select or deselect the boxes on the left side. Click the appropriate button on the right.

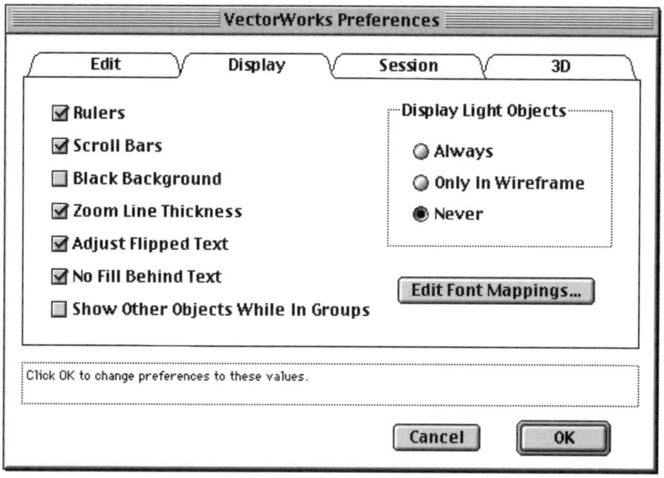

Click the *SESSION* tab and select or deselect the boxes on the left and the appropriate button on the right. Highlight the edit boxes and type in the appropriate numbers. If you have a small monitor, you may want to change the *PALETTE MARGINS* to *NONE*. Also, if your machine has a limited amount of RAM you may want to make the number in the *MAXIMUM NUMBER OF UNDOS* somewhat smaller than 20.

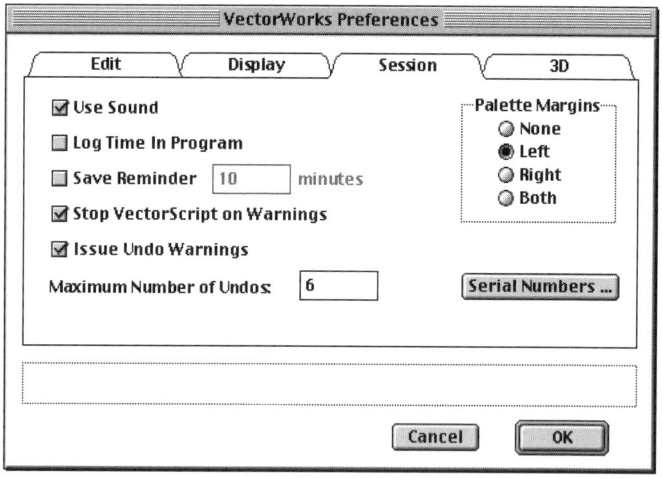

Click the *3D* tab, select *SHOW 3D AXIS LABELS*, and select the appropriate pop-out choice on the bottom. Click the *OK* button when done.

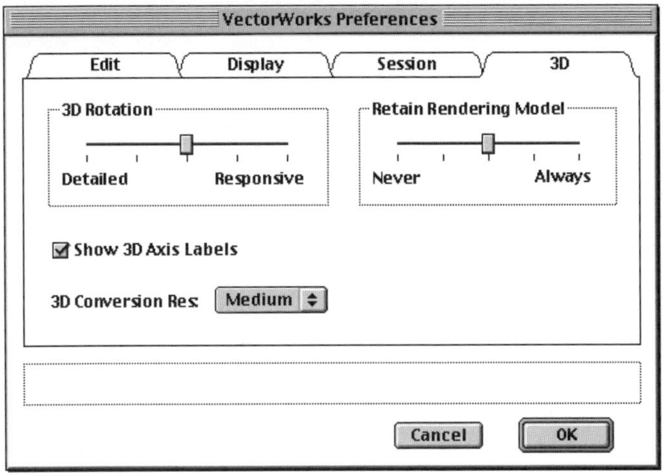

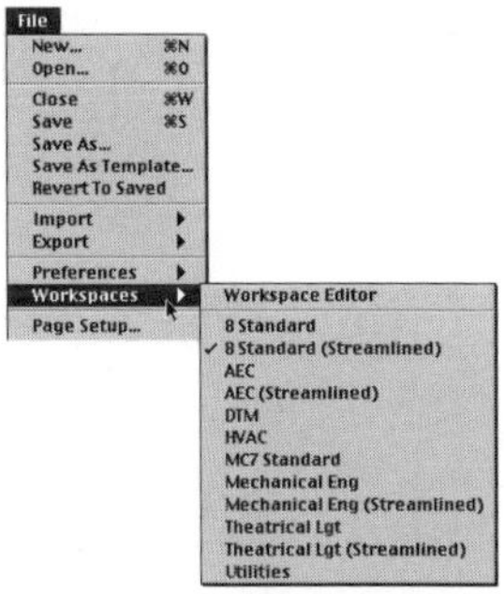

Workspaces

Under *FILE>WORKSPACES*, verify that *8 STANDARD (STREAMLINED)* has a check mark next to it, otherwise, press/drag to select it. The palettes and *command menu titles* will momentarily disappear. Do not worry, they will reappear but in a new arrangement. As a note, what use to be called *OVERLAYS* is now called *WORKSPACES*.

Unit Format

Select *PAGE>UNITS*. When the *SET UNITS* dialog box opens, select *FEET & INCHES* in the pop-out menu, the *DISPLAY AS FRACTIONS* button, and press/drag to $^1/_2$" under *DISPLAY PRECISION*. Do not change the value for *DIMENSION PRECISION*. Change the *ANGULAR ACCURACY* to *0° 0'*.

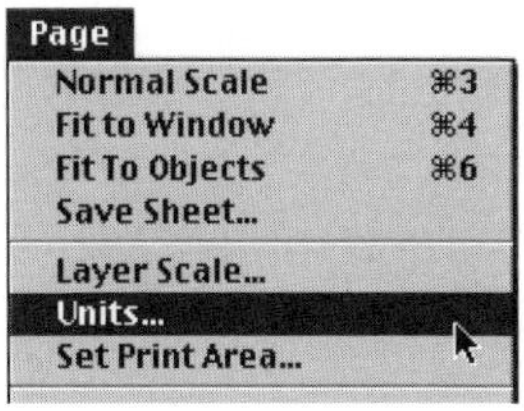

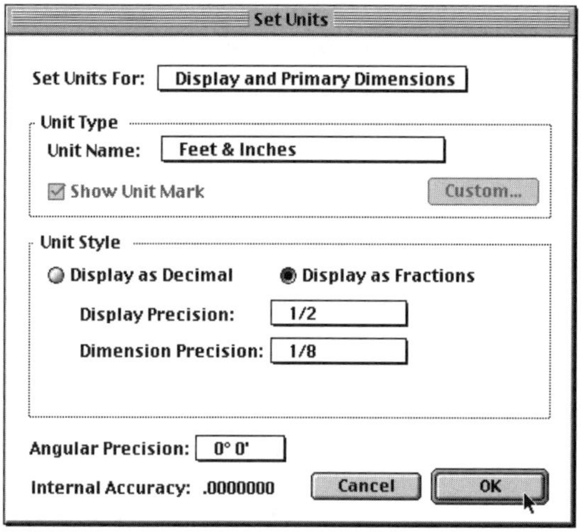

For those of you who are really set on the metric system, we will do our best to provide the equivalents which will follow in parenthesis. The diagrams though, will remain in the Imperial system of measurement. So, under *Set Units*, disregard *feet & inches* and select *meters* instead in the pop-out menu. Also select the *show unit mark* box, click *display as decimal*, and press/drag to *.00* for *display precision* and again, do not change the *dimension precision*. Select the *.XX0* for *decimal format*, and change the *angular accuracy* to *0° 0'*.

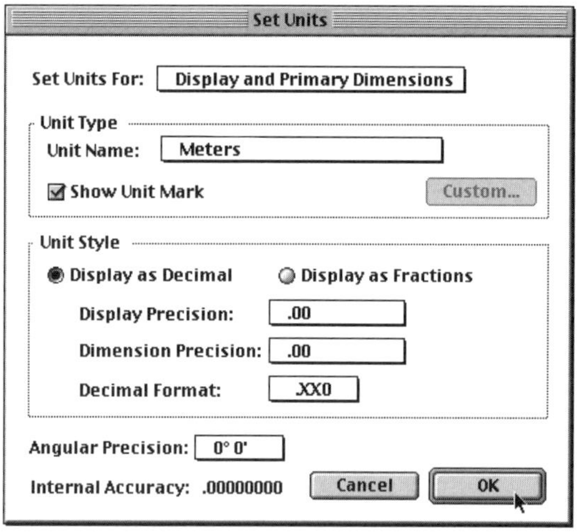

Line Thickness

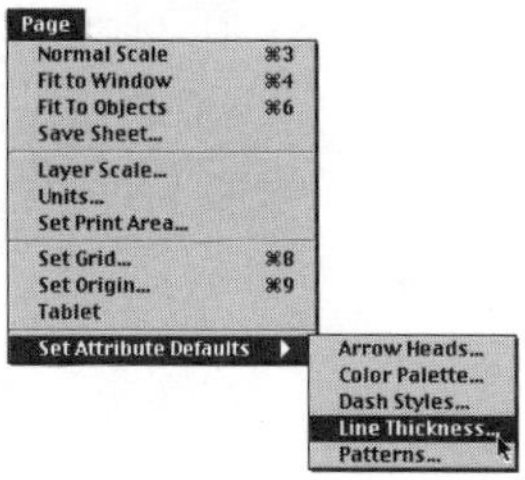

Open the *Preferred Line Thicknesses* dialog box under *PAGE> Set Attribute Defaults>Line Thickness.* Select the *mm* button and press/drag in each edit box to highlight the existing text, or use the *Tab* key to move from one box to the next which also automatically selects the text. Type in the numbers so that the *new* boxes correspond to the following example. As a note, the numbers entered may automatically get revised a small amount when the dialog box closes and is reopened later. Do not worry about this.

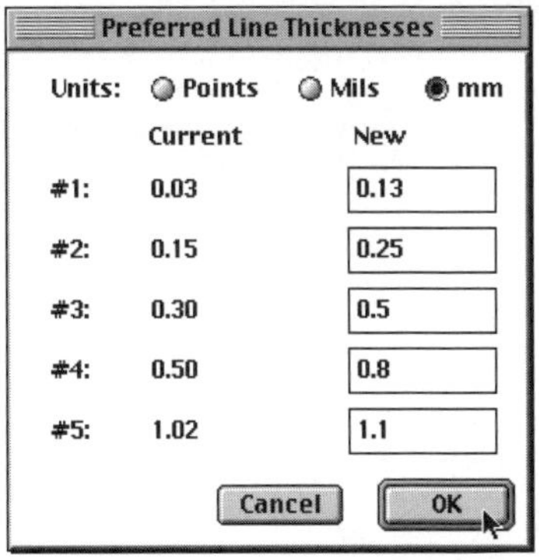

Arrow Marker

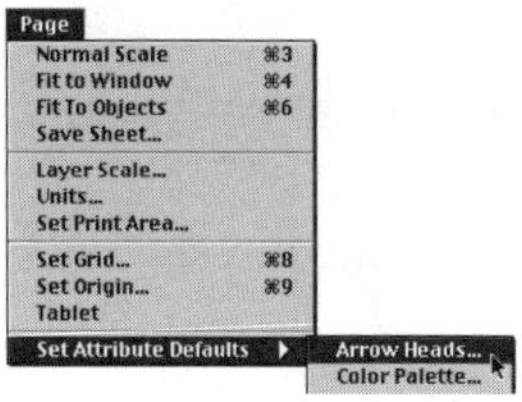

We will change one of the default arrow markers. Open the *Set Arrow Attributes* dialog box under *PAGE>Set Attribute Defaults>Arrow Heads.* Select the marker style from the pop-out menu and change the *angle* and *length* so that it appears the same as the following dialog box.

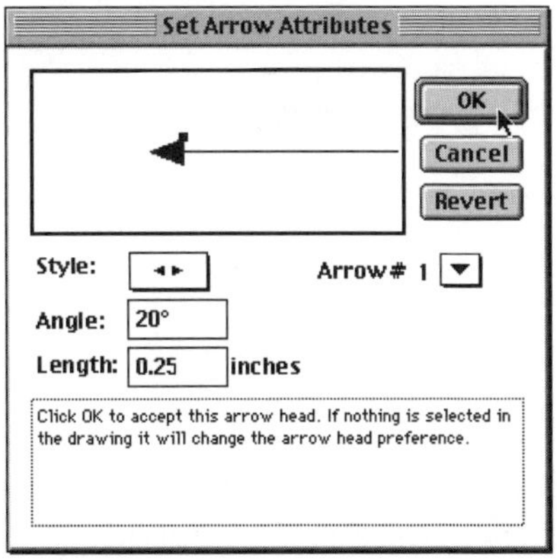

Text

Go up to *TEXT*, press/drag down to *Font* and over to the desired font on the pop-out menu. We are using a font called *Graphite* by Adobe in this book. If you do not have that particular font, select *Tekton*, or *Helvetica*, or another one appropriate for drawings instead. Now go up to *TEXT>Size* and press/drag down to *12* on the pop-out menu to set 12 points as the default size.

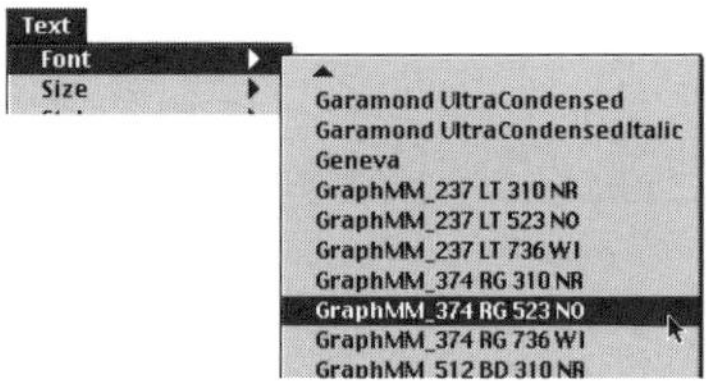

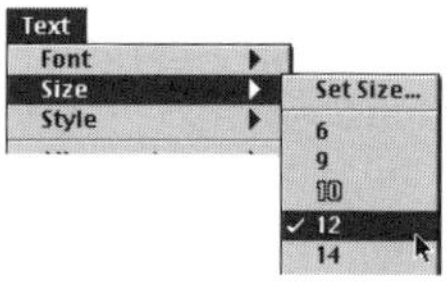

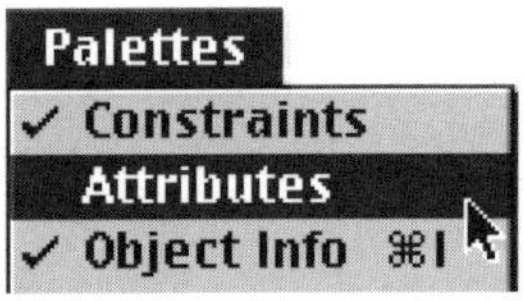

Attributes Palette

Go to the *Attributes* palette. If the palette is not open, select *PALETTES>Attributes*, then press on the *line thickness* button. When the pop-out menu opens, drag over and down to the third solid line and release. The selected line weight now appears on the line style button. Also note, that the newly selected line weight will have a check mark next to it the next time the pop-out menu is opened.

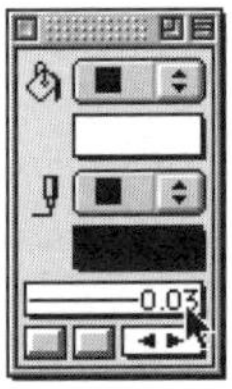

On the Mac side, the right button is a window shade shortcut. The middle button is an expand/contract resize button. The left button is the close box. On the Windows side, the right button is the close box. To use window shade, just double-click the title bar. To resize the palette, use the right mouse button and click the title bar then go to *size*.

Constraints Palette

Go to the *Constraints* palette. If it is not open, select *PALETTES>Constraints*, then click to select the *Snap To Grid* (top left), the *Snap To Object* (top right), and the *Snap Points* (third down on left) icons. As a note, always leave these three constraints selected, at least for this tutorial, even when other constraints are used.

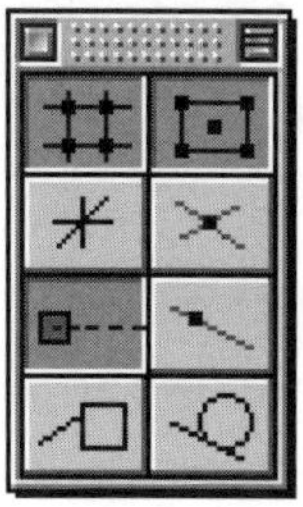

Snap Points

Double-click the *Snap Points* icon to open the *Smart Points* dialog box. Select the *horizontal/vertical extensions* and *use floating datum* boxes.

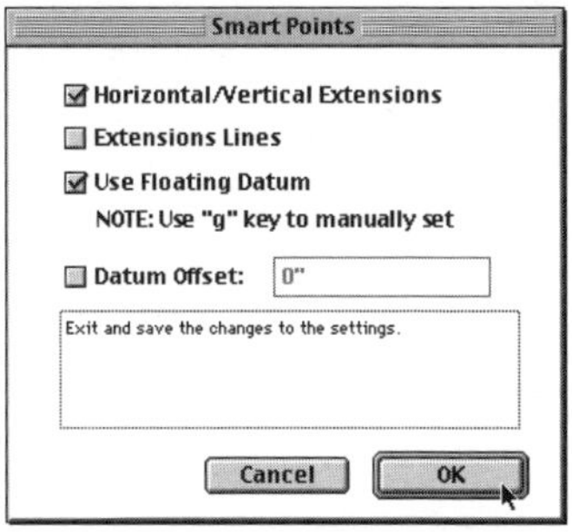

Angle Constraint

Double-click the *Angle* constraint (2nd down on the left) to open the *Angle Snaps* dialog box. Select the *30,60*, and *45* boxes. *Enter angle* should have 0° entered and the *extension lines* box should be deselected. It is not necessary to leave this constraint selected.

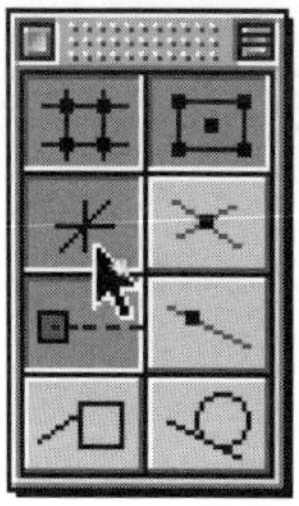

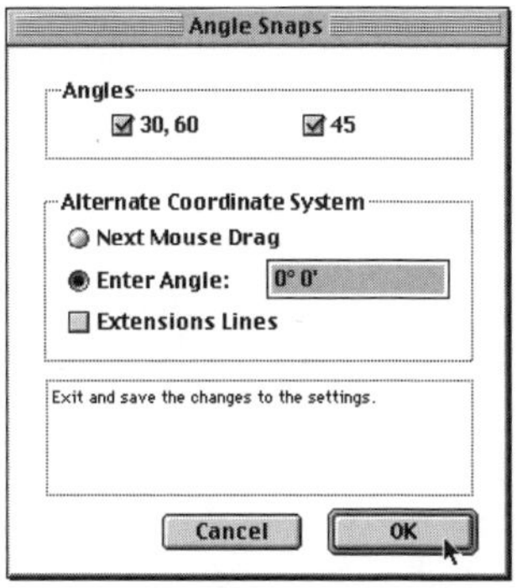

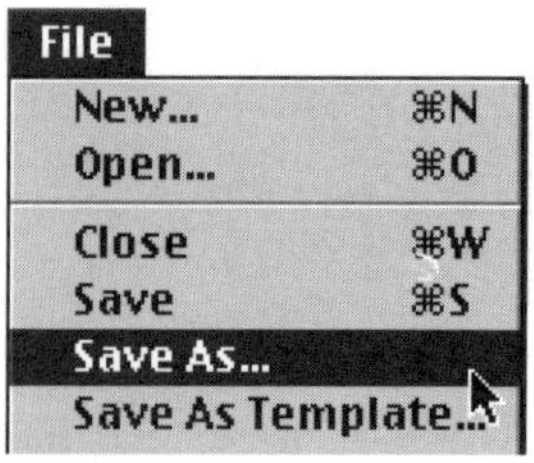

ENOUGH FOR NOW

At this point you can quit the program and come back later. Even though we really have not drawn anything, it is necessary to save this document in order for some of the settings to be remembered. Select the *FILE>Save As* command. A dialog box opens allowing you to navigate to a particular folder as well as an edit box for *NEW FILE NAME*. Type *chapt 1 [chapt 1.mcd]* for the name and make sure *VectorWorks 8 ƒ* appears at the top of the pop-out menu, then click *SAVE*. Once done, select *FILE>Quit [Exit]*.

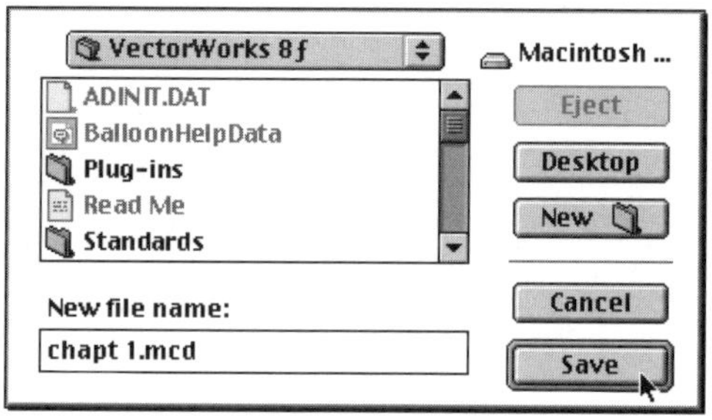

THE ENVIRONMENT IN SUMMATION

All of the selections made for the environment in this chapter are for the purposes of this tutorial only. After you have gone through the lessons, do play around and change them. Some items I always keep the same, but many I do change from file to file, or even task to task, or just because. These formatting items are easy to change and each has a reason for selecting or not selecting depending on their use or your comfort level. There is a disk included in the back of this book which includes a finished file for each chapter – so check yourself as you progress through the book.

The only default settings to watch out for are the *3D CONVERSION RES* in the *VectorWorks Preferences* dialog box and all of the unit formatting in the *Set Units* dialog box, since they both are global, which means they affect all items even those already drawn. Remember also, if someone else is using your computer, they may change the defaults for these settings. So it is a good habit to check each of these items that have been set up in this chapter every time you start.

Chapter 2

LET'S LEARN HOW TO DRAW

DRAWING IN VECTORWORKS

There are basically four different methods used in creating objects. The first most obvious method is with the mouse and making use of the *smartcursor*. The second is using the *data display bar* which can also be used in conjunction with the mouse. The third is using a dialog box which might make use of a *script* or a *plug-in* tool. And the fourth method is to duplicate an existing object.

The tools, commands, and other items we will be exploring are;

2D Selection Tool
Mirror Tool
Rectangle Tool
Single Line Tool
Sphere Tool
Table Plug-In Tool
Zoom In Tool
Zoom Out Tool
Copy Command
Duplicate Command
Duplicate Array Command
Fit To Objects Command
Fit To Window Command
New Command
Normal Scale Command
Paste Command
Quit [Exit] Command
Set Grid Command
Snap Points Constraint
Cursors
Data Display Bar
View Bar

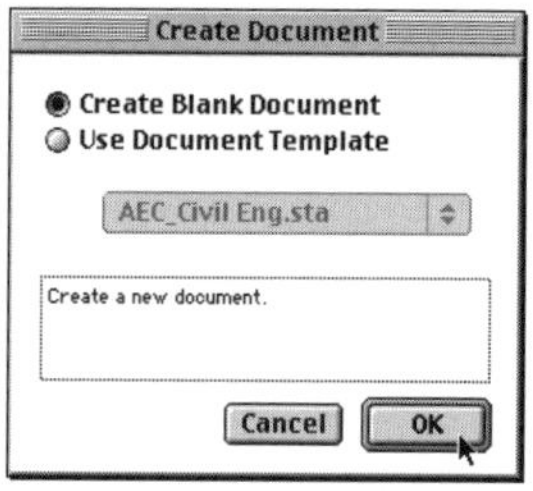

LET'S DRAW

The first thing is to open *VectorWorks 8* by double-clicking the program icon. Then, if a blank sheet does not automatically appear, select *FILE>NEW*. In this case, the *CREATE DOCUMENT* dialog box opens. Just select the *CREATE BLANK DOCUMENT* button and *OK*. You now have an unformatted sheet called *"untitled 1" [untitled 1.mcd]*. As a note, many of the floating palettes may open. The ones that you might need now are the *2D TOOLS*, the *3D TOOLS*, the *ATTRIBUTES*, the *CONSTRAINTS*, and maybe the *OBJECT INFO* palettes. The rest you can click the *close* box to have them disappear.

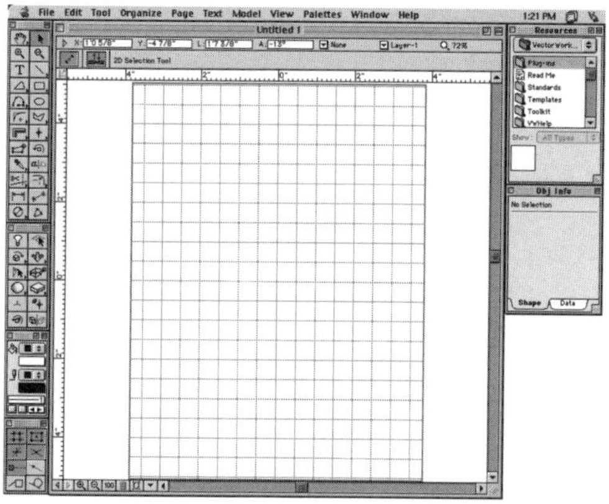

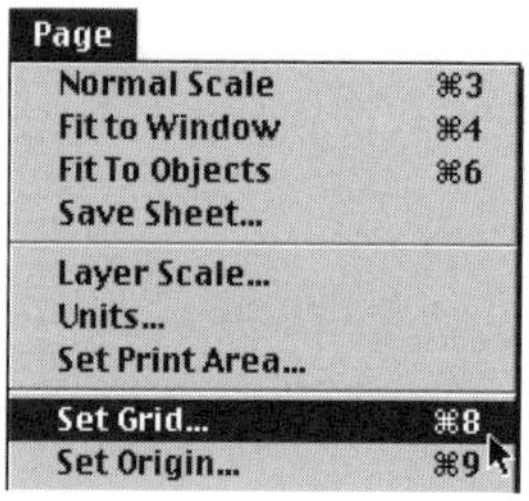

If no grid appears on the document, open the *SET GRID* dialog box by going to *PAGE>SET GRID*. Make sure *GRID OPTIONS>SHOW GRID LINES* is checked and the dialog box matches the example shown below. The other thing you should verify is that all of the settings and defaults established in the previous chapter have not changed with special note of the units, default line weights, and the selected constraints.

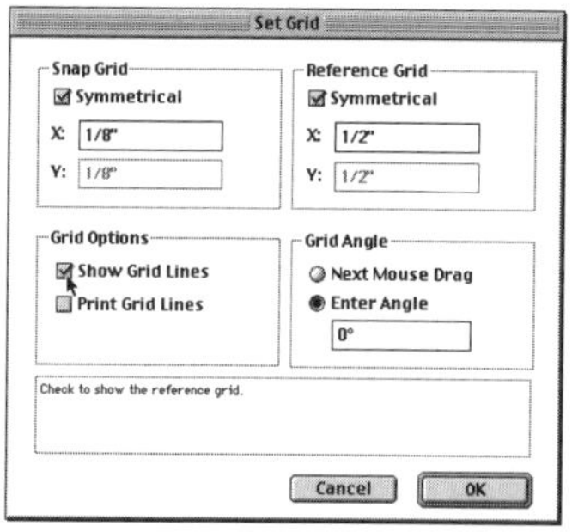

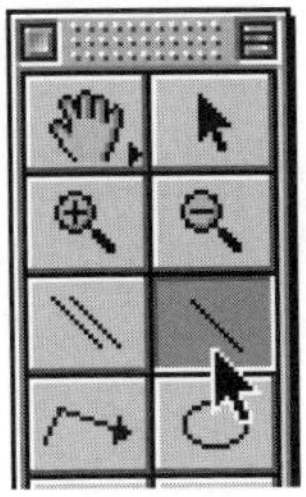

Drawing With The Mouse

Let's take the first method of creating objects which is the one most commonly used.

Step 1- press/drag & release

Select the *SINGLE LINE* tool along with the *UNCONSTRAINED MODIFIER* icon, press with the mouse at one point, drag it to the second desired point, and then release the mouse. So in other words it is press, drag, and release.

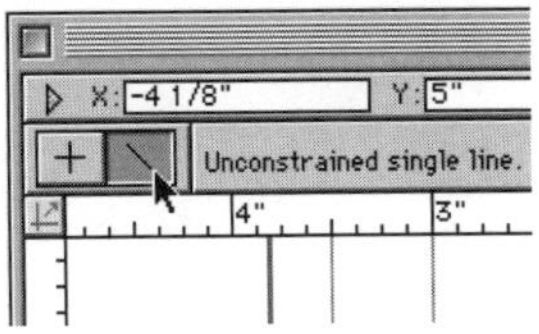

If *CLICK DRAG DRAWING* was not checked in the *VECTORWORKS PREFERENCES* dialog box, then you would click the first point which would be the starting point of the line, move the mouse to the desired end point and click again. So you would click and click, but for this tutorial do select *CLICK DRAG DRAWING* in the *VECTORWORKS PREFERENCES* dialog box.

Notice when press/dragging, how the Δ*X [±X]* and Δ*Y [±Y]* change in the *data display bar*. If you are moving the mouse downwards, the Δ*Y [±Y]* becomes a negative number and turns positive when moving upwards. The Δ*X* turns negative if moved to the left of its starting point and positive if moved to the right.

Using The Data Display Bar To Draw

When drawing with this method, an object is placed at an exact location and/or in an exact size. This is the easiest method to create an object having a specific size or location that needs to align or correspond somehow with another existing object.

With the *SINGLE LINE* tool selected, hit the *Tab* key. Notice the first edit box is highlighted in the *data display bar*. Hit the *Tab* key again to highlight the next box and again until you have cycled through the boxes and nothing is highlighted.

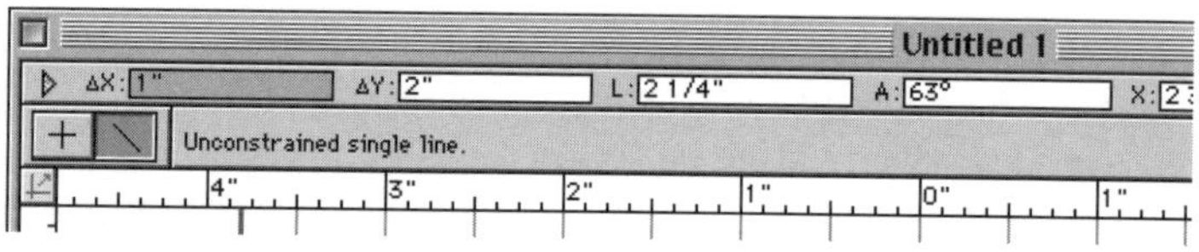

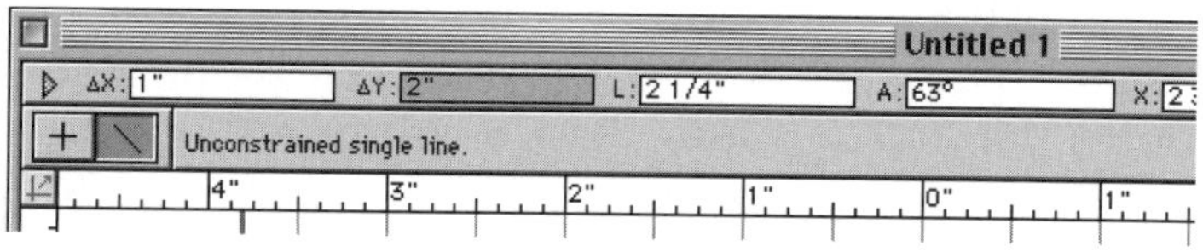

Step 1 - creating an object of a certain size

To start drawing, press the mouse at a starting point, and while still pressing the mouse button hit the *Tab* key until the L edit box is highlighted. You may need to move the mouse around a little once the button is pressed in order to *Tab* across.

Type in a length, 2" (.05m) using the key board, and hit the *Return [Enter]* key. Now while still keeping the mouse pressed move the mouse around. See that the line is now constrained to the length entered into the L edit box no matter what direction the mouse is moved or where the cursor is located. Also note the *smartcursor cue, length* on the drawing window and the grayed outline on the L edit box in the *data display bar* (Mac side only) to clue you into what information is set. Do not release the mouse button yet.

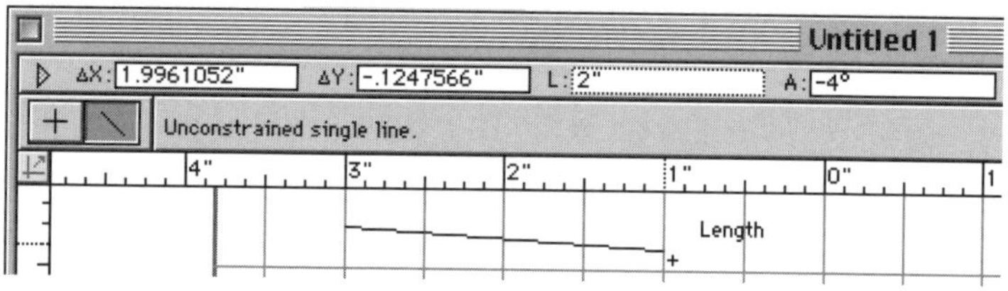

Step 2 - changing a dimension

If you enter the wrong dimension or for some reason change your mind it is easy to revise. While still keeping the mouse button pressed, *Tab* across the *data display bar* until the L edit box is again highlighted. Enter another dimension, 1.5" (.03m) and hit the *Return [Enter]* key. Then tab across again, this time to the A edit box, enter -20°, hit

Return [Enter], and release the mouse button. You do not need to use the ° mark since it is assumed for the angle edit box. In this case it does not matter which modifier icon is selected for the line, whether *CONSTRAINED* or *UNCONSTRAINED*, since data bar dimensioning does override the constraining.

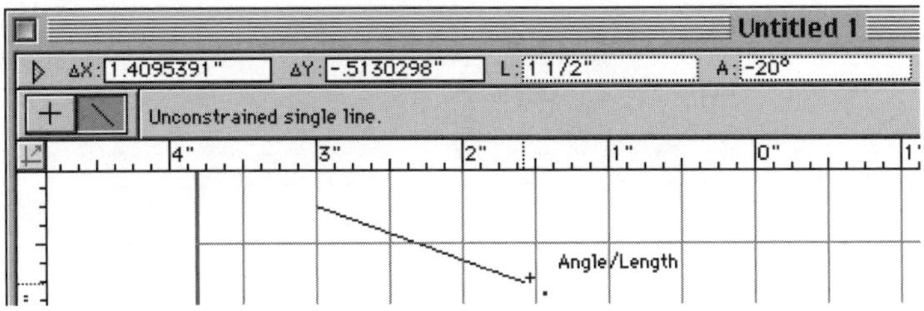

Step 3 - creating a guide line

Now to create another line that has a certain *ΔY [±Y]* dimension, but not length. The *ΔY [±Y]* means the change in the length along the Y axis from the initial point the mouse is pressed. If the number entered is positive, the guide line will appear above the starting point and if negative, then below that point.

With the *SINGLE LINE* tool still selected, press at a starting point and move the cursor a little off of that initial point, hit the *Tab* key until the *ΔY [±Y]* edit box is highlighted in the *data display bar*, use the keyboard to type in the dimension -.75" (-.02m), then hit the *Return* [*Enter*] key.

A horizontal dashed guide line crosses the Y axis. The point you actually release the mouse button will establish the *ΔX [±X]* dimension. The end of the line snaps to the guide line, aligning with the wherever cursor may be.

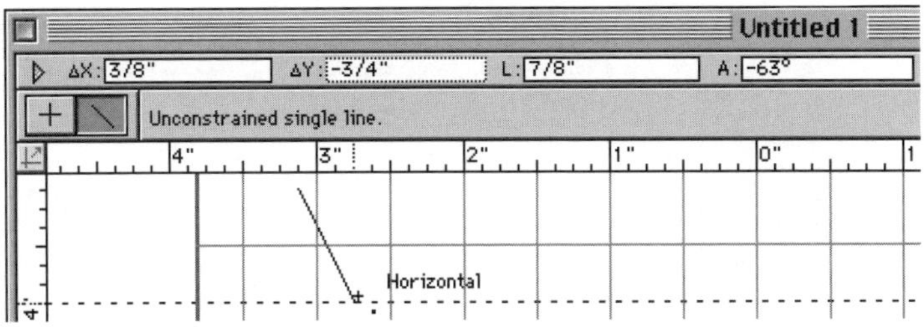

The guide line location can be changed before you release the mouse by again tabbing and entering the revised dimension into the same edit box. Another edit box can also have a dimension entered so two guide lines appear. This creates a snapping point where the two guides intersect.

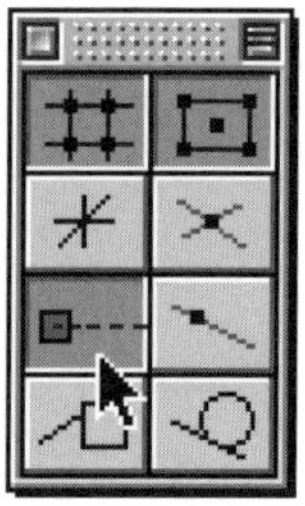

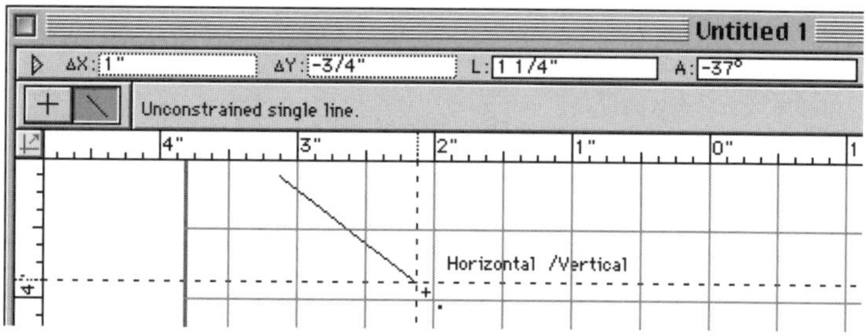

Step 4 - creating and aligning an object

A new object can be drawn to align with other existing objects by using the *smartcursor* to extend horizontal and vertical guide lines. First double-click the *SNAP POINTS* icon in the *CONSTRAINTS* palette. When the *SMART POINTS* dialog box opens, verify that the *HORIZONTAL/VERTICAL EXTENSIONS* box is checked, and that *EXTENSION LINES* is not, then click *OK*. For that matter, double-click the *CONSTRAIN ANGLE* and verify that only *30,60* and *45* are selected.

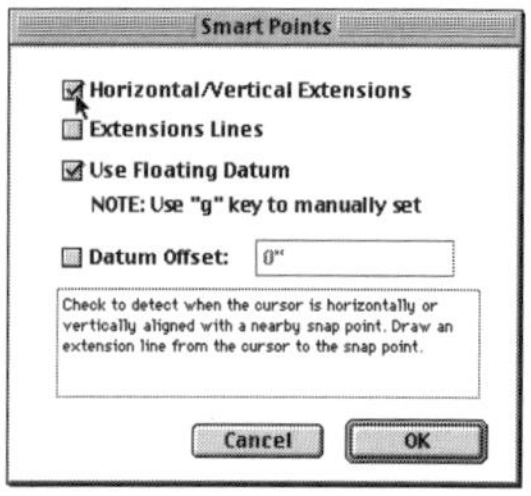

Make sure there are two lines already drawn, and with the *SINGLE LINE* tool selected, place the cursor on a point or vertex of the object, such as an endpoint of one of the lines. Move it around a little if necessary until the *X* and *Y* edit boxes in the *data display bar* are both 0. If it gets stubborn, just hit the *G* key to set the point instead.

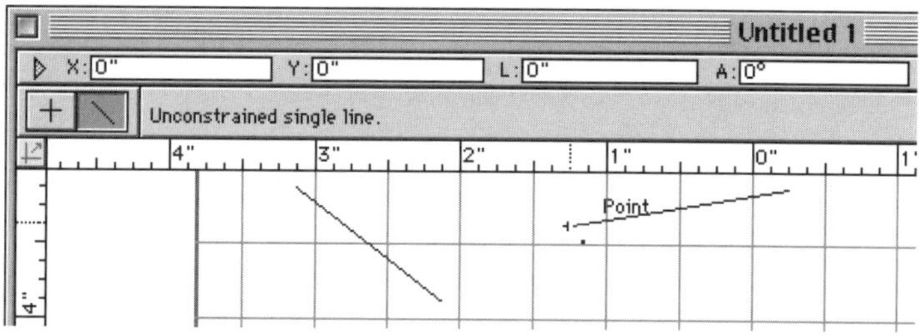

Then move the cursor to another point. Notice that the first point will be circled and the *smartcursor cue* changes to *datum* and the second will now have the *smartcursor cue, point.*

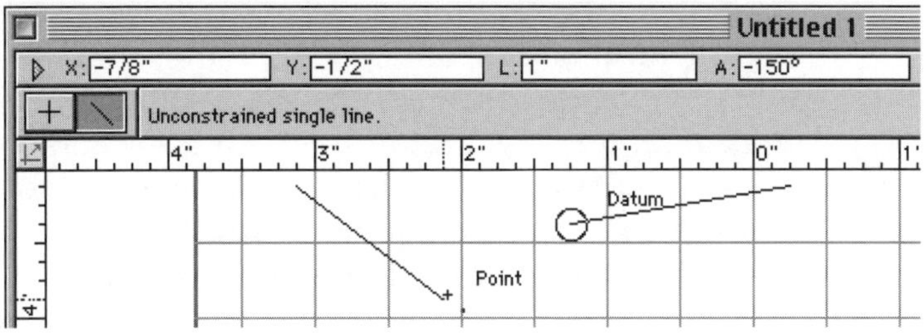

Now move the cursor so that a guide line appears. The guide line only shows when the cursor is directly horizontally over from, or vertically above/below that point.

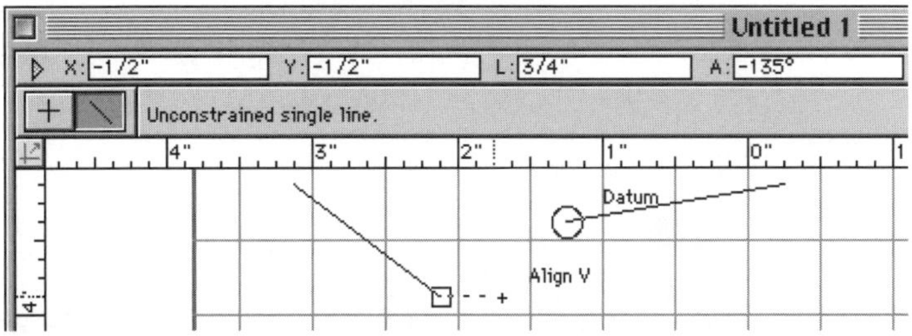

When the *smartcursor* passes over the location where the vertical and horizontal guides meet, extending from both objects, the *smartcursor cue, align h/align v* appears with guide lines going back to the original points. If you press/ drag at this point, the new object will align with the points on the original objects.

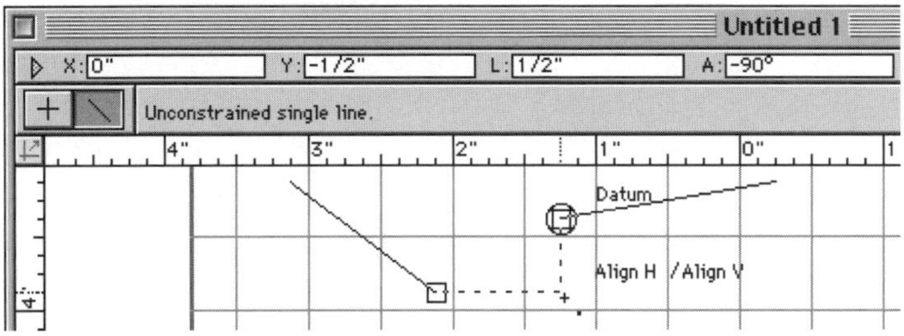

Step 5 - creating and locating an object

You can also use the *floating datum point* to draw an object a specific distance from an existing point on an object. With the *Single Line* tool still selected, create a floating datum point on an existing object (where the x and y coordinates change to 0), hit the *Tab* key to highlight the *x* edit box, type in a distance, 1" (.025 m) and hit the *Return [Enter]* key. Do the same for the *y* edit box entering -.5" and (-.01m) for the distance. Notice that guide lines are shown at the designated offset. When you then press the mouse to start drawing, the starting point of the new object will automatically snap to the intersection of these two guides.

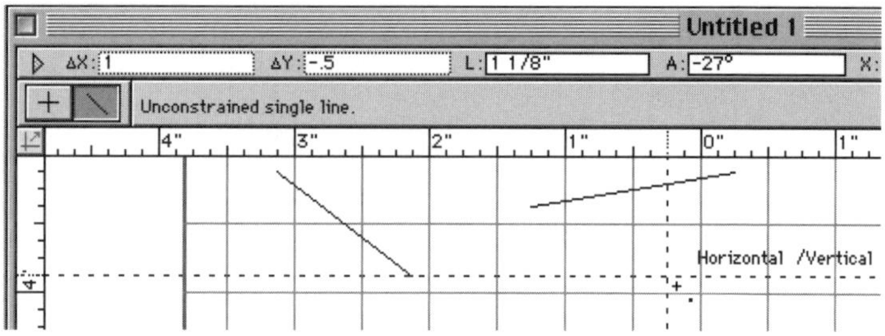

If only one guide line was entered (ie. entering either the *x* or *y* edit box, not both), when you press the mouse, the starting point of the new object will snap to the guide line, aligning with the location of the cursor when pressed.

Objects By A Dialog Box

The third method of creating objects uses a dialog box. Most creation tools when double-clicked will open some variation of a *Create "object"* dialog box. The options within a dialog box change depending on the object type and whether or not it is a 2D object, a 3D object, or a *plug-in*. In some cases you can also select the *class* and *layer* location from the pop-out menu from the existing ones in the file; or set the location of the object itself either by setting coordinates or by clicking the mouse when the dialog box closes; or set the size for the object you are creating.

Step 1 - dialog box for a 2D object

To access the dialog box for a 2D tool, just double-click the tool icon, in this case the *SINGLE LINE* tool. The *CREATE LINE* dialog box opens with two buttons, the top one for *CARTESIAN* and bottom one for *POLAR*.

cartesian

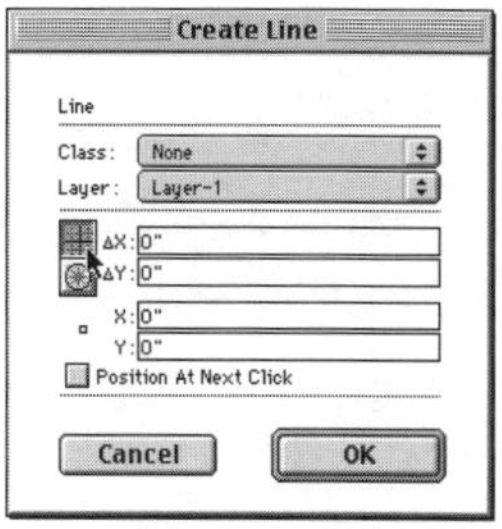

With the *CARTESIAN* button selected, the Δx *[±x]* and Δy *[±y]* edit boxes need to be filled. They represent the change in *x* and change in *y* directions from the first point, not the length of the line. When both boxes have numbers entered, the numbers represent the legs of a right triangle whose hypotenuse is the actual length of the line. If one of the boxes has 0 the other box actually does give the line length.

polar

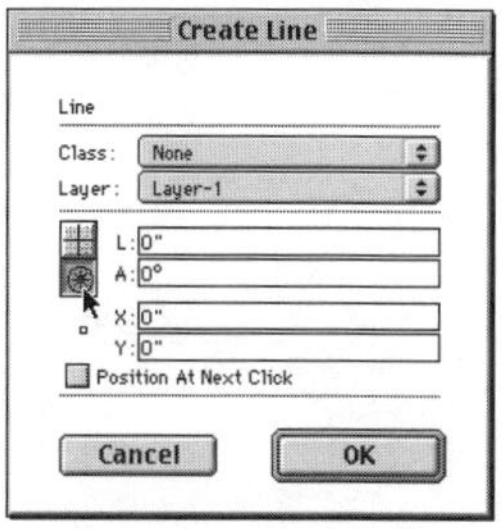

With *POLAR* selected, you enter an amount for the length of the line, *L* and the angle, *A*. If 0° is entered, the line goes towards the right (due east or the 3 in the 3 o'clock position).

location

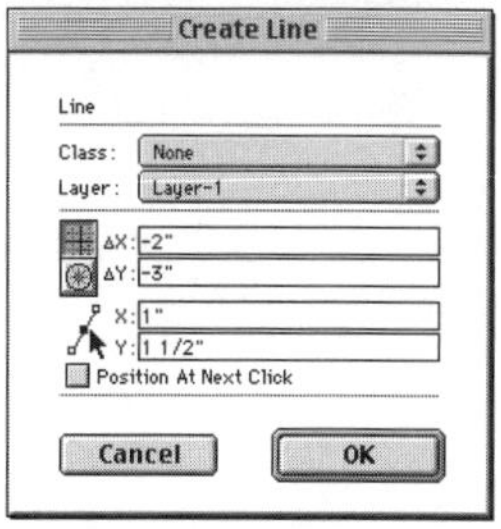

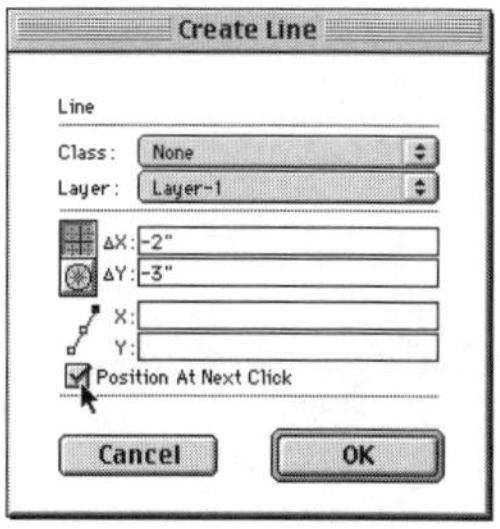

In both cases, *CARTESIAN* and *POLAR*, the *x* and *y* edit boxes represent the location of the line. This is in relationship to the *origin* where 0 is marked on the vertical and horizontal rulers. When a value is inserted for Δx and Δy *(±x, ±y)*, a diagram appears so that you can select which point of the line, center or either end, that the *x* and *y* edit boxes locate. When *OK* is selected, the object will automatically be created and placed at the designated location. If you do not know the exact *XY* coordinates, then select the *POSITION AT NEXT CLICK* button and leave the *x* and *y* edit boxes blank. When you exit the dialog box, the *bulls eye* cursor appears and you would click to place the object visually.

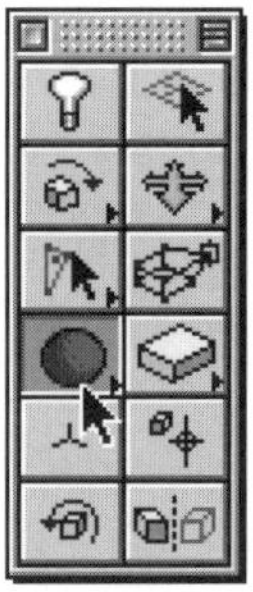

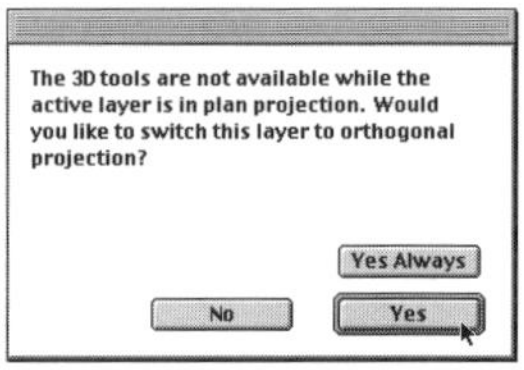

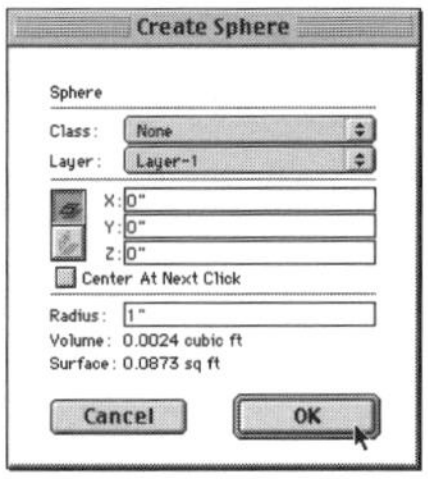

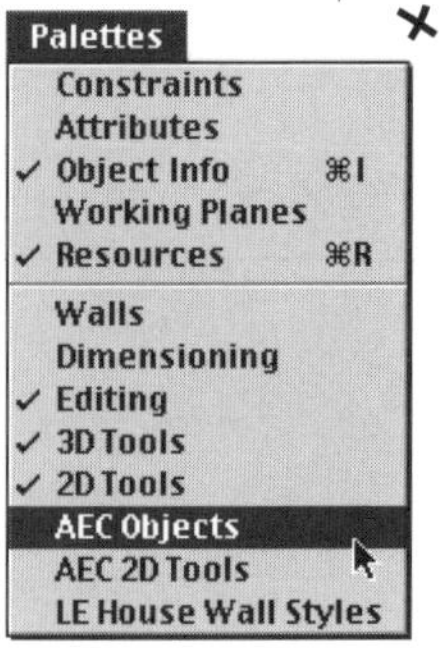

Step 2 - dialog box for a 3D object

The new 3D tools can be used to create a 3D solids object via a dialog box. To access a dialog box, just double-click the tool icon in the *3D TOOLS* palette, in this case the *SPHERE* tool. When a dialog box appears asking if you wish to change to an orthogonal projection – just select *YES*. The *CREATE SPHERE* dialog box then opens. If it does not, just double-click the tool again in the new projection.

location

There are several options for locating a 3D solids object. One is its location within the file which can be placed in an existing *CLASS* and *LAYER* via the two pop-out menus. The next two buttons control the actual placement of the center of the sphere, whether by coordinates using the *ground plane, xyz,* if the first button is selected, or the *working plane* coordinates, *ijk* for the next button. If the *CENTER AT NEXT CLICK* box is selected instead, the object will be centered on the cursor when clicked after exiting the dialog box. Select the *CENTER AT NEXT* click box.

size

The *RADIUS* edit box controls the size of the object. The *VOLUME* and *SURFACE* are automatically displayed in the dialog box providing information on the object. Enter 2" (.05m) for *RADIUS* and click *OK*. When the dialog box closes, click the drawing to create a sphere.

Step 3 - dialog box for a plug-in object

To access one of the *plug-ins*, change the *FILE>WORKSPACES* to *AEC*. It is necessary to change to *VIEW>STANDARD VIEWS> TOP/PLAN* for all *plug-ins*. Also, access the *LAYER SCALE* dialog box under *PAGE>LAYER SCALE* and change the scale to 2"=1'-0" (1:5). Everything that was already drawn gets reduced in size. The blue grid disappears, but do not worry about this now. As an example, double-click the *TABLE* plug-in tool in the *AEC OBJECTS* palette. If the palette is not open, select *PALETTES>AEC OBJECTS*. The *CREATE TABLE* dialog box opens. The plug-ins have many more options than just size and location since they generally create complex object types. The objects created are hybrid as well – having both a 2D and a 3D component.

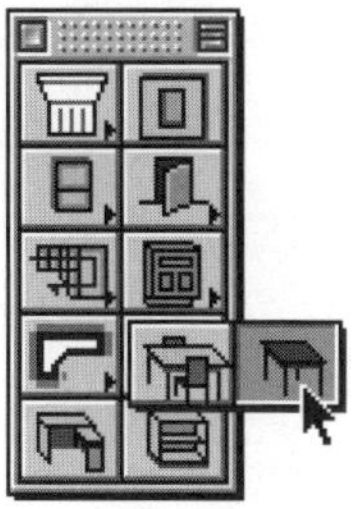

location

The *XYZ* or *IJK* edit boxes, depending on which of the two top buttons are selected, locate the coordinates for the bottom center of the object whether on the *ground plane* or *working plane*. The *ROT* edit box allows you to enter an angle for the rotation of the object in plan. The table is automatically placed as you create it. Be aware that the *plug-in* tools automatically create new classes to place these objects in. Even if you click the *CANCEL* button in the dialog box or deselect the tool, the class is still automatically created.

size and shape

The *CONFIG* pop-out allows you to select the shape of the table, whether *SQUARE* (rectangular), *OVAL*, or *ROUNDED*. Unfortunately it does not allow for a either a boat or raceway (bullet) top, but this may be added with later releases. The *HEIGHT*, *WIDTH*, and *LENGTH* edit boxes set the size of the *plug-in* object. You can also enter a height for the skirting and its location from the edge of the table top under *SKIRT* and *INSET*. If you do not want a skirting just enter 0 into the *SKIRT* box, although one will still be created but without height.

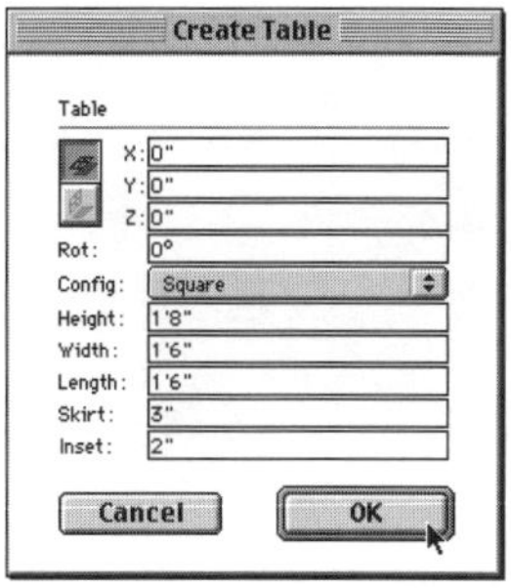

As a note, leaving the *HEIGHT* at 0 places the table top on the *ground plane*, but it still creates a hybrid object. Also, four square legs are automatically created without other options.

Enter 20" (.50m) for *HEIGHT*, 12" (.30m) for *WIDTH* and *LENGTH*, 3" (.07m) for *SKIRT* and 2" (.05m) for *INSET*. The table will be created when you select *OK*. Change back to *WORKSPACES>8 STANDARD (STREAMLINED)*.

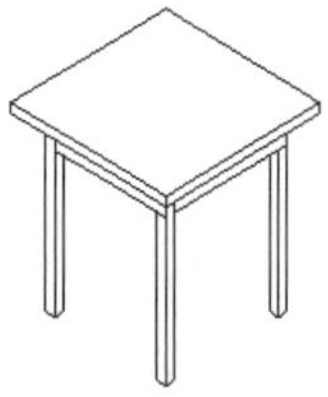

Creating Objects By Duplicating

Another method of creating objects is to duplicate an exact replica of an existing object. There are various techniques to duplicate object(s).

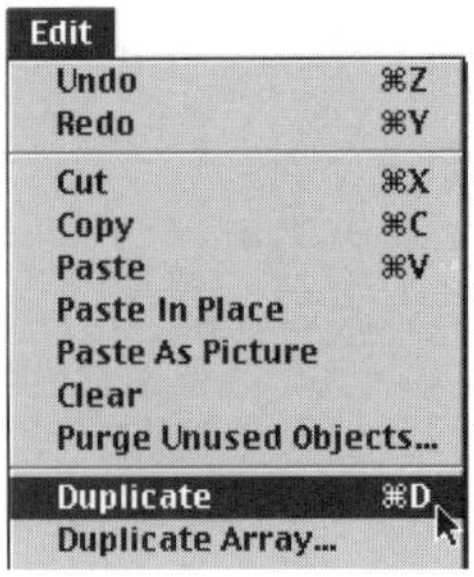

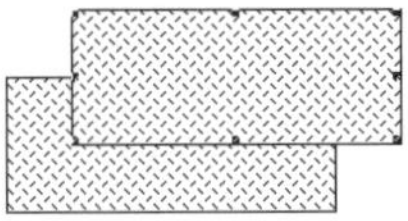

Step 1 - duplicate command

First select the *Rectangle* tool, then press/drag diagonally to create a rectangle. With the rectangle selected (notice the 8 selection handles), select the *EDIT>Duplicate* command. Since *offset duplications* is checked in *VectorWorks Preferences*, the original object remains and the duplicate is placed usually to the upper right. The duplicate becomes the selected object. If *offset duplications* is not checked, the duplicate is placed on top of the original.

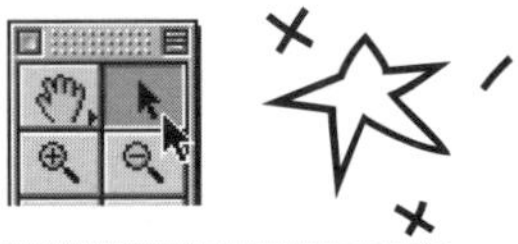

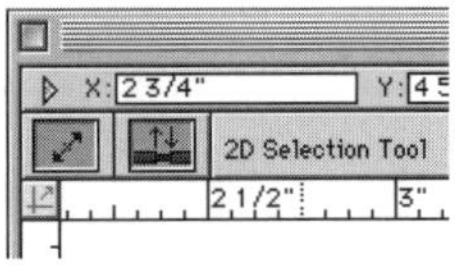

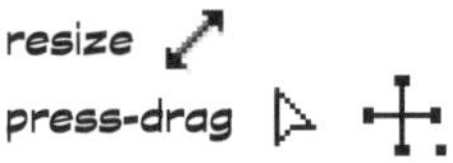

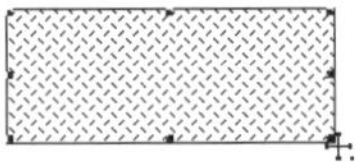

Step 2 - duplicating using option [control]

Another easy way of creating a duplicate is with the *2d Selection* tool. Move the mouse over a corner, end, or center of an object until a *press-drag* cursor appears (not a *resize* cursor). If you hit the *U* key to deselect the first icon in the mode bar, only the *press-drag* cursor will be available. As a default, though, leave this icon selected. When it does appear, without moving the mouse, press the *Option [Control]* key, press/drag the mouse then release the key. It will automatically move a newly created duplicate without affecting the original.

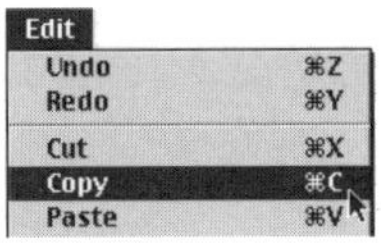

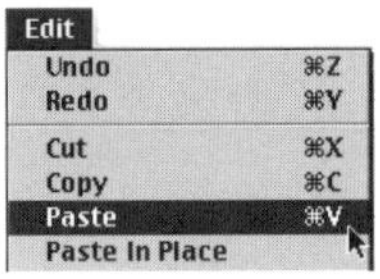

Step 3 - copy & pasting duplicates

You can also select an object and the *EDIT>Copy* command. A duplicate is placed in the clipboard. Now, every time you select *EDIT>Paste* a duplicate is placed on the drawing. The duplicate is usually placed to the upper left of the object that was copied unless you move to a different area where the original object is no longer visible. In this case the copy usually is centered. As a note, the clipboard will remember the high resolution of VectorWorks as long as it remains the active program. If you inadvertently click the desktop, the resolution drops down to 72 dpi for the pasted copy.

Step 4 - duplicate array

You can also create a series of duplicates by specifying the quantity and arrangement for placement. First, select an object(s) and the *Edit>Duplicate Array* command. The *Duplicate* dialog box opens. The types of duplication layouts, or *duplication shape*, can be *linear* (along a line, whether vertical, horizontal, or on an angle), *rectangular* (a series of horizontal and vertical *rows* and *columns*), or *circular array*. Under each of the options, you can designate the quantity and the distance each duplicate is offset. The *offset* distance is center-line to center-line, not a clear dimension, and can be set by entering in a specific *xy* dimension under *manual*, or by the *next mouse click*. There is also a choice for *resize* and *rotate duplicate(s)* which affect each instance of duplication.

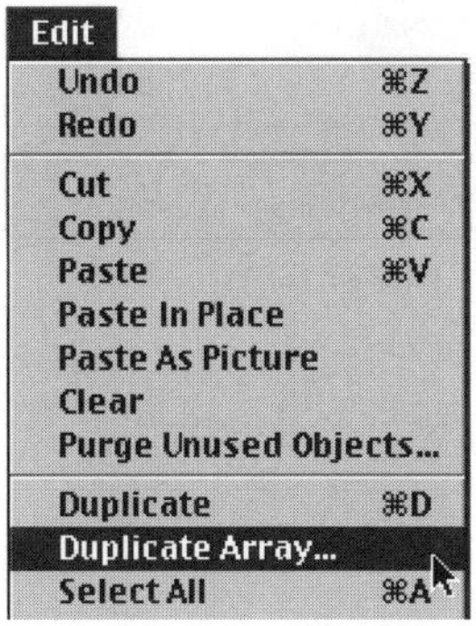

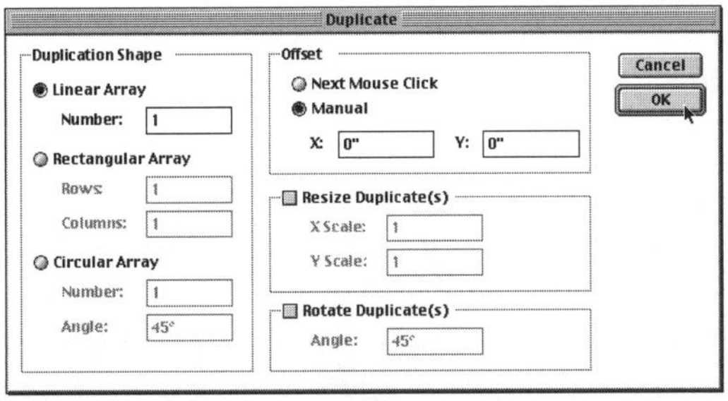

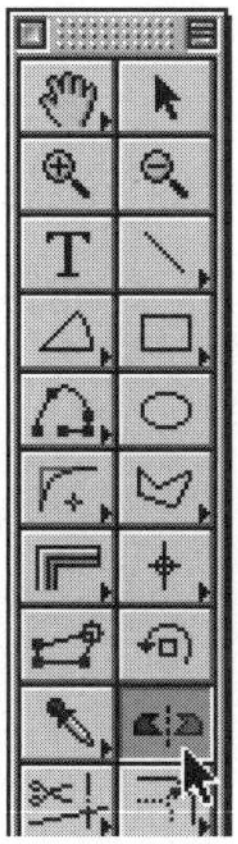

Step 5 - mirrored duplicates

If you want to create an object that is identical to an existing object, but a mirrored image, select the object, in this case one of the diagonal lines already created, then select the *Mirror* tool. In the mode bar across the top there are two modifier icons. Click the second icon to select the *mirror and duplicate* modifier. With the tool selected, press/drag a line which serves as an axis for the mirroring of the duplicate.

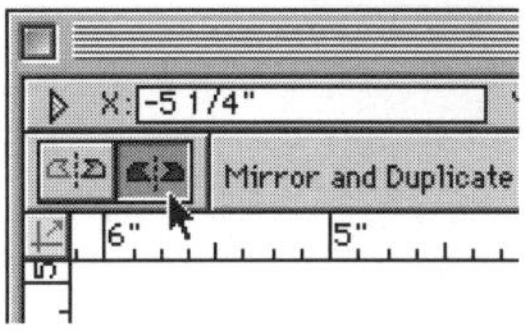

When you release the mouse, the axis line disappears and the duplicate will be created using this as a center-line between the duplicate and the original. The angle of the axis line can be constrained vertically or horizontally by pressing the *Shift* key before you release the mouse.

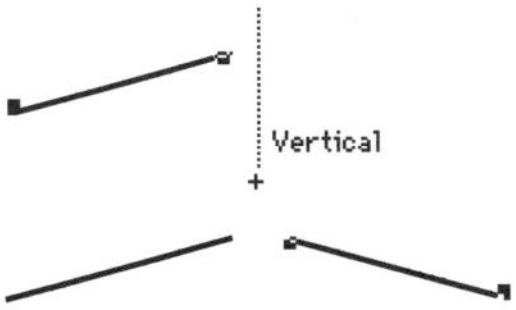

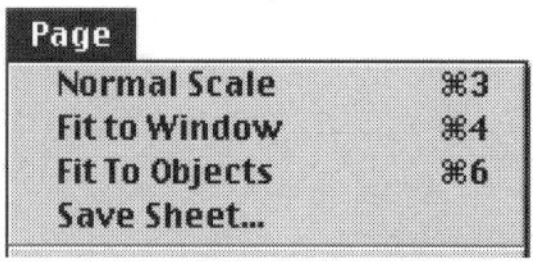

Looking At Objects

One other thing you should know about at this point are the *Zoom-In* and *Zoom-Out* tools, and the *Normal Scale, Fit To Window,* and *Fit To Objects* commands located under *PAGE*. All of these tools and commands allow you to move in closer to an object or farther away so that the object appears magnified or reduced. With any of these tools or commands except the *Fit To Window*, if an object(s) is selected it will affect what is centered on the screen and what will be visible. Play with these tools and commands both with objects selected and not selected. What you do will not affect the drawing, just how it looks on the screen. Also notice the magnification in the *data display bar* when you change the amount of zoom. The *views bar* located in the bottom left of the scroll bar has several icons making it easier to access these commands or tools with just a click as well as to navigate to previous views.

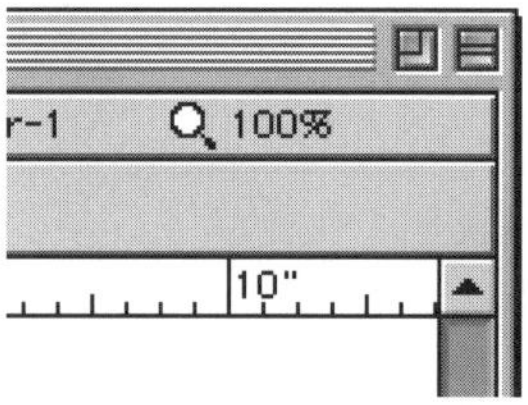

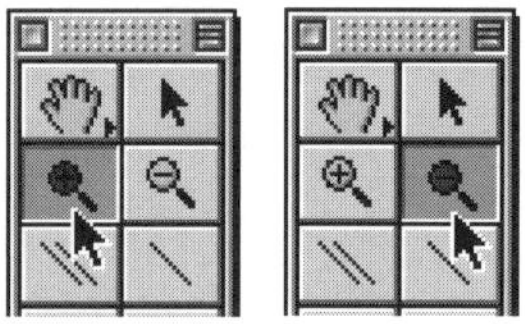

The Zoom Tools

The *Zoom-In* tool allows you to press/drag a marquee around an area or an object. When the mouse is released the area within the marquee fills the whole drawing window. With both the *Zoom-In* and *Zoom-Out* tools, double-clicking the tool either brings you in twice as close or twice as far away. The two small magnifying icons in the *view bar* when clicked once do the same thing as double-clicking the tools but without deselecting the previous tool.

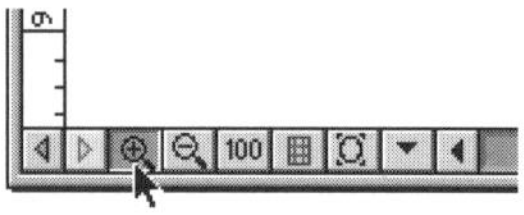

Viewing History Arrows

The two arrows on the left in the *view bar*, allow you to move back and forth between the nine previous views in your drawing just by clicking. The previous projection, positioning of the view, and magnification are remembered as well. Do not confuse this with multiple undos.

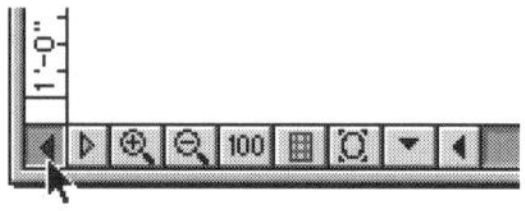

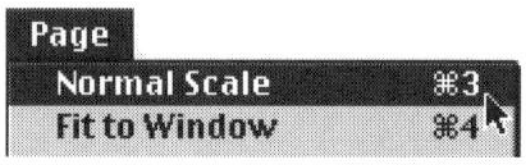

Normal Scale Command

Selecting the *Normal Scale* command changes the view to 100% magnification. If your sheet size is small enough and your monitor big enough you can see the whole drawing at one time, otherwise only part of the drawing will appear on the screen. It will be the same size as what actually gets printed. If an object or several objects are selected when the command is used, the object(s) will be centered on the screen. Clicking the *100* in the *view bar* does the same thing and is easier to access.

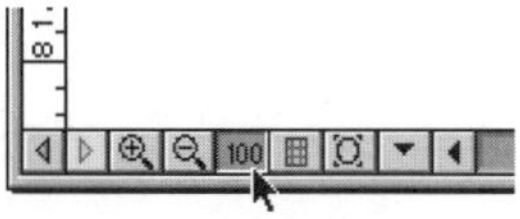

Fit To Window Command

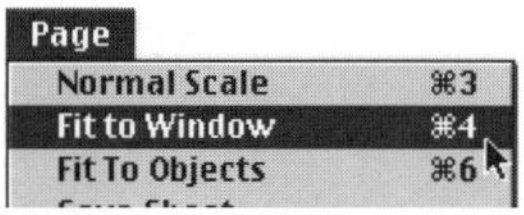

The *Fit To Window* command either reduces or enlarges the magnification of the drawing so that the whole sheet can be seen at one time regardless of the scale. The *view bar* icon does the same thing with one click.

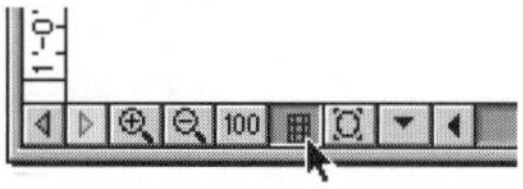

Fit To Objects Command

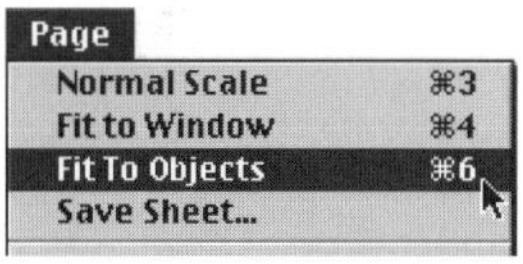

The *Fit To Objects* command will change the magnification size so that all objects are visible. If an object or several objects are selected when the command is used, the object(s) will enlarge to fit the screen. The icon in the *view bar* does the same thing with one click.

QUITTING

Once you have gone through these methods of creating objects and are comfortable with each, you are ready to quit the program. Just select the *FILE>Quit [Exit]* command. The computer will ask you if you want to save the untitled document.

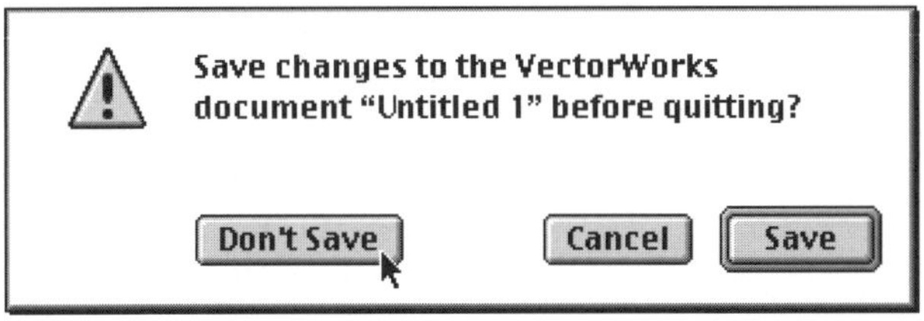

Since there really is nothing to save but computer scribbles, select the *DON'T SAVE* button. If you are not ready to quit VectorWorks, just click the *close* box instead in the upper left [upper right] corner of your document and answer *DON'T SAVE* when it asks the same question about saving.

This is probably the most important chapter in the book. If you are having trouble with any of the following chapters or you are not **extremely** comfortable with the information contained in this one, do repeat it again, and again, and again...

DRAWING IN SUMMATION

In summary, the different methods we have learned for creating or drawing objects have different advantages. You should become fluent and feel comfortable with each of these methods for creating objects as well as viewing the object and moving around within the drawing. When actually drawing, if you can easily switch from one method to another, you will make the most use out of the computer and take advantage of its inherent time-saving abilities.

- You can just use the mouse to eyeball an object and make use of the *smartcursor* to align it with a point on an existing object.

- If you need to draw an object of a specific size and/or location and would like to align it with an existing object, use the *data display bar.*

- If you need to create an object of a specific size and/or location but do not need to view the drawing to create it, use a dialog box.

- If you need to create a complex object, use an existing *plug-in* tool if one exists. Remember that you may need to change the *Workspaces* in order to find the *plug-in.*

- If several objects need to be made that are identical then duplicate them.

TEMPLATE - WHAT'S THAT?

WHY TEMPLATES

A template, previously known as a stationery pad, allows standardized information and formatting to open in a new untitled document every time the file is opened. Basically, once a sheet is set up, you save time by skipping all of the setup steps every time after and really take advantage of the computer which is what this is all about in the first place. You can tell the difference between a template and a regular file in VectorWorks. The template icon is similar to the file icon except that it has a frame around the outside.

file

template

The tools, commands, and constraints we will be exploring are;

2D Selection Tool
Rectangle Tool
Single Line Tool
Text Insertion Tool
Align Objects Command
Center Command
Duplicate Array Command
Group Command
Layer Options Command
Layers Command
Nudge Command
Page Setup [Print Setup] Command
Rotate Command
Save Command
Save As Command
Save As Template Command
Scale Objects Command
Select All Command
Text Commands
Snap To Distance Constraint
Snap To Edge Constraint

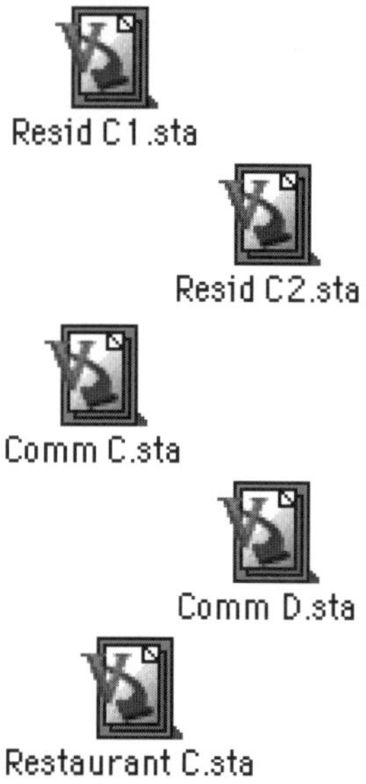

WHAT GOES INTO A TEMPLATE

Usually I have several template files that are used for different project types. Each template can have a different standardized sheet size with the title block adjusted and placed accordingly. It can also have different formatting depending on how many stories the building has or include general notes specific to whether it is a commercial or residential project. Even standardized details and symbols can be included within a template. If you make use of classes and layers, they can also be integrated.

Typically I have several residential template files - "Resid C1" (residential project, C size sheet, 1 story), "Resid C2" (residential, C sheet, 2 story), etc. I also have a "Commercial C," a "Commercial D," and a "Restaurant C." Other templates get added as other project types come up and are often based on an existing file with some slight modifications.

CREATING A STANDARDIZED FILE

The first thing we are going to do is create a file which includes a title block and other information that might typically be used on a drawing. Open a blank sheet by double-clicking the *VectorWorks 8* icon or if it is already open, select the *FILE>NEW* command and select *CREATE BLANK DOCUMENT* in the *CREATE DOCUMENT* dialog box that opens. Again verify the settings and defaults, particularly for constraints, default line weight, and units. Remember to check your default settings.

The Sheet Itself

Depending on your printer driver there might be all kinds of options. Some of the typical ones are, *PAPER SIZE* which is self-explanatory, whether letter, legal, etc. *REDUCE OR ENLARGE* or *SCALE* allows you to resize all information on a sheet to fill another size sheet when printed or faxed. *ORIENTATION* allows you to have portrait or landscape (vertical or horizontal formatting). *HI-RESOLUTION PRINTING* should be checked if drawing any curves or diagonals. *EDGE TO EDGE PRINTING* allows you to eliminate the margins on a sheet of paper. Again, whether these options are available to you depends on the printer driver you have available.

Step 1 - setting up a sheet

Go to *FILE>PAGE SETUP [PRINT SETUP]* to open your printer's *PAGE SETUP* dialog box. Click the *LANDSCAPE* button under *ORIENTATION*. Select the drawing size 8.5 x 14 (*US LEGAL*) or *A3* for metric. If you do not have that capability in your printer, then select 8.5 x 11 (*US LETTER*) or *A4* or *B4*. Look for *EDGE-TO-EDGE PRINTING* or larger printable area usually under *OPTIONS* or *PAPER* and select. Also on the Mac, look for *VECTORWORKS 8* options and change the setting to *HI-RESOLUTION PRINTING* and select *MAXIMUM*. On Windows, go to *PROPERTIES>ADVANCED>GRAPHICS RESOLUTION* and change the resoution to *HIGH*. Remember what you see in the *PAGE SETUP* dialog box depends on which printer driver you are using, since each driver will show a different dialog box.

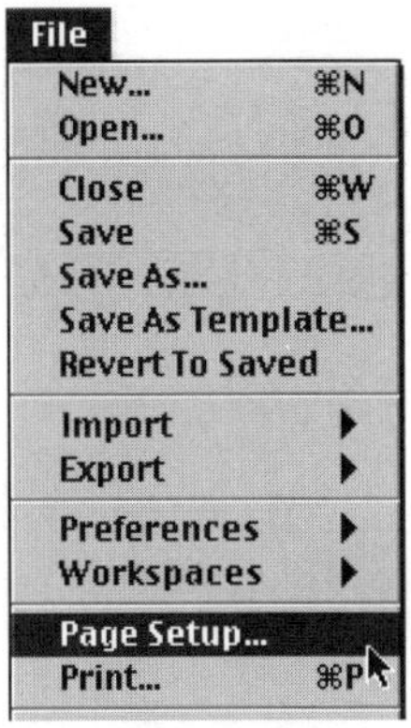

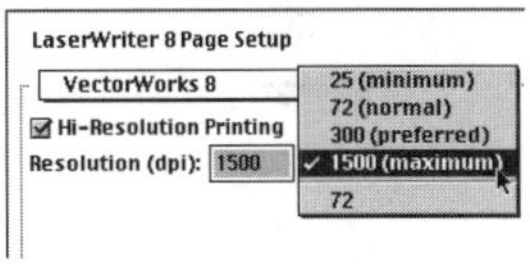

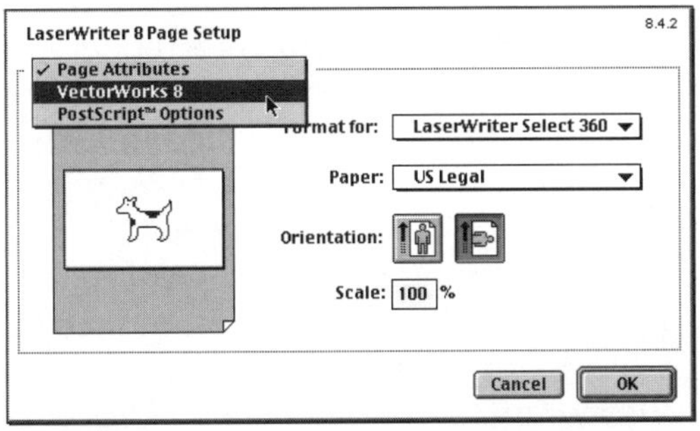

Step 2 - saving

This is also an appropriate time to name the file by selecting *FILE>SAVE AS*. When the dialog box opens give it the name *chapt 3 [chapt 3.mcd]*. Navigate through the scrolling list so that *VectorWorks 8 ƒ* folder is at the top of the pop-out menu.

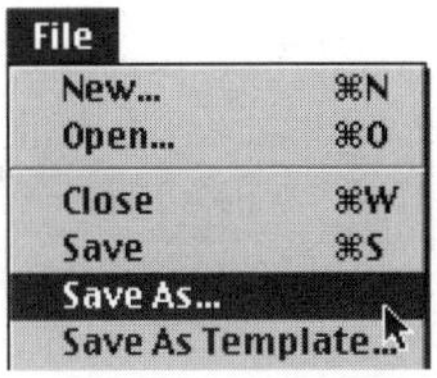

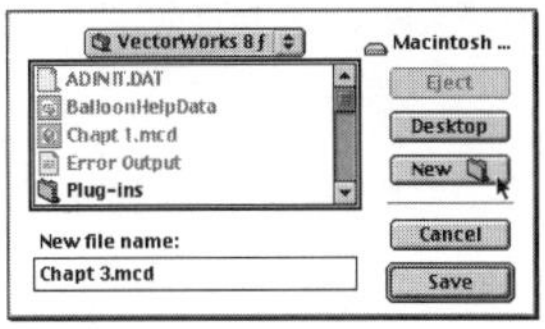

Select the *NEW FOLDER* button. When the dialog box opens, name it *experiments* and click *CREATE*. This folder name now replaces *VectorWorks 8 ƒ* folder and the scrolling list will be empty. Click the *SAVE* button. Do just a little filing now before we go any further. Open the *VectorWorks 8 folder* on your desktop, find the icon for the *chapt 1 [chapt 1.mcd]* file, and drag it to the new *experiments* folder so that it is placed inside.

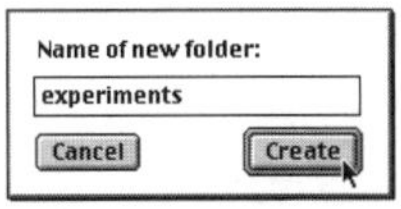

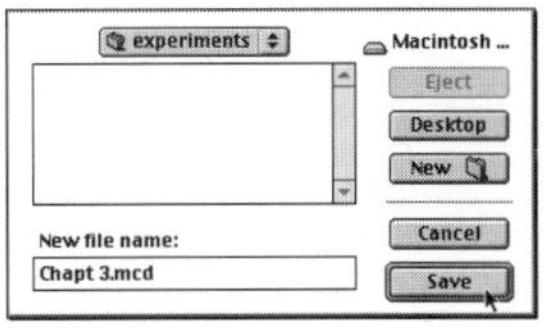

This new file, *chapt 3 [chapt 3.mcd],* as well as the previous *chapt 1 [chapt 1.mcd]* file will be located within the *experiments* folder which is within the *VectorWorks 8* folder. As you go through the following steps make sure you frequently save the document by either selecting the *FILE>SAVE* command or pressing the *Command [Control]* and *S* keys.

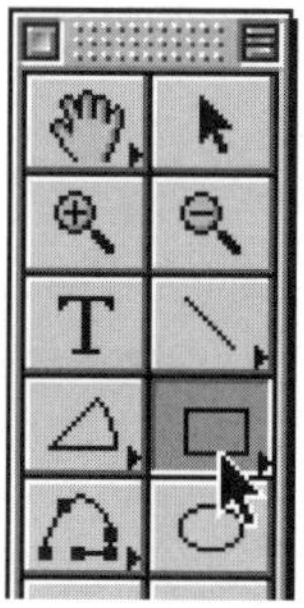

Creating A Title Block

The next thing is to create a title block. A title block is usually made up of several components; the firm information, the project information, the drawing information, and the graphic component. We will start with the last item.

Step 1 - the graphic components

With the *RECTANGLE* tool selected, create a rectangle that is 8" x 1.25" (.20m x .03m). Either use the *data display bar* to enter exact dimensions or double-click the tool to open the *CREATE RECTANGLE* dialog box.

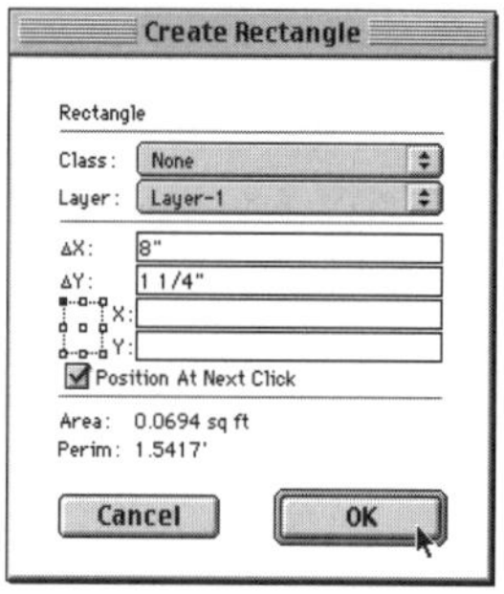

Remember when placing fractions to leave a space between the fraction and the whole number. Most times, it is easier and less steps to just enter a decimal point number instead and let VectorWorks convert it to fractions. Also, with our setup, VectorWorks automatically assumes inches unless the foot marker is actually placed. For example, enter 5.5' instead of 5'-6" or 1.75 instead of 1 3/4". If using metric, no designation needs to be placed.

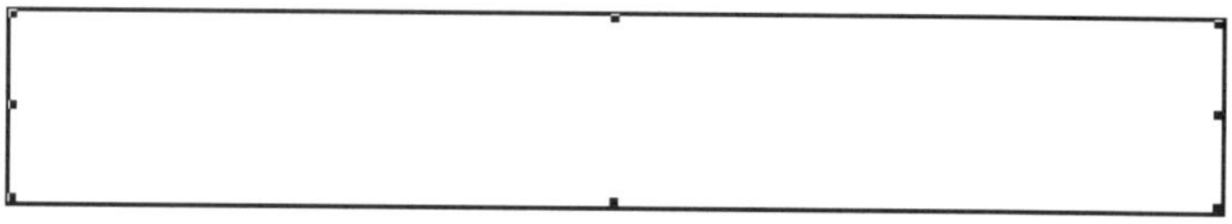

With the new rectangle selected, go to the *ATTRIBUTES* palette and select the thickest line (5th solid line down). This will change only the rectangle line weight and not the default setting.

Next we will want to place vertical lines at specific locations to divide up the information. To assist us in locating the lines, double-click the *Snap To Edge* constraint. When the *Edge Snaps* dialog box opens, select *use 2nd vector* and *use floating edge* then select *ok*. This constraint should remain selected on the *Constraints* palette.

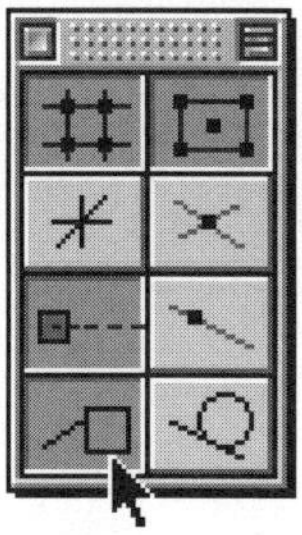

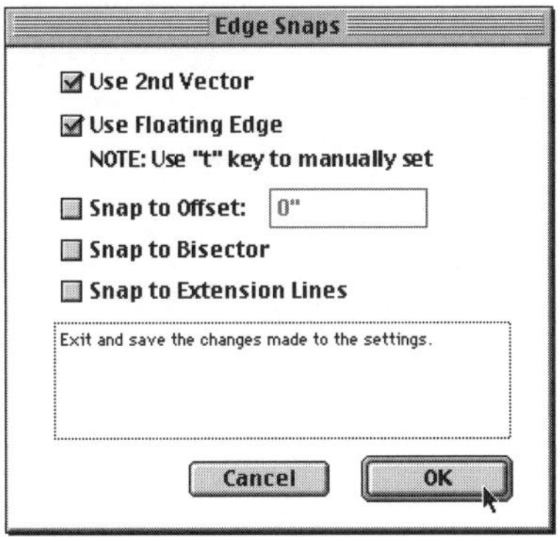

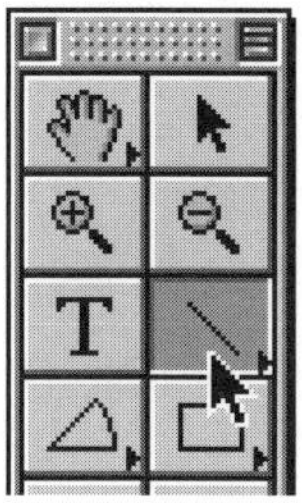

Select the *Single Line* tool with the *constrained line* modifier icon. Do not press the mouse button yet. We will want to draw a vertical line 3" (.08m) over from the left edge.

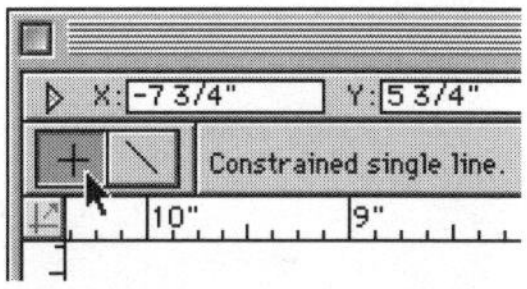

Make use of the *smartcursor* capabilities by placing the cursor on the upper left corner of the rectangle, moving it around a little, to make the corner the floating datum point. Both the *x* and *y* edit boxes should now be changed to 0. If VectorWorks gets a little stubborn and you are having trouble making that point the floating datum, just hit the *G* key to manually set the point.

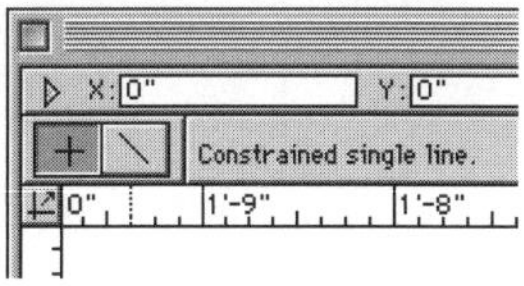

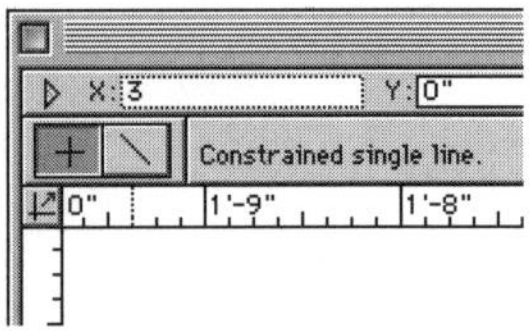

Hit the *Tab* key until the *x* edit box is highlighted, use the keyboard to enter 3" (.08m) and hit the *Return [Enter]* key. You will now notice a dashed guide line.

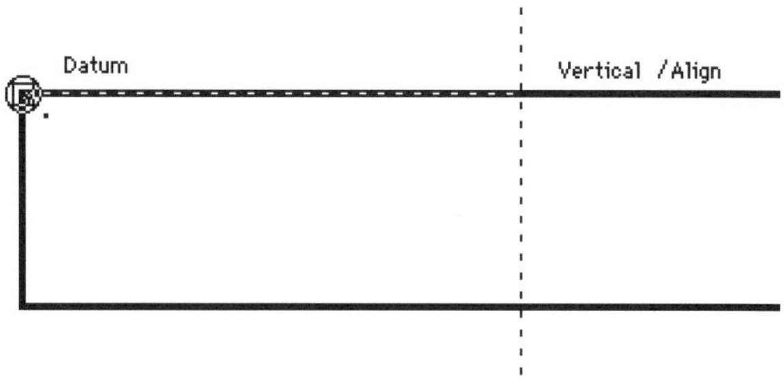

Place the cursor where the guide line touches the top surface of the rectangle and press when the *smartcursor cue* becomes *object/vertical*.

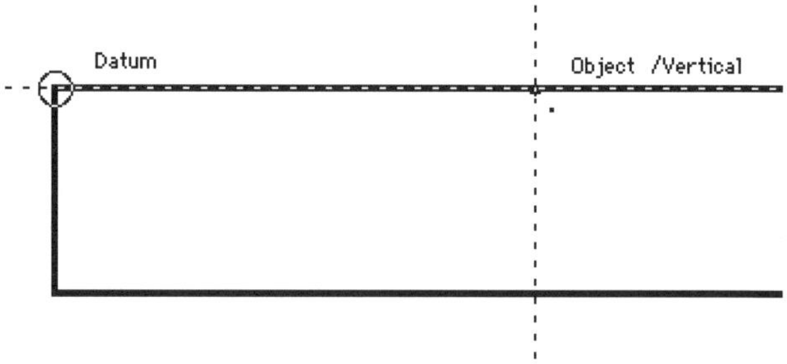

Press/drag the cursor from that point downwards. When the line is vertical and touches the bottom of the rectangle the *smartcursor cue, object/vertical* appears again. You may not get the second horizontal guide line or edge lock. This does not matter if you get the cue, *object* which shows you are snapping to the edge of the rectangle. Release the mouse. The line is now created at the right location and in the correct length.

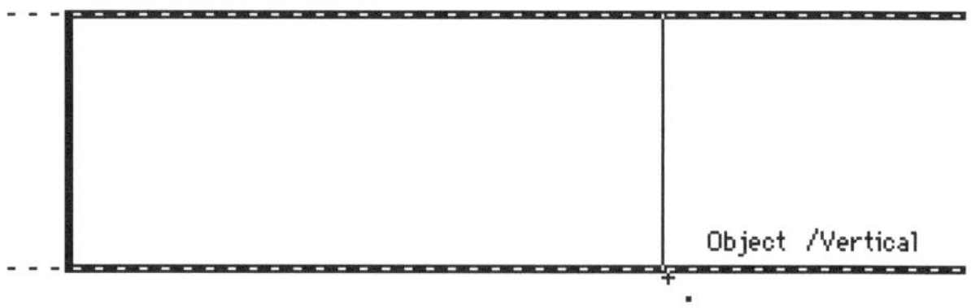

With the line still selected, change the line weight to the 4th weight down in the *ATTRIBUTES* palette. Now, select the *EDIT>DUPLICATE ARRAY* command. Under *LINEAR ARRAY*, leave the default of 1 under *NUMBER* and click *OFFSET>MANUAL* and enter 2.25 (.06m) for *X*.

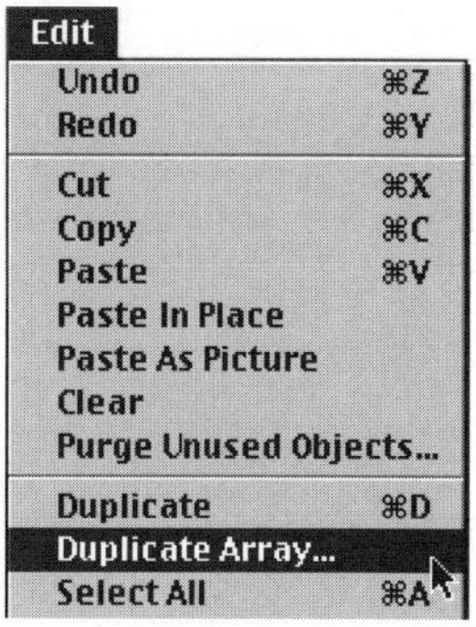

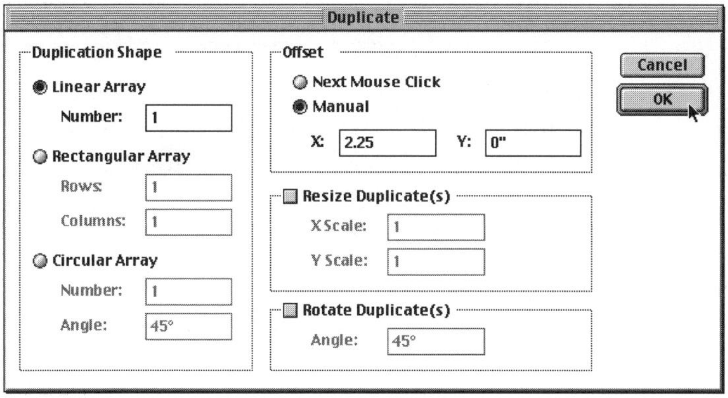

When the *OK* button is selected, the duplicated object is automatically placed in the correct location. With the duplicate still selected, go through the same steps and place the next line at a 1.5" (.03m) for the *X OFFSET*.

Click anywhere on the drawing to deselect all objects and select the fourth line weight down on the *ATTRIBUTES* palette. This will change the default line weight. With the *SINGLE LINE* tool selected and the *UNCONSTRAINED* modifier icon, place the cursor on the first line and move it until the *smartcursor cue, center,* appears. Press the mouse, drag to the right until you get the *smartcursor cue, center,* to also appear on the second line. When you release the mouse a horizontal line is created that aligns exactly with the centerpoints.

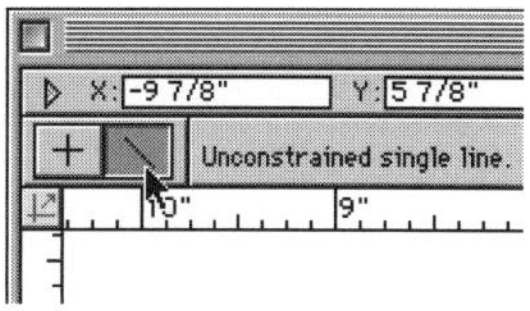

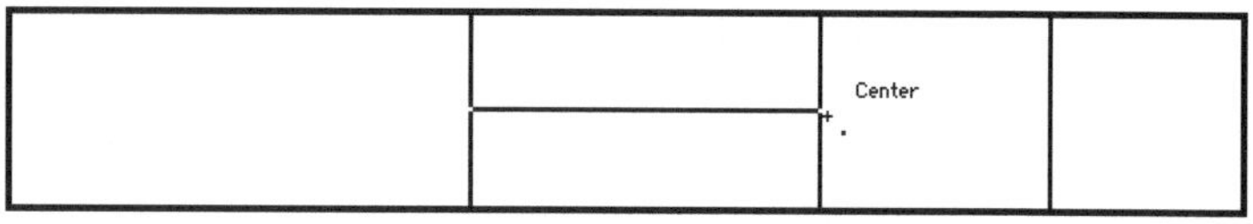

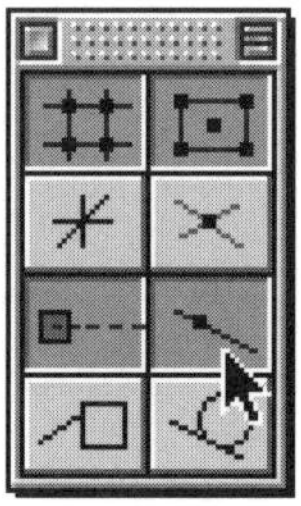

Click to deselect everything and again select the *Single Line* tool. Deselect the *Snap To Edge* constraint and double-click the *Snap To Distance* icon on the *Constraints* palette. The *Snap Distance* dialog box opens. Select the *by fraction* button and enter 1/3 and also select the *multiple divisions* box.

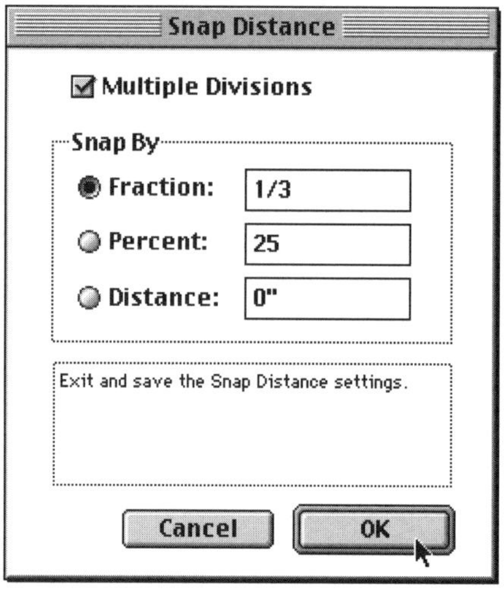

When the dialog box closes, the *Snap to Distance* icon is selected. Run the cursor along the middle vertical line and press/drag when the *smartcursor cue, along line,* appears. Press/drag to the last line and release it when the same *smartcursor cue* appears. The new line will snap to these points which are exactly 1/3 from the end. Do the same from the other end of the middle line so that two horizontal lines are placed dividing the space in thirds.

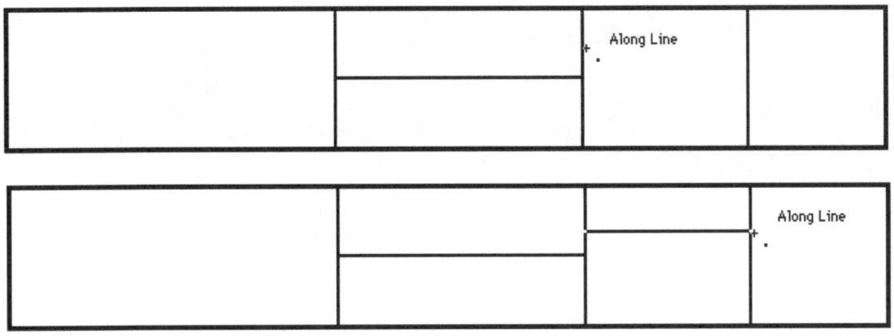

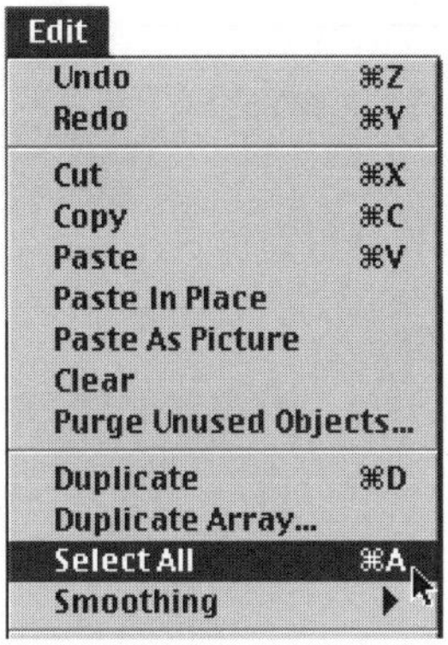

In order to organize all of these individual objects, use the *EDIT>SELECT ALL* command to select all of the component pieces and use the *ORGANIZE>GROUP* command. Notice that all of the individual handles for each line disappear into one object. Also, deselect the *SNAP TO DISTANCE* constraint icon.

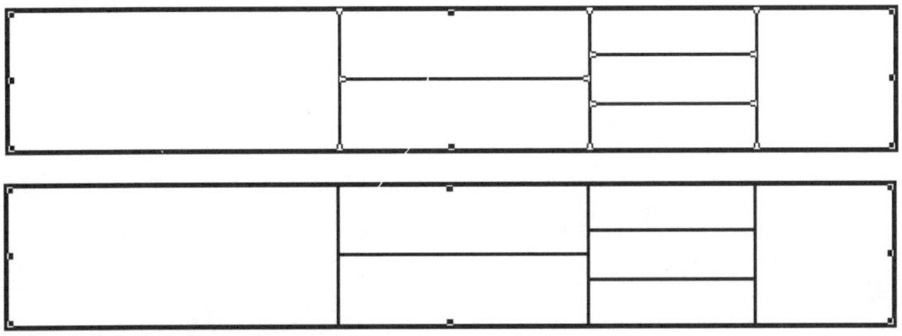

The Text Components

The next steps will be adding text information blocks to the graphic element and placing them appropriately.

Step 1 - creating the text

With the *TEXT INSERTION* tool selected, click the drawing, the location not being important, and using the keys, type the firm name and address below. Place a hard return by hitting the *Return [Enter]* key each time you need to get to the next line.

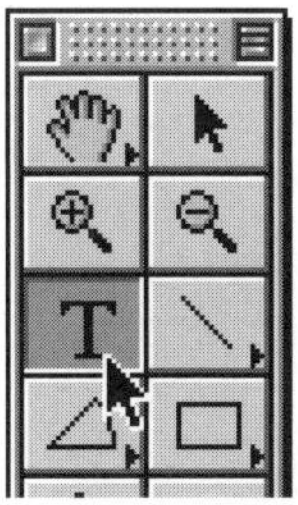

The Furf & Grinch Studios
3579 Snowball Lane
North Pole, Arctic 00000

Step 2 - adding style and changing size

Now with the *TEXT INSERTION* tool still selected, press/drag just through the name to select it. The selected text will be highlighted.

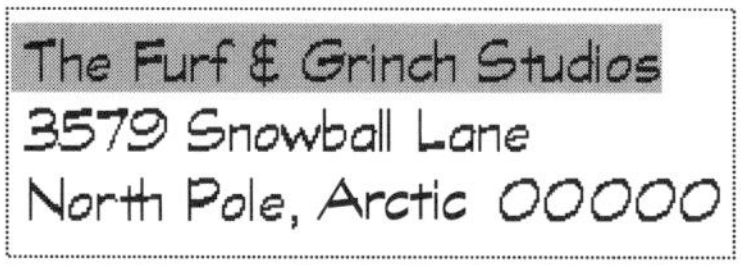

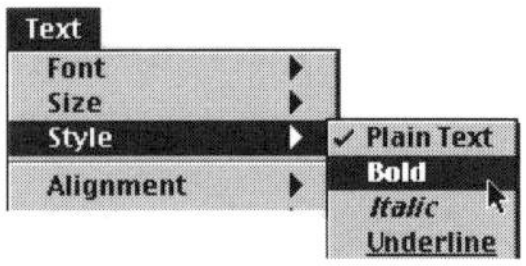

Select *TEXT>STYLE>BOLD* and then *TEXT>SIZE>SET SIZE.* When the *SET TEXT SIZE* dialog box opens enter 13 *POINTS.*

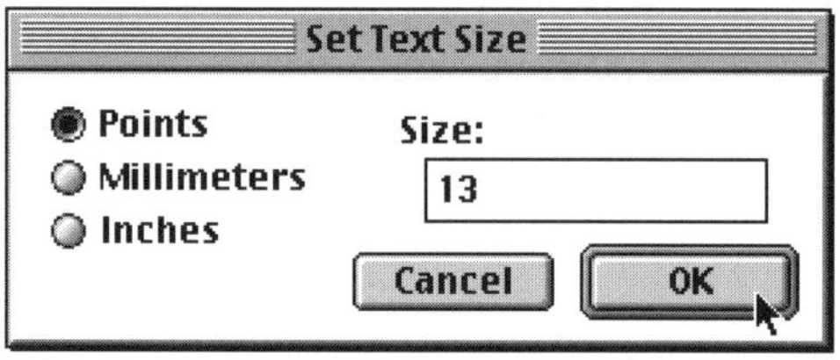

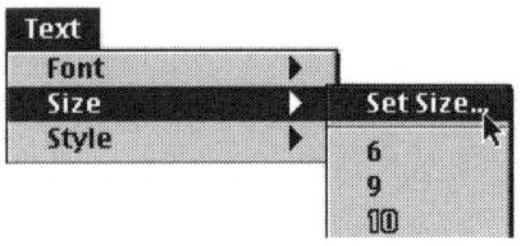

With the *TEXT INSERTION* tool still selected, press/drag through the remainder of the text to select. This will automatically deselect the name and select the rest of the text. Select *SIZE>SET SIZE* and change the font to 11 points.

Step 3 - changing the alignment

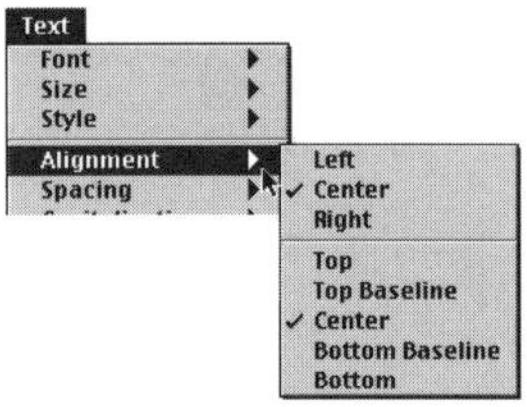

Change to the *2D SELECTION* tool and click the text as an object. With this text object now selected, change the alignment to *TEXT>ALIGNMENT>CENTER* and again select *TEXT>ALIGNMENT* and change from *TOP* to *CENTER* as well. Notice how the X changes position on the selected text object showing you the insertion point for the text object.

Now *Shift*-select both the text and the grouped graphic object by clicking the text object, pressing the *Shift* key, clicking the graphic object, and then releasing the *Shift*

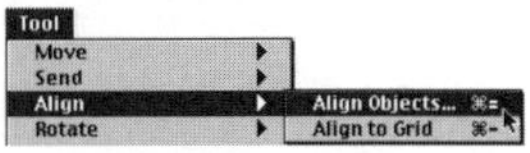

key. Go up to the *TOOL>ALIGN>ALIGN OBJECTS* command and when the *ALIGN OBJECTS* dialog box opens, click the *LEFT SIDES* button, and the *T/B CENTERS* button, then select *OK*.

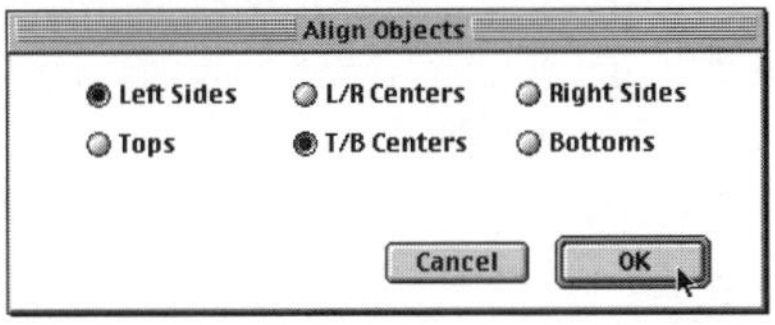

Depending on where the rectangle is and where the text is, one or both objects will relocate. To center the text within the left box, select just the text block with the *2D SELECTION* tool and with the *resize* cursor, press/drag the right corner of the block to align with the first line. The text automatically adjusts to center within the first box.

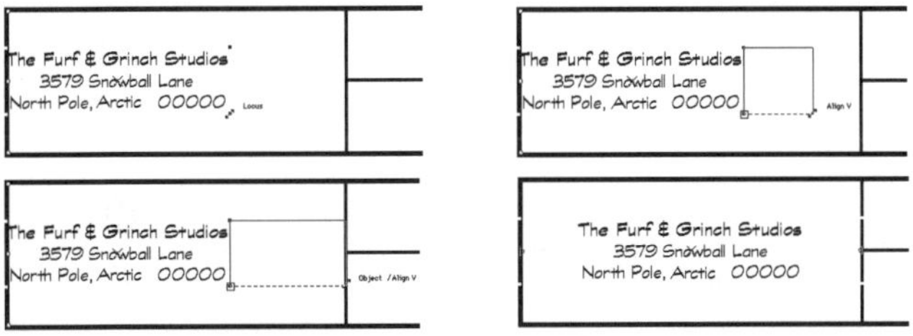

With the *TEXT INSERTION* tool, select the firm name and then the *TEXT>CAPITALIZATION>UPPER CASE* command.

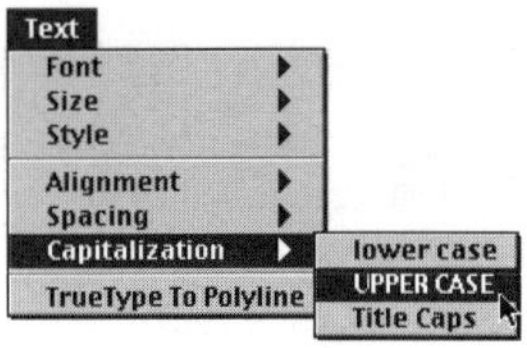

Step 4 - more text

With the *TEXT INSERTION* tool, click approximately where each text object goes as shown by the next illustration, and type the words, *project, sheet title, date, scale, project no,* and *sheet no. Shift*-select each of these blocks and change the *SIZE* to 8.

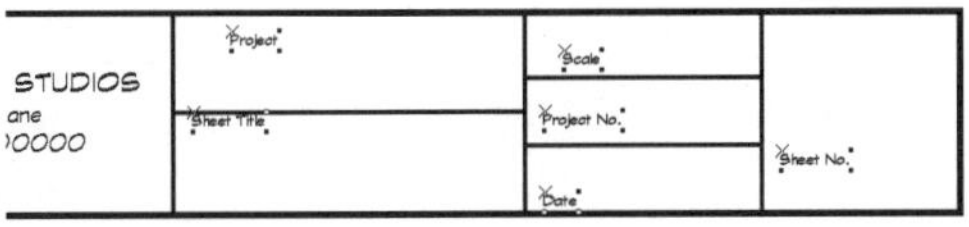

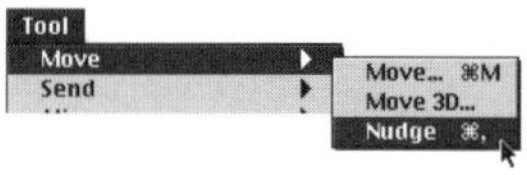

Click to deselect all and then *Shift*-select both *project* and *sheet title*. Use the *ALIGN OBJECTS* command with *LEFT SIDES* selected. Once both are aligned on their left sides, press/drag them to place the left side location near the first line. Deselect both and select just one of these text blocks. Select the *TOOL>NUDGE* command. Use the *Arrow* keys to move it up or down as needed, then click the drawing to stop the command. *NUDGE* the other text block up or down as needed. Now both of these objects are aligned on their left sides and eyeballed to be approximately the same distance below the top and middle line.

Follow the same steps with the rest of the text, aligning the left sides for *scale, project no,* and *date* and then the bottoms of *date* and *sheet no.* Use the *NUDGE* command where appropriate. As a note, in order to use the *ALIGN OBJECTS* command at least two objects need to be selected. Also type in the typical project information so that the text location and font size can be formatted. Change the fonts size of the project information to 10 points.

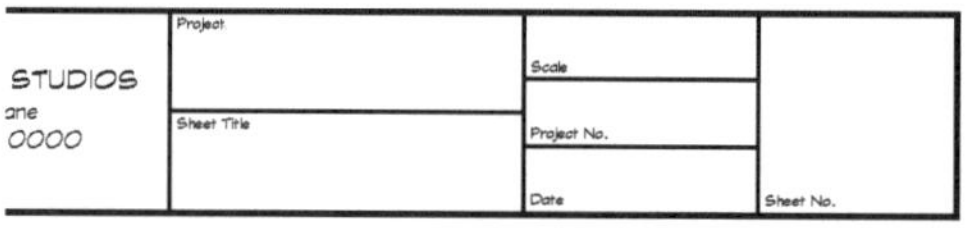

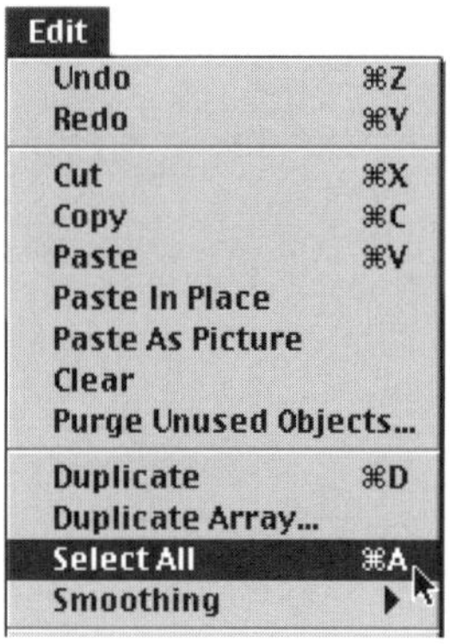

Step 5 - organizing the title block

Now choose the *EDIT>SELECT ALL* command and then the *ORGANIZE>GROUP* command again. This allows for a group within a group or a nested group. It can then be moved together as one object and the careful formatting does not get inadvertently messed up. You can always revise individual elements by selecting the grouped object and then the *ORGANIZE>EDIT GROUP* command.

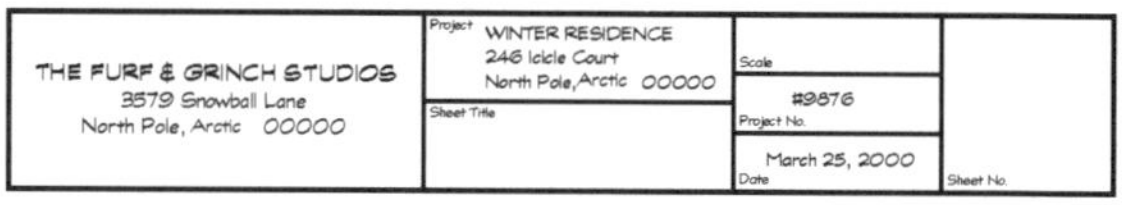

As a note, if you did not have an option for a edge-to edge printing or larger print area under *FILE>PAGE SETUP [PRINT SETUP]*, the title block will stick out beyond the printable area when we rotate the text block into position. If this is the case, with the title block selected, go to *TOOL>SCALE OBJECTS*. When the *SCALE OBJECTS* dialog box opens, select *SYMMETRIC* and enter .95 for the *X,Y,Z FACTOR*, select the *SCALE TEXT* box and then *OK*.

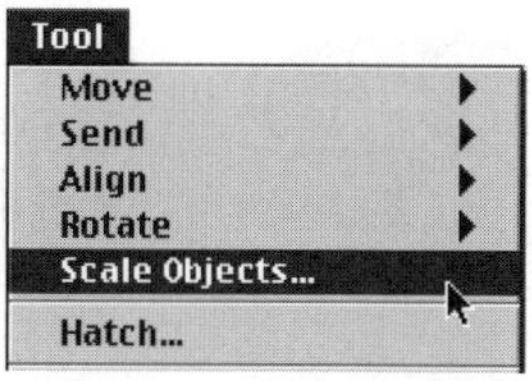

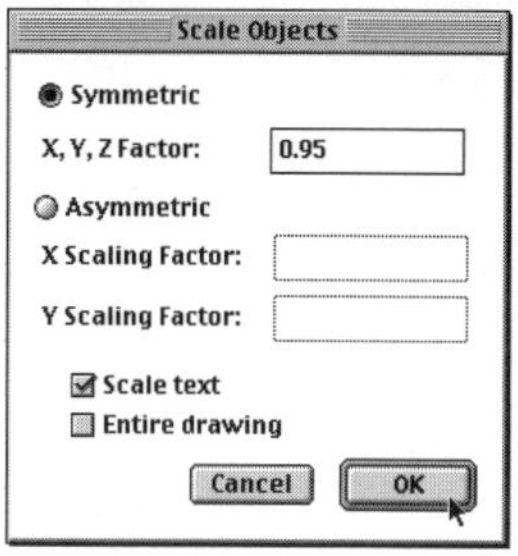

With the grouped title block selected, choose the *TOOL> ROTATE>ROTATE LEFT 90°* command. Press/drag the title block so that it is centered on the sheet top to bottom and over to the right side.

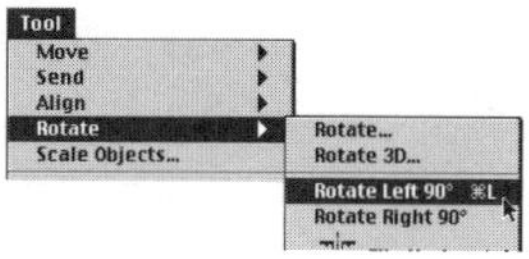

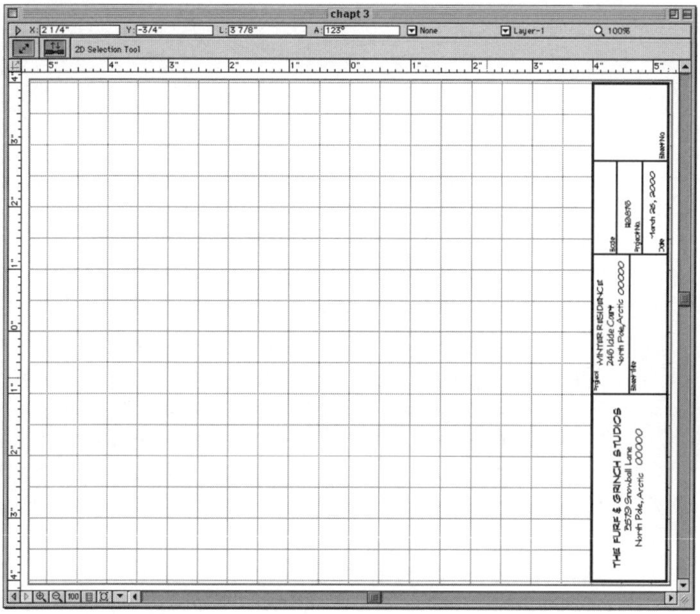

Setting Up Layers

Making use of different layers allows you to organize information within a drawing. There are complex organizing systems developed by different organizations that VectorWorks now comes with or you can develop your own standards that are more Mac-like [intuitive].

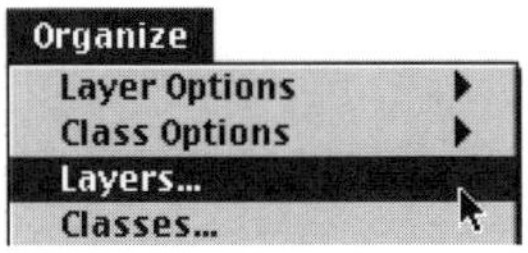

Step 1 - creating layers

Go up to the *ORGANIZE>LAYERS* command. When the *LAYERS SETUP* dialog box opens and the default layer name, *layer-1,* appears under NAME, select it and replace it with the word *title.*

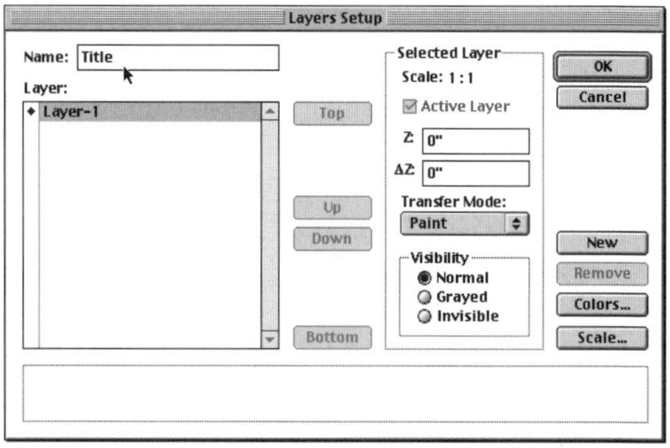

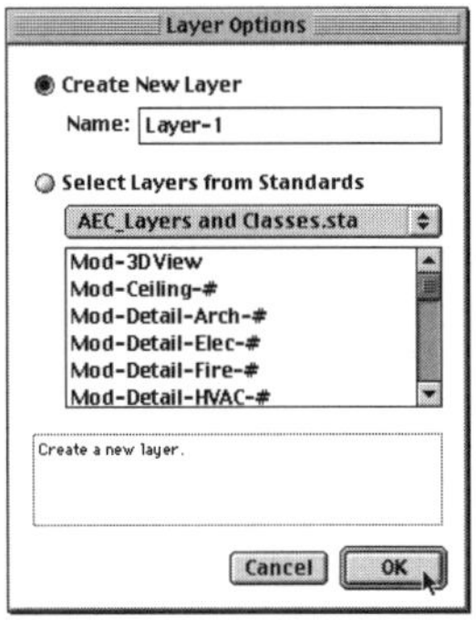

Select the NEW button. When the *LAYER OPTIONS* dialog box opens, select the CREATE NEW LAYER button and click OK. A new layer with the default name of *layer-1* is automatically created. Click the NEW button again, this time type to replace *layer-2* with *eighth scale [hundredth scale]* next to NAME in the *LAYER OPTIONS* dialog box and then click OK. Click to select *layer-1* in the LAYER scrolling list in the *LAYERS SETUP* dialog box, and *Tab* to highlight the edit box next to NAME and type to rename it, *quarter scale [fiftieth scale].*

With this last layer still selected, select the SCALE button. When the *LAYER SCALE* dialog box opens select 1/4" (1:50) making sure the SCALE TEXT box is deselected and click OK.

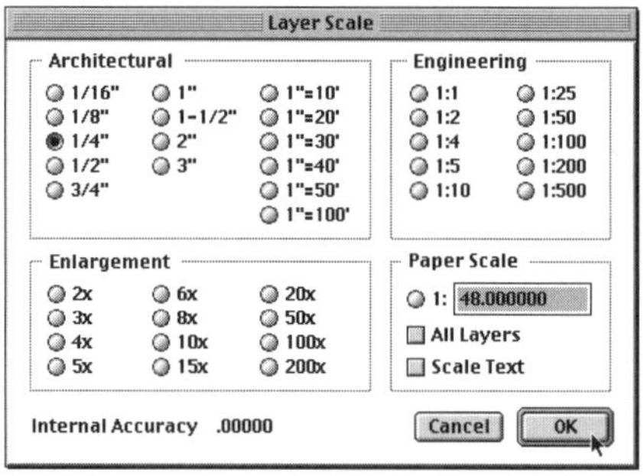

Click the *eighth scale [hundredth scale]* layer in the *LAYER* scrolling list and then the *SCALE* button and select 1/8" (1:100) for the scale. If you select the *title* layer you will notice that the default scale is 1:1 or Full Scale which is fine for this layer. In the *LAYERS SETUP* dialog box select *OK*.

Notice that if you press on the right arrow in the *data display bar,* a pop-out menu appears displaying all layers. Also, you can press/drag to *LAYERS* here instead of going up to *ORGANIZE>LAYERS* to open the *LAYERS SETUP* dialog box. The active layer has a check mark next to it.

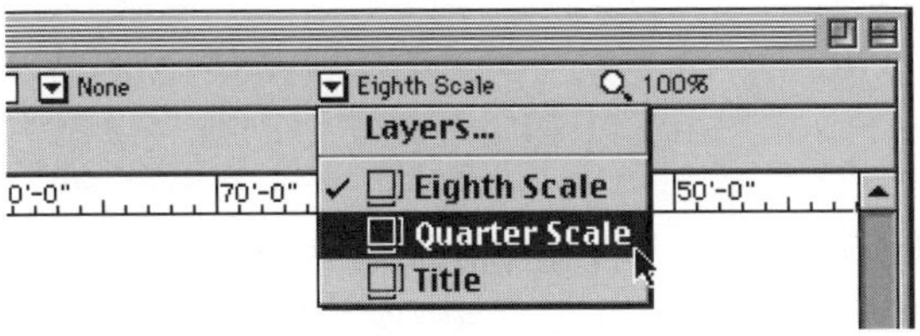

Press/drag down to *quarter scale [fiftieth scale]* to make it the active layer if it is not already. Do not worry if all of the information previously drawn is gray or not visible. Select the *TEXT INSERTION* tool, click the drawing, and type 1/4"=1'-0" (1:50). With the *2D SELECTION* tool, select this text block, change the *SIZE* to 10 point, and rotate it 90° following the same steps as the title block. Go to *ORGANIZE> LAYER OPTIONS* and select *SHOW OTHERS* if it is not already selected.

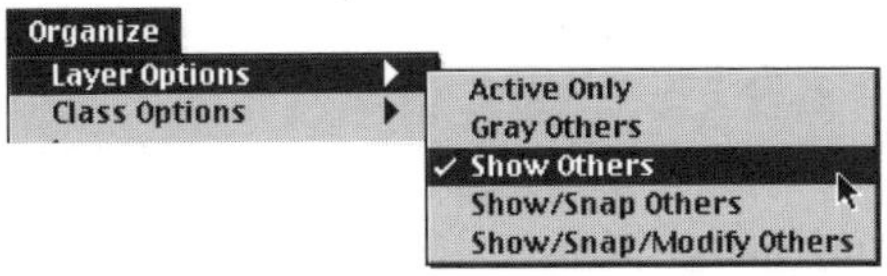

Now press/drag the rotated text block to its designated place for scale in the title block. After making *eighth scale [hundredth scale]* the active layer, follow the same steps, but typing in 1/8"=1'-0" (1:100). Notice that the two scale designations are placed on top of each other. Do not worry about that now.

Creating Templates

Before we save this file as a template, change the default line weight to the middle weight and the active layer to *title*. Select the *FILE>SAVE AS TEMPLATE* command. Type the name *chapt 3 [chapt3.sta]*. Do not use *VectorWorks default [default]* for the file name until you know more about the program. Navigate through the scrolling list so that you are within the *experiments* folder.

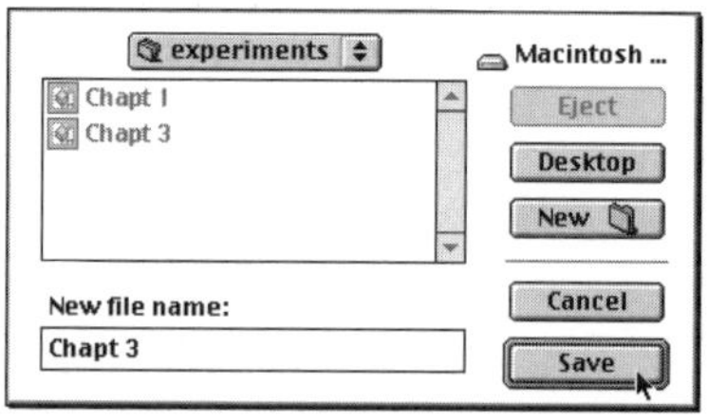

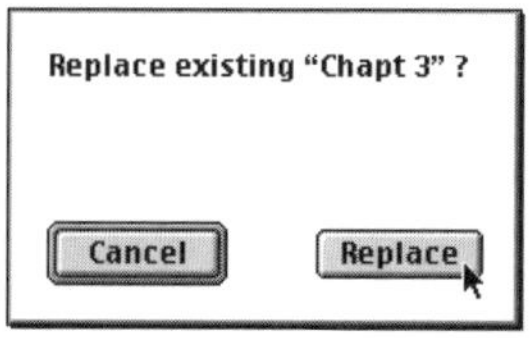

When *SAVE* is selected, a new dialog box opens asking if you want to replace the existing file. Click the *REPLACE* button. When you select *REPLACE*, this new template file, *chapt 3 [chapt3.sta]* replaces the previous file and saves it as a template within the *experiments* folder within the *VectorWorks 8f folder*. The name of the current file you have been working in has been changed to *untitled 2*. *QUIT [EXIT]* the program and do not bother saving the untitled file when asked. As a note, if you had named the file *chapt 3.mcd*, when you save it as a template called *chapt 3.sta*, it will not ask you if you wish to replace the file since the name is different. So, just go back and trash the original *chapt 3.mcd* file.

TEMPLATES IN SUMMATION

We have gone through the steps of creating a template with some minimal formatting. The most helpful item initially is to include the title block so that every time a new document is opened from this file, the block already exists. We also created several layers that already have a designated scale. If this template is used to open a new file and one of these layers is not needed, you can always delete the layer, or change the scale and its designation. The thought to keep in mind, is to include within a template what is most commonly used in order to minimize the set up time.

Chapter 4

CREATING OBJECTS

OBJECT TYPES

We will go through the steps of creating a series of objects that will provide an overview of some of the different tools and commands and how to put them together. Objects can be created that are just 2D, just 3D, or both 2D and 3D. Most of the objects we shall create are 3-dimensional, so that you get right into taking advantage of the 3D aspects of VectorWorks. Objects can be divided into different categories, each with its own characteristics. Polygons and non-polygons are 2D objects. Plug-in and hybrid objects are both 2D and 3D. 3D solids, VectorWorks native and meshes are the different types of 3D objects.

The tools, commands, and constraints we will be exploring are;

2D Reshape Tool
Ellipse Tool
Mirror Tool
Rectangle Tool
Rounded Rectangle Tool
Shelving Unit Plug-In Tool
Text Insertion Tool
Add Solids Command
Align Objects Command
Convert To 3D Polys Command
Duplicate Array Command
Extrude Command
Group Command
Move Command
Move 3D Command
Nudge Command
Rendering Commands
Rotate Command
Send Commands
Set Grid Command
Standard Views Command
Trim Command
Constrain Angle Constraint

FIRST THE SHEET

We will need to open a new file to create the objects in this exercise. By double-clicking the template we previously set up, *chapt 3 [chapt 3.sta]*. VectorWorks (if it is closed) as well as a new file, will both open. The file will open with *untitled 1* across the top, that is, unless another untitled document was opened, in which case it could be *untitled 2* or *untitled 3* or whatever. Verify your default settings, in particular the selected icons on the *CONSTRAINTS* palette.

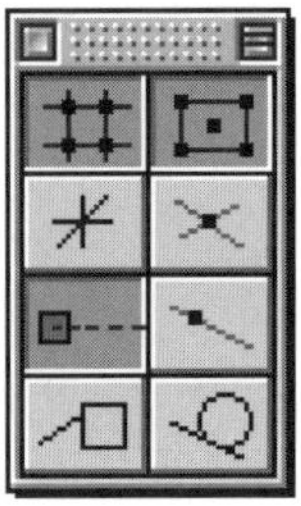

Setting Up The Environment

Go to *PAGE>SET GRID* and select 1" (.01m) for *SNAP GRID* and 1'-0" (.50m) for *REFERENCE GRID* in the *SET GRID* dialog box. Check the *SYMMETRICAL* box in both. The *SHOW GRID LINES* box should also be checked before selecting *OK*.

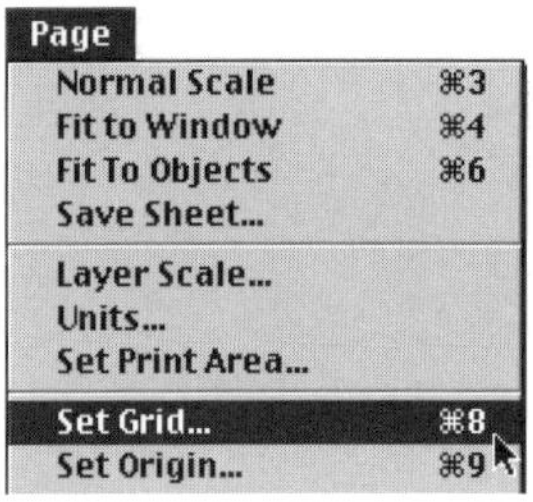

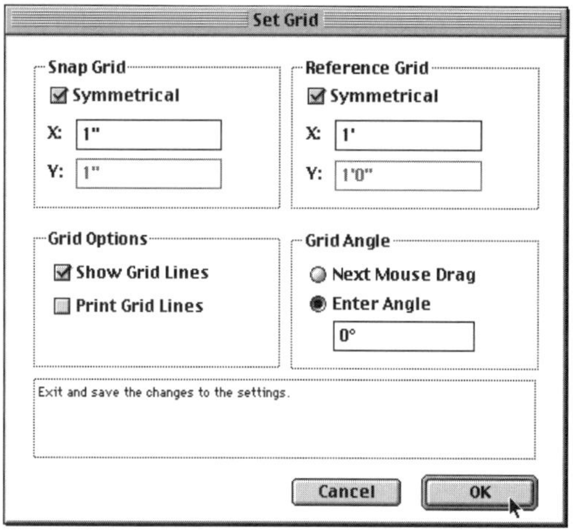

Look at the line weight in the *ATTRIBUTES* palette and select the second weight down as the default. The line weight of .25 should show on the line button and a check-mark appears next to it when the pop-out menu is reopened. Also select *ORGANIZE>LAYER OPTIONS>ACTIVE ONLY*.

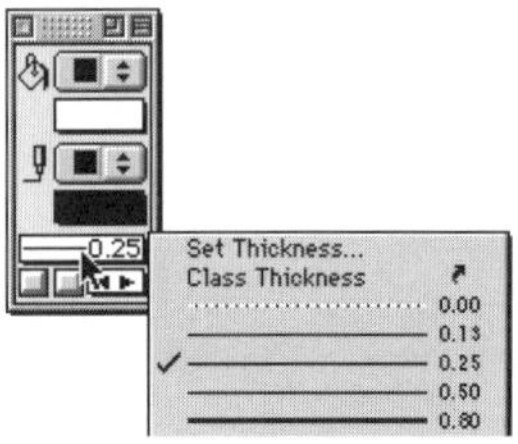

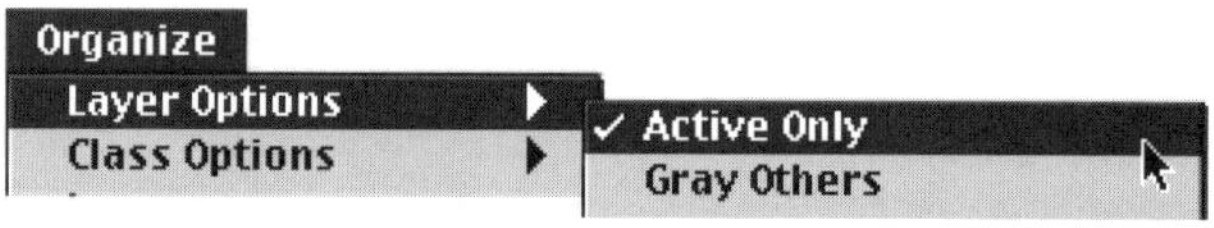

Saving

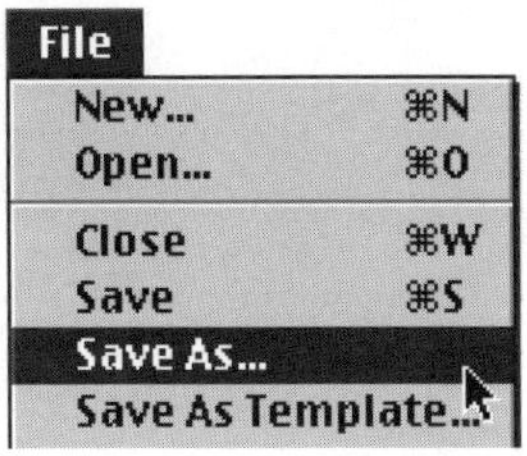

This is also an appropriate time to name the file by selecting *FILE>SAVE AS*. When the dialog box opens type in the name *chapt 4 [chapt 4.mcd]* under the NEW FILE NAME edit box. Navigate through the scrolling list, as you did in the previous chapter, to have the document placed in the *experiments* folder within the *VectorWorks 8 ƒ* folder. As you go through the following steps make sure you frequently save the document by either selecting the *SAVE* command or pressing the *Command [Control]* and *S* keys.

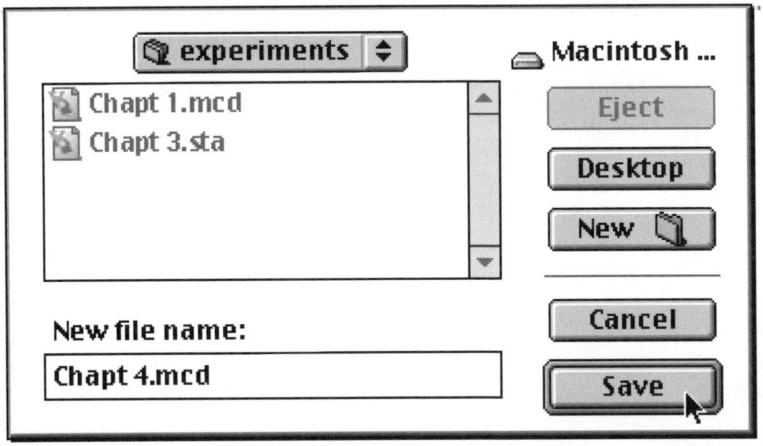

CREATING SIMPLE OBJECTS

Each of the examples illustrated in the following exercises shows a method of creating an object. You should be aware that an object can be created in a multitude of ways as shown in the previous two chapters. Where appropriate, rather than duplicating the same method for each object, another way is shown. Again, the more comfortable you are with the various methods, the quicker you will be able to draw.

ARCHITECTURAL DESIGNATORS IN 2D

Our first exercises will be creating 2-dimensional architectural symbols or designators. (Note that we are using the word, symbols, in the architectural sense, not what VectorWorks means for an object type called symbol.)

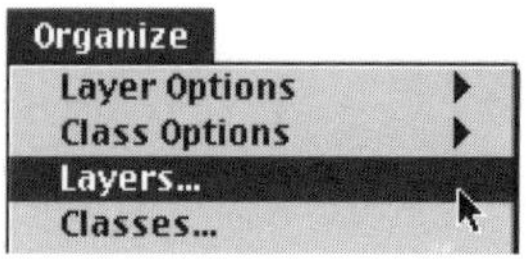

Open the *Layers Setup* dialog box under *ORGANIZE>Layers*. When the dialog box opens, click the layer name, *eighth scale* in the *layer* scrolling list to select. Rename it to say *arch symbols* by highlighting *eighth scale* (*hundredth scale*) in the *name* edit box and retyping. You can highlight the edit box by either press/dragging or hitting the *Tab* key. With this layer selected, also select the *active layer* button before selecting *ok*. The following are some examples of often used symbols.

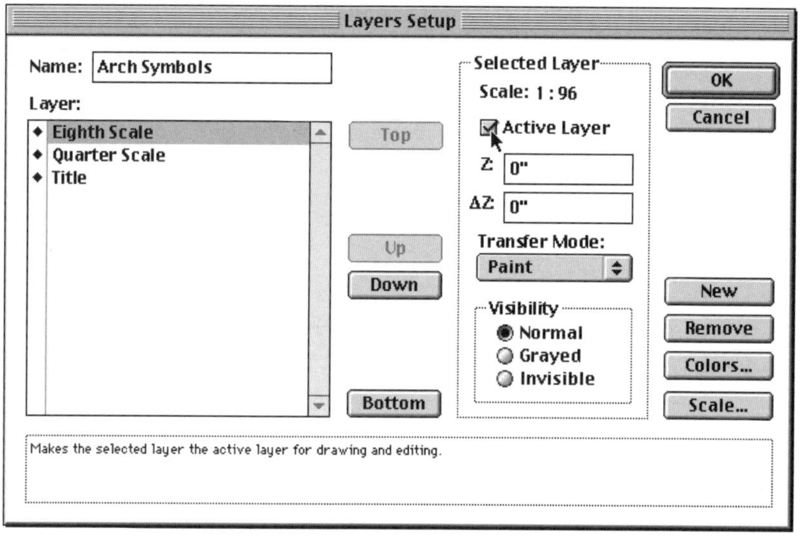

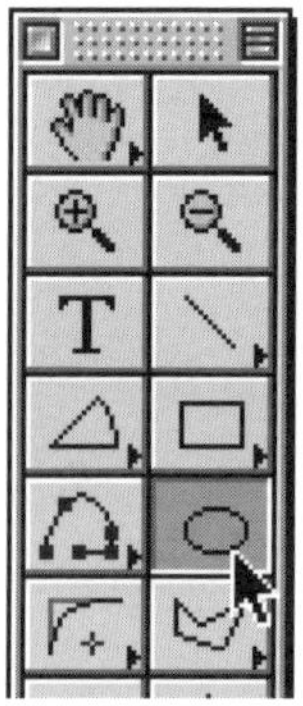

North Arrow

There are many different styles of north arrows. We will create one that is composed of a heavier line segment within a circle to represent north.

Step 1 - the circle

With the *Ellipse* tool and the *circle by diameter* modifier icon selected, draw a scaled circle that is 5' (1.50m) in diameter creating a circle of 5/8" (.06m) world dimension. Remember that you can either use the mouse and eyeball the dimension; or *Tab* across the *data display bar* and enter the diameter into the *L* edit box; or double-click the tool itself to open a *Create Circle* dialog box.

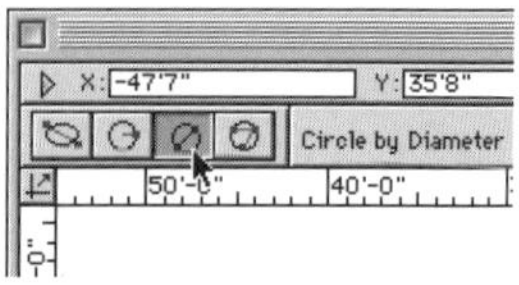

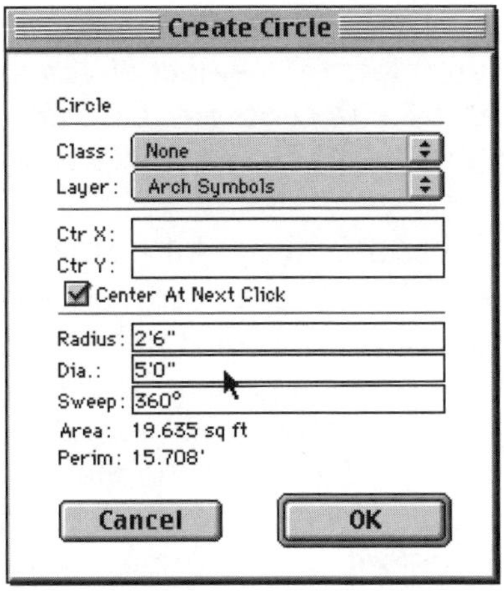

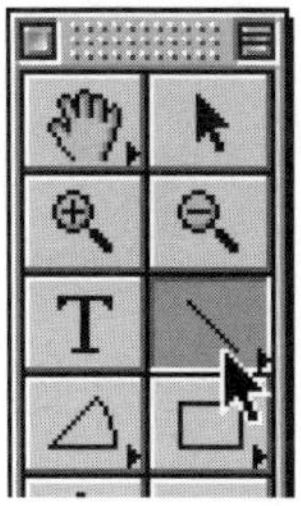

Step 2 - the lines

With the *Single Line* tool and the *unconstrained* modifier icon selected and making use of the *smartcursor cues* along with its snapping dot, draw two lines bisecting the circle. Look for the *cues, top center* and *center left,* before you press/drag and *bottom center* and *center right* before you release.

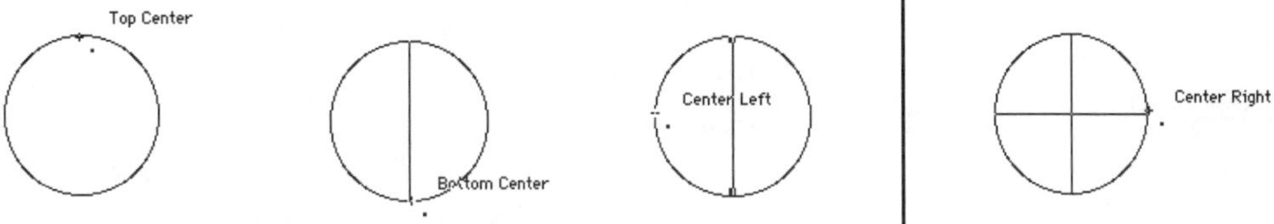

Step 3 - the north designation

Select both lines by *Shift*-clicking (selecting one object, press the *Shift* key, and click the second object) and choose the *TOOL>Trim* command. When the *pick* cursor appears, click the line that is horizontal which will be used as the cutting line. This will separate the vertical line into two separate pieces without affecting the horizontal cutting line.

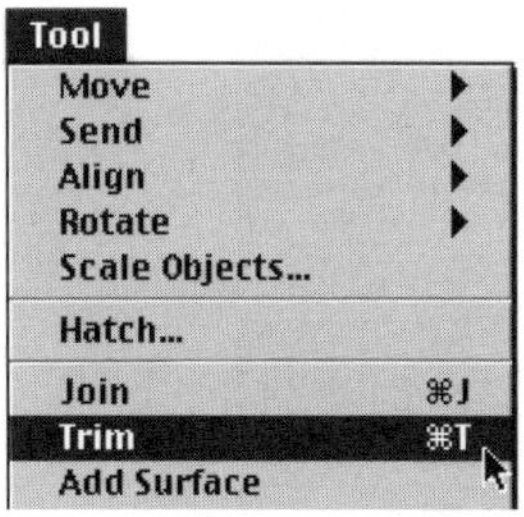

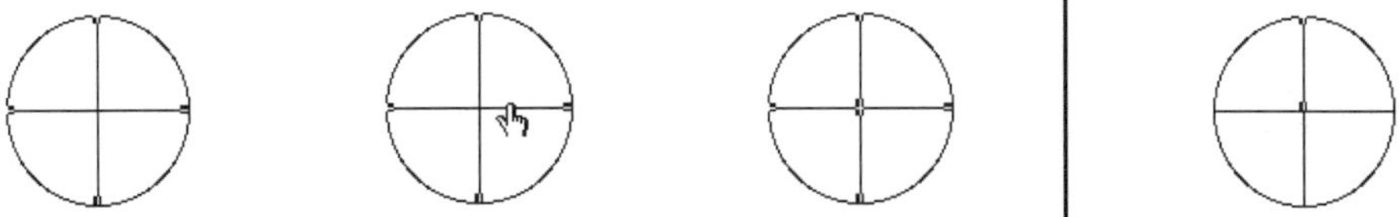

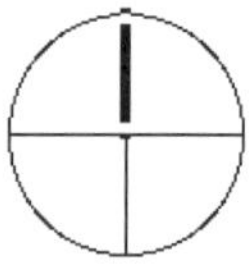

Now, click anywhere in the drawing area except on another object to deselect all lines and then select just the top vertical line segment. Go to the *Attributes* palette and select the fourth heaviest line weight.

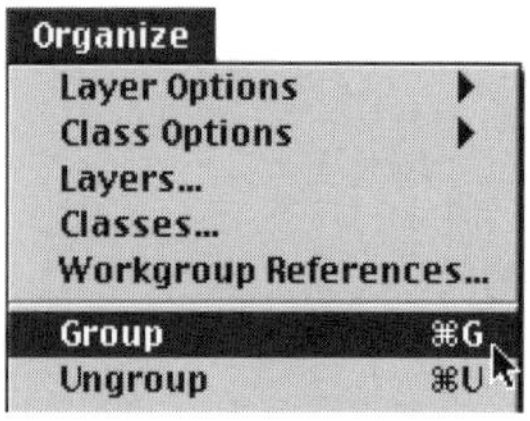

step 4 - combining the components

We have now made a north arrow composed of four components. Since we carefully arranged all pieces, we do not want them inadvertently misaligned when the north arrow is moved. To treat the individual pieces as one object, select all of the pieces and choose the *ORGANIZE>Group* command. The component pieces are now joined into one grouped object that safeguards their position. You can always go back later and use *Edit Group* to revise any one of the component pieces.

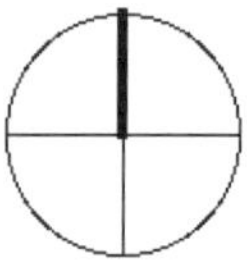

Entry Arrow

Like the north arrow, there are many different styles of entry arrows. We will create one that is composed of a patterned triangle with some text.

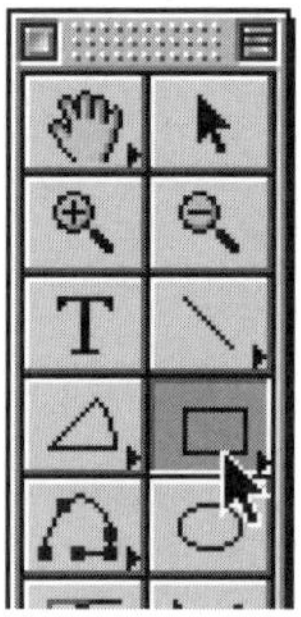

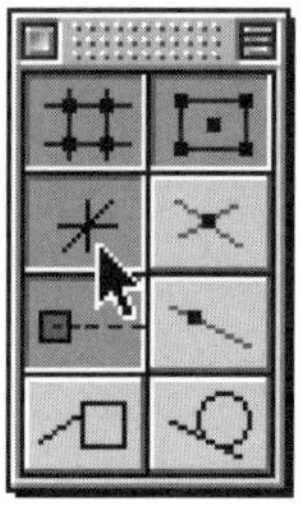

Step 1 - creating the arrow

First you will create a square that is 5' (1.50m) in scale per side. Press/drag diagonally with the *Rectangle* tool and enter the dimension into the *data display bar* in the Δx *[±x]* edit box. Before you release the mouse keep it constrained to a square by pressing the *Shift* key, looking for the *cue, angle/vertical,* or you can hit the *S* key to select the *Constrain Angle* constraint but look for the *cue, vertical/symmetric* instead. Both of these methods set a side of the rectangle to a given dimension and keep it constrained to be a square.

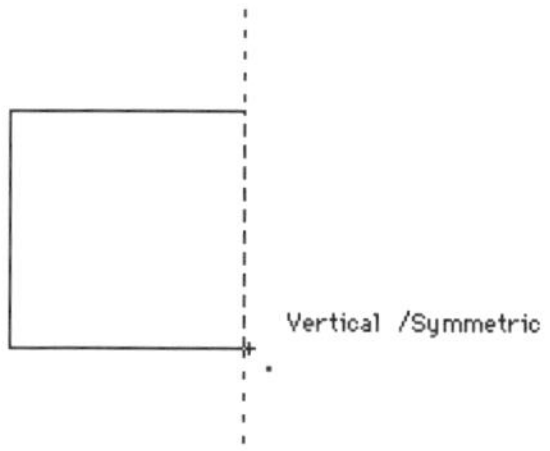

With the square selected, choose the *TOOL>ROTATE>ROTATE* command to open the *ROTATE OBJECT* dialog box. This allows you to enter a custom rotation of 45° under *ANGLE*. Do not worry if the ° mark gets deleted, since it assumes the measurement is in degrees with or without it.

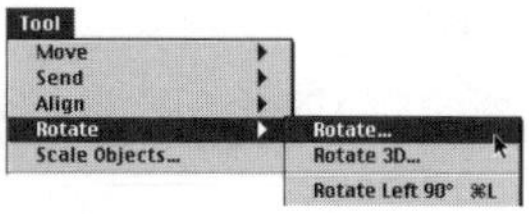

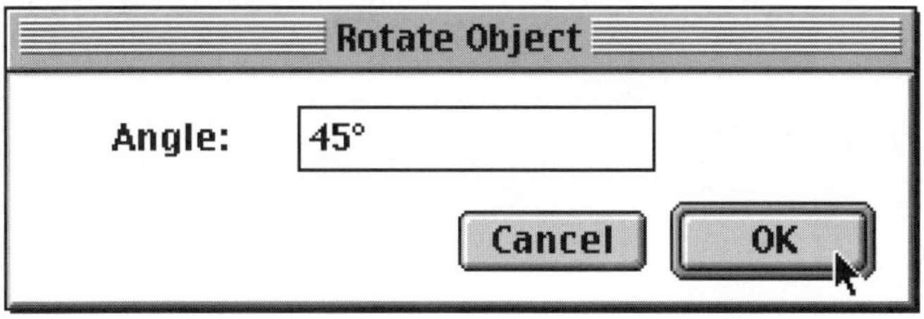

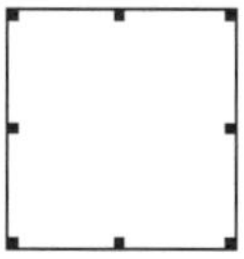

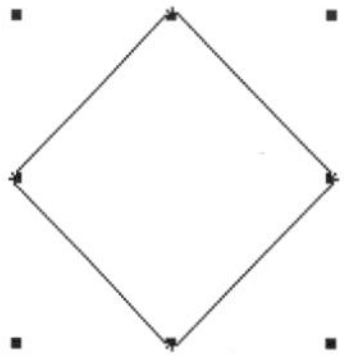

By rotating the square, it automatically becomes a polygon which, although it looks the same, is a different kind of object in the eyes of VectorWorks. Notice that the handles are no longer at each corner of the object, but at the corner of an invisible box that surrounds the rotated square called the bounding box.

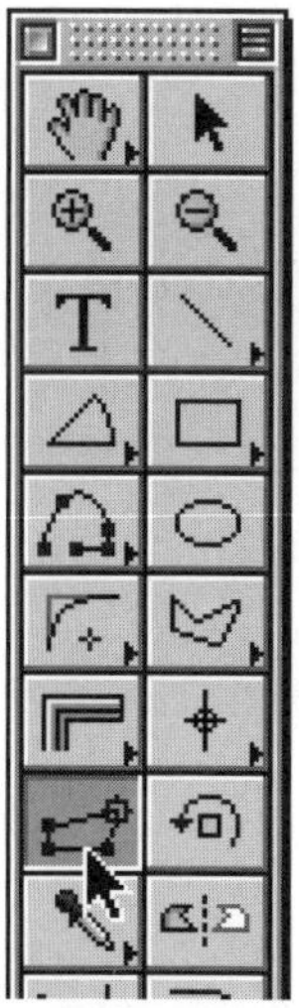

Now with the object selected, choose the *2D RESHAPE* tool. Notice that the handles are again at each corner. Select the *DELETE A VERTEX* icon and place the cursor over the bottom handle. When the *delete* cursor appears just click and that corner will disappear, changing the object to a triangle.

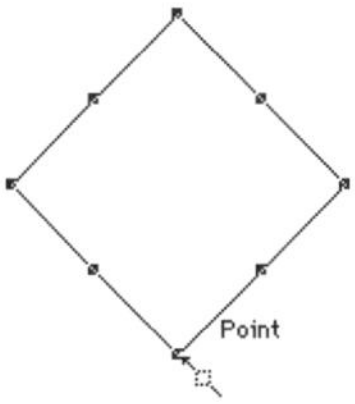

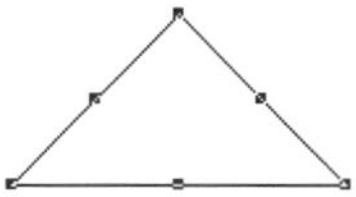

Step 2 - creating the text

With the *TEXT INSERTION* tool selected, click anywhere in the drawing area and type the word *entry*. Change to the *2D SELECTION* tool and with the text object selected go to *TEXT>SIZE* and change the text size to 10 point.

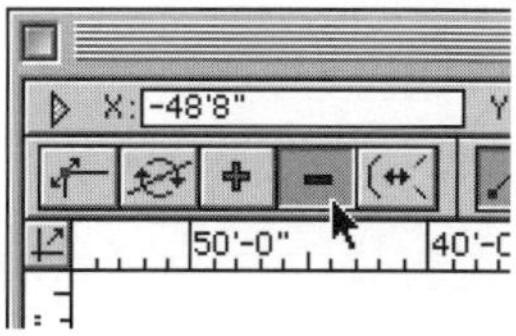

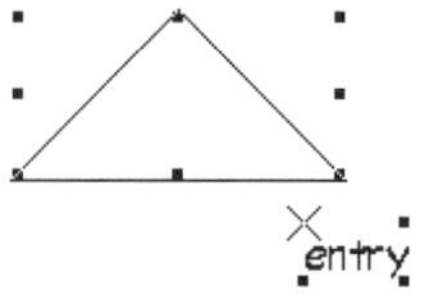

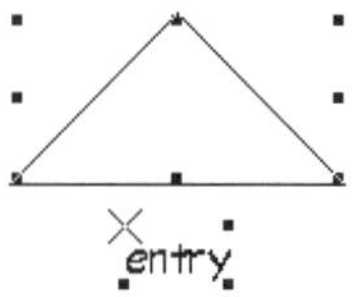

Step 3 - aligning text

Shift-select the triangle and the text then the *TOOL>ALIGN> ALIGN OBJECTS* command. Select the *L/R CENTERS* and click to deselect any other alignments. When *OK* is selected, the dialog box closes and both of these elements will relocate so that they are centered on each other in the one direction only.

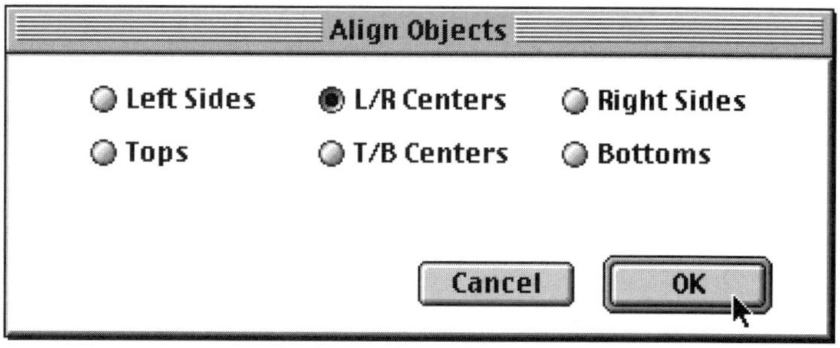

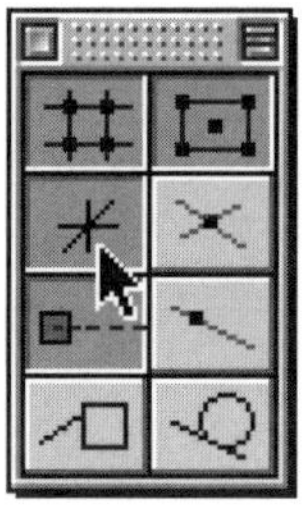

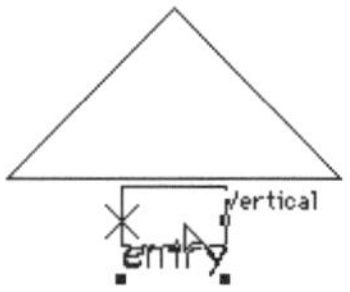

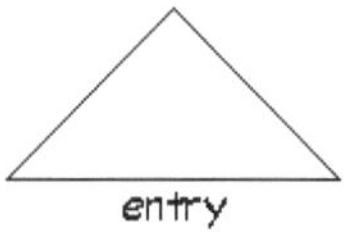

Click the drawing to deselect the objects and click the text object. With the *press-drag* cursor, press the object and then the *Shift* key. Drag the text to position it just below the triangle. Notice the *cue, vertical.* You could have also hit the *S* key to select the *CONSTRAIN ANGLE* constraint. In this case be sure to hit the *S* key again to deselect the constraint. Holding the *Shift* key or hitting the *S* key while moving an object keeps the object constrained to either move vertically or horizontally (or at 30°, 45°, or 60° angle) but not both. This will keep the left/right alignment accurate.

Step 4 - adding pattern

With the triangle selected, go to the *ATTRIBUTES* palette and press/drag on the *SOLID* fill button, down to *PATTERN* in the pop-out menu. Then press/drag on the *FILL PATTERN* button that appears on the left to the desired pattern. Select both the triangle and text and the *ORGANIZE>GROUP* command.

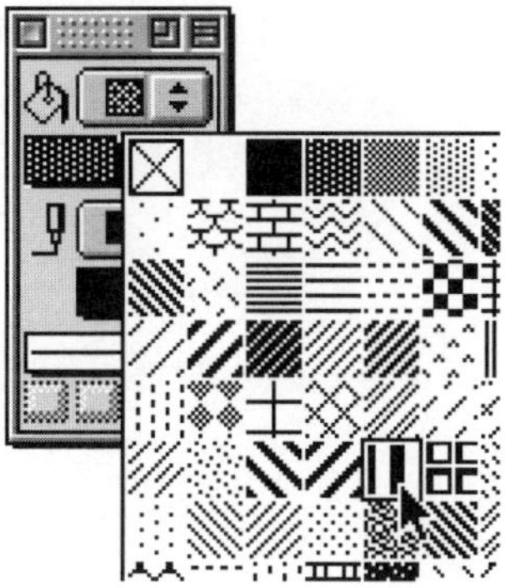

Elevation Arrows

The following example of an elevation arrow combines some of the steps we used in the previous examples.

Step 1 - the circle

Create a 6'-0" (1.80m) diameter circle, again by using the mouse, *data display bar*, or dialog box.

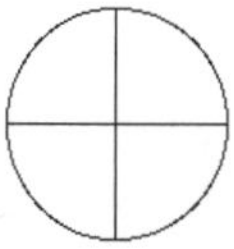

Step 2 - the lines

Use the *Single Line* tool and the *smartcursor cues* to place 2 lines, one vertical and the other horizontal, bisecting the circle. You might want to use the *Group* command at this point for the three objects just created.

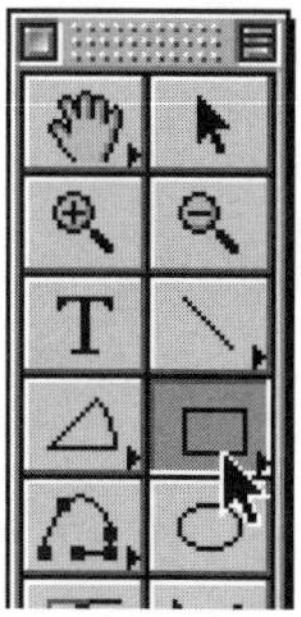

Step 3 - the arrows

Select the *Rectangle* tool and use the *smartcursor* to create guide lines for the starting point of the square. Align the top left corner of the rectangle with the top and left sides of the circle's bounding box.

Hint — make one point of the circle the floating datum point, move to the second alignment point, and move the cursor so that the guide lines appear, then press the mouse and start drawing when the *cue, align h/align v,* appears. Do the same for the ending point of the square by resting the cursor on the other two points to get the guide lines and then release the mouse. You might get the *cue, top left* and *bottom right*, meaning it is snapping to the bounding box instead, which is fine.

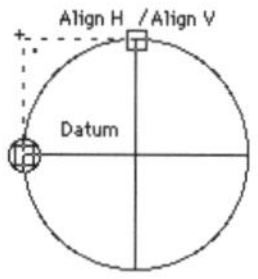

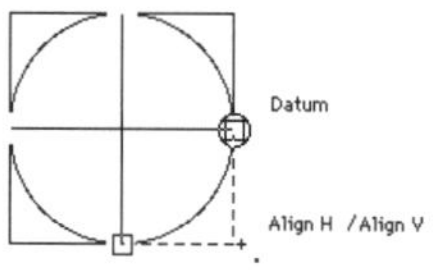

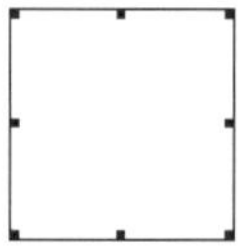

The square is placed on top of the circle and lines because objects are placed in stratums in the order they are actually drawn. The square will also obscure the objects below it. Normally you could just change the fill to *NONE*, but in this case we want the fill *PATTERN* to be a solid black.

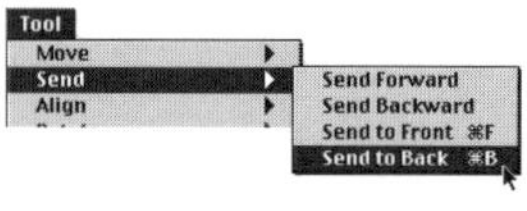

In order to move the square underneath the other objects, select the square and choose the *TOOL>SEND>SEND TO BACK* command. With the square still selected, press/drag the *FILL COLOR* button on the *ATTRIBUTES* palette to black.

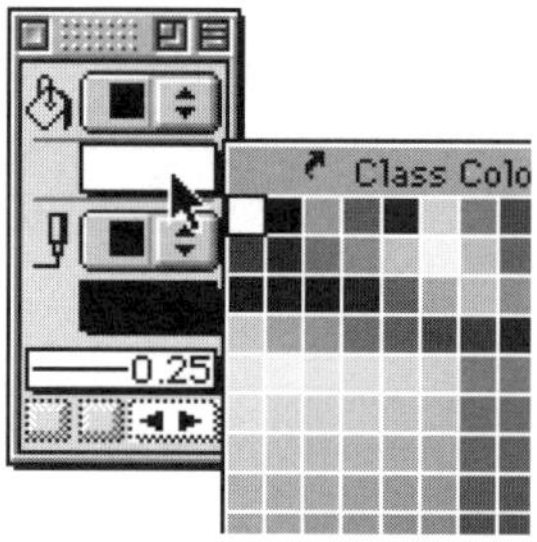

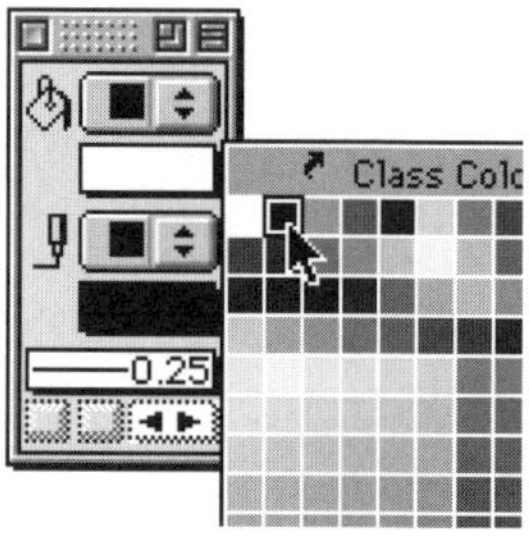

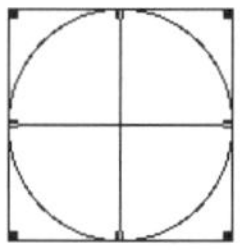

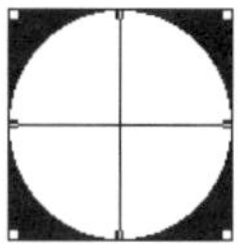

Since the circle is opaque it appears as if a hole is cut through the square. Press/drag a marquee around the square and the grouped object and *GROUP* again. It may look as if nothing is selected since the selection handles are placed exactly on top of each other, but it is selected. If you are not sure, just select again. Now use the *ROTATE>ROTATE* command and rotate it 45° when the *ROTATE OBJECT* dialog box opens.

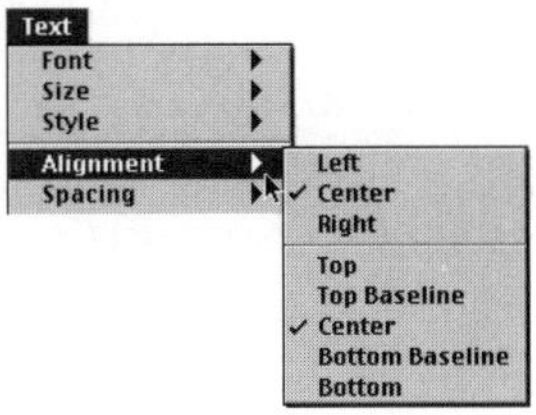

Step 4 - the elevation designators

With the *2D Selection* tool and nothing else selected, change the default alignment to *TEXT>Alignment>Center* selecting both *Center* commands. Click the *Text Insertion* tool to place a numerical designation for each of the elevations. Do not worry about exact locations. *Shift*-select the object and the 1 and 3 and use the *TOOL>Align> Align Objects* command and choose *l/r centers.*

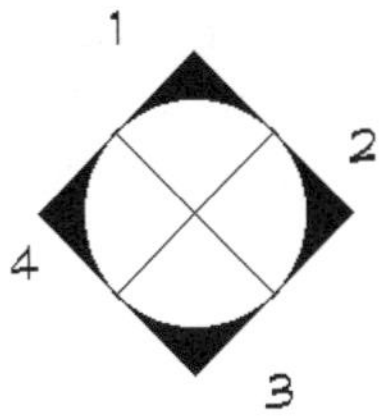

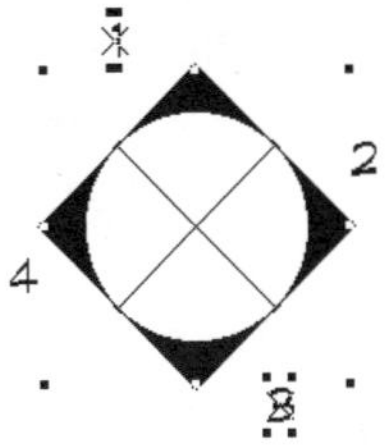

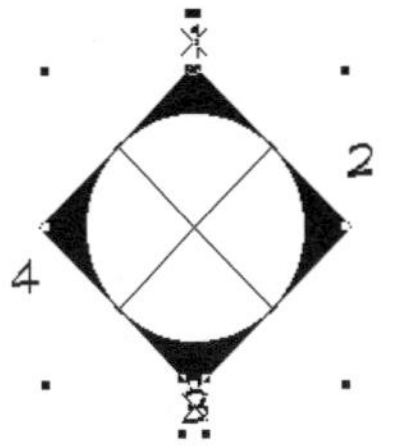

Notice that the pieces within the grouped object will not align individually but will keep their respective places within the group. Select just the number 1 and with the *Shift* key pressed, move it downwards to its placement within the marker. Do the same with the number 3 moving it upwards. Pressing the *Shift* key keeps the selected object constrained allowing it to move only vertically, horizontally or 30°, 45°, or 60°. Select the grouped object and the 1 and 3 markers and *Group* again. With it still selected, use the *Send To Back* command.

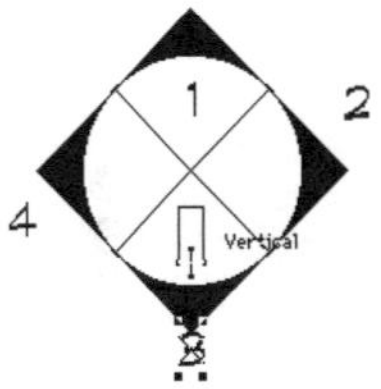

Follow these same steps for the 2 and 4 numbers using the *Align Objects* command but this time, select *t/b centers* and make sure the *l/r centers* button is deselected. The grouped object and the second and fourth designators should be selected. Once everything is positioned, select all of the components and *Group* again.

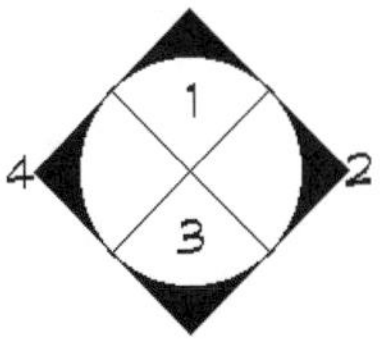

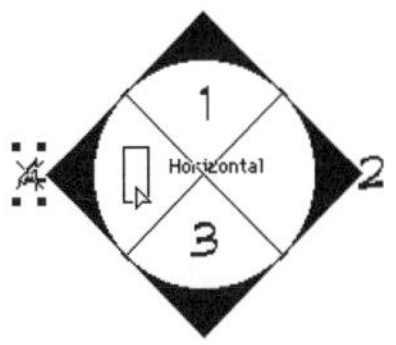

Hint – when the *Align Objects* command is used with either of the *center* options, all of the selected objects will relocate to the overall midpoint unless one of the selected objects actually encompasses the others. The encompassing object will not move and the others will relocate around it. So in the preceding pictured example, since the 4 and 2 fall within the grouped object (top to bottom) and we are using *t/b centers*, the grouped object stays stationary and the numbers move to center on it. In this case it would not have been necessary to use the *Group* command on the object and the 1 and 3 markers to hold the formatting before centering the 4 and 2.

FURNITURE IN 3D

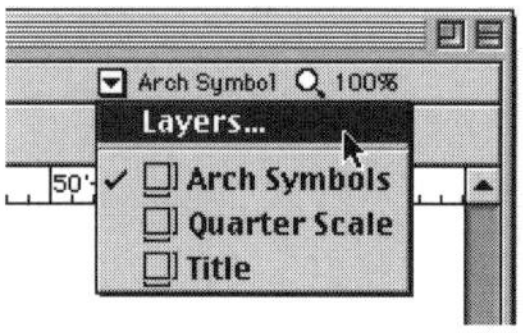

We will create a series of 3-dimensional furniture pieces so that you can see the steps involved in going right into 3D. Go into the *Layers Setup* dialog box and click *quarter scale* in the *layer* scrolling list. You can access the dialog box by press/dragging down to *layers* in the layers pop-out menu in the *data display bar.*

Highlight *quarter scale (fiftieth scale)* in the *name* edit box and type in *furniture* to rename it. With this layer still selected, also check the *active layer* box before selecting *ok.* This renames the layer and makes it the active layer, so any objects created are placed in this layer until another layer becomes active. The other objects will disappear.

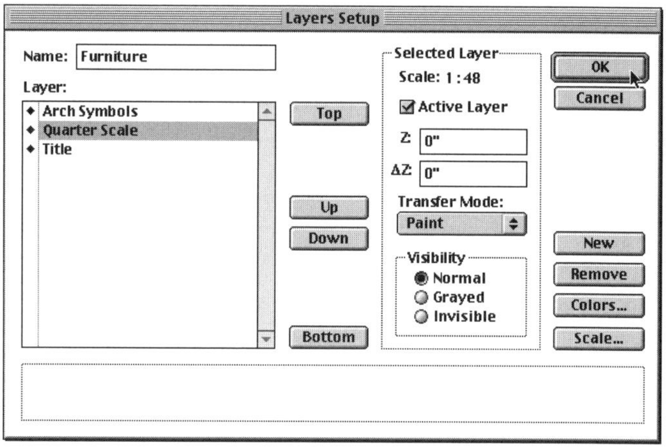

End Table

The first object we will create is a cubed end table with a recessed base.

Step 1 - creating the cube

With *VIEW>STANDARD VIEWS>TOP/PLAN* selected, select the *RECTANGLE* tool and press at a starting point. Create a 2'-6" (.75m) square by tabbing across so the *Δx [±x]* edit box is highlighted. Enter 30 (.75) and hit the *Return [Enter]* key. Notice that one side of the square jumps to that dimension. The 30 should automatically change to 2'-6" in the *data display bar*, although with version 8.0 it remains at 30 - a small bug. Tab across again to the *ΔY [±Y]* edit box for the other side and enter the same dimension so that the object becomes constrained to a square.

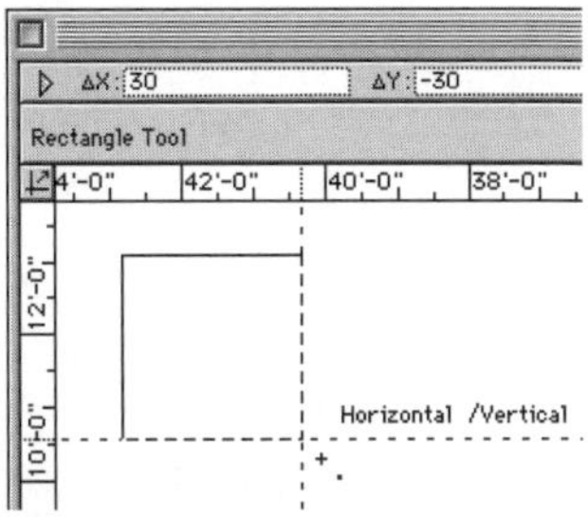

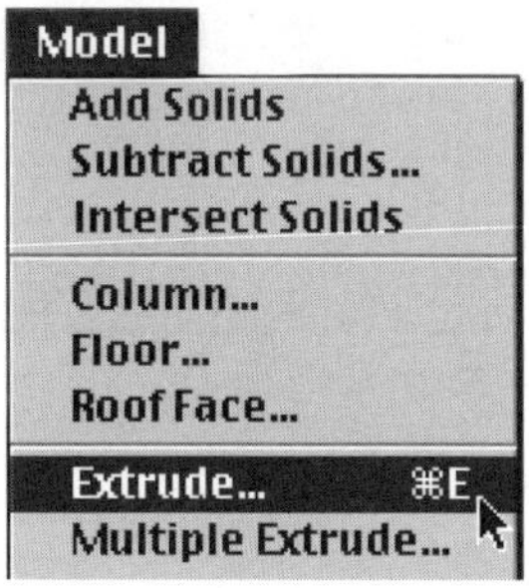

Select the square and then the *MODEL>EXTRUDE* command. The *CREATE EXTRUDE* dialog box opens. With the *EXTRUSION* edit field highlighted, enter or type in the number 16" (.40m) and select *OK*. The square has now been converted to a 3D cube which you can see by looking at one of the *ISOMETRIC* views under *VIEW>STANDARD VIEWS*.

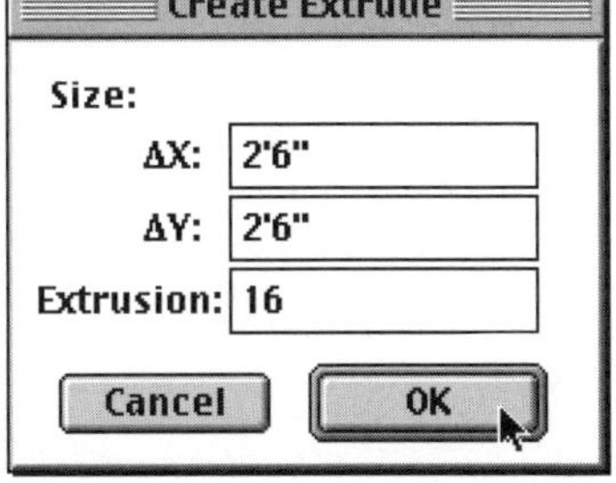

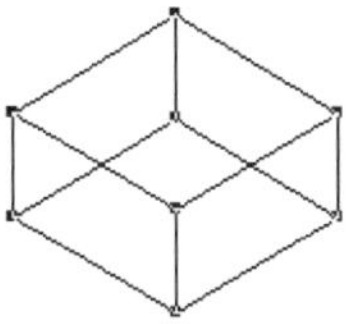

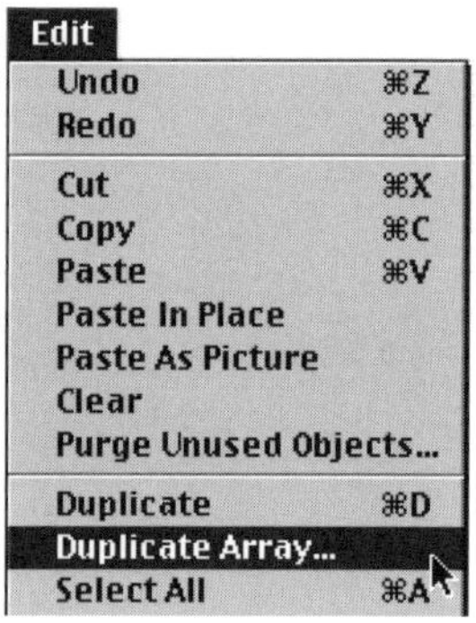

Step 2 - creating the base

Now go back to *Top/Plan* view and we will create another element for the base measuring 24" x 24" (.60m x .60m). Select the first cube and then the *EDIT>Duplicate Array* command. Select *linear array* with 1 for *number*. The *offset* should be *manual* with 0 entered into both the *x* and *y* boxes. Select *resize duplicate(s)* and enter .8 for both the *x* and *y scale* boxes and then *ok*.

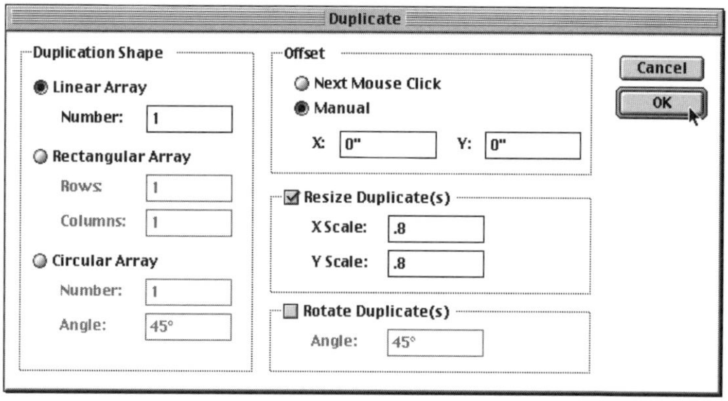

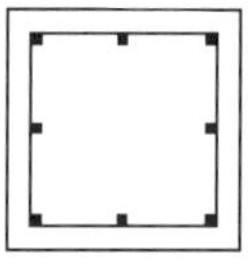

This creates a duplicate of the original object but the duplicate has now been resized to 24" x 24" (.60m x .60m) which is 80% of the original cube.

Step 3 - adjusting heights

Select *VIEW>Standard Views>Right Isometric*. The duplicate is centered in the x and y direction on the original since 0 was entered for *offset*. Since the height of the duplicate does not change from the original, it would need to be revised to an appropriate base height by using the *Object Info* palette. If it is not already opened, select *PALETTES> Object Info*. With the duplicate selected, enter 4" (.10m) in the *extr* edit box and hit the *Tab* or *Return [Enter]* key. The base will adjust to the correct height.

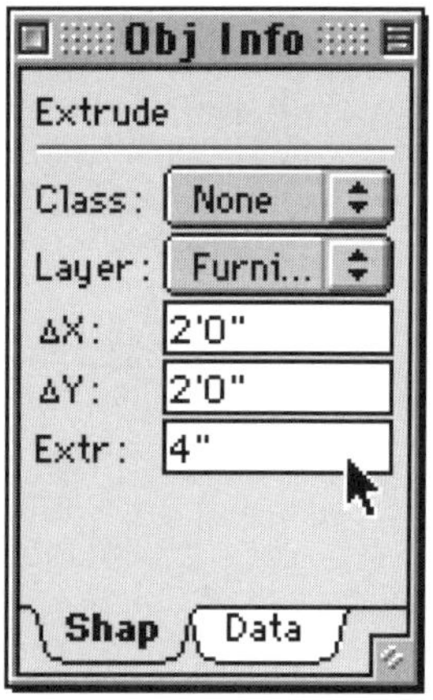

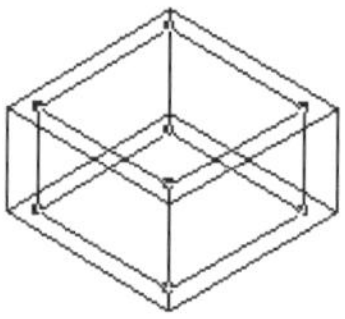

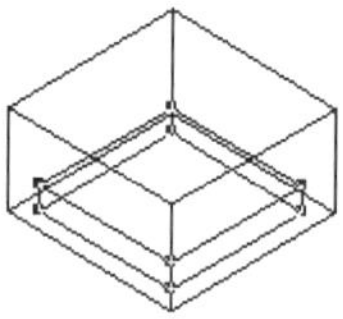

Step 4 - aligning the components

Now select *VIEW>Standard Views>Front.* Notice that although the two objects are centered on each other they both touch the horizontal colored line which is the *ground plane.*

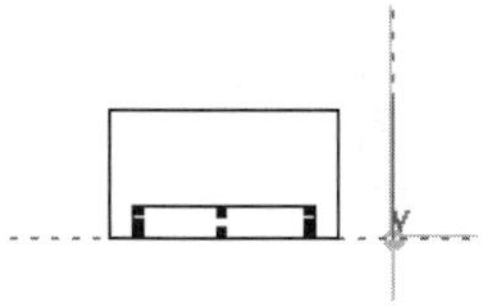

Since we do not want them to overlap, select just the larger cube and then select the *TOOL>Move>Move* command. You will need to click the wireframe itself, not the surface of the plane, in order to select the object. When the *Move Selection* dialog box opens, enter 4" (.10m) into the *y offset* edit box and select *ok.* If you do not see the *y offset,* make sure the *Cartesian* button is selected. This places the larger cube so that it sits on top of the base.

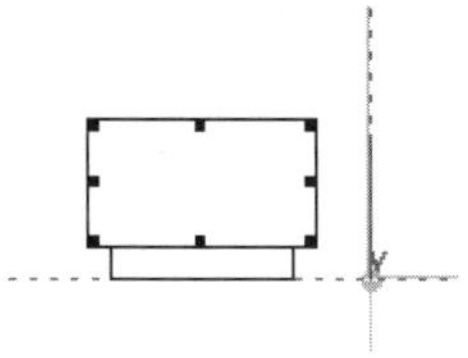

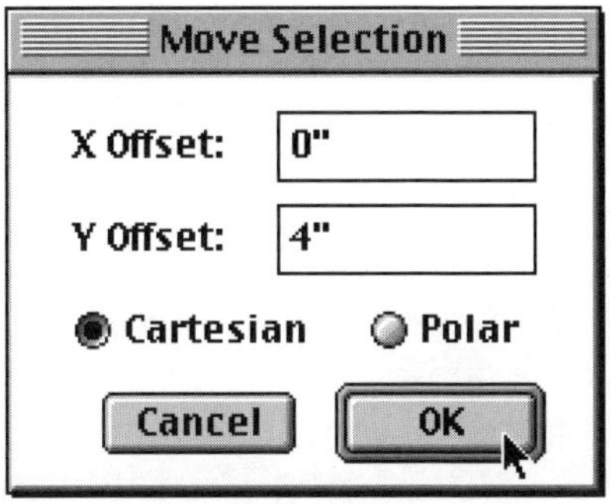

Step 5 - rendering and grouping

Change to *VIEW>Standard Views>Right Isometric* and then go up to *VIEW>Rendering>Solid.* This will change the object from a transparent wireframe object where you can see all lines to a solid opaque object. Select both pieces and choose the *Group* command. This time you can click the plane rather than the wireframe edge to select, since it is now rendered solid.

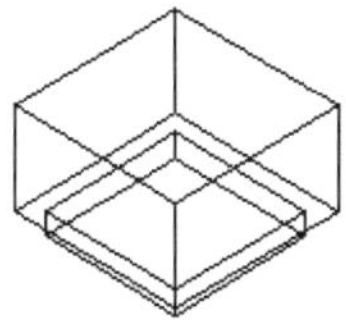

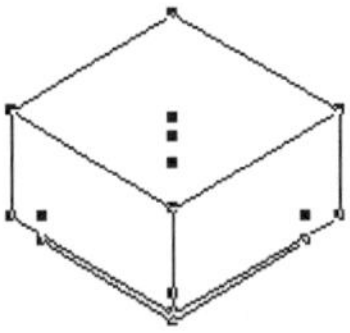

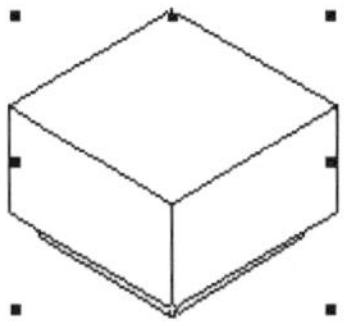

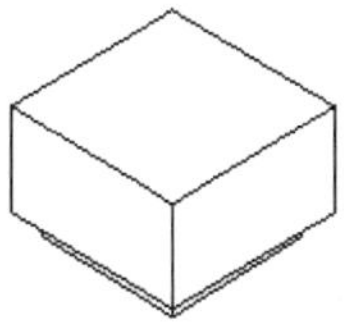

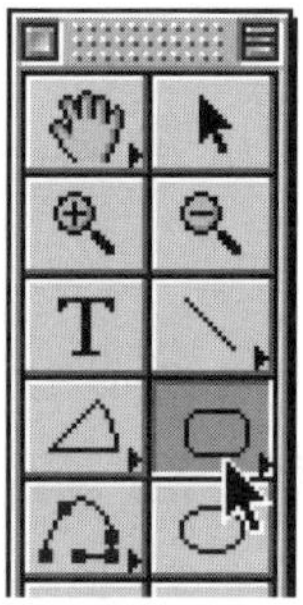

Dining Table

The next piece of furniture we create will be a boat shaped dining table with cylindrical legs.

Step 1 - creating the tabletop

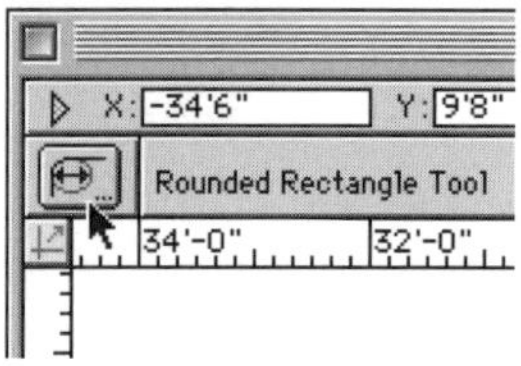

In *Top/Plan* view select the *Rounded Rectangle* tool and then the icon in the mode bar. When the *Round Rect Pref* dialog box opens, select *proportional corners* and then *ok*.

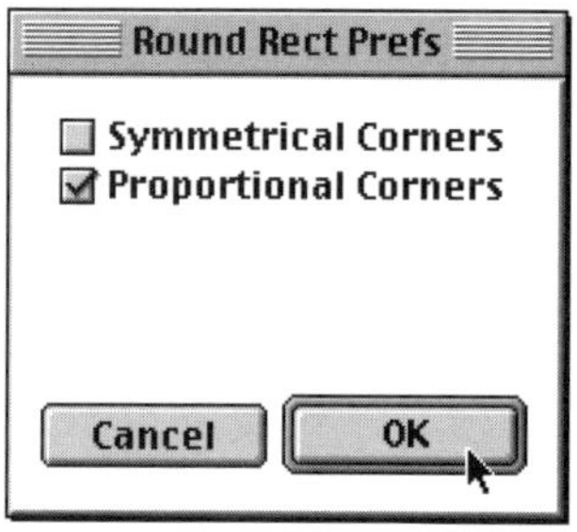

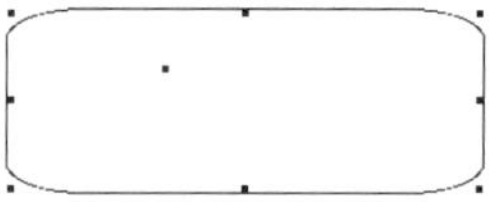

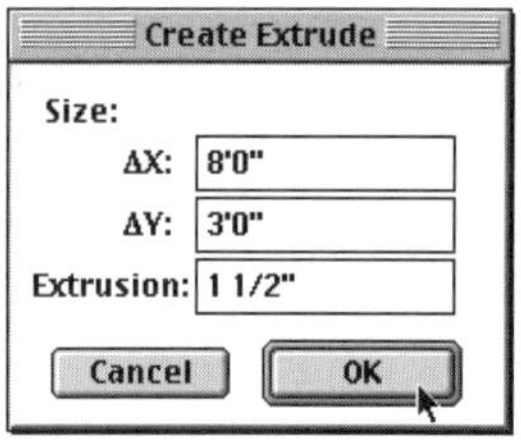

Create a rounded rectangle that is 36" (.90m) in the Y direction by 96" (2.40m) in the X direction. Select this object and the *MODEL>Extrude* command. When the *Create Extrude* dialog box opens, enter $1^{1}/_{2}$" (.04m) into the *extrusion* edit box.

Step 2 - positioning the tabletop

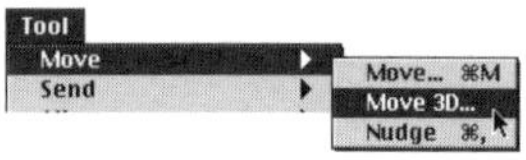

Select the object and the *TOOL>Move>Move 3d* command. The *Move 3d Selection* dialog box opens. Enter 28.5 (.71m) into the *z offset* edit box and select *ok*. This allows you to move an object in 3d space without changing views. Also, since the bottom of the object sits on the *ground plane*, when it moves upwards $28^{1}/_{2}$" (.71m), the top surface will be at 30" (.75m) due to the table top thickness.

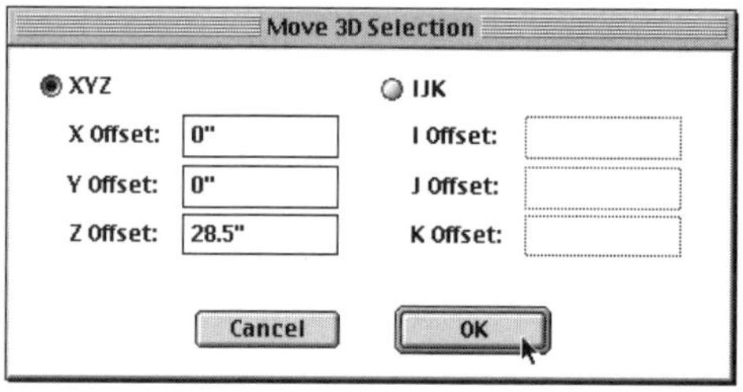

Step 3 - creating the legs

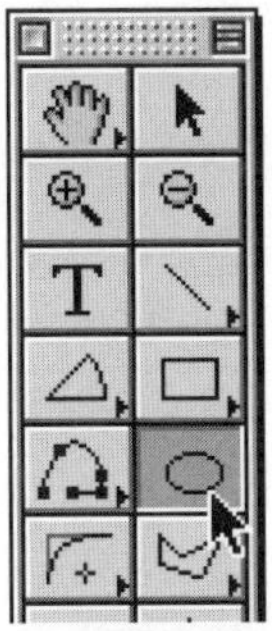

Now with the *Ellipse* tool and the *circle by diameter* icon selected, create a circle that is 3" (.08m) in diameter. Once you press/drag with the tool selected, you can enter the diameter into the *L* edit box in the *data display bar* with the *Tab* and *Return [Enter]* keys.

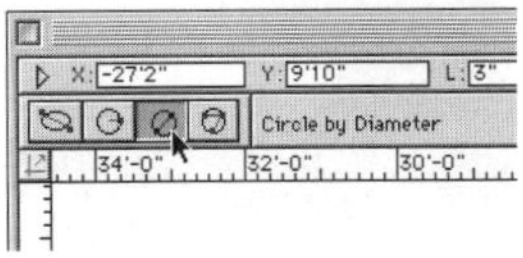

With the circle selected, change the line weight in the *Attributes* palette to the fist line weight, then select the *EDIT>Duplicate Array* command. When the *Duplicate* dialog box opens, select *rectangular array* and insert 2 *columns* and 2 *rows*. Select *offset>manual* and enter for *x offset* the dimension 4'-0" (1.20m) and for *y offset* 18" (.45m). Then select *ok*. Make sure the *resize duplicate(s)* box is not checked.

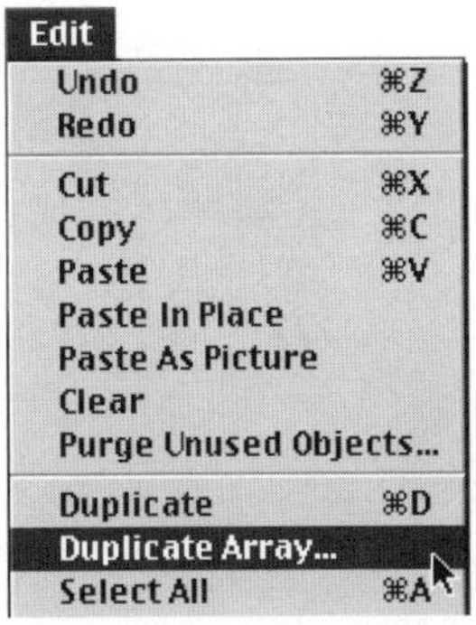

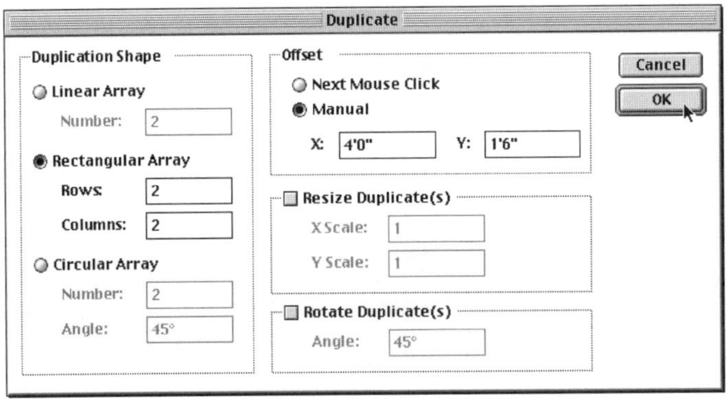

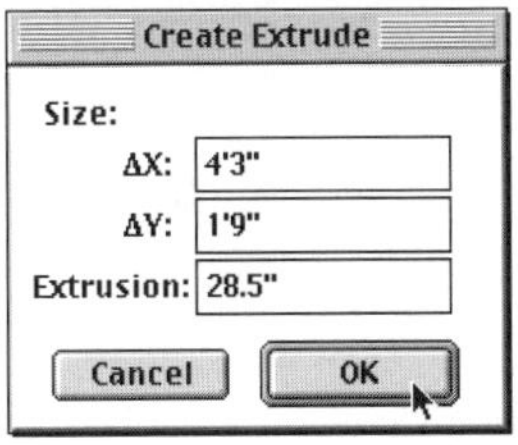

Now select all four circles (only the three duplicates are currently selected) and use the *Extrude* command. Enter 28.5 (.71m) in the *extrusion* box. When several objects are extruded together they are automatically grouped as one object.

Step 4 - aligning and combining

Select the legs, the table top, and then *TOOL>Align>Align Objects* command. The *Align Objects* dialog box opens. Notice that with 3D objects, there are now three alignment options in the dialog box, whereas there were only two options for the 2D objects. Click to select the *L/R centers*

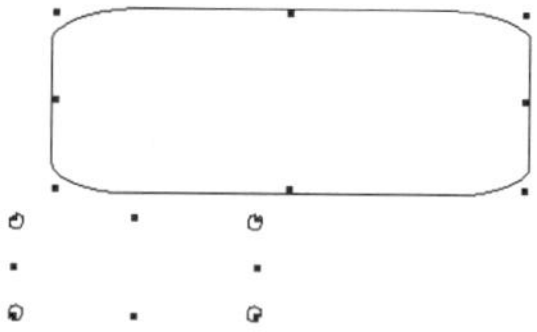

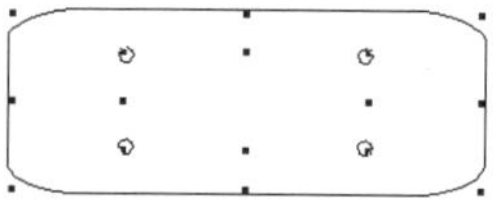

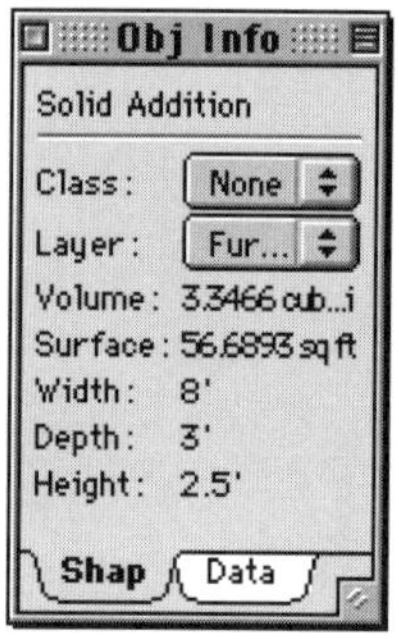

and *T/B CENTERS* only, and then select *OK*. The dialog box closes and both objects center on each other. Also notice that both of the objects actually move to align. This is true for the centering options if one object is not located within the other before aligning.

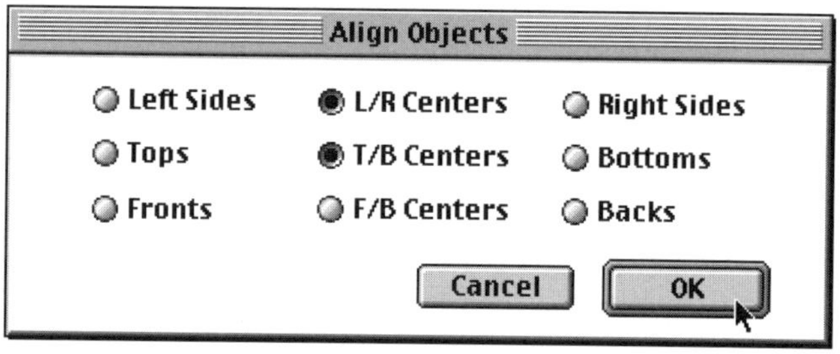

Now with both objects still selected (the extruded legs and the table top) choose the *MODEL>ADD SOLIDS* command. All components are now joined into one object identified as a *SOLID ADDITION* in the *OBJECT INFO* palette with information on its overall dimensions, area, and volume. Look at the table you created in other views and renderings.

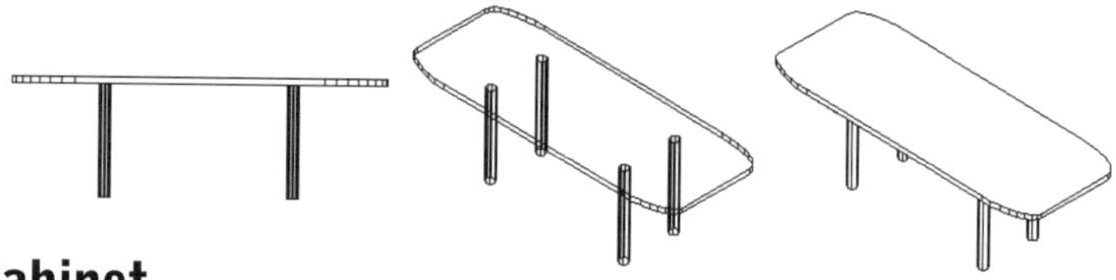

File Cabinet

The next object we shall create is a 2-drawer legal vertical file cabinet.

Step 1 - creating the cabinet

This time let's try a different view. Select *VIEW>STANDARD VIEWS>FRONT*. With the *RECTANGLE* tool selected, draw a rectangle that is 18" (.45m) wide by 29" (.75m) tall making sure the bottom of the rectangle is resting on the *ground plane,* the colored horizontal line, and that the rest of the rectangle is above it. The *Y* edit box in the *data display bar* should be 0 when you press/drag the bottom of the rectangle.

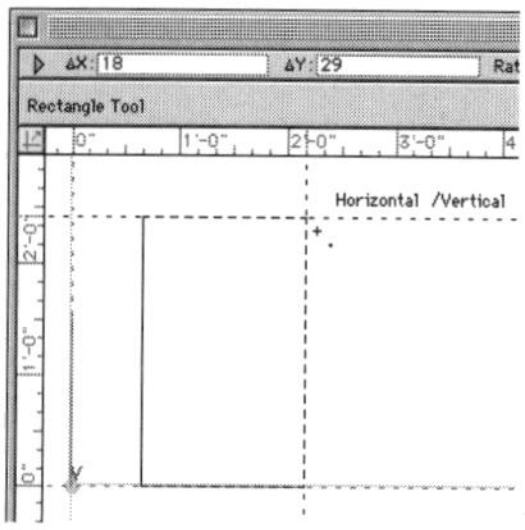

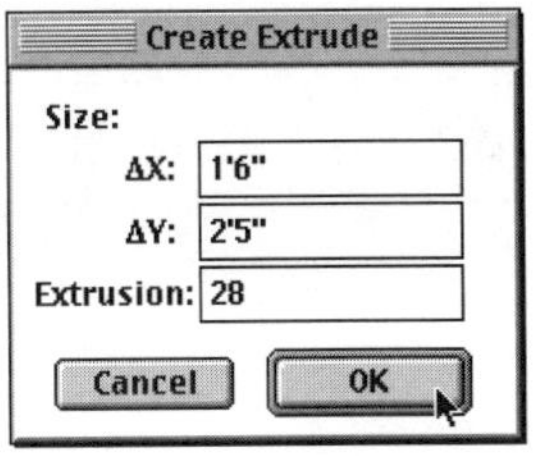

With the rectangle selected use the *Extrude* command and enter 28 (.70m) for the *extrusion* then select *ok*. Because we are working in the *Front* view the dimension extruded is actually the object's depth not its height.

Step 2 - creating the drawer fronts

In order to create the drawer fronts, we would need to create two rectangles 12" (.30m) high by 16" (.40m) wide. First, change the default line weight to the thinnest weight in the *Attributes* palette, then select the *Rectangle* tool.

Next, in order to find the starting point of the drawer front, create a floating datum point at the upper left corner of the cabinet, then use the *data display bar* to find the offset location so that it starts 1.5" (.04m) down and 1" (.025m) in from the top left side. Remember to enter the two dimensions into the *data display bar* and then press the mouse.The starting point will snap to the point where the guide lines meet.

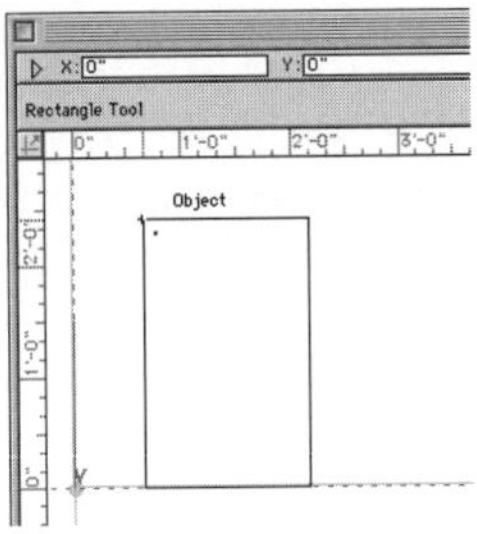

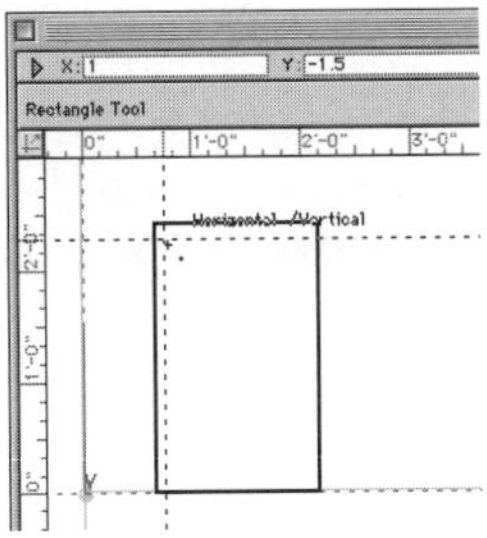

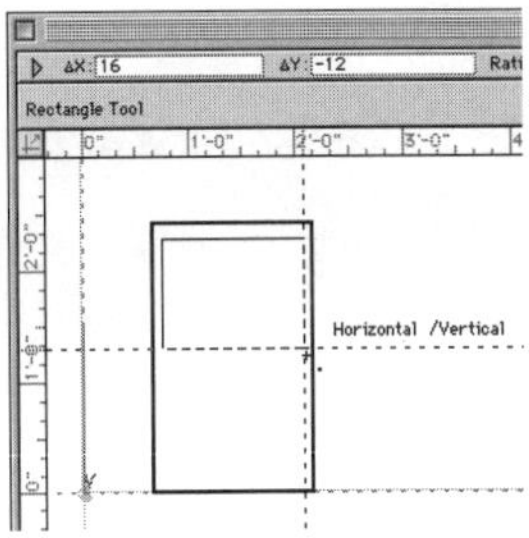

Once you find the starting point and the mouse is pressed, use the *data display bar* again to enter the size of the drawer front of 12" (.30m) high by 16" (.40m) wide. Use the *Zoom-In* tool as necessary to see the accuracy.

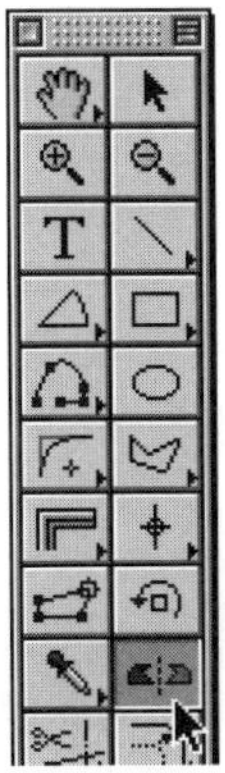

Now, with this rectangle selected, choose the *Mirror* tool and select the *mirror and duplicate* modifier icon. Press from the lower left corner of the drawer, making sure you have actually located that corner with the *smartcursor*

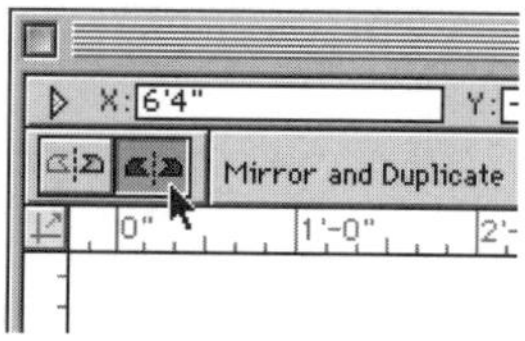

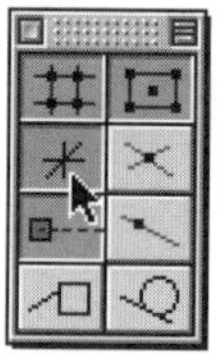

(look for the snapping dot), and drag towards the right. Hit the *S* key to select the *Constrain Angle* icon on the *Constraints* palette. When the *cue, horizontal,* appears, release the mouse button. The duplicate is now created and selected. Hit the *S* key again to deselect the *Constrain Angle* icon.

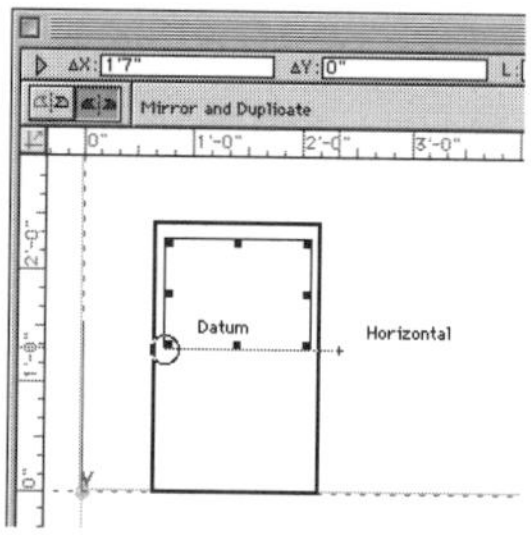

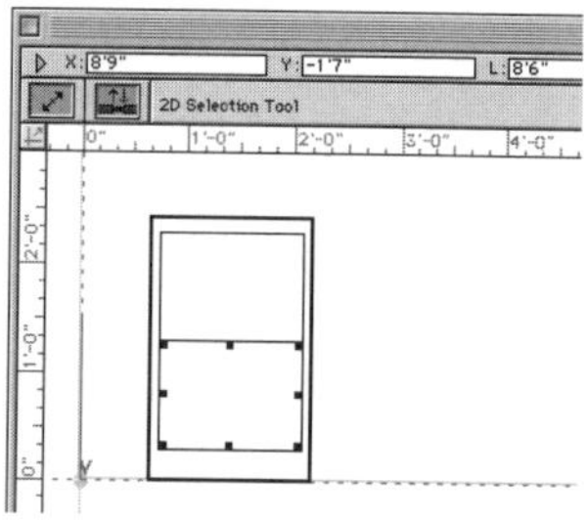

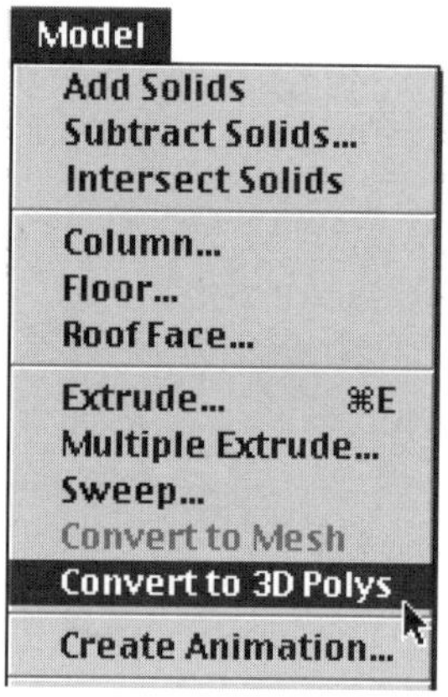

Shift-click to select the other drawer front. With both drawer fronts selected, choose the *MODEL>Convert To 3D Polys* command. This changes a 2D object to a 3D without any depth allowing it to be projected into 3D space. Also, since two objects were selected with this command both will be treated together as one converted 3D object. As a note, if you had created a drawer with the actual depth, it would take up much more memory, and in this case it is not necessary.

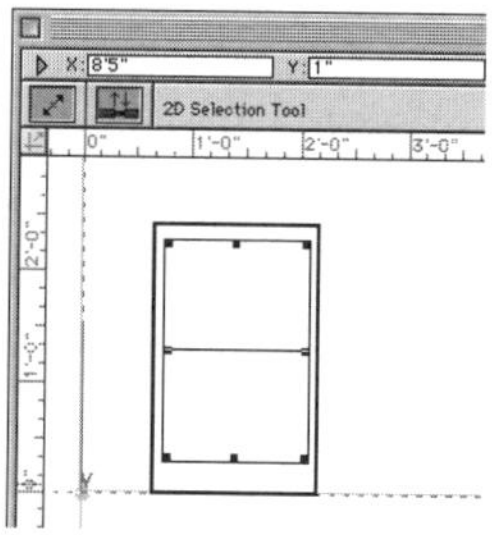

Step 3 - aligning the components

Now with the drawer fronts selected, change the *Standard Views* to either *Left* or *Right*. Notice that the drawers show as a line in this view. The line should be moved so it appears to be resting on the cabinet itself and not within it. Select the *TOOL>Move>Nudge* command and by hitting

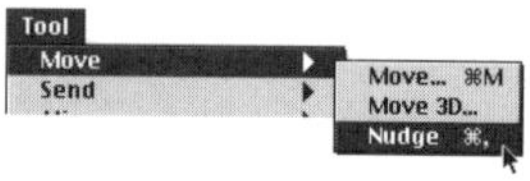

the *Arrow* keys on your keyboard move the drawers to the left or right. The command will be deactivated when you click once with the mouse.

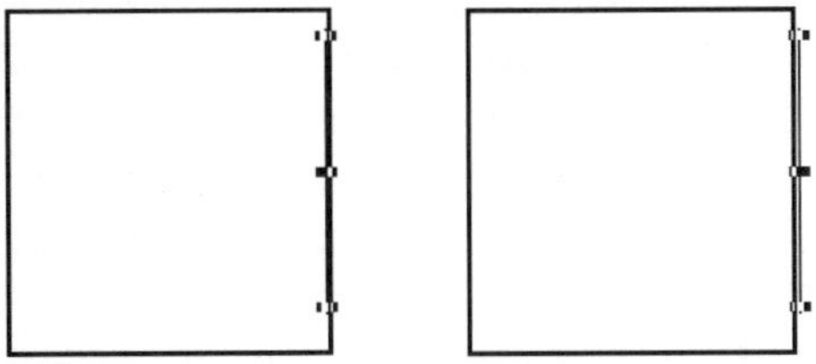

Select *VIEW>RENDERING>SOLID* and *VIEW>STANDARD VIEWS>BACK*. If the drawers disappear, then they are actually located within the cabinet and need to be moved to the surface. Change back to the *LEFT* or *RIGHT* view, select the drawers, and then the *NUDGE* command again. Hit the *Arrow* key in the direction the drawers should move. Click anywhere on the drawing to deselect the command and view the cabinet again. Do this until it is aligned satisfactorily. Now select the drawer fronts and the cabinet and *GROUP* the object. View it in *LEFT REAR ISO.*

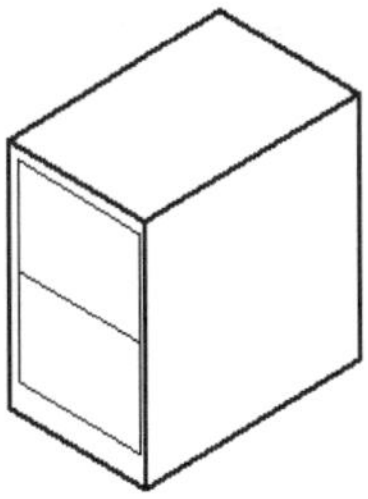

Shelving Unit

VectorWorks now comes with a new type of tool called *plug-in* tools, that creates complex hybrid objects. The plus side of using these *plug-in* tools, is that 3D objects are created very quickly via a dialog box and can easily be modified with the *OBJECT INFO* palette. The drawback is that you do not have as much control of different line weights, styles or colors within the object itself as you may want. Another drawback is that a *plug-in* tool also automatically creates new classes which may not be desirable once you start working more with the program and want to create your own setup. These items can be modified, although it may take a few more steps and may not make the *plug-in* as time efficient as possible, but it is still a good starting point.

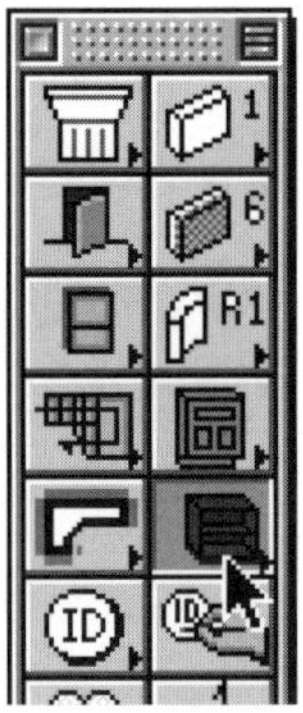

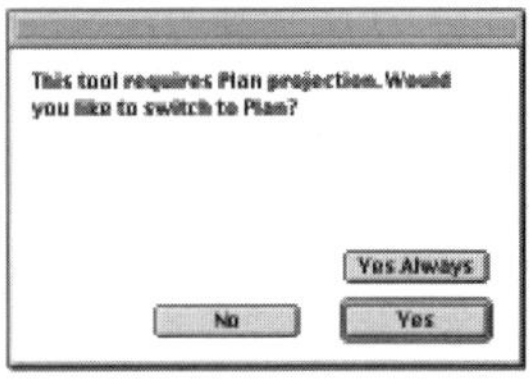

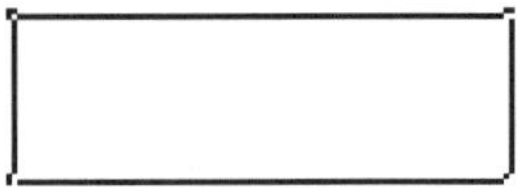

Step 1 - creating the unit

The first thing to do is to change *FILE>WORKSPACES* from *8 STANDARD (STREAMLINED)* to *AEC (STREAMLINED)*. This will take a moment or two depending on the speed of your computer. When *WORKSPACES* has changed, there will be new tools and commands available and locations of many of the previous commands will have changed. Make sure *PALETTES>AEC OBJECTS* has a checkmark and is open, if not just select it. Also, change the default line weight to .25. Double-click the *SHELVING UNIT* tool to open the *CREATE SHELVING UNIT* dialog box. An alert box may open saying to change the view to *TOP/PLAN* - just select *YES*. Enter the different options to match the dialog box below and then select *OK*. The object will automatically be created and be placed centered on the *X* and *Y* coordinates in the drawing area in *TOP/PLAN* view.

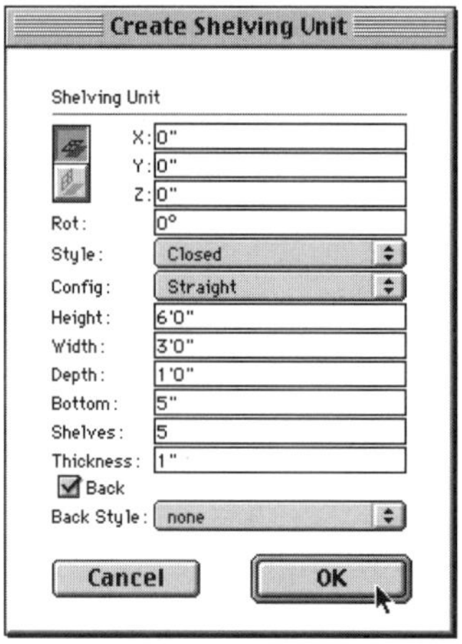

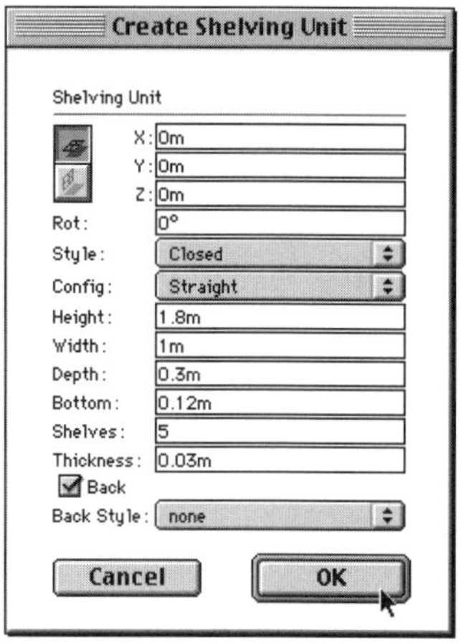

Step 2 - modifying the unit

Change the view to *RIGHT ISOMETRIC* and the *RENDERING* to *SOLID*. If the *OBJECT INFO* palette is not open, select *PALETTES>OBJECT INFO*. Look for the *HEIGHT* edit box and change it from 6'0" to 5'-6" (1.65m). Notice how the shelving unit immediately changes heights and all of the shelves automatically reposition. Also notice that it will re-render on its own as well.

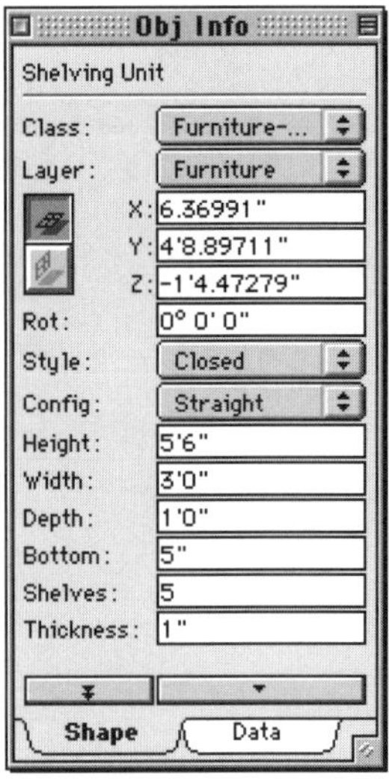

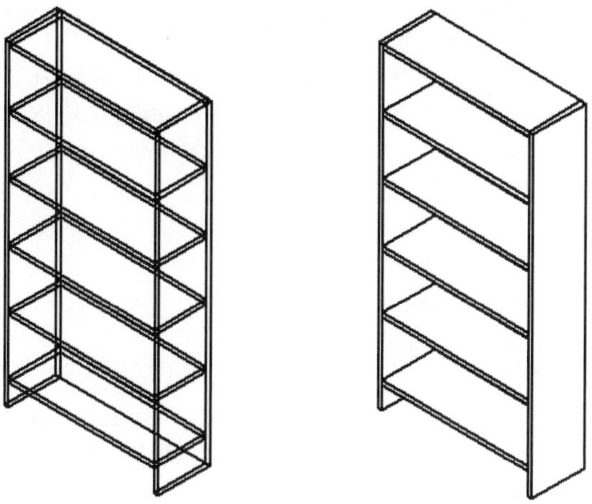

Go to the class pop-out menu on the *data display bar* and press/drag to *furniture-main*. Notice that when using these plug-in tools that classes are automatically created. Go to *CLASSES* in the pop-out menu and when the *CLASSES* dialog box opens, select this new class and then the *REMOVE* button. An alert box opens asking whether you are sure that you want to delete the class. Just select *YES* and then *OK* to exit the *CLASSES* dialog box.

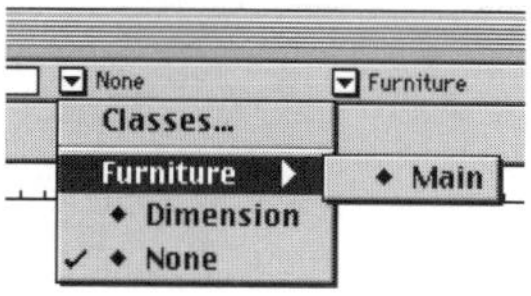

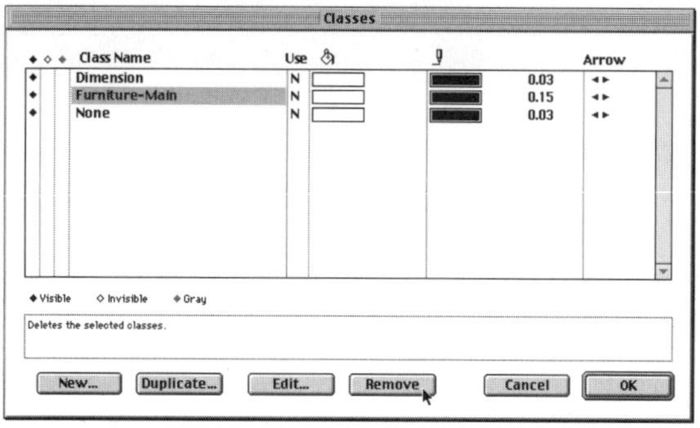

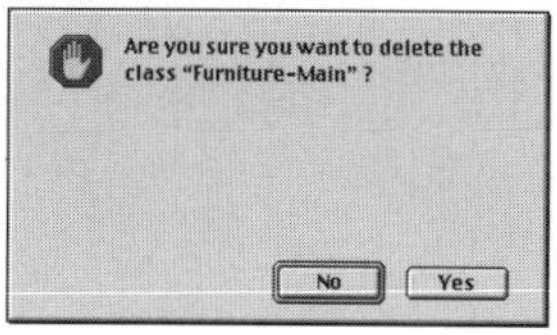

The shelving unit has not been deleted along with the class, but notice in the *OBJECT INFO* palette that it has changed location to the *none* class. When a class is deleted, all objects located in that class automatically get relocated to the *none* class. Change the *WORKSPACE* back to *8 STANDARD (STREAMLINED)* and the *LAYER OPTIONS* to *SHOW OTHERS*.

CREATING OBJECTS IN SUMMATION

Now that you have created a variety of 2D and 3D objects, *QUIT [EXIT]* the program making sure you save this file. With this quick whirlwind tour through creation of simple objects, you should now be able to use many of the tools and commands to create other objects. There are many points to remember.

- Be aware that, the order the different elements are drawn in can block objects below.

- Pressing the *Shift* key has many valuable uses from making circles and squares to moving an existing object so that it is constrained to be either directly above/below its starting place or to the right/left of it.

- Learn the key equivalents for quickly selecting or deselecting a *CONSTRAINT* icon will save you time while drawing.

- Remember to use the *GROUP* command to hold together an object constructed out of multiple pieces so that parts are not left out when moved.

- To see objects projected in other views, the objects have to be converted to 3D.

- The view an object is extruded in, affects whether the extrusion dimension or *ΔZ [±Z]* is a depth or height or width.

- To change the *TEXT* defaults, make sure only the *2D SELECTION* tool is selected with nothing else.

- When using the *ALIGN OBJECTS* command and the *CENTER* options, all objects will relocate to a center point unless one object encompasses the others.

- Be aware that just selecting a *plug-in* tool automatically adds new classes to your file even if no object was created.

- When classes are deleted, the objects located on that class are automatically moved to the *none* class.

Chapter 5

CREATING SYMBOLS

SYMBOL TYPES

Symbols are useful object types, particularly when using many duplicates of the same thing. There are many reasons for changing an object, grouped or otherwise into a symbol, such as, the ease of revising multiple placements, less memory usage, and the ability to have the 2D component entirely different from the 3D. Also, a symbol becomes a resource for a file and is easily replaced or imported into another file, whereas an object needs to be cut and pasted. The other aspect is that symbols and some of the *plug-in* objects such as doors, windows, and columns placed within walls created with the *WALL* tool, automatically cut the walls and heal them if they are removed.

The tools, commands, and palettes we will be exploring are;

- *2D LOCUS* Tool
- *3D LOCUS* Tool
- *2D SYMBOL INSERTION* Tool
- *ARC* Tool
- *DOUBLE LINE POLYGON* Tool
- *MIRROR* Tool
- *QUARTER ARC* Tool
- *SELECTION* Tool
- *WALL* Tool
- *CLASSES* Command
- *CONVERT TO 3D POLYS* Command
- *CREATE SYMBOL* Command
- *EDIT GROUP* Command
- *MOVE* Command
- *RENDERING* Commands
- *ROTATE* Command
- *SWEEP* Command
- *SYMBOL TO GROUP* Command
- *ATTRIBUTES* Palette
- *OBJECT INFO* Palette
- *RESOURCES* Palette

CREATING SYMBOLS

We will need to open a new file from the original template we had created, *chapt 3 [chapt 3.sta]*. This time, with the VectorWorks program opened use the *FILE>OPEN* command. Navigate in the scrolling list until you are in the *experiments* folder, select *chapt 3 [chapt 3.sta],* and then the *OPEN* button. Notice in this scrolling list, the icon is for a normal file rather than the template icon you would see within the folder. Why this happens is anyone's guess. You either need to remember which file is a template or double-click the icon itself rather than using the *OPEN* command in VectorWorks.

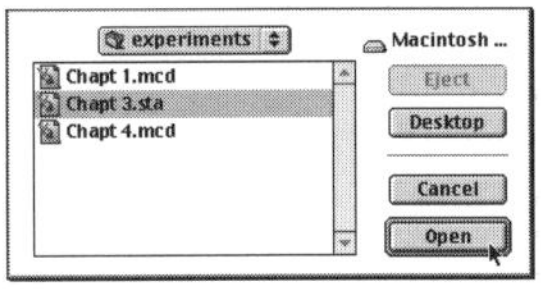

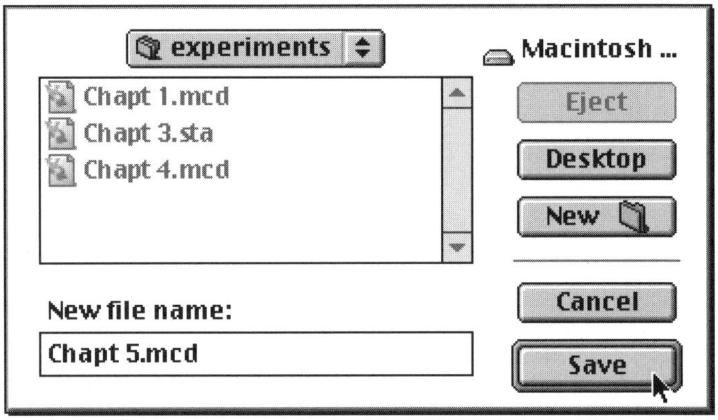

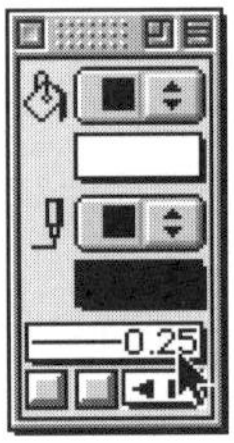

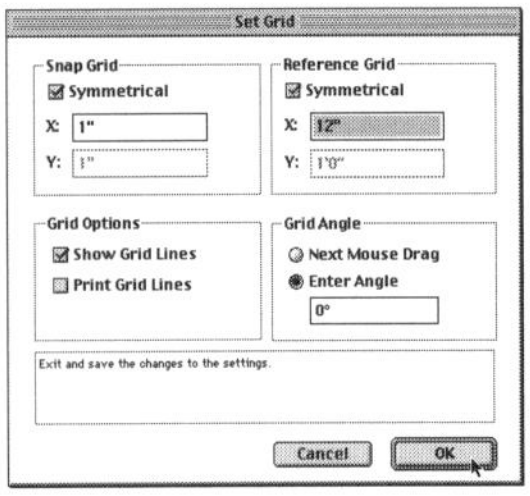

Once the new untitled file is opened, name it *chapt 5 [chapt 5.mcd]* and place it in the *experiments* folder by selecting the *SAVE* command. If a file has not yet been saved, you can use the *SAVE* command rather than the *SAVE AS* command. The same dialog box will open. Another untitled document may be open with no formatting, depending on how you had opened VectorWorks. Just make it the active file and click the *close box* in the upper left. Remember to continually *SAVE* as you go along. Also, check the default line weight in the *ATTRIBUTES* palette and verify that the third line weight, .5 and the three constraint icons are selected on the *CONSTRAINTS* palette. Select *PAGE>SET GRID* and enter 1" (.01m) for *SNAP GRID* and 1' (.5m) for *REFERENCE GRID* in the *SET GRID* dialog box with the *SYMMETRICAL* and *SHOW GRID LINES* boxes selected.

Basically, to create a symbol, you first have to actually make the object, then convert it into a symbol. If you want a hybrid symbol, one having both a 2D as well as a 3D component, it is easier to start with the 3D object. Then once the 3D symbol is made, edit it in the *symbol edit window* and add the 2D aspect.

CREATING DOORS

Make *eighth scale (hundredth scale)* the active layer and select *ORGANIZE>LAYER OPTIONS>ACTIVE ONLY*.

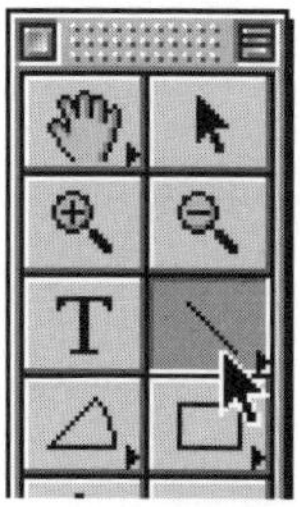

Quick Door

The first door symbol that we will create will be a simple 3' (.90m) wide door. It can only be used for 2D plans since it will not have a 3D component.

Step 1 - the door

Select the *SINGLE LINE* tool with the *CONSTRAINED* modifier icon. Draw a vertical line that is 3' (.90m) and change its line weight to .25.

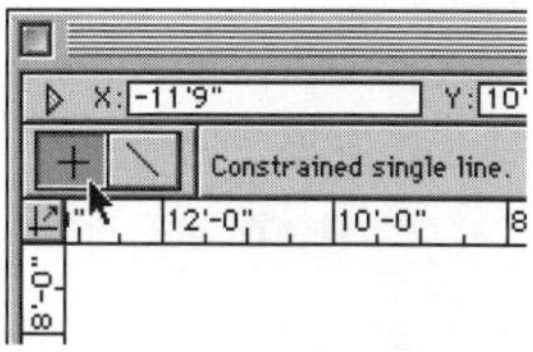

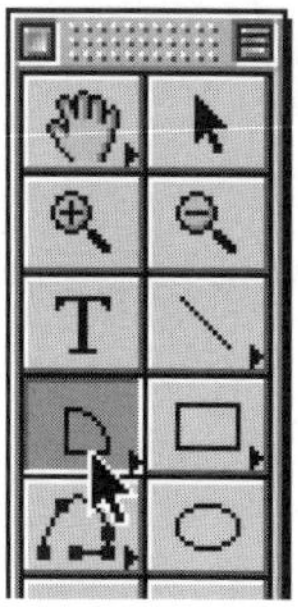

Step 2 - the door swing

Select the *QUARTER ARC* tool. Now place the cursor on the top of the line and when the *smartcursor cue, point* appears, press/drag horizontally to the right. While still pressing the mouse, hit the *Tab* key to highlight the Δx *[±x]* edit box in the *data display bar*. Enter 3' (.90m) (don't forget to hit the *Return [Enter]* key). Then press the *Shift* key or hit the *S* key so the arc is constrained symmetrically to a quarter of a circle rather than a quarter of an ellipse, and then release the mouse. The *cues* will differ depending on how you constrained the arc. Also, you may find the arc may have the centerpoint on the wrong side. Since there is really no way to control this, either delete it and start again or use the *TOOL>ROTATE>FLIP HORIZONTAL* and then the *FLIP VERTICAL* commands.

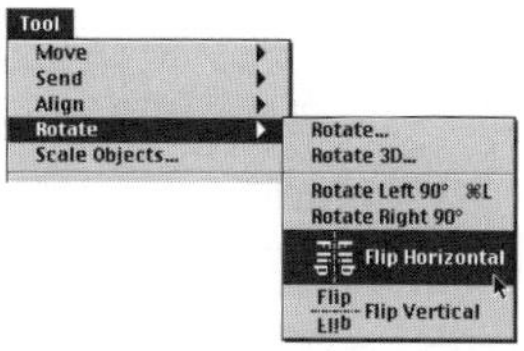

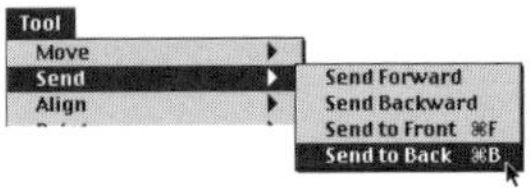

With the arc selected, use the *TOOL>Send>Send To Back* command. This keeps the door swing ($^{1}/_{4}$ arc) from obscuring the door (line). With the arc still selected change the line weight to the thinnest line and the fill to *none* in the *Attributes* palette.

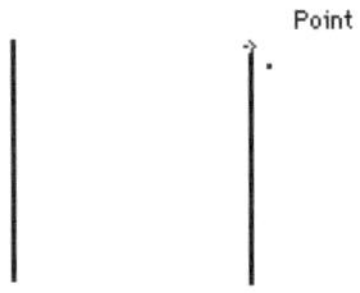

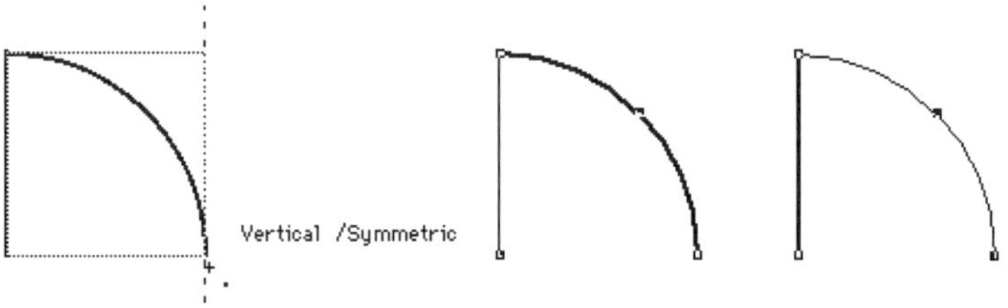

Step 3 - creating a symbol

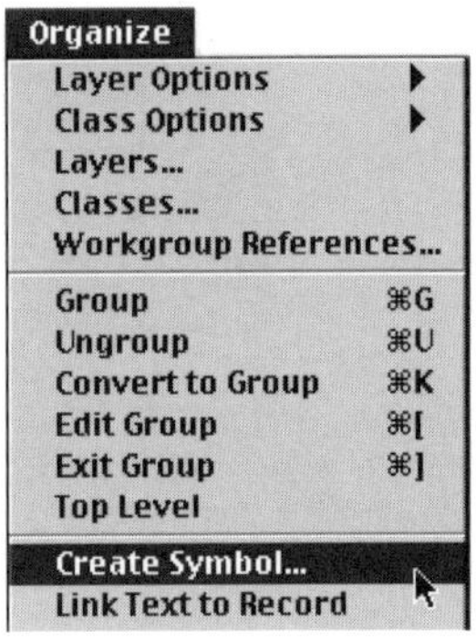

With both objects selected, go to the *ORGANIZE>Create Symbol* command. The *Create Symbol* dialog box opens. A default name is automatically given and highlighted, in this case *symbol #1* since it is the first symbol.

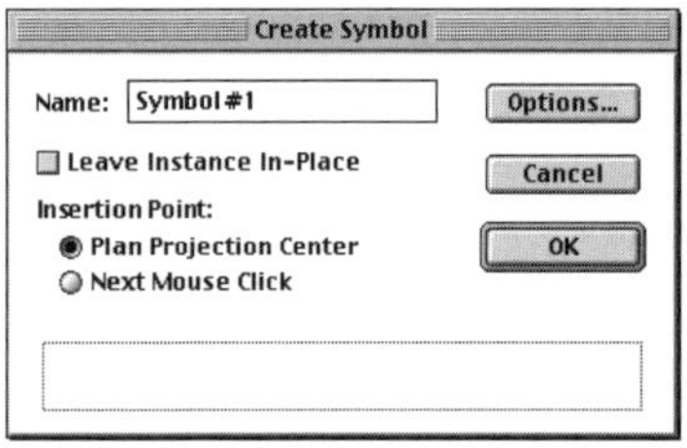

Rename the symbol *door quick*. Select the *options* button. When the *Insertion Options* dialog box opens, click the *on edge* button, the *full break with caps*, and then *ok*. When the dialog box closes, select the *leave instance in-place* box, the *next mouse click* button for the *insertion point*, and click *ok* again.

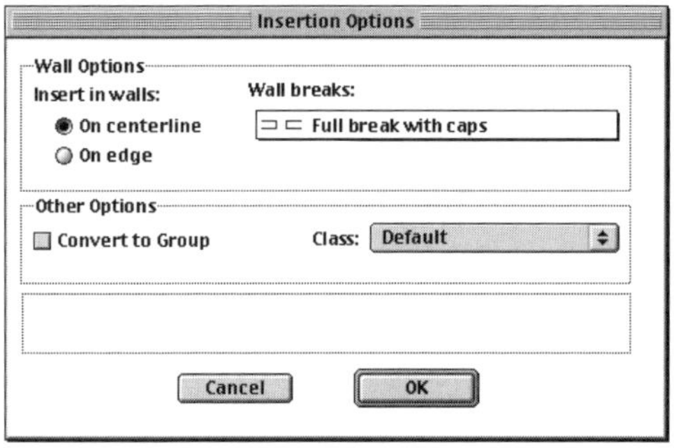

When the dialog box closes, place the cursor on the hinge part of the door. Move the cursor until it snaps to that point and the *cue, point* appears and then click. The door will disappear from the screen and then reappear and will automatically be placed as a symbol in the *RESOURCES* palette for this particular file.

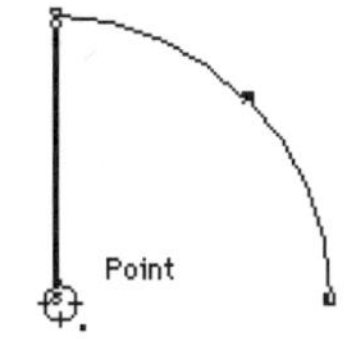

Symbols placed in walls will have their locus or insertion point actually centered on the wall unless you select the *OPTIONS* button which allows you to designate and place the symbol on the wall's edge. This way, you can now use the same symbol for different wall thicknesses.

Slab Door

The next door symbol that we will create will be a hybrid symbol - in other words it has both a 2D and a 3D component. The door will be a typical 3' x 7' (.90m x 2.00m) slab door. Make *quarter scale (fiftieth scale)* the active layer. By the way, the only reason we are changing layers is to go to a larger scale for the more complex symbols, although it really does not make a difference which scale is used. A symbol or object when placed or pasted will always resize according to the current scale for that layer.

Step 1 - the slab

Change to *VIEW>STANDARD VIEWS>FRONT*. With the *RECTANGLE* tool selected, press/drag along the horizontal line on your screen upwards, so that it sits on the line designating the *ground plane*. The rectangle should be created to measure 3' (.90m) in the X direction and 7'-0" (2.00m) in the Y by either eyeballing with the mouse or entering information into the *data display bar*. Change the line weight of the rectangle to the second weight down in the *ATTRIBUTES* palette.

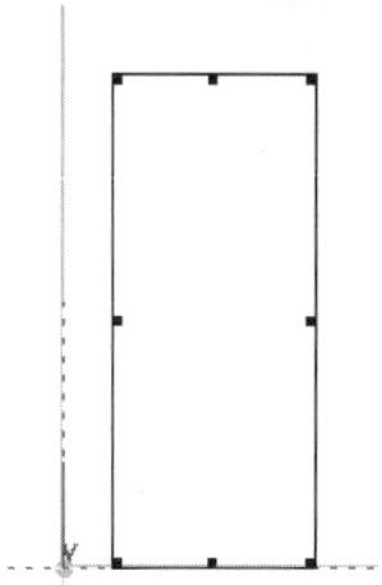

With the rectangle selected, use the *MODEL>EXTRUDE* command. When the *CREATE EXTRUDE* dialog box. Enter 1" (.025m) into the *EXTRUSION* edit box and select *OK*.

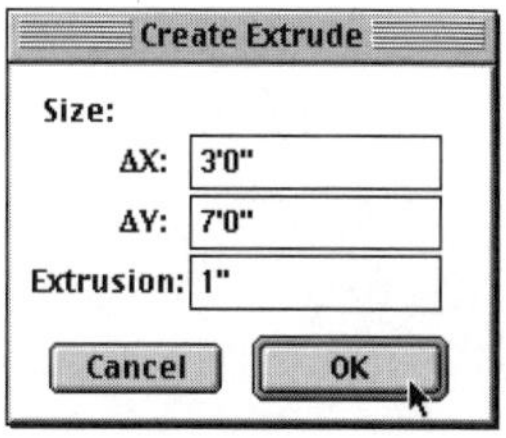

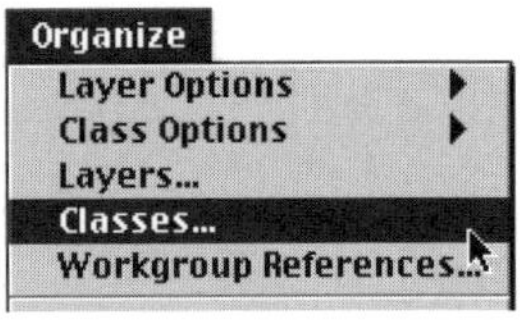

Step 2 - the knob and shank

Change to *Top/Plan* view and zoom in to get a closer look at the door. With nothing selected, change the default line weight to the first or lightest weight on the *Attributes* palette. Create a new class by going to *ORGANIZE> Classes* and when the *Classes* dialog box opens, click the *new* button.

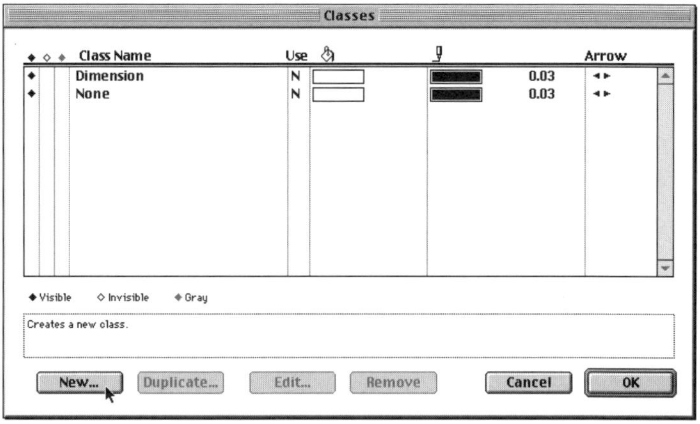

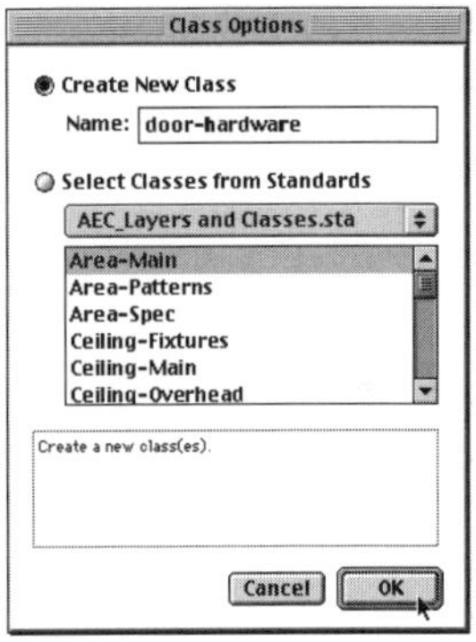

In the *Class Options* dialog box enter *door-hardware* under *name*. The *create new class* button should be selected, then click *ok*. This brings you back to the *Classes* dialog box. Click *ok* again to exit. Now, notice when you press on the class pop-out menu in the *data display bar* how the new class, *door-hardware*, appears. Placing a hyphen without spaces allows you to have class submenus. Press/drag down to it to make it the active class.

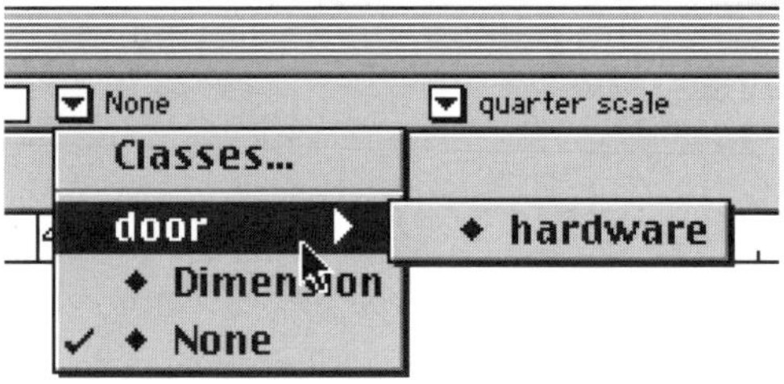

With the *Arc* tool and *arc by radius* modifier icon selected, draw an arc with a 3/4" (.02m) radius. You would need to press the mouse and drag it downwards, *Tab* across to the *L* edit box, enter 3/4" (.02m), and then press the *Shift* key to keep it constrained vertically, and finally release the mouse button. After the button is released the *data display bar* changes. Move the mouse and when the *sweep* in the *data display bar* is 180° and the *smartcursor cue, vertical* appears, just click. So in other words, it is press, drag, release, and click. If this does not seem to work, you are not zoomed in far enough. Try getting the magnification up to at least 800%. You can quickly hit the *C* key twice to double the magnification if you have not already started drawing the object.

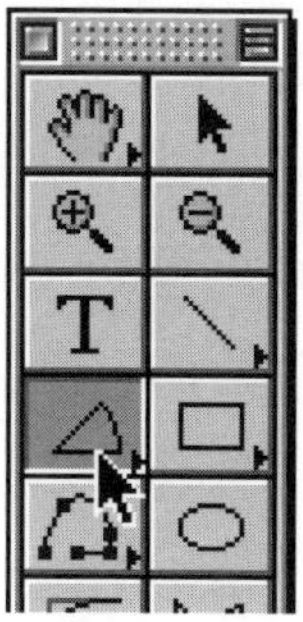

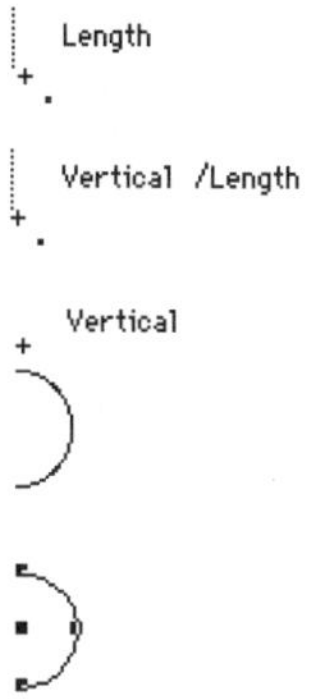

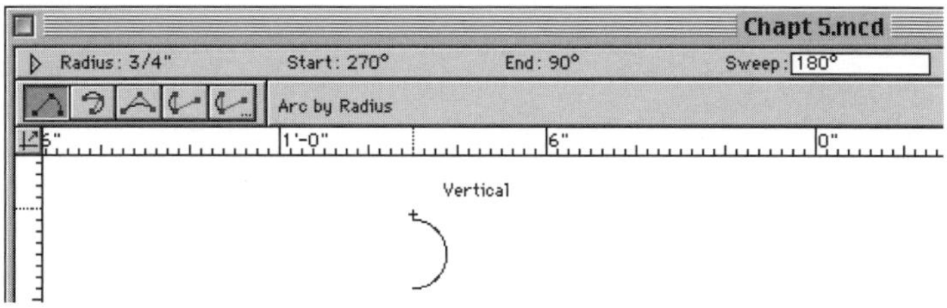

Create the shank by drawing a single line 4" (.10m) long snapping to the end of the arc for the starting point and constraining it vertically. The shank should be in a vertical position on your screen. If it is not already, select both the knob and the shank and use the *TOOL>Rotate>Rotate Left 90°* command.

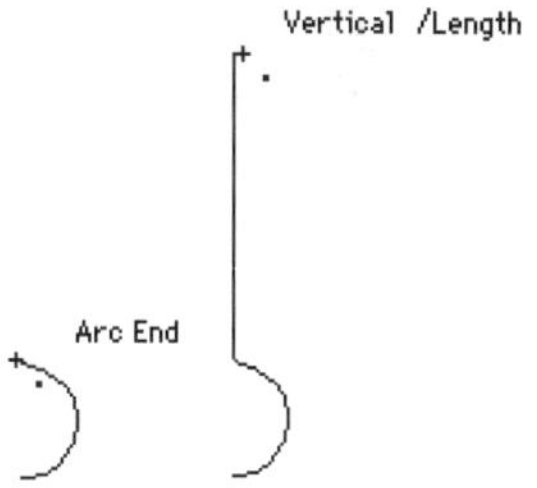

You will need to make a duplicate of the arc which will be used for the other knob. First select the arc and place the *selection* cursor over it, moving the mouse around on the bottom part until the *press/drag* cursor appears. You can also just hit the *U* key so that the *resize* cursor is not an option with the *2D Selection* tool. When the *cue, arc end* appears, press the *Option [Control]* key, press/drag with the mouse, and then release the key. The original arc remains and a duplicate is created. While still pressing the

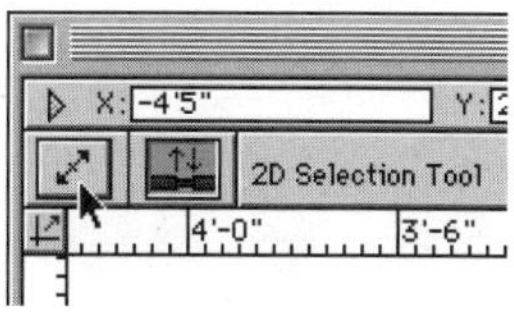

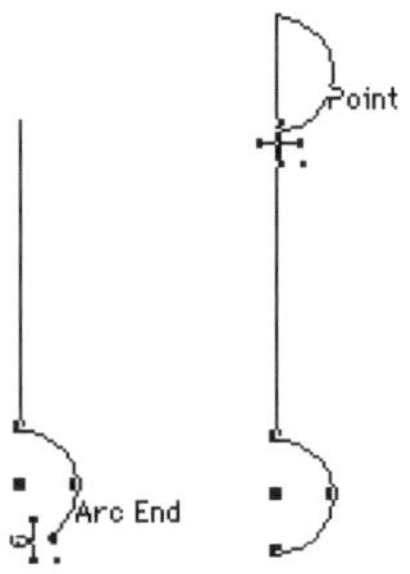

mouse drag it to the other end of the line and release when the cursor snaps to the end and the *cue, point* appears. Hit the *U* key again so that the *2D SELECTION* tool goes back to its normal mode of *resize* and *press-drag.*

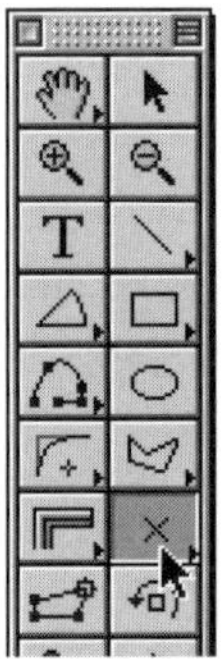

Now with the *2D LOCUS* tool selected, click to place a loci at the end of the shank line making use of the *smartcursor cues* to find the exact location. With the locus point selected, use the *TOOL>MOVE>MOVE* command to offset it 3/4" (.02m) in the x direction away from the arc side. Remember to insert a minus sign to move it towards the left.

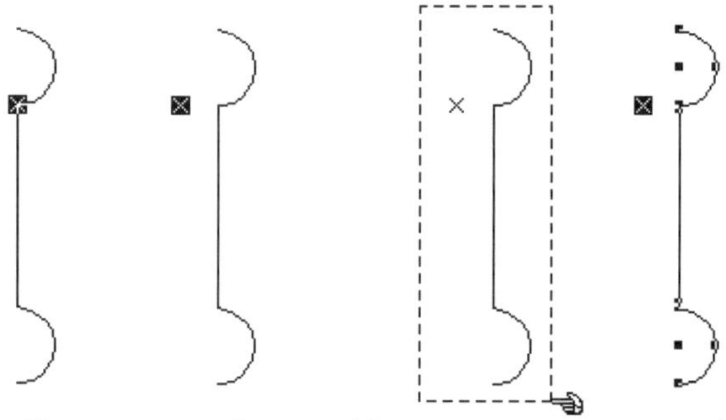

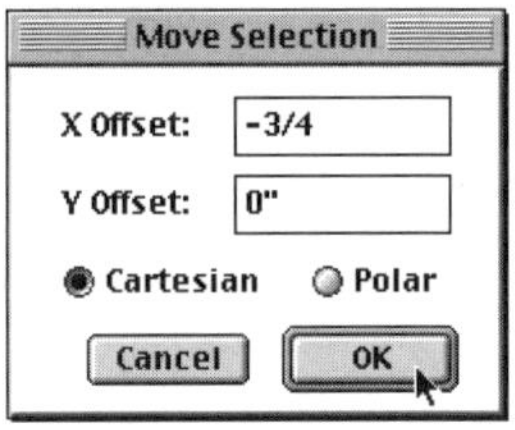

With the *2D SELECTION* tool press/drag a marquee to select both arcs, the line, and the locus point. Select the *MODEL>SWEEP* command. The *CREATE SWEEP* dialog box automatically opens. Change the *SEGMENT ANGLE* to 30°. If the dialog box does not hide this object, you can see what happens when you change the *SEGMENT ANGLE* and *Tab* out of the edit box. The *SEGMENT ANGLE* controls how many degrees each facet has. The higher the degrees the more faceted an object looks. Click *OK* to exit. The *SWEEP* command automatically groups all of the objects.

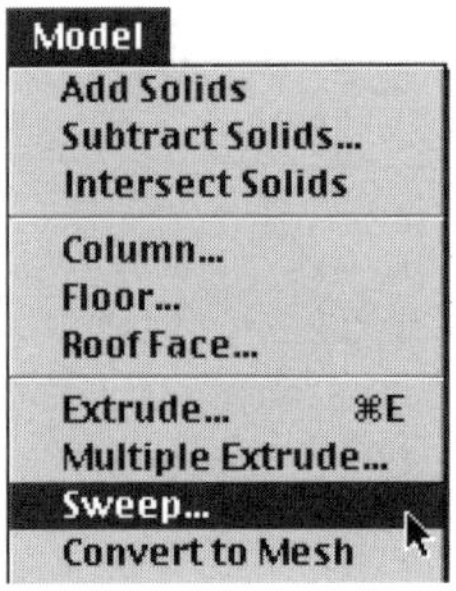

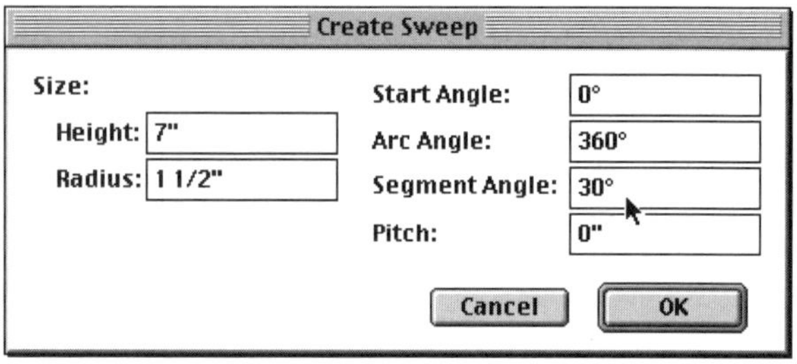

With the swept object still selected, change the line to a custom weight by selecting *SET THICKNESS* in the line button pop-out menu in the *ATTRIBUTES* palette. Enter .03 in the *SET THICKNESS* dialog box.

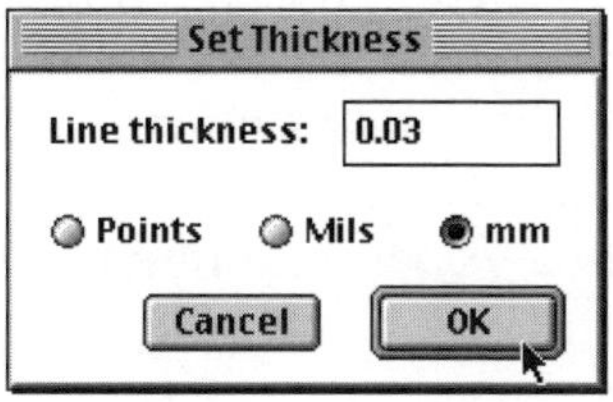

Open the *OBJECT INFO* palette under *PALETTES*. Select the swept object, type 60° into the *SEG* box and hit the *Return [Enter]* or *Tab* key. Now compare the before and after. The facets are more easily noticed on the shank. As a note, if you see the arrows across the bottom of the *OBJECT INFO* palette, click the double arrow on the left to move a pane length downwards or click the single arrow to move one edit box down. You could also press/drag the *resize* box on the lower right.

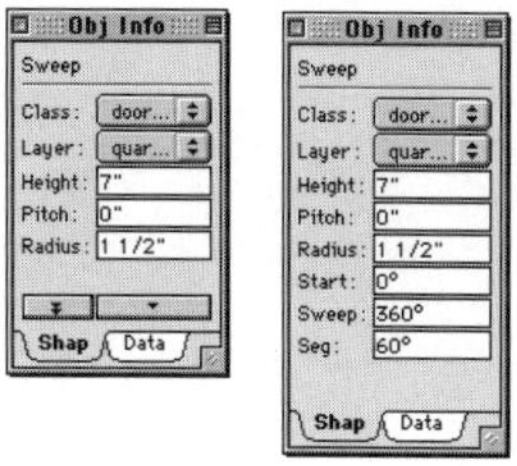

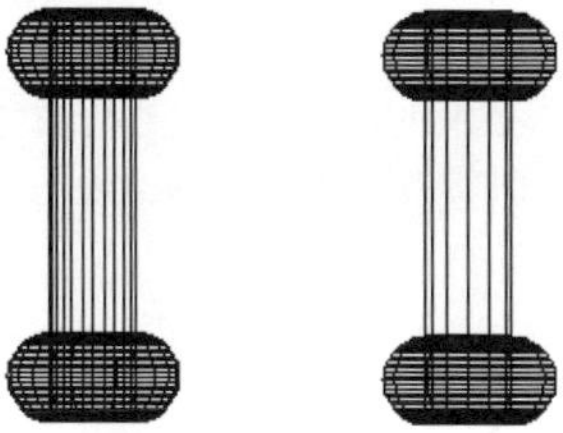

Step 3 - the door assembly

Zoom-out and select both objects, the door and hardware, and then the *TOOL>ALIGN>ALIGN OBJECTS* command. When the *ALIGN OBJECTS* dialog box opens click the *LEFT SIDES, T/B CENTERS,* and *BACKS* buttons and then *OK*.

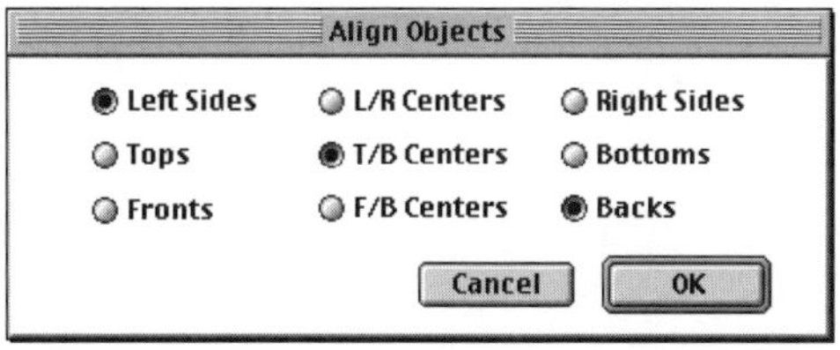

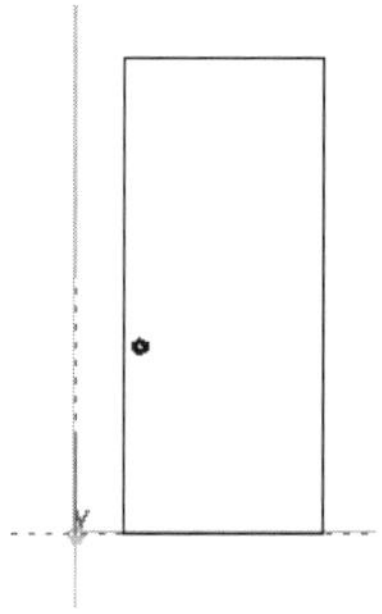

Wireframe

Solid

Shaded No Lines

In order to fine tune the placement of the knob change back to *VIEW>Standard Views>Front.* With just the hardware selected move it over 1 1/2" (.04m) from the edge and up to a height of 33" (.82m) with the *TOOL>Move>Move* command. Moving over from the edge in the x direction is straight forward, but moving it so that the center is at a 33" (.82m) height takes some calculation. Since the object is 3" (.08m) in diameter and the bottom rests on the *ground plane* you would need to move it up 31 1/2" (.78m) or +31 1/2" (+.78m) in the *y offset* box in the *Move Selection* dialog box.

Also check to see that the door is on the *ground plane* and that it did not inadvertently move when it was aligned. Press/drag it to position if necessary.

Step 4 - finishing touches

With the door assembly selected, go to the *Attributes* palette and select *pen* colors for the outline of the door and the knob, and a different *fill* color for the door plane. If you look at the door in any of the 3D views, the outline will be in the selected *pen* color but the *fill* color does not show and it appears transparent even though the *fill* has *solid* selected. This is because it is in *Wireframe* rather than rendered *Solid.*

Now choose *VIEW>Rendering>Solid* in order to view it as an opaque object. It will appear in the selected *fill* color, outlined with the *pen* color. If you select *Shaded No Lines,* it will appear in different shades of the *fill* color.

You can also make the hardware disappear by again accessing the *Classes* dialog box and clicking in the *invisible* column next to the name *door-hardware,* so that an open diamond appears. When you exit the dialog box, the knobs will appear if *door-hardware* is the active class and disappear when it is not.

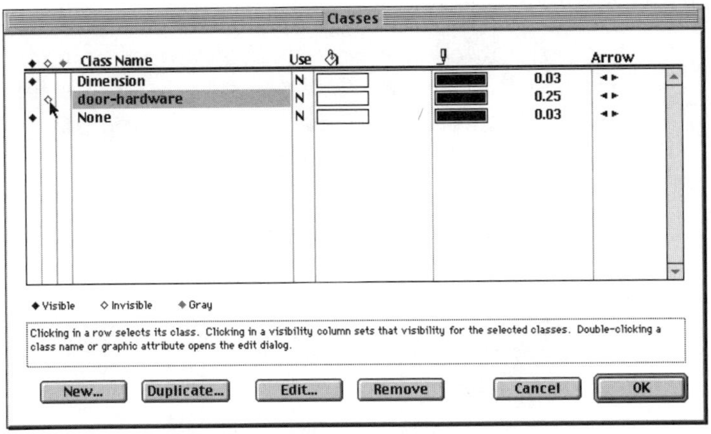

Step 5 - creating a symbol

Make the *door-hardware* class VISIBLE in the *CLASSES* dialog box by clicking in the VISIBLE column next to its name so that a black diamond appears, go back to *RIGHT ISOMETRIC* view, marquee select both objects, select *ORGANIZE> CREATE SYMBOL*. When the *CREATE SYMBOL* dialog box opens, name it *door 36x84 (door 90x200)*. Select OPTIONS and when the *INSERTION OPTIONS* dialog box opens, select ON CENTERLINE, then OK. Choose the NEXT MOUSE CLICK button and then OK. Click the door on the hinge side. Do not worry about placing it exactly since we will edit it. The door disappears from the screen and is saved as a resource for this document.

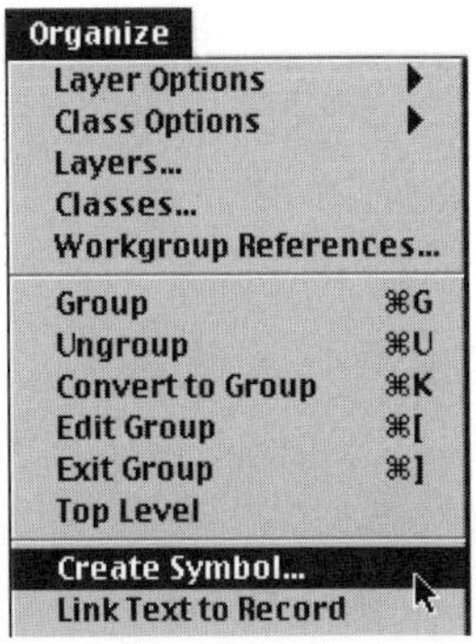

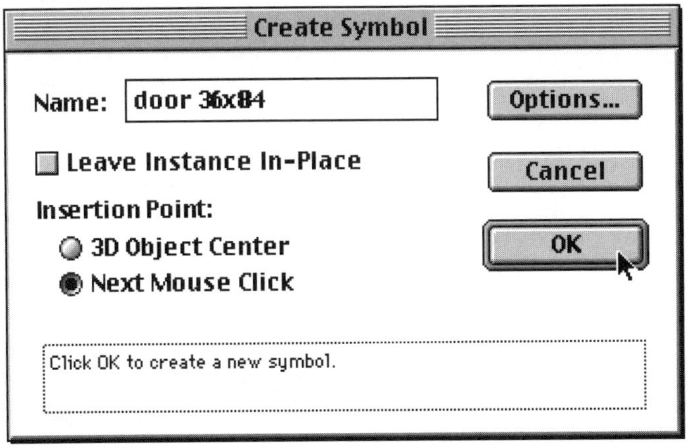

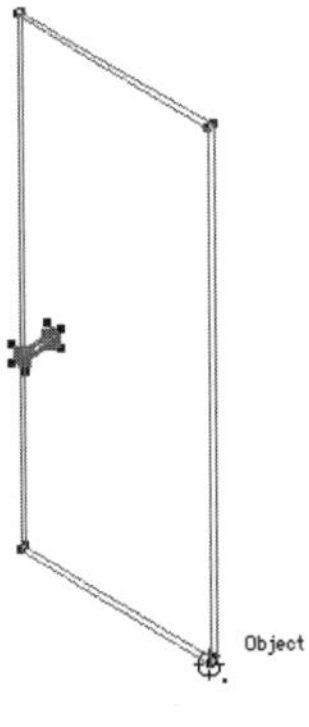

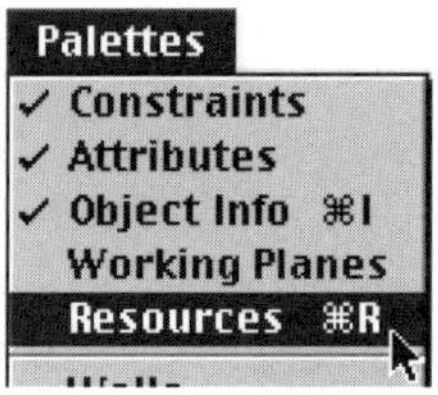

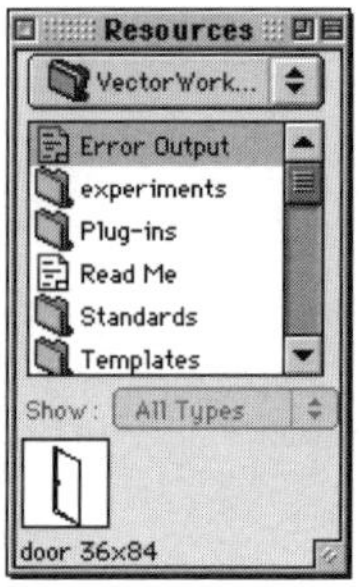

Step 6 - modifying a symbol

In order to change an existing symbol you would need to access it in the *Resources* palette. Open the *Resources* palette under *PALETTES>Resources* and navigate to the *chapt 5 [chapt 5.mcd]* file at the bottom. With *door 36x84 (door 90x200)* selected, click the *edit* button. If the buttons are not visible on the right, click the top button second from the right to expand the palette.

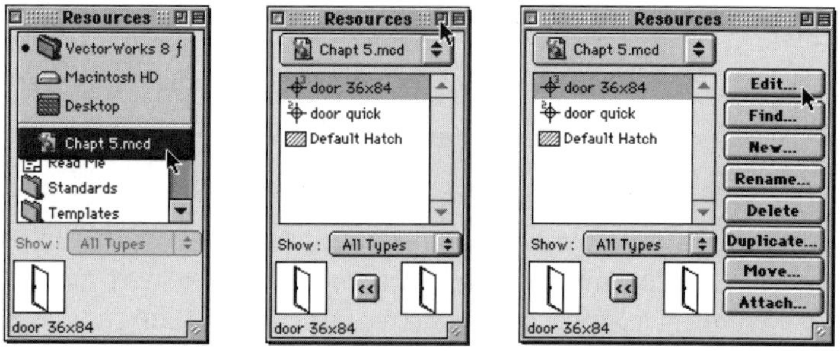

A dialog box opens asking whether you wish to edit the *2d* or *3d component* of the symbol even if you had not created both views.

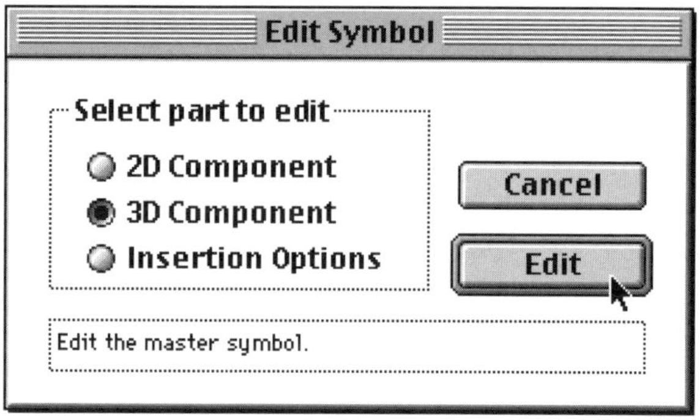

revising the symbol

Select the 3d button and then *edit*. The door appears in the *symbol editing window*. Change the view to *Top/Plan* and with the door and hardware selected, use the *TOOL>Rotate>Rotate* command. When the *Rotate Object* dialog box opens, enter -30° under *angle*.

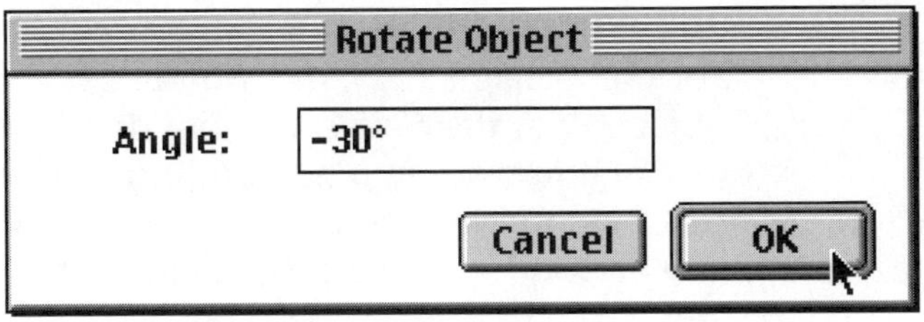

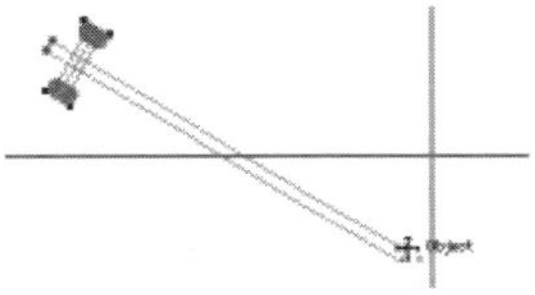

Once rotated, press/drag the door so the hinge rests on the intersection of the guide lines. This intersection is the insertion point when placing symbols. With the door rotated, it will appear partially ajar in 3D views.

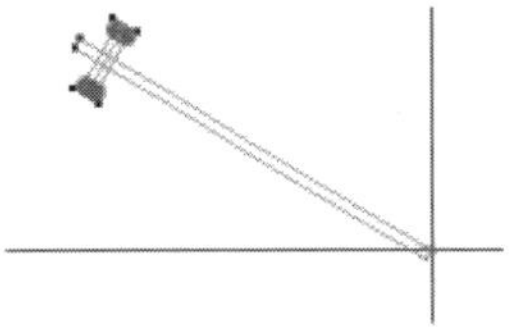

To take into account a wall thickness of 6" (.15m), use the *Move* command to place the door 3" (.075m) up in the Y direction, so when inserted it will be flush with the wall. Change the view to *Front* and verify that the bottom of the door is resting on the *ground plane*. If not, select the door and hardware and position it. Change back to *Top/Plan*.

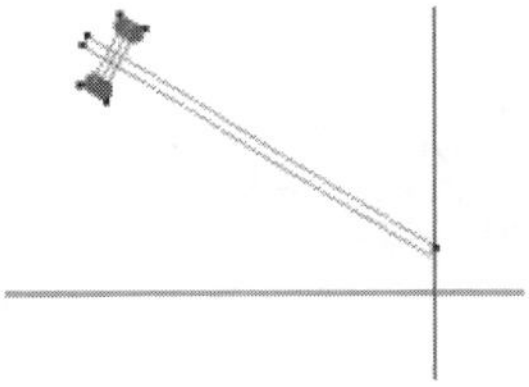

adding an opening

Change the default line weight to the second weight in the *Attributes* palette. Change the active class back to *none*. For the casing, draw a rectangle 6" x 3'-0" (.15m x .90m) and place the center right edge at the insertion point. Change the fill to *NONE*, and extrude it to 7'-0" (2.00m). This piece needs to be added if you want to see the full opening demarcated in a 3D view.

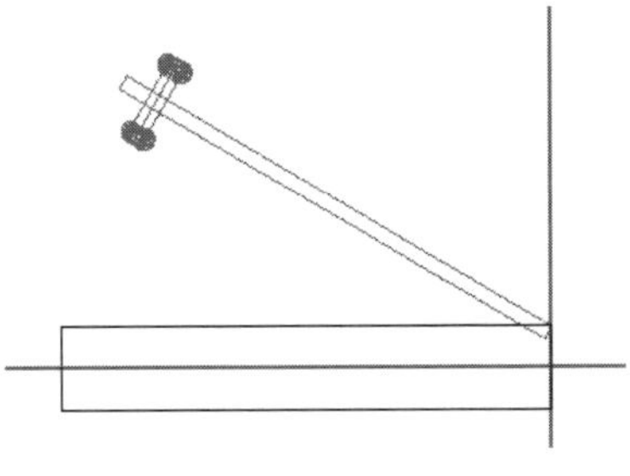

adding the 2D portion

For the 2D aspect just draw on top of the existing object. With the *Single Line* tool draw a vertical 3' (.90m) line starting 3" (.075m) up from the insertion point where the guide lines intersect. Make sure the line or door is on the same side as the 3D door. Now with the *Quarter Arc* tool draw an arc with a 36" (.90m) radius in the thinnest line weight, send it to the back so it does not block the line, and change the fill to *NONE*.

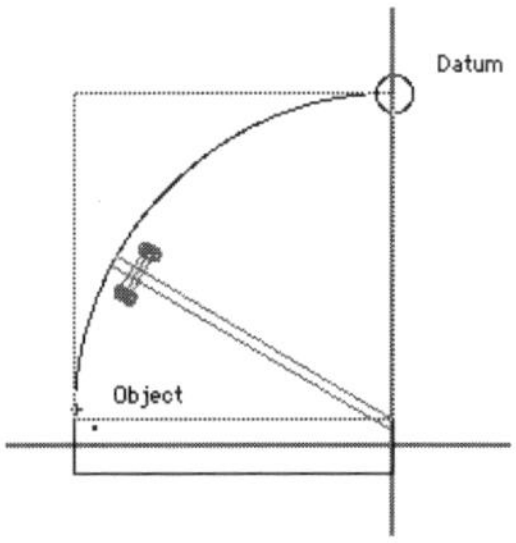

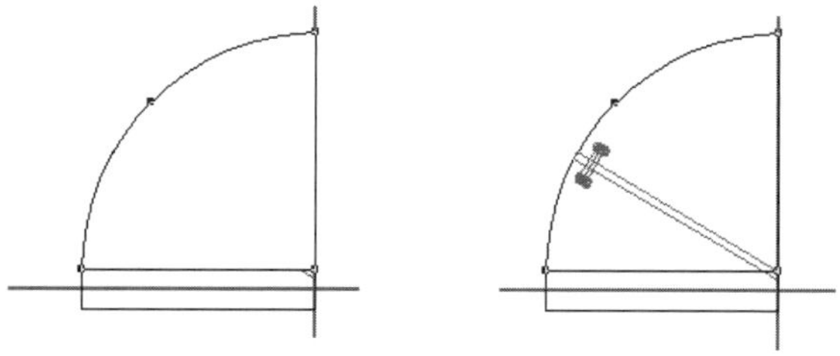

To add more detail, such as trim around the door opening in plan view, create a rectangle 3" x 1/2" (.075m x .013m) snapping to one of the outside corners. Change the line weight of this object to .13.

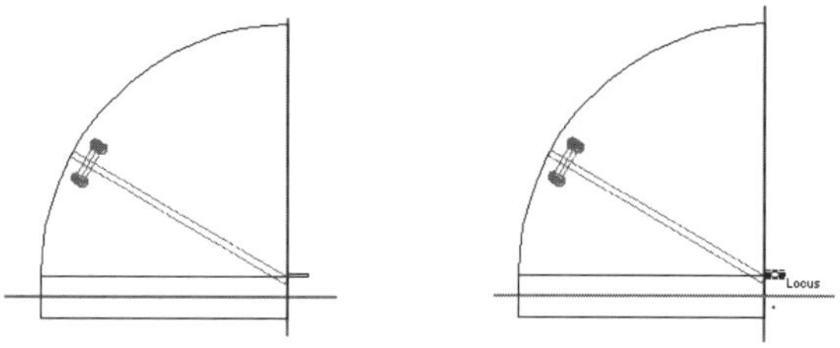

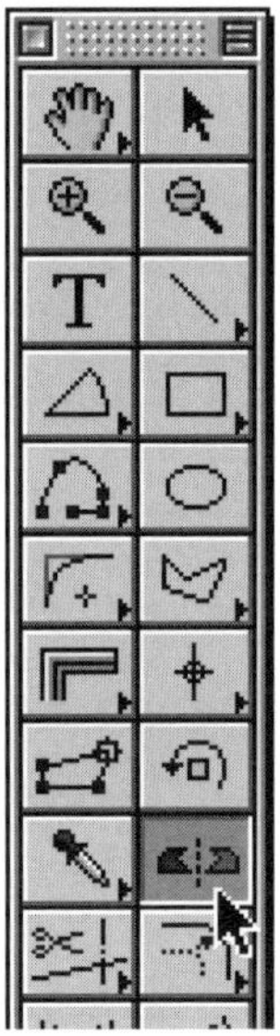

Select the rectangle and use the *Mirror* tool with the *MIRROR AND DUPLICATE* icon. Snap to the centerline of the door opening to draw the axis line for the duplicate keeping it constrained with the *Shift* key.

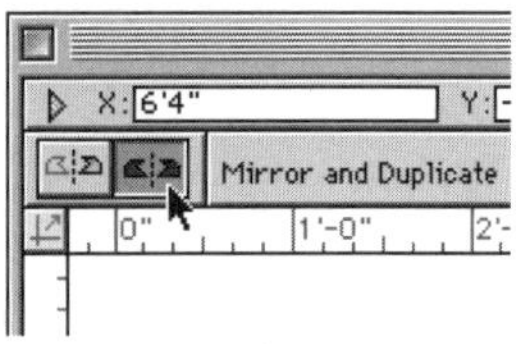

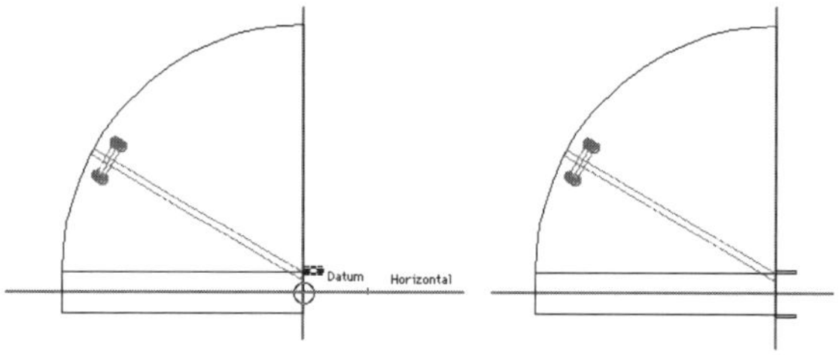

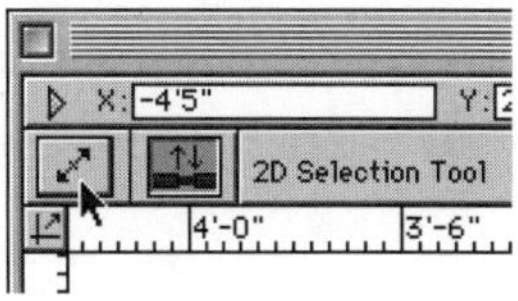

With the *Selection* tool, deselect the first icon with the *U* key so that you only get the *press-drag* cursor. Marquee select the two rectangles, press the *Option [Control]* key then press/drag from the right inner corner of one of the rectangles to make a duplicate. Press/drag the duplicates over to the left and release when the *cue, object* appears and it is snapped to the other side of the door opening. Change the view to *Right Isometric*, then click the *exit symbol* button. If you need to edit the 2D portion again, which we will, you will need to select *edit 2D* to access this part of the hybrid symbol. Hit the *U* key so that the *resize and reshape* mode are both available on the *2D Selection* tool.

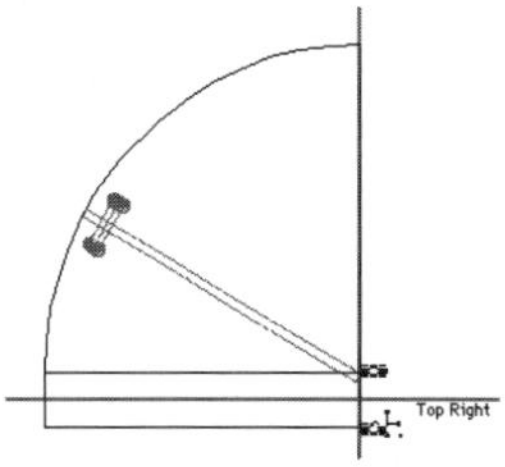

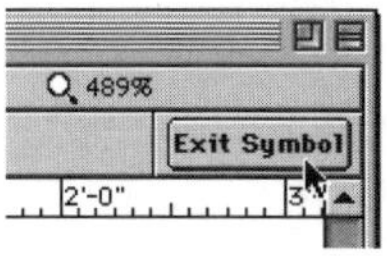

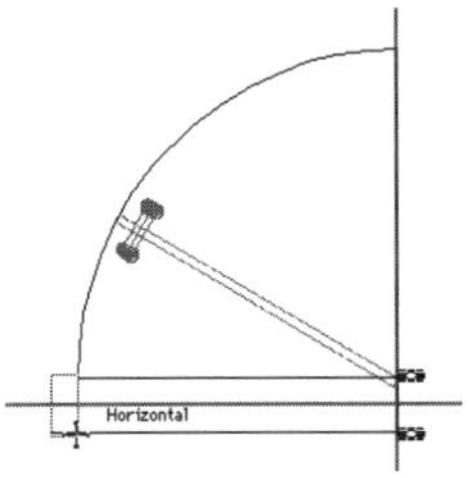

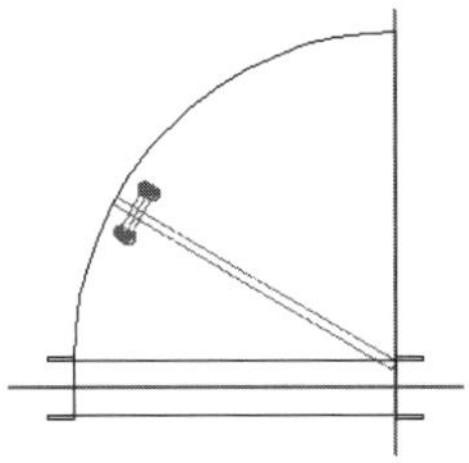

viewing the symbol

Change the view to *Top/Plan*. Select the *Wall* tool and click the right most icon to open the *Wall Preferences* dialog box. Enter 6" (.15m) for *separation*.

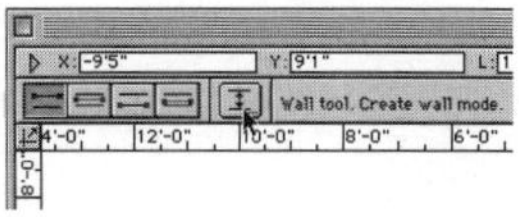

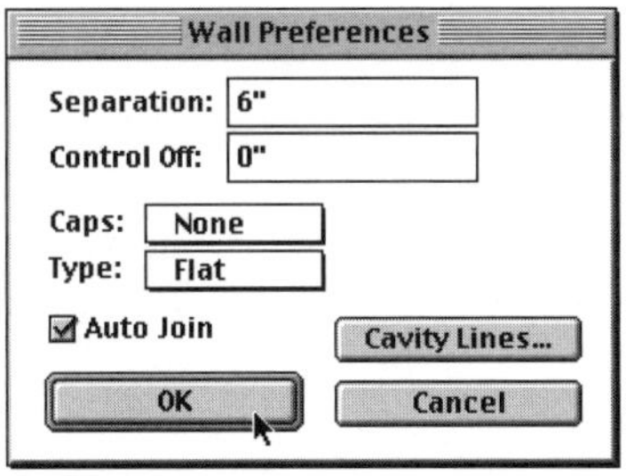

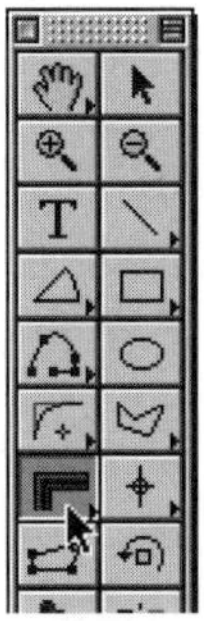

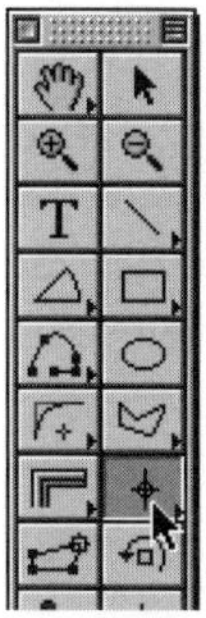

Draw a segment of wall by clicking at one point and double-clicking at the end point. Then with the *2D Symbol Insertion* tool selected and the first icon in the mode bar, click once within the wall. This new symbol

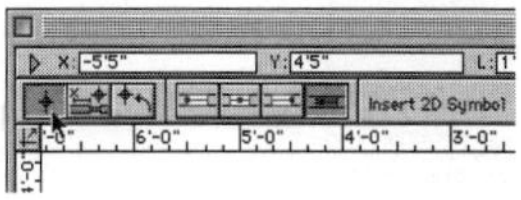

will be selected and placed in the wall since it was the last symbol created. If no symbol is selected, you will need to double-click the symbol name in the *Resources* palette to select this symbol for placement. If the *Resources* palette is not open, go to *PALETTES> Resources*. In the pop-out menu in the upper part of the *Resources* palette, press/drag down to the active document on the bottom. Notice how the symbol cuts the wall at the outside edge of the trim rather than at the inner side in *Top/Plan* view.

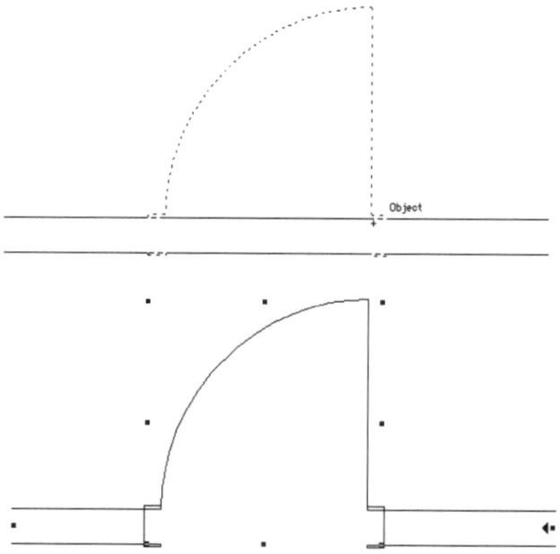

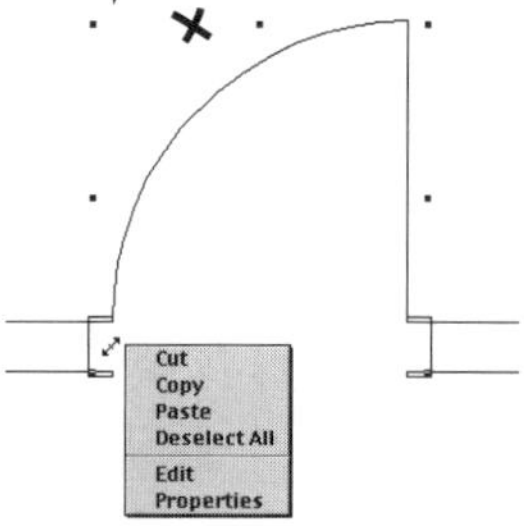

editing the 2D portion

In this case we will need to go in and edit the 2D portion so that the wall is cut at the inner side of the trim. Press the *Control* key *[right-click on the mouse]* and press a point on the symbol to open the *object edit mode* pop-up menu. Press/drag down to *Edit* to open the *2D symbol edit window*. With the *2D Locus* tool selected, click to place a locus along the *x* axis aligning it on the inner side of the trim - one on each side for a total of two locus points.

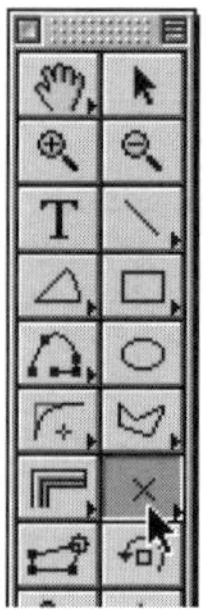

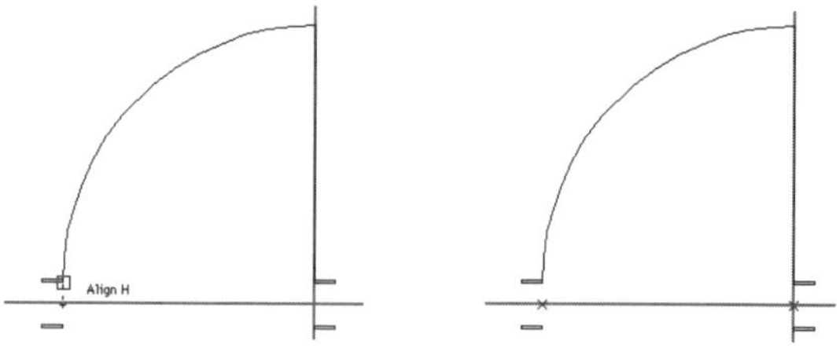

Click the *EXIT SYMBOL* button in the upper right of your screen and then view how the symbol cuts the wall now. It is necessary to have two locus points to control how the 2D portion of a symbol cuts a wall when placed. The loci will not print.

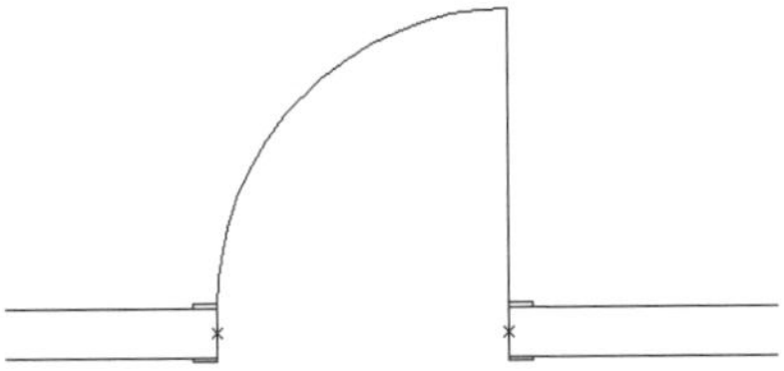

Another Slab Door

If you need another symbol similar to an existing one, you can now create it very easily. Just select the symbol name in the *RESOURCES* palette and then the *DUPLICATE* button. Once the duplicate is created, you can then go in and modify it. Let's say you need another slab door, but this one is only 2'-8" (.80m) rather than 3'-0" (.90m) wide.

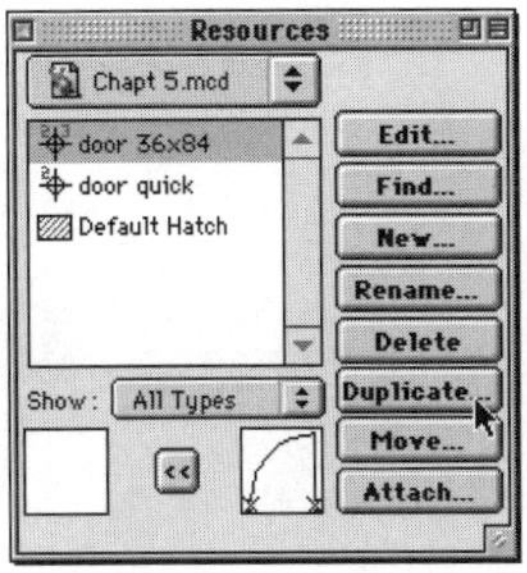

Step 1 - duplicating an existing symbol

Select the symbol called *door 36x84 (door 90x200)* in the *RESOURCES* palette and then the *DUPLICATE* button. When the *ASSIGN NAME* dialog opens, enter *door 32x84 (door 80x200)* in the *NEW NAME* edit box for the symbol and then click *OK*.

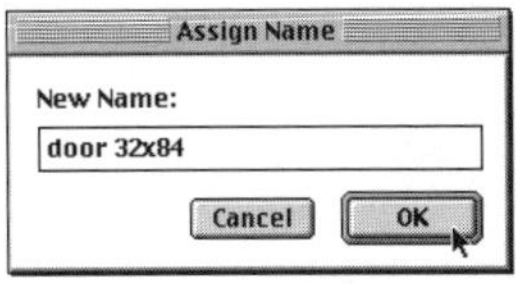

Step 2 - editing the 3D portion

Select the new symbol name in the *RESOURCES* palette and then the *EDIT* button. When the *EDIT SYMBOL* dialog box opens click the *3D COMPONENT* button and then *EDIT*. The *symbol edit window* will open allowing you to edit just the 3D aspect of the symbol.

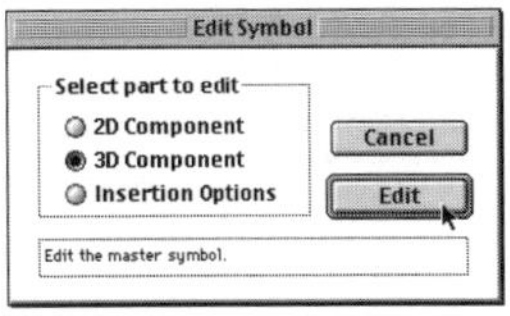

With just the rectangular opening selected, open the *OBJECT INFO* palette, highlight the *Δx [±x]* edit box where it says 3'-0" (.90m), click the right arrow on the keyboard so the cursor is placed at the end of the number, and type in -4" (.10m). The formula will automatically calculate when

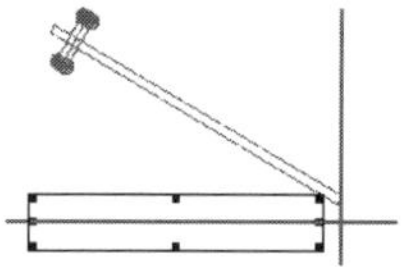

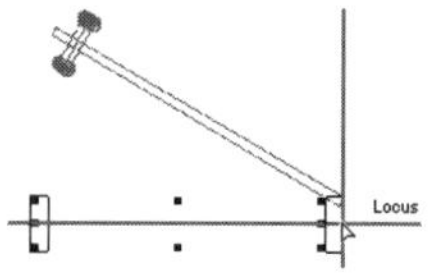

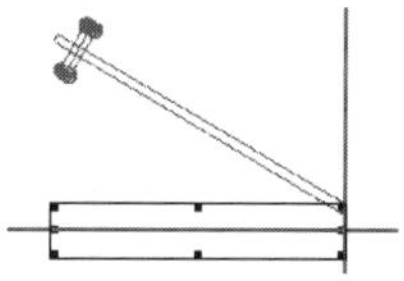

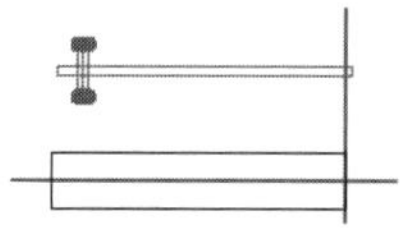

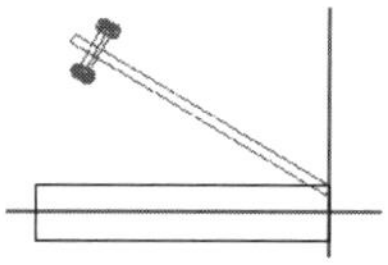

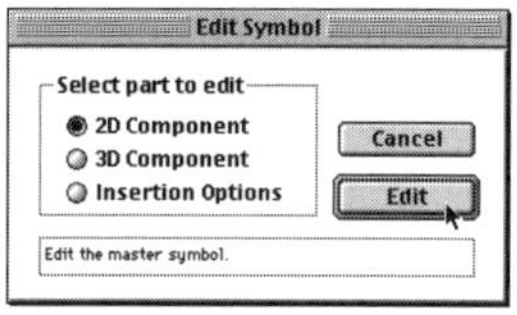

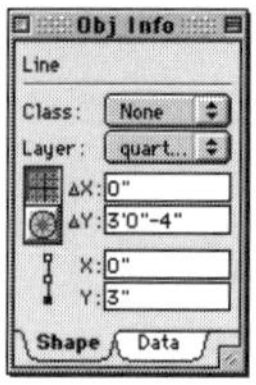

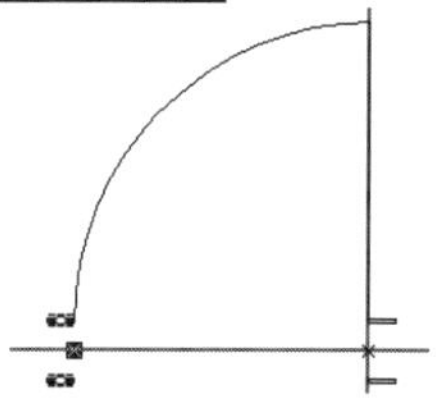

you hit the *Tab* or *Return [Enter]* key. Move the rectangle over to rest on the insertion point where the *X* an *Y* axis cross. Now use the *TOOL>Rotate>Rotate* command and rotate the door and hardware 30° to a horizontal position.

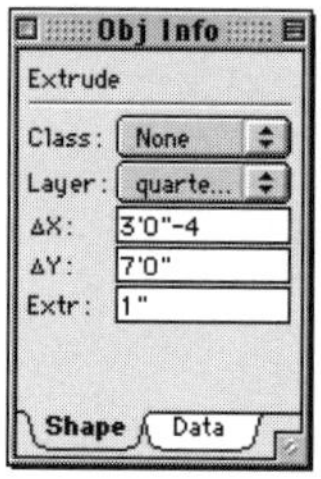

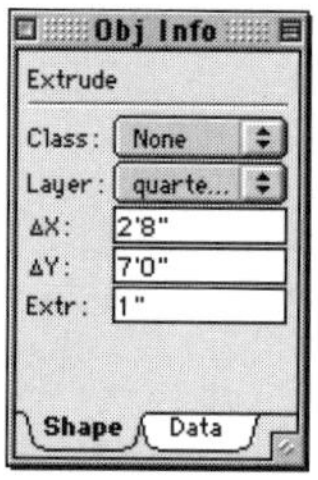

Select just the door and change the dimension to 32" (.80m) also using the *Object Info* palette. Select the hardware and use the *Move* command to move the knob over 2" (.05m). Rotate the door and hardware back -30° and adjust both as necessary for the door to spring from the correct point on the opening. Now select the *Edit* button again in the *Resources* palette. When the *Edit Symbol* dialog box opens click the *2D Component* button. The *symbol edit window* will open allowing you to edit the 2D aspect.

Step 3 - editing the 2D portion

To shorten the line to 32" (.80m), select the line and look for the diagram of the line in the *Object Info* palette. Click the lower box in the diagram to select which point of the line sets the coordinates or location of the line. Then enter the length 32" (.80m) in the ΔY *[±Y]* edit box, and hit the *Tab* or *Return* key. Select the arc and change the *Obj Info>Radius* subtracting 4" (.10m). Select the two rectangles for the trim pieces and the locus point on one side and move it 4" (.10m) along the X axis towards the insertion point with the *Move* command. Then click the *Exit Symbol* button in the upper right.

CREATING WINDOWS

Window symbols are made in the same manner as doors. When placed in a wall they also automatically cut the wall and heal it when removed.

Quick Window

The first task is to create a window that can only be used in *Top/Plan* view. Since this symbol will only be 2D, it will not project into any of the 3D views. Make *eighth scale [hundredth scale]* the active layer, *none* the active class, and the second line weight the default weight.

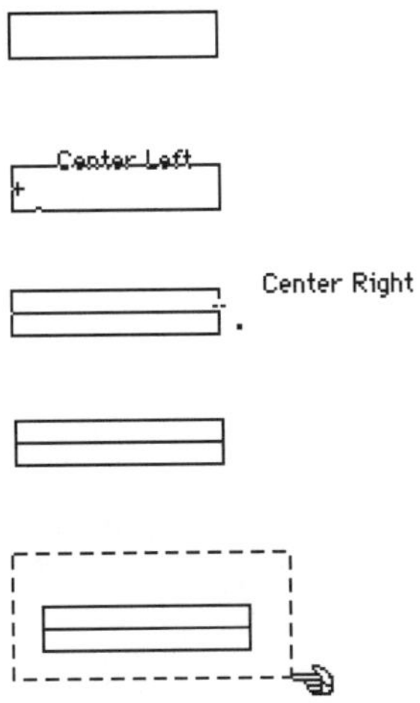

Step 1 - creating the window

In *Top/Plan,* create a 30" x 6" (.75m x .15m) rectangle with the *Rectangle* tool. *Zoom-In* to the window and with the *Single Line* tool and the *unconstrained* modifier icon, place a line snapping to the center of both ends of the rectangle for the glass. With the line selected, change the weight to the middle weight on the *Attributes* palette.

Step 2 - creating the symbol

With both the rectangle and the line selected choose the *Create Symbol* command. Enter *window quick* for its name and then select the *plan projection center* button. When you click *ok,* it disappears and is placed as a resource for this document.

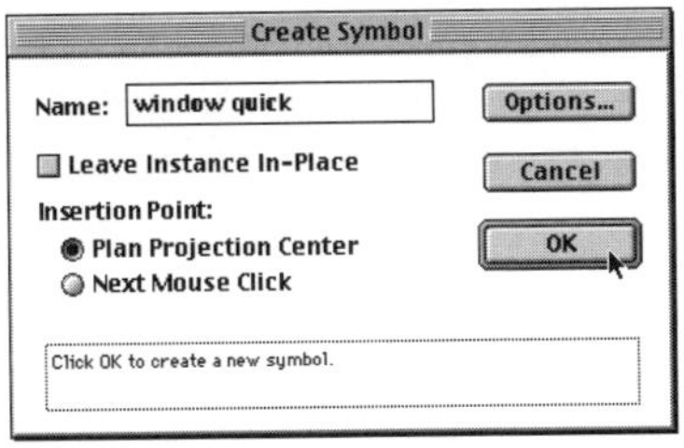

Creating A Double Hung Window

The next symbol we will create will be a hybrid double-hung window which is 2'-6" (.75m) wide by 4'-0" (1.20m) high. Go back to the *quarter scale (fiftieth scale)* layer and change to *Front* view.

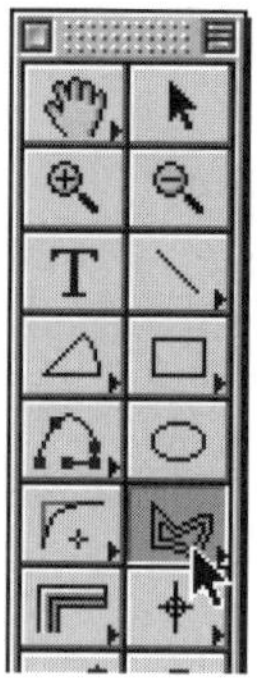

Step 1 - creating the lower window

Select the *Double-Line Polygon* tool. Click the modifier icon on the far right of the mode bar to open the *Double Line Preferences* dialog box. Set the *separation* at $2\frac{1}{2}$" (.06m), choose the *create polygons* button, and *ok*.

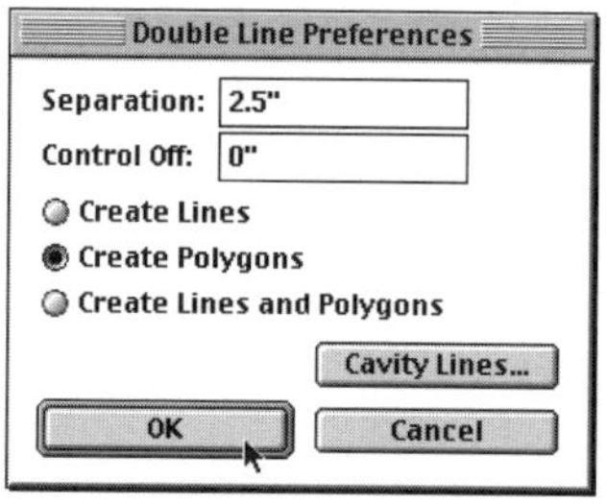

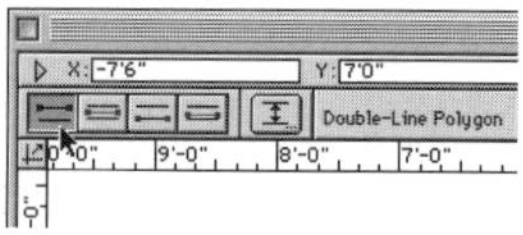

Select the first icon in the mode bar to set the control line then click with the mouse to set the starting point. Use the *Tab* key to enter 30" (.75m) in the Δ*x [±x]* edit box. Press the *Shift* key to keep it constrained and click again to create the first segment.

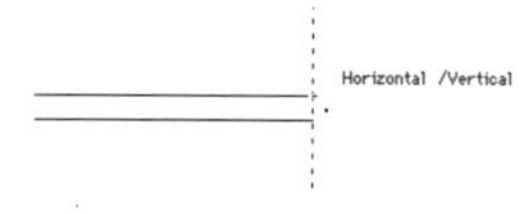

Use the *Tab* key to again enter a distance but this time enter -25.25" (-.63m) into the Δ*y [±y]* edit box. Press the *Shift* key again before and while you click to establish the second segment keeping it constrained vertically.

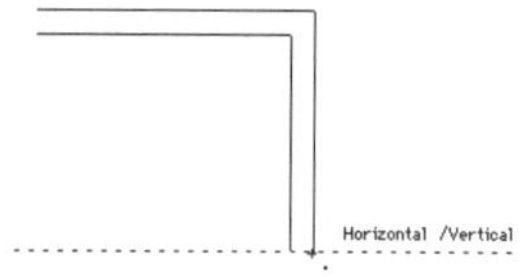

Move the cursor to sit on top of the starting point and then move it downwards. Notice that the starting point becomes a *datum* point and that a dashed guide line appears with the *smartcursor cue, align h.* Press the *Shift* key making sure the guide line is still visible, then click again.

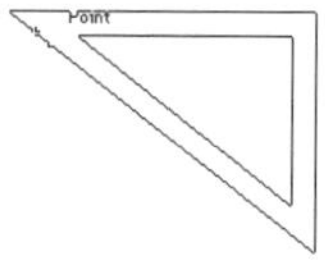

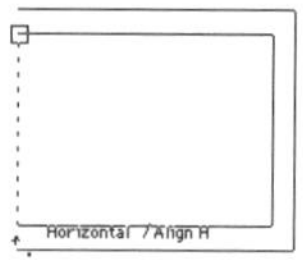

Finally for the last segment bring the mouse to the starting point and when the *cues, vertical* and *datum* or *point* appear, click again to end the frame. If you have trouble ending it with a single click, delete it and start over, but this time *Zoom-In* further so you have a larger magnification.

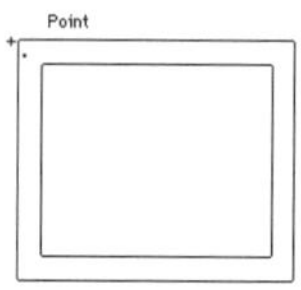

With the object selected select the *MODEL>EXTRUDE* command to open the *CREATE EXTRUDE* dialog box. Enter 1.5 (.03m) into the *EXTRUSION* edit box and click *OK*.

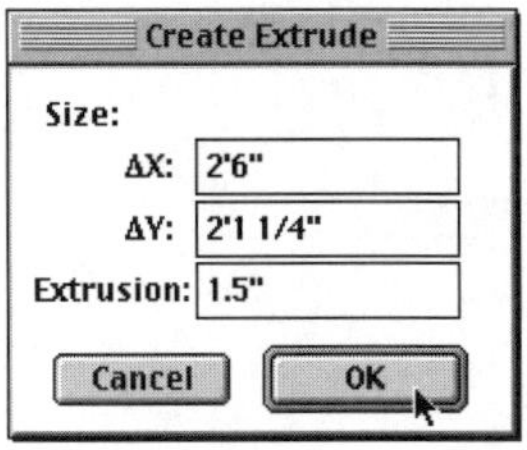

Step 2 - the glass

With the *RECTANGLE* tool selected, draw a rectangle using the *smartcursor cues* to match the inner part of the frame. With the rectangle selected change the fill to *NONE* in the *ATTRIBUTES* palette and then use the command *MODEL> CONVERT TO 3D POLYS.* This way, although you can not see the glass itself, in a 3-dimensional view, you can see where the glass hits the frame.

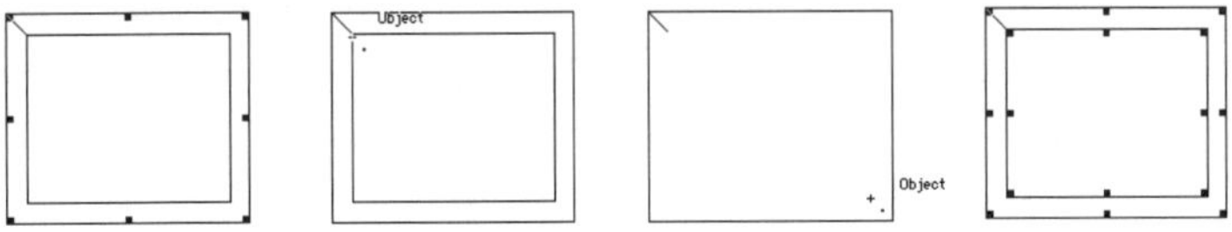

Select both the frame and the glass and the *TOOL>ALIGN> ALIGN OBJECTS* command. Select just *F/B CENTERS* in the *ALIGN OBJECTS* dialog box that opens and then *OK*. Now with both still selected use the *GROUP* command.

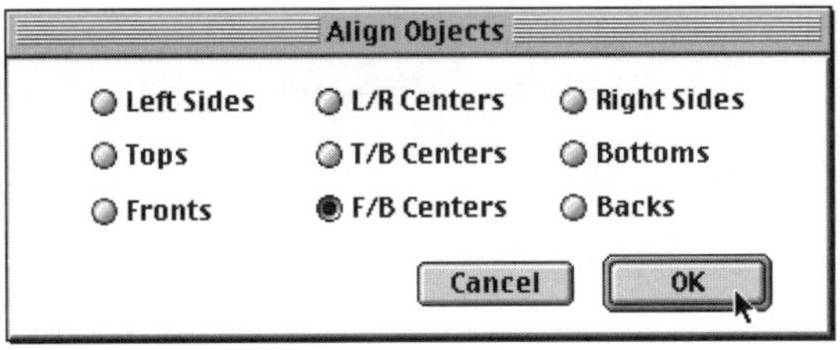

Step 3 - the upper window

You will need to duplicate this object. Place a guide point by clicking with the *2D LOCUS* tool on the corner. Use the *MOVE* command to move it down -1.25" (-.03m) to mark the halfway point of the top part of the frame.

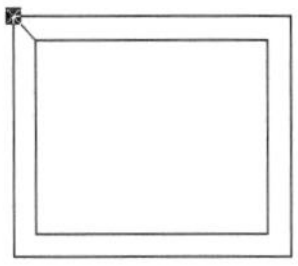

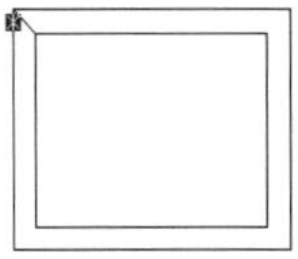

Select the window and the *MIRROR* tool with the *MIRROR AND DUPLICATE* modifier icon. Press/drag from the locus point and press the *Shift* key to keep it constrained horizontally. You do not need to drag it all the way across the object

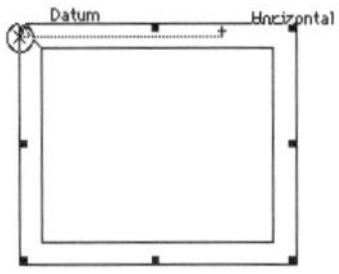

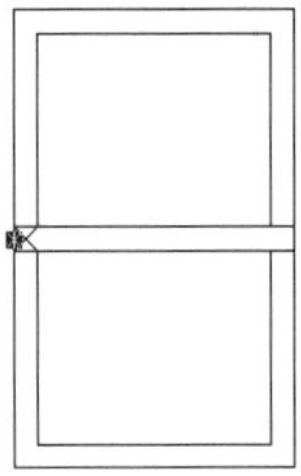

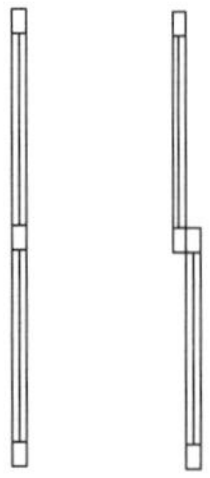

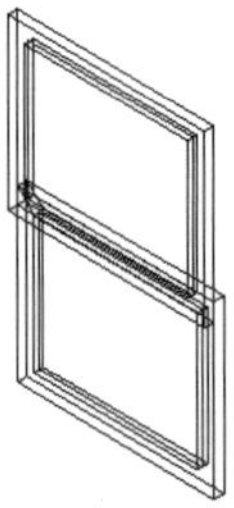

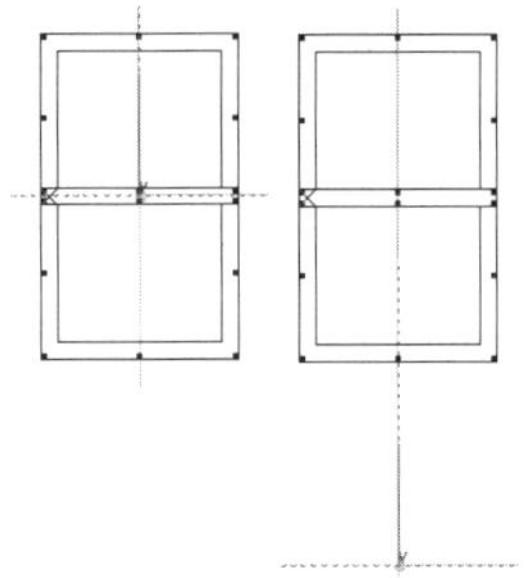

before you release the mouse, just enough to create an axis line for the duplicate to locate itself. Select the locus point by press/dragging a marquee around it and *Delete*.

Step 4 - organizing the windows

Select both windows and use the *Group* command. Now view it in *Right* elevation and use the *ORGANIZE>Edit Group* command. Select just the lower window and using the *Move* command relocate it 1.5" (.03m) in the x direction. Now click the *exit group* button.

Step 5 - creating the 3D symbol

Change the view to *Right Isometric* and with the window selected, use the *Create Symbol* command. When the *Create Symbol* dialog box opens, name it *window dh 30x48* (*window dh 75x120*). Select *3D object center* and click *ok*.

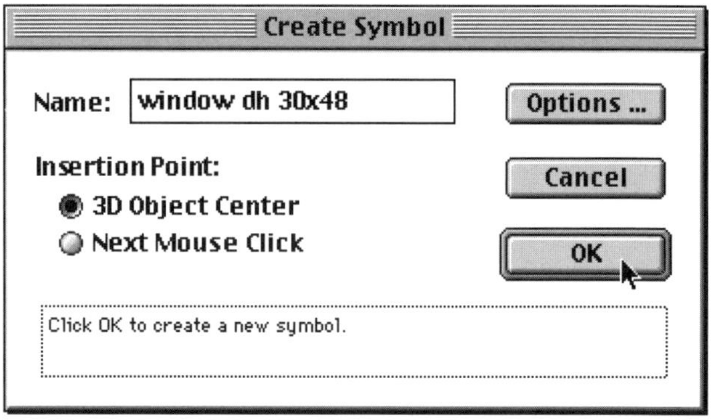

Step 6 - editing the 3D

Click this new window symbol in the *Resources* palette, then the *edit* button and then *3D component*. Change the view to *Front*, *Select All*, and use the *TOOL>Move* command to move it 30" (.75m) above the *ground plane* which works out to 54" (1.35m) total.

Select the *Double Line Polygon* tool and change the *separation* in the *Double Line Preferences* dialog box to 3$^{1}/_{2}$" (.08m). Select the *bottom control line* icon in the mode bar. To apply the trim to three sides, click at the lower left corner, top left, top right, and double-click at the lower right corner to end. Change the *separation* to 2" (.05m), then snap to lower right of the trim and click, then double-click at the lower left of the trim to end. *Extrude* the first trim piece to 1" (.025m) and then the second trim piece to 3" (.075m).

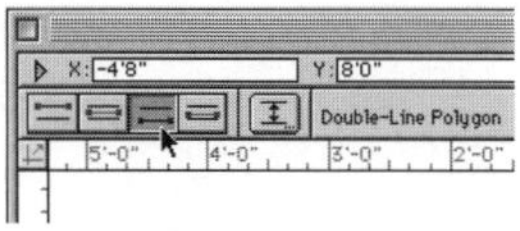

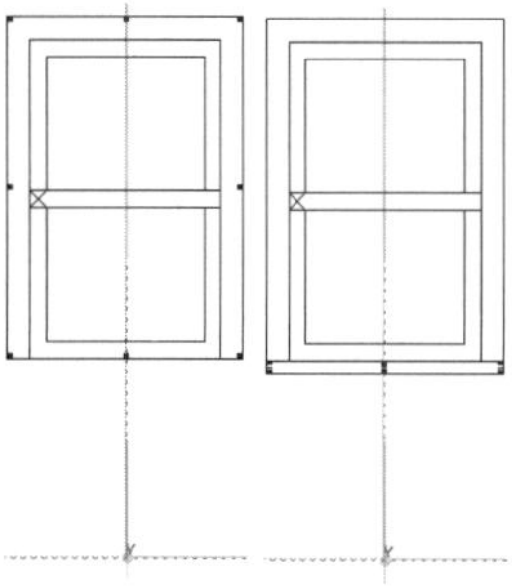

Change to *Top/Plan* view and move the trim downwards in the *y* direction 3" (.04m) – this is assuming a 6" (.075m) thick wall. Select both trim pieces and the *MODEL>Add Solids* command. With the trim piece selected, which is now called a *solid addition* in the *Object Info* palette, use the *Mirror* tool with the *mirror and duplicate* icon, and draw a horizontal axis line snapping to the *cue, locus,* at the center.

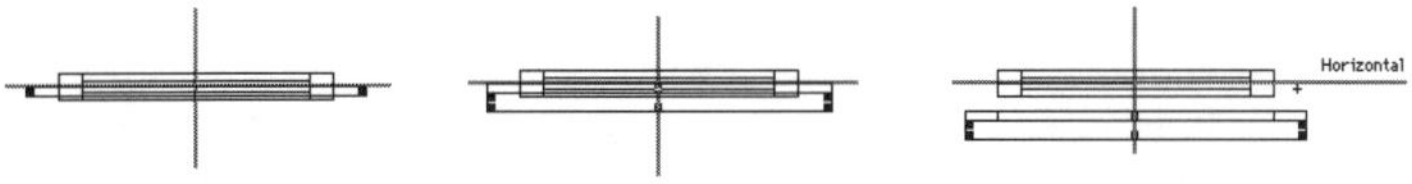

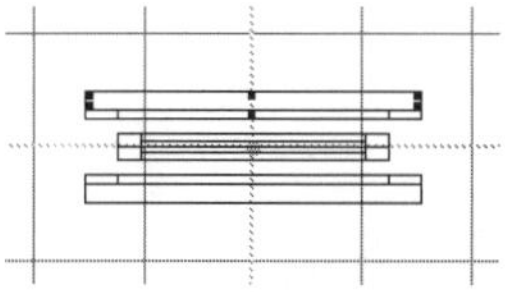

Select the *3d Locus* tool on the *3d Tools* palette. If it is not open, then select *PALETTES>3d Tools*. An alert box will open telling you to change the view – just click *yes*. The view will change to *Top* view.

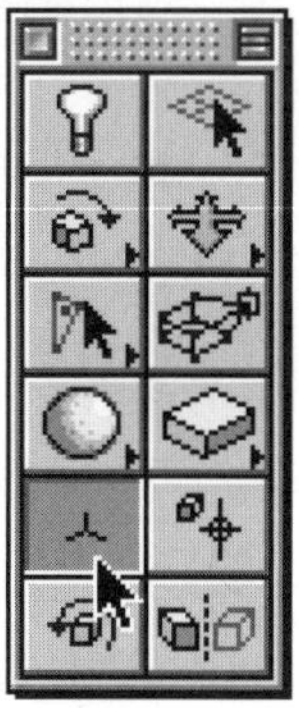

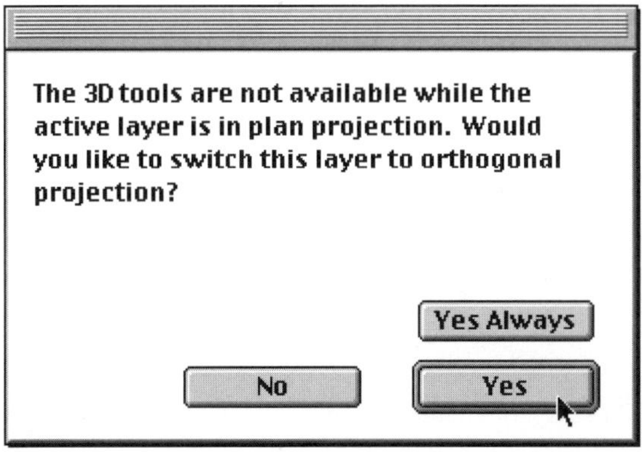

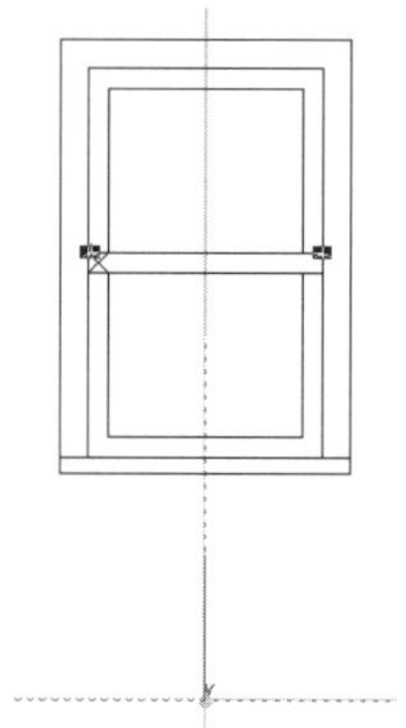

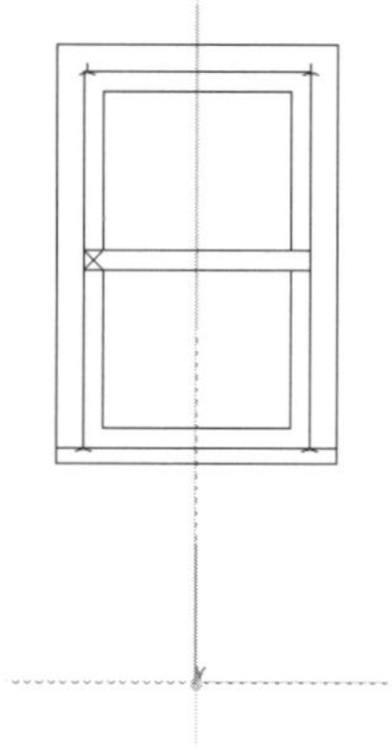

With the *3D Locus* tool, place a loci at each end of the window, not the end of the trim. Change the view to *Front*. Press/drag both loci, which are centered, down to the bottom of the window, not the trim. With the loci still selected, press the *Option [Control]* key and press/drag the duplicates, then release the key and press the *Shift* key keeping it constrained, to the top of the window, again not to the trim. So there are now four locus points placed on the symbol. The 3D loci serve the same purpose as the 2D loci we had used in the 2D portion of the door symbol - setting where the symbol actually cuts the wall.

Step 7 - creating the 2D

Change the view to *Top/Plan*. With the *Rectangle* and *Single Line* tools draw a 6" x 30" (.15m x .75m) rectangle with a line centered, similar to the *quick window* symbol, paying attention to the line weights. This should be drawn directly on top of the 3D window. Click the *Exit Symbol* button in the upper right corner.

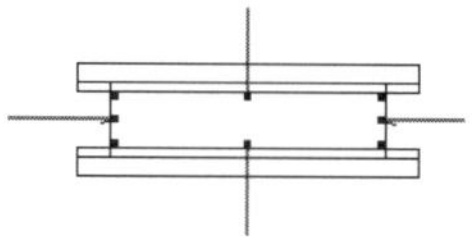

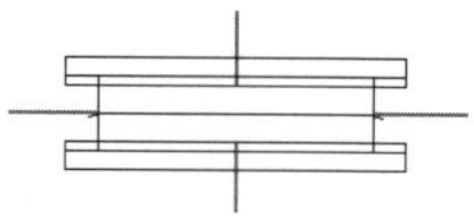

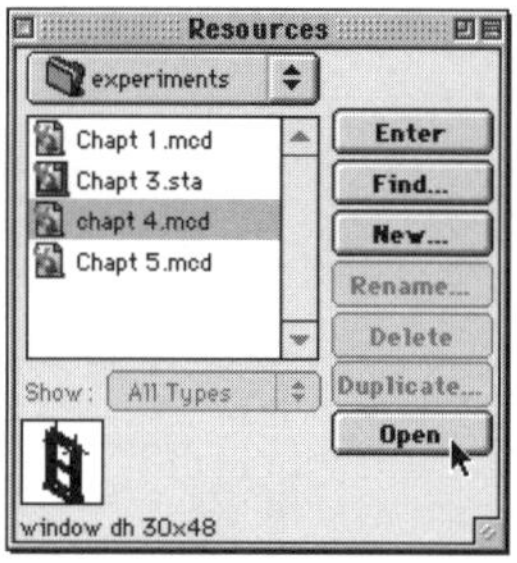

SYMBOLS FROM EXISTING OBJECTS

You can change an existing object from another file into a symbol. Use the *Resources* palette to navigate to the correct file, in this case the previous drawing we were working in called *chapt 4 [chapt 4.mcd]* located in the *experiments* folder. Select the file in the scrolling list and click the *Open* button. The document will open as the active window.

File Cabinet

We will create a hybrid symbol out of the file cabinet previously created.

Step 1 - pasting the object

Go to the *furniture* layer and select the file cabinet you had created, then choose *EDIT>COPY*. Now go up to *WINDOW* and press/drag down to *chapt 5 [chapt 5.mcd]* to make it the active file. In *TOP* view, not *TOP/PLAN*, select the *PASTE* command. Go back to *WINDOW*, select the *chapt 4 [chapt 4.mcd]* file to make it active, and then click its *close* box. If the dialog box appears asking if you want to save, just click the *DON'T SAVE* button.

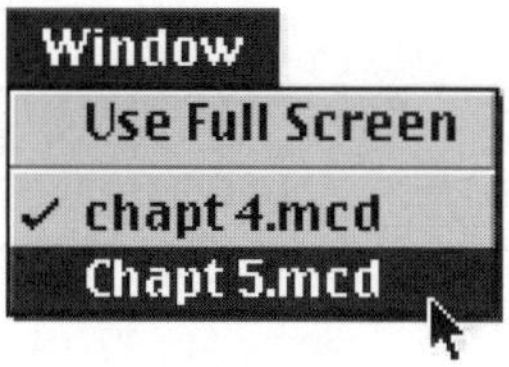

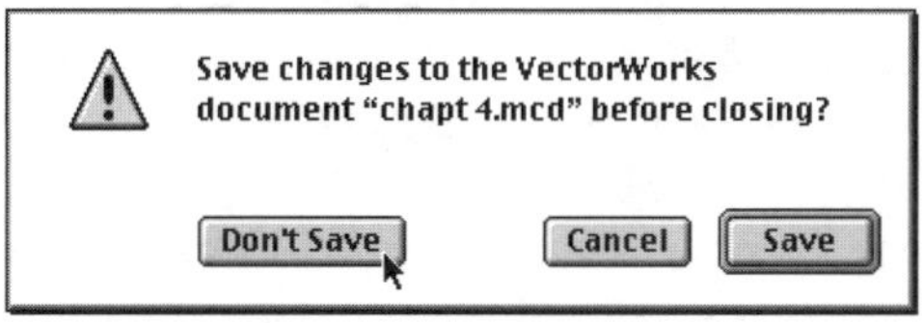

Step 2 - creating the 3D symbol

Change the view to *RIGHT ISOMETRIC* and with the object selected, use the *CREATE SYMBOL* command and name it *file 2drw ver.* Click the *OPTIONS* button and select *INSERT IN WALLS>ON EDGE* and *WALL BREAKS>NO BREAK*, then *OK*.

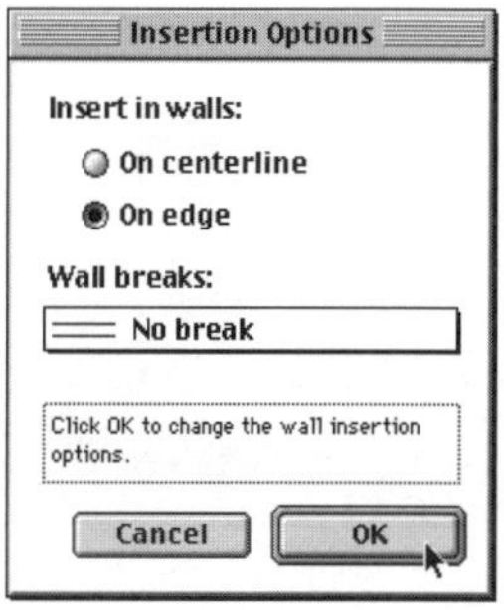

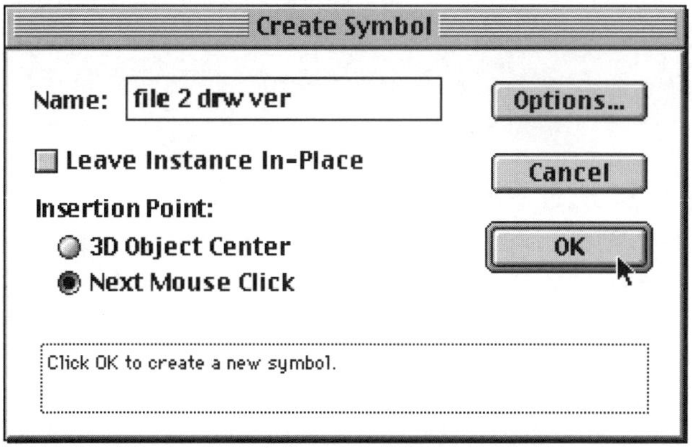

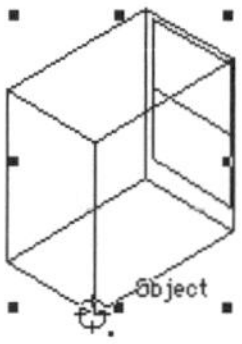

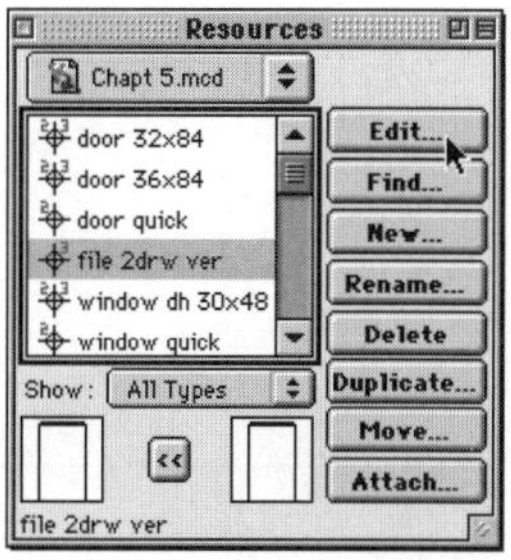

With the *NEXT MOUSE CLICK* selected and then *OK*, click the lower back left corner of the cabinet. Navigate back to the current file in the *RESOURCES* palette. Access the new symbol and select *EDIT* and then the *3D COMPONENT*. Verify in various views that the back lower corner of the cabinet is placed at the insertion point where the guide lines meet.

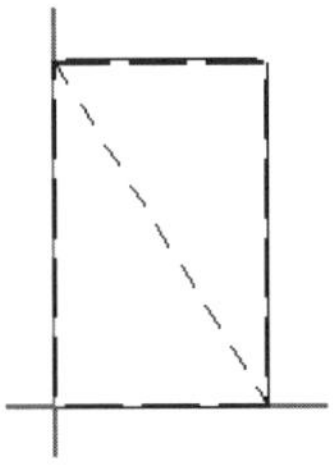

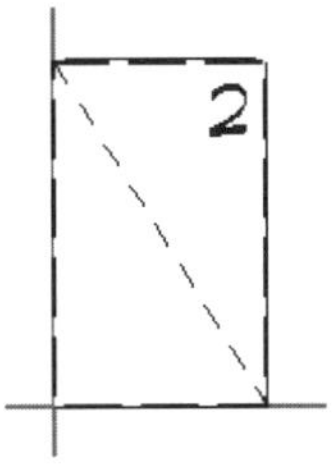

Step 3 - creating the 2D symbol

In *Top/Plan* view and with the *Rectangle* tool selected, draw a rectangle on top of the 3D file. With the rectangle selected, verify that the line weight is the second weight and change the line style from the solid to the second dashed line in the *Attributes* palette. Use the *Single Line* tool with the *unconstrained* modifier icon to draw a diagonal on top of the rectangle and change it to the first line weight and the first dashed line style. Then with the *Text Insertion* tool place the number 2 in the front corner of the cabinet. Select the text and change the *Size* to 10 point. Click the *exit symbol* button.

This symbol allows you to have a file cabinet that appears one way in a 3D view and as a dashed object in a 2D *Top/Plan* view (as if it is sitting under a counter).

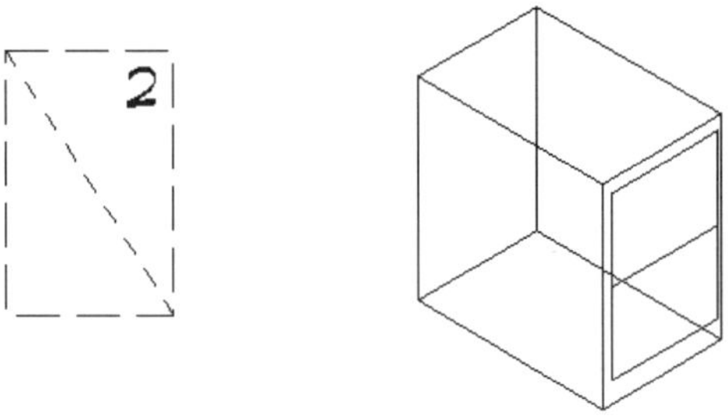

SYMBOLS FROM PLUG-INS

VectorWorks has a new type of object called a plug-in. As we have already seen, these hybrid objects are more complex and are created with a tool and a series of parameters set by a dialog box. Some of the plug-in objects work similarly to symbols having the ability to automatically cut walls as well. If you need to place several of the same plug-in object, it saves memory and makes revisions easier if it is converted into a symbol. It is also easier to attach information and track symbols within a worksheet rather than individual objects. The *plug-in* tools are located in the *AEC Objects* palette which is available when either the *Workspaces>AEC* or *AEC (Streamlined)* is selected.

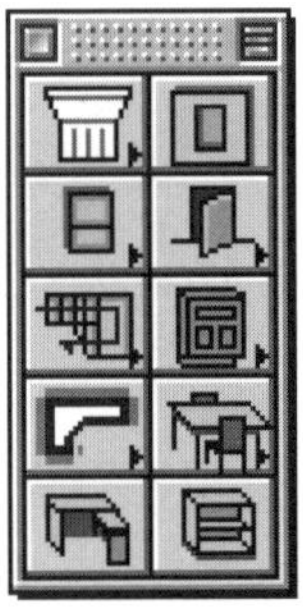

You would create the object with the *plug-in* tool, select it and use the *Create Symbol* command like any other object. Since it is a hybrid object, the symbol is also hybrid. To modify the symbol, select the *edit* button like any other symbol and then use the *Object Info* palette to modify the different plug-in components.

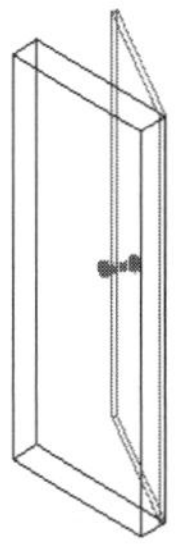

PLACING SYMBOLS

Before closing the file, use the *2d Symbol Insertion* tool to place one of each symbol we made onto the drawing. Open the *Resources* palette and click a symbol in the scrolling list so that it is visible in the lower right *preview window*. Click the arrow box in the center to select the symbol. It should now be visible along with its designation in the lower left *selection window*. You can also just double-click the symbol so it is selected in one step.

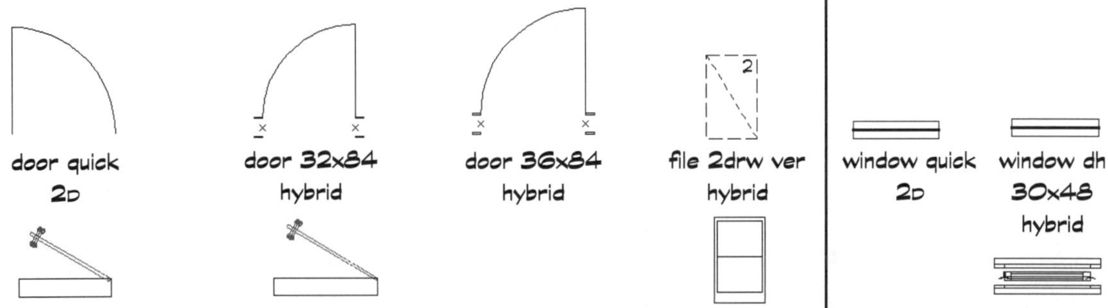

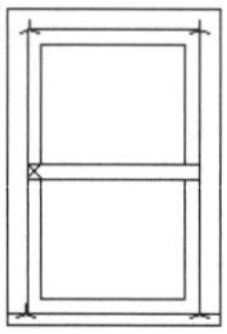

Then with the *2d Symbol Insertion* tool click the drawing to place a copy. You can also use the *Text Insertion* tool to type the names of the symbols as well and whether it is 2D or hybrid for future reference. Before you *Quit [Exit]* look at these symbols in different views and with different rendering options. I also tend to make the *title* layer active, the view *Top/Plan*, and the *Layer Options>Show Others* before quitting unless there is a good reason not to.

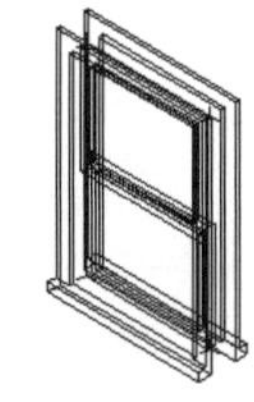

CREATING SYMBOLS IN SUMMATION

From the above examples, you can see the difference in time and ease in creating 2D verses hybrid symbols. Although it initially does take much longer to create hybrid symbols, in the long run it allows you more flexibility and does save time.

• Once the object is saved you can reuse it and import it into another document regardless of the scale.

• A symbol when placed will always resize to the scale of the layer it is placed on.

• Save time by modifying an existing symbol to create a new one rather than starting from scratch.

• Sometimes it is easier to keep a file just of your custom symbols. This way when you need to import a symbol, it is obvious where it is located rather than hunting through individual project files.

• If you want to change one instance of a symbol into a grouped object use the *Symbol To Group, Convert To Group* in v8.5, command. If the symbol is in a 3D view when the command is used, the object will be 3D only and if the command is used in a 2D view it will be a 2D object only.

• The preview window for hybrid or 3D symbols will show in a 3D view if the symbol was initially saved in this view and if every time the symbol edit window is opened it is in that view when *exit symbol* is selected.

• The *Object Browser* palette is new with v8.5 and provides a slightly larger preview of the symbol. Just select the *add* button and navigate to a desired file. When the symbol is selected in this palette and placed on the drawing with the *Symbol Insertion* tool, it is automatically imported into the file as a resource.

• And the final thing to note, is the importance of where the insertion point is located. Typically, I find it easier to locate doors at the hinge side, windows at the center, furniture that gets placed near a wall at a back corner, fixtures at the back center, and tables at the center. Whatever you decide, keep it consistent. There is nothing more frustrating than carefully placing a symbol and finding that it does not align where you think it should.

Chapter 6

WALLS, FLOORS, ROOFS, AND STAIRS

ARCHITECTURAL ELEMENTS

We will go through a series of exercises to create various architectural elements and look at the advantages of using 3D. Drawings done just in 2D do take less time than adding the 3D components, but the advantage to creating the 3D elements is that it takes much less time to create any of the 3D views which includes elevations and sections.

The tools, commands, and constraints we will be exploring are;

Mirror Tool
Single-Line Polygon Tool
Straight Stair Tool
Wall Tool
Wall Join Tool
AEC Command
Convert To 3D Polys Command
Create Polygon From Interior Walls Command
Create Polygon From Exterior Walls Command
Floor Command
Guides Commands
Roof Face Command
Show/Snap/Modify Others Command
Undo Command
Constrain Angle Constraint

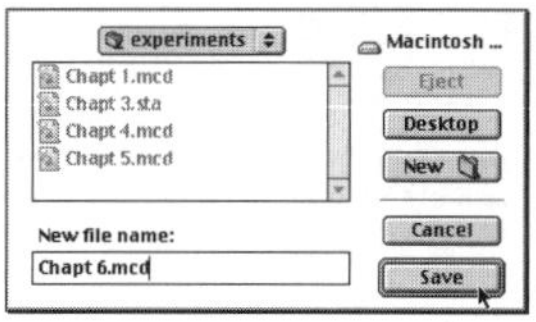

CREATING ARCHITECTURAL ELEMENTS

First open a new file from your template called *chapt 3 [chapt 3.sta]* and use the *Save As* command naming it *chapt 6 [chapt 6.mcd]*. Remember to continually save as you go along. Gee, have I said this before? It must be **important**! Go to *FILE> Workspaces* and change to *AEC [Streamlined]*. All of the commands and tools will disappear and it will take a few moments before they reappear in the new configuration so do not panic.

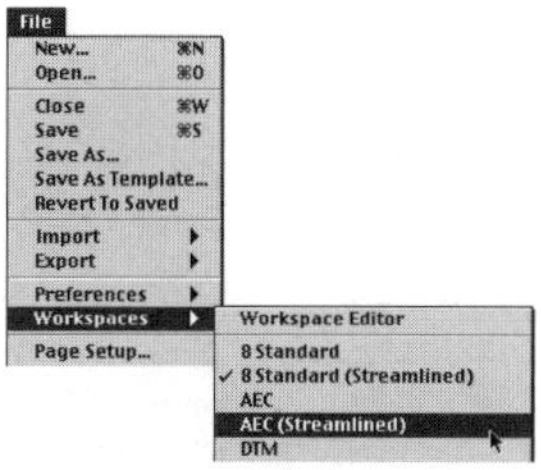

The active *Workspace* now has a check mark placed in the pop-out menu. Make sure the default line weight is the middle weight and the appropriate constraints are selected. Select *Page>Set Grid* and set the *snap grid* to 1" (.01m), the *reference grid* to 1'-0" (.5m), and *show grid lines* and the *symmetrical grids* boxes should be checked.

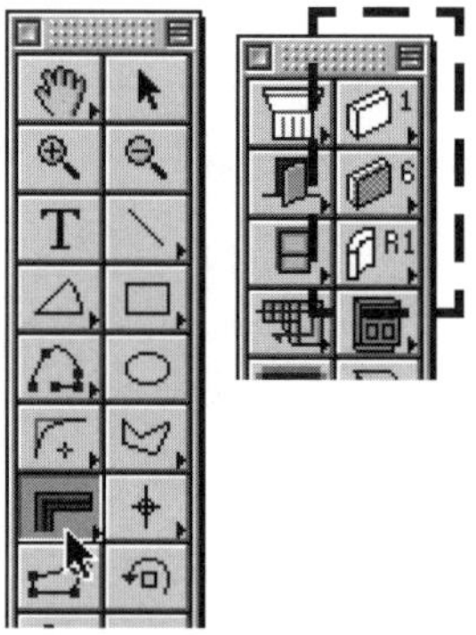

WALLS, FLOORS, ROOFS, AND STAIRS

There are several commands and tools that are used specifically to create architectural elements. We will go through the steps to create walls, floor, a roof, and a stairs, but you should be aware of the other specific tools, plug-ins, and commands to create architectural elements such as doors, windows, revision clouds, structural shapes, property bounds, cabinetry, amongst others.

WALLS

One of the special tools in VectorWorks is the *Wall* tool, now a series of separate tools. They are hybrid tools that create walls having both a 2D and 3D component. Any of the *Wall* tools can only be used in *Top/Plan* view and can only be placed perpendicular to the *ground plane*. Straight walls are created by clicking each end point no matter whether *click-drag drawing* in the *VectorWorks Preferences* dialog box is selected or not. To end a series of segments you would double-click unless the ending point is also the starting point, in which case it would be a single click.

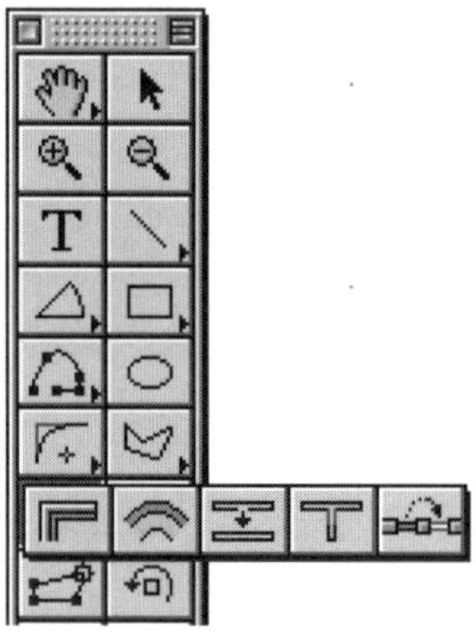

Walls Without Height

As an experiment, let's draw a wall without any height to see the difference between a hybrid object and a 2D object. With the *quarter scale (fiftieth scale)* layer active, select the *Wall* tool and then the right most icon in the mode bar.

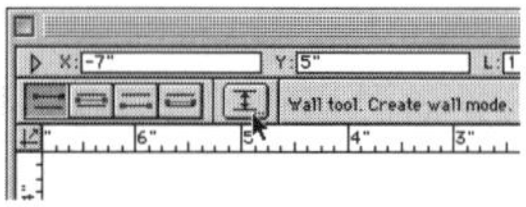

When the *Wall Preferences* dialog box opens enter 6" (.15m) for *separation* (or wall thickness), *caps* should be *both* and *type* should be *flat*. Then select *ok*. Select the first icon in the first group of modifier icons for the control line location.

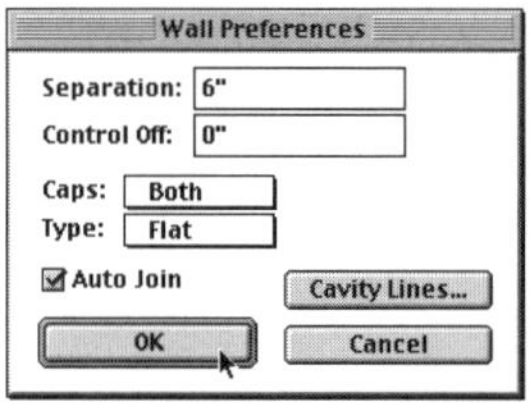

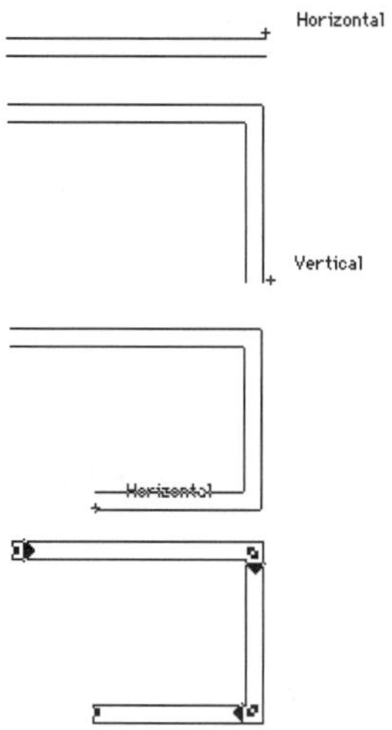

Click anywhere on the drawing to start and move the mouse towards the right. If you are zoomed in close enough, you will notice that the cursor is on the top of the wall matching the icon in the mode bar. Hold the *Shift* key to keep it constrained, click again. Move the cursor downwards, and pressing the *Shift* key, click again. Notice that the cursor is on the right side of the wall when moving downwards. Move the cursor towards the left and notice the cursor location is now on the bottom of the wall, or the opposite of the icon. Now, press the *Shift* key and double-click to end this run of three wall segments.

The important thing to note is that the cursor aligns with the control line icons when moving from left to right. The caps are placed once the wall run is ended. Also note that when the walls are selected there is a small arrow at the beginning of each wall segment showing the direction the wall was created in. This direction of the wall affects symbol placement within the wall.

With the *RECTANGLE* tool, draw a rectangle near the walls, then change the view to a *RIGHT ISOMETRIC*. Notice that the walls will project into 3D space since they are hybrid objects even though they do not have a height. The rectangle is a 2D object remaining true to the screen and does not project or move in 3D space.

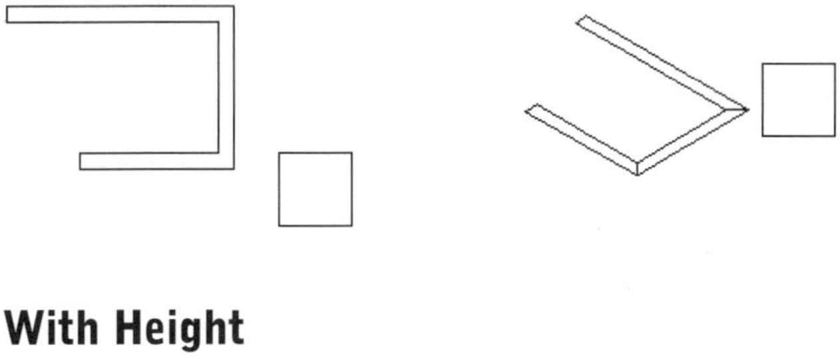

Walls With Height

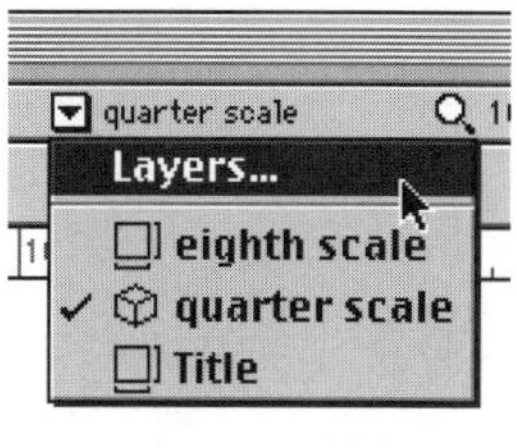

We will now create a rectangular space where the outside dimension is 25' x 35' (7.50m x 10.50m) and the wall height is 8' (2.40m). Go to *LAYERS* in the mode bar to open the *LAYERS SETUP* dialog box. Select the *quarter scale (fiftieth scale)* layer in the scrolling list and click the *VISIBILITY>INVISIBLE* button.

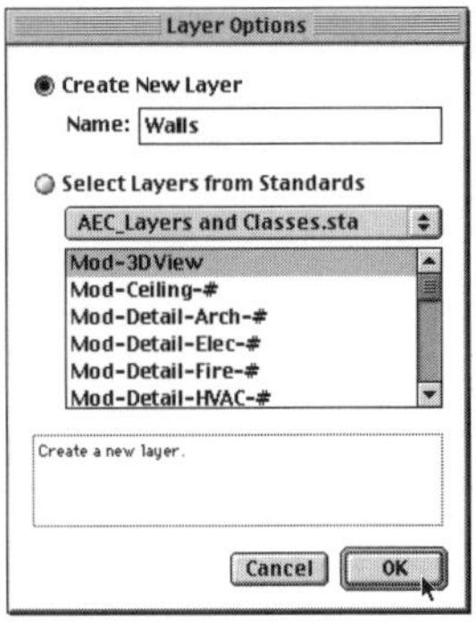

Create a new layer by clicking the *New* button. When the *Layer Options* dialog box opens, hit the *Tab* key until the *Name* box is highlighted, and type in *walls*. Make sure that the *Create New Layer* button is selected and click *OK*. With the *walls* layer selected in the *Layer* scrolling list, click the *Scale* button and change the scale to $^1/_8$" (1:100), making sure the *Scale Text* button is not checked.

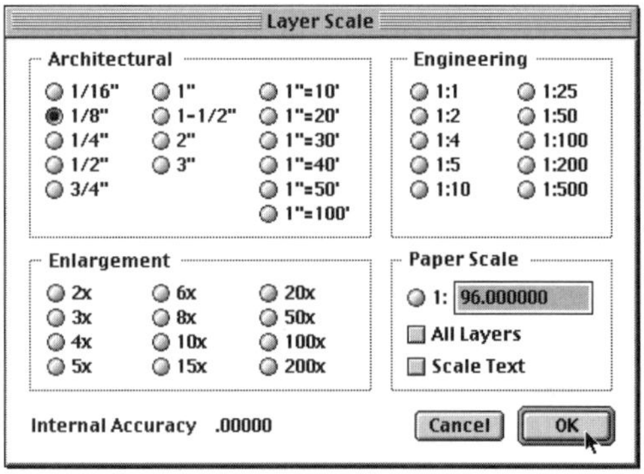

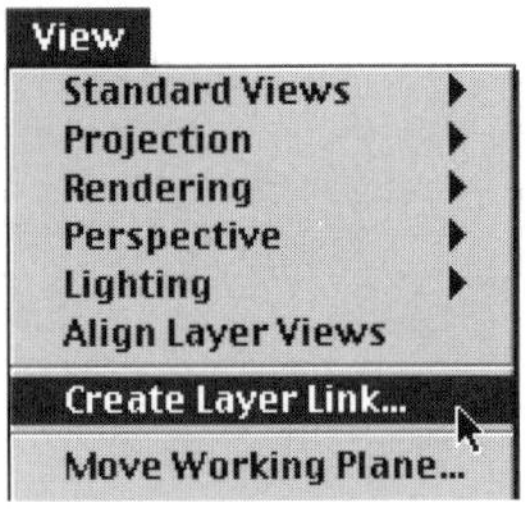

With the *walls* layer still selected, enter 8' (2.40m) into the Δz *[±z]* edit box for the actual height of the layer and enter 18" (.45m) into the *z* edit box for the height above the *ground plane.* This amount above the *ground plane* only comes into play when you use the *View>Create Layer Link* command. Otherwise the layer is placed on the *ground plane* at 0. Make sure the *Active Layer* box is checked, then select *OK*. Notice that *walls* is the active layer in the *data display bar* and that the objects created on the *quarter scale (fiftieth scale)* layer are no longer visible.

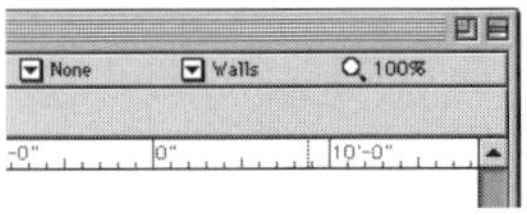

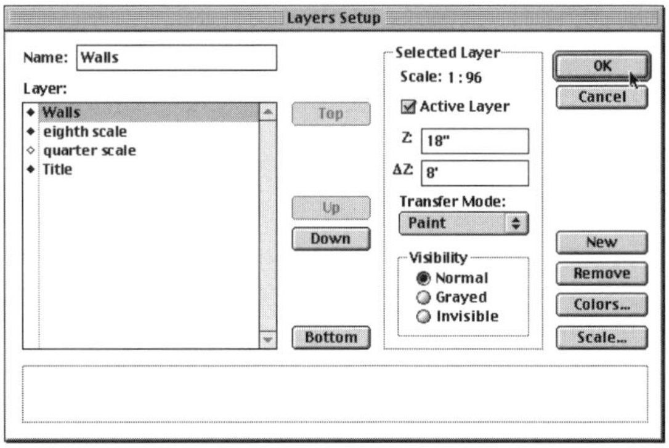

Step 1 - exterior wall setup

Select the *Wall* tool. Since *Top/Plan* was not selected, a dialog box opens asking if you want to switch views. The *Wall* tool can only be used in *Top/Plan*, so click *yes*. Open the *Wall Preferences* dialog box again by clicking the right most icon in the mode bar. Change the *caps* to *none*, deselect *auto join*, and select *ok*. Leave the first control line icon selected. Also, before you start drawing, change the *fill* color in the *Attributes* palette from the default white to a light gray.

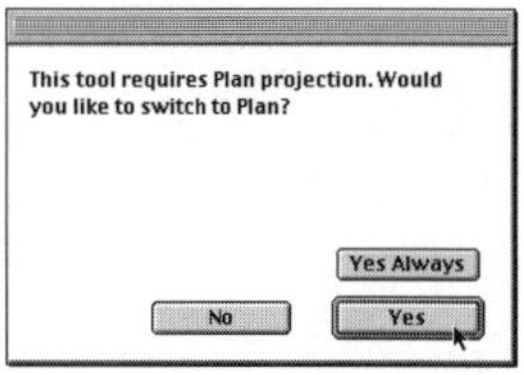

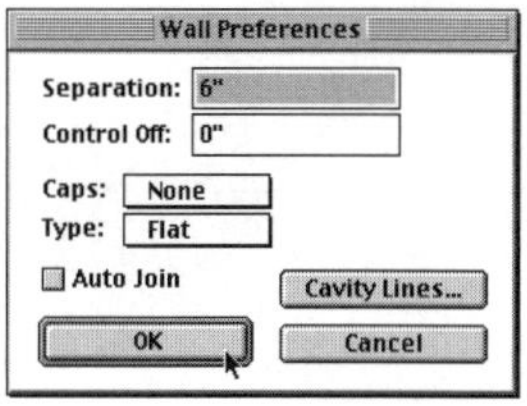

Step 2 - creating the walls

With the *Wall* tool selected, click on the upper left of the drawing. Move the cursor to the right and use the *Tab* and *Return [Enter]* keys to enter 35' (10.50m) into the ΔX [$\pm X$] edit box in the *data display bar*. Press the *Shift* key and click.

Again, move the mouse and enter -25' (-7.50m) into the ΔY [$\pm Y$] box, press the *Shift* key and click. Place the mouse at the starting point to engage the *smartcursor*. A guide line appears when the mouse is moved. Move the mouse downwards until it is almost horizontal and with the guide line still showing, press the *Shift* key and click. Bring the cursor back to the starting point and when the *smartcursor cue, point* appears, click once to end.

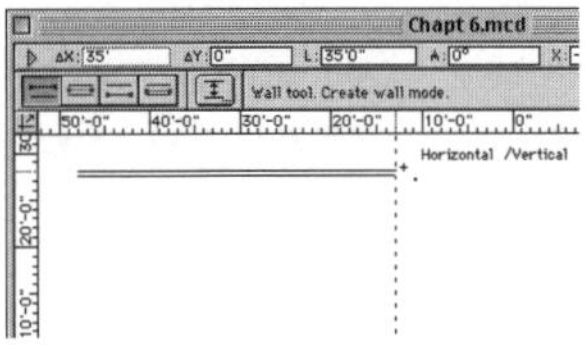

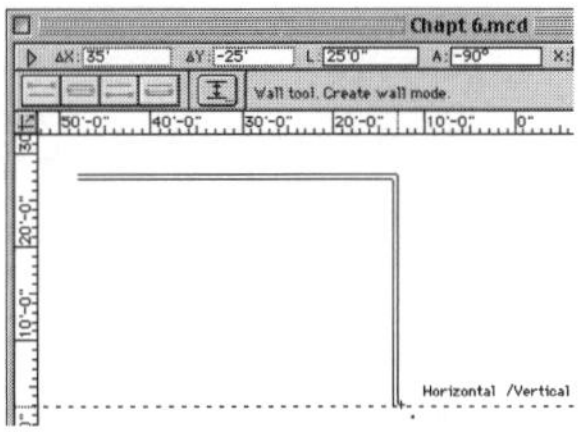

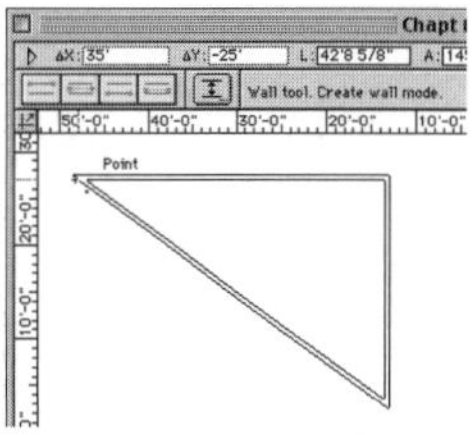

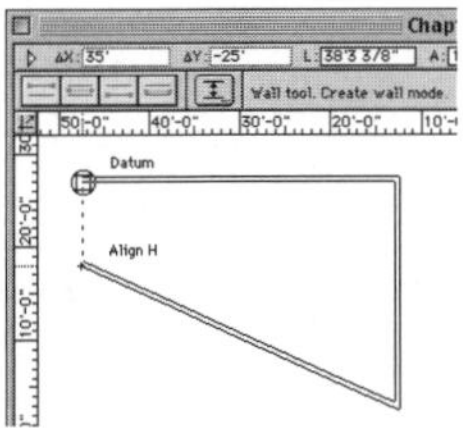

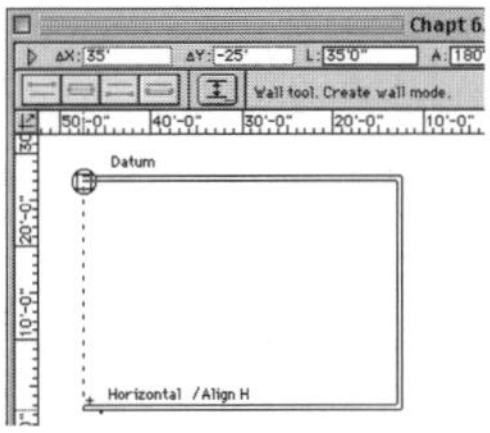

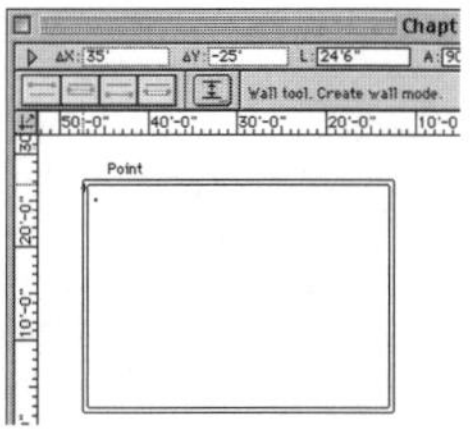

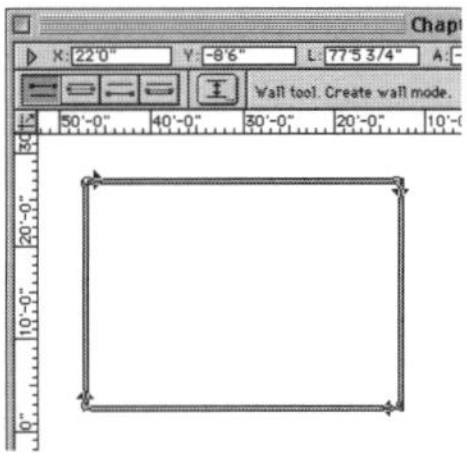

Do not panic if the run of walls does not end with this single click. Sometimes, if you are not zoomed-in close enough, you might think you are at the starting point and when you click to end the run of wall segments, it does not end but seems as if it will go on forever. Just double-click to end. You can always deselect all of the walls, then select just the unwanted segment(s) and *Delete* them. To join the first and last wall segment, just select the *Wall Join* tool and the second icon in the mode bar and press/drag from within the ending wall segment to the beginning wall segment or visa versa. The wall automatically joins when the mouse is released.

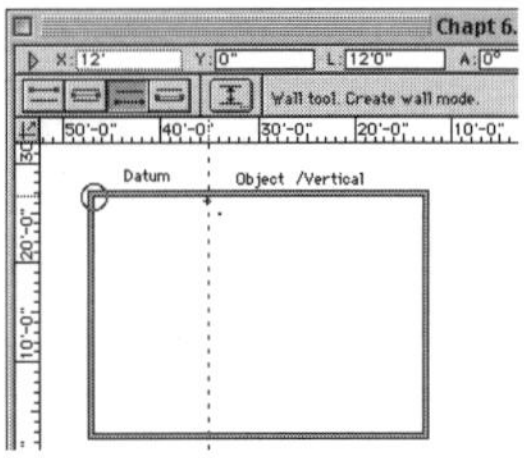

Step 3 - creating interior walls

With the *Wall* tool selected, click the right most icon to open the *Wall Preferences* dialog box again and change the separation to $4^{1}/_{2}$" (.12m). Remember to leave a space between the fraction and whole number. The first interior wall will run along the Y axis allowing a 12' (3.60m) clear dimension or space from the left wall.

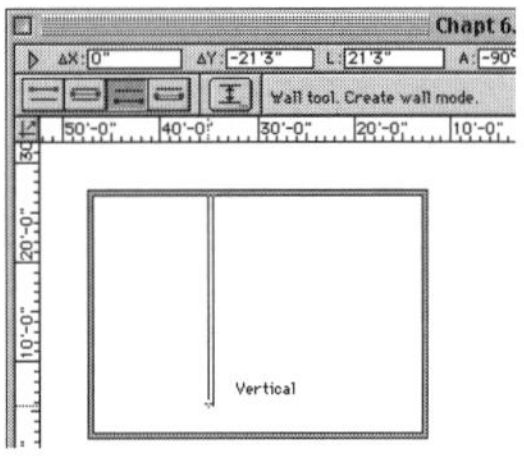

Select the icon showing the bottom control line. Place the cursor on the inside upper left corner until it turns into a floating datum point in the *data display bar*. Use the *Tab* and *Return [Enter]* keys to enter 12' (3.60m) into the *x* box. A guide line appears.

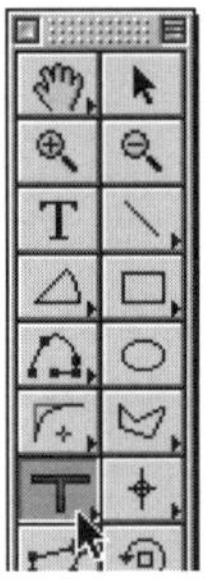

Place the cursor below the top wall at the guide line. When the *smartcursor cue, object/vertical* appears, click. Move the mouse downwards towards the bottom wall but do not touch the bottom wall. Hold the *Shift* key and double-click to end the wall segment. Now select the *Wall Join* tool with the first icon in the mode bar.

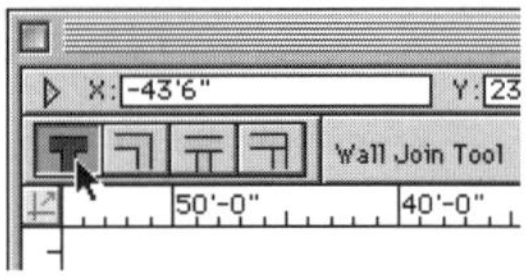

Press/drag from within the new interior wall and release anywhere within the bottom wall. The wall will automatically join. Although the top wall appears as if it is joined, it is not actually joined, but rather just placed exactly on top. Press/drag the interior wall away to see the difference between the two situations. Use the *EDIT>UNDO* command and then with the *WALL JOIN* tool, press/drag again from the new wall and release on the top wall.

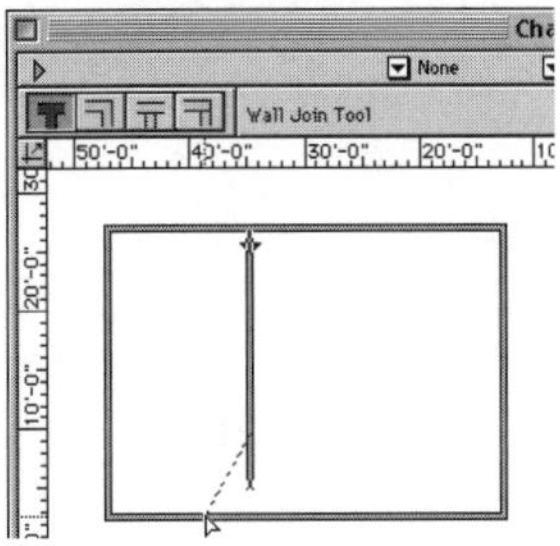

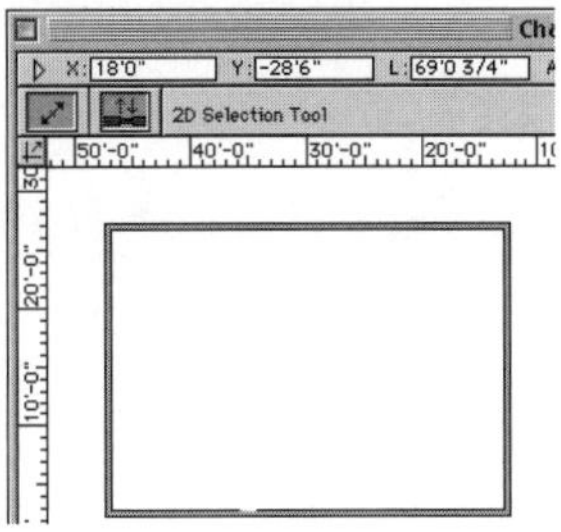

FLOORS

We will look at a series of objects to create a floor slab, floor finishes, and stairs. All of these objects will be created in 2D and then converted so that they can project into 3D. Access the *LAYERS SETUP* dialog box under *LAYERS*. Select the layer *eighth scale (hundredth scale)* in the scrolling list, *Tab* to highlight it under *NAME* and change the name to *floor*. Change the amounts in the *Z* box to 0", the *ΔZ [±Z]* box to 18" (.45m), and check the *ACTIVE LAYER* button. Notice that when the *Command [Control]* key is pressed, the quick key short cuts appear. You can use these key combinations instead of clicking buttons with the mouse. Select *OK* and then go up to *ORGANIZE>LAYER OPTIONS>SHOW/SNAP/MODIFY OTHERS*. Also change the default *FILL* to another light color on the *ATTRIBUTES* palette.

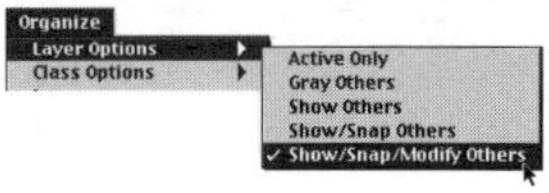

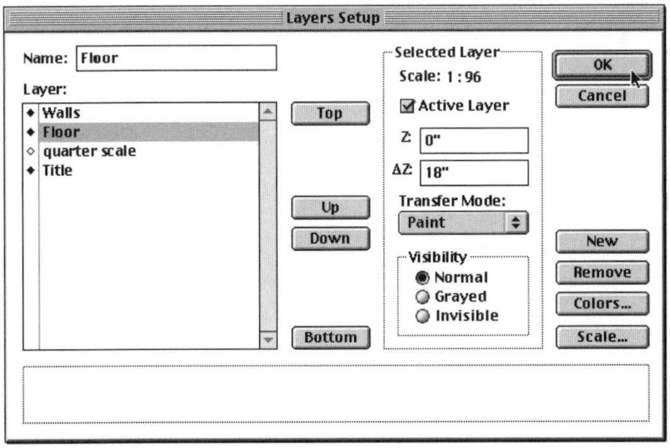

The Slab

We will create an object for the floor where the floor slab sits on the *ground plane* and the top of the slab aligns with the bottom of the walls. In other words the walls will actually sit on top of the floor.

Step 1 - the floor in 2D

There are several ways you can create the 2D object that will then be converted into a floor. Either you can use the *Rectangle* or *Single-Line Polygon* tools snapping to the outside corners of the walls or you can use the new *Create Polygon From Exterior Walls* command which is simpler. In order to use this new command, just marquee-select all of the walls we have created and then the *AEC>Create Polygon From Exterior Walls*.

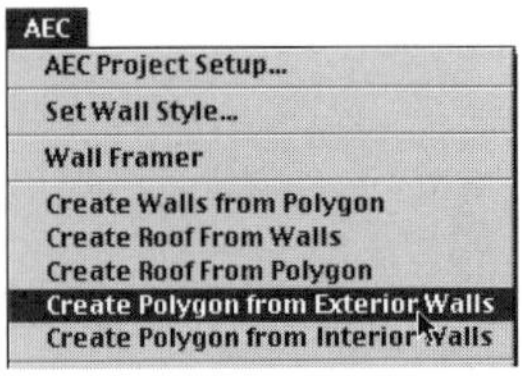

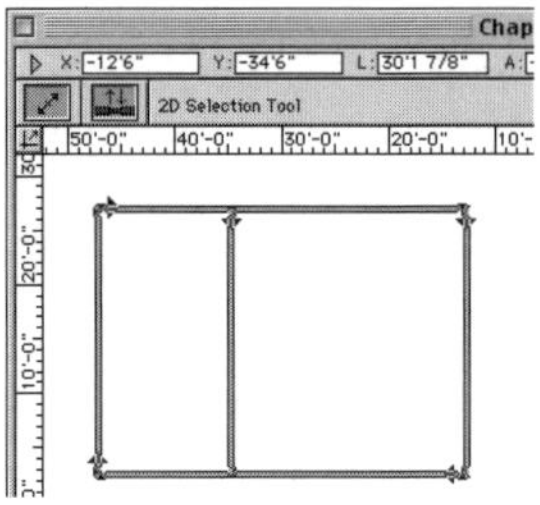

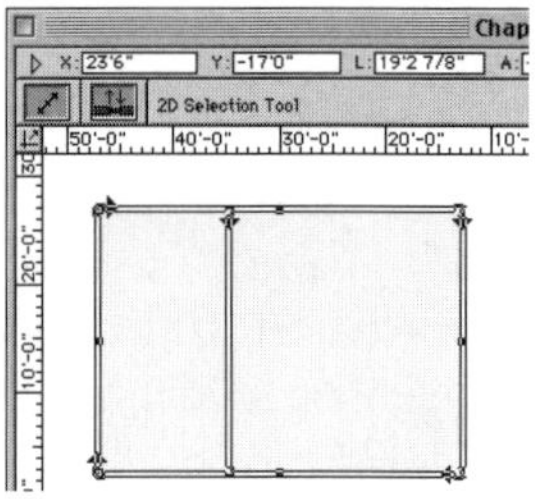

Step 2 - the floor in 3D

With only this new polygon selected choose the *MODEL>Floor* command. When the *Create Floor* dialog box opens. Enter 18" (.45m) for *thickness* and leave *bottom z* at 0". This command converts the 2D polygon into a hybrid object having both a 2D and a 3D component. The floor will not look any different unless you view it in one of the 3D views.

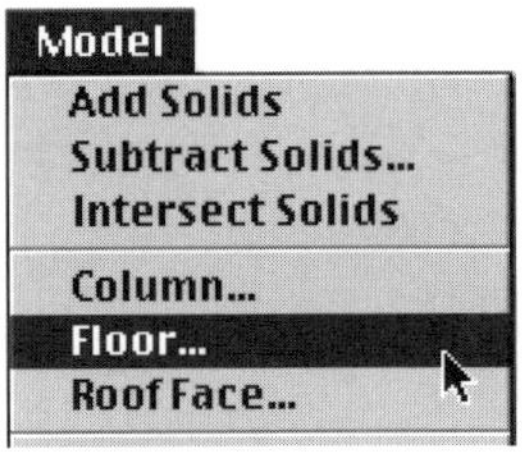

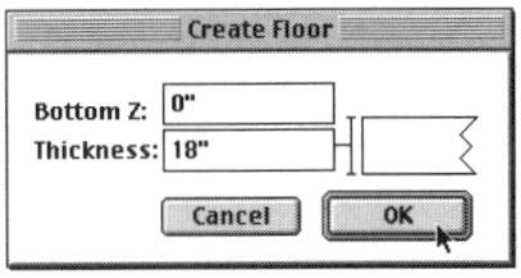

Flooring Patterns

We will create an object that can be used to display a floor pattern. *Floor* should still be the selected layer and *Layer Options>Show/Snap/Modify Others* should still be selected.

Step 1 - creating the flooring pattern

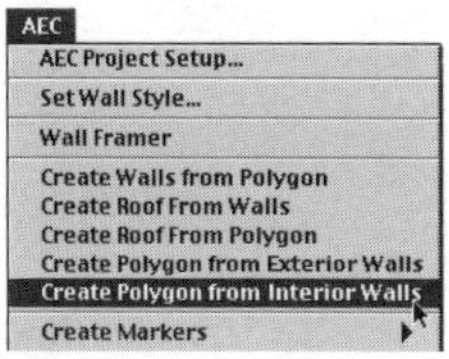

Change the fill color on the *ATTRIBUTES* palette to white. *Shift*-select all of the walls and then the *AEC>CREATE POLYGON FROM INTERIOR WALLS* command. A polygon will automatically be created to match the right space aligning with the interior face of the walls. Click to deselect and *Shift*-select all of the walls except the right exterior wall and use the command again. A polygon will be created in the left space. Select one of the polygons and then the fill *PATTERN* button on the *ATTRIBUTES* palette. Then press/drag to a pattern. Select a pattern for the other polygon.

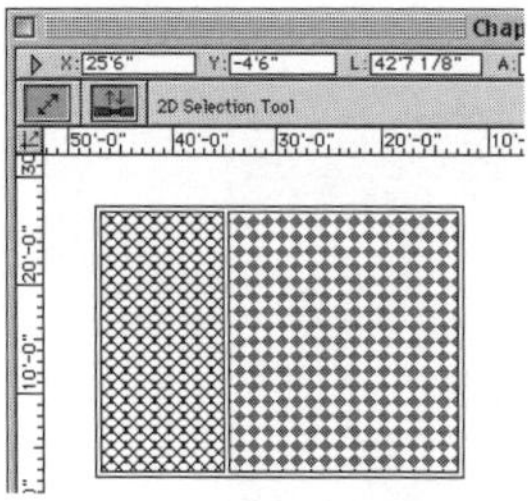

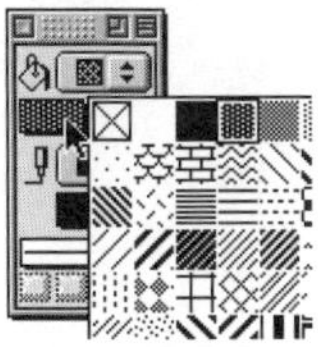

Step 2 - creating a 3D flooring pattern

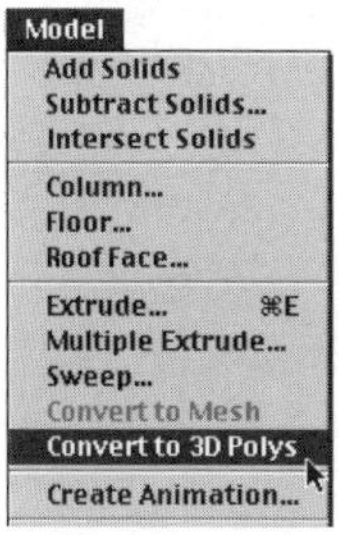

Select both of the polygons and then the *MODEL>CONVERT TO 3D POLYS*. The patterns will disappear since both of these objects have been converted into one 3D object, not a hybrid object. A pattern is not visible on a 3D object until rendered *SOLID*. Change the view to *FRONT*. Notice that the selected object is on the *ground plane*. It needs to be move upwards in the *Y* direction 18" (.45m) so that it sits on top of the slab. Use the *TOOL>MOVE>MOVE* command to do so. Then use the *MOVE>NUDGE* command and the *Up Arrow* on the keyboard to move it one pixel more so that the pattern rests just above the slab. Change the view to *RIGHT ISOMETRIC* and render it *SOLID* to view. If the pattern is not visible, you will need to go back to *FRONT* view and *NUDGE* it upwards another pixel. Change back to *TOP/PLAN*.

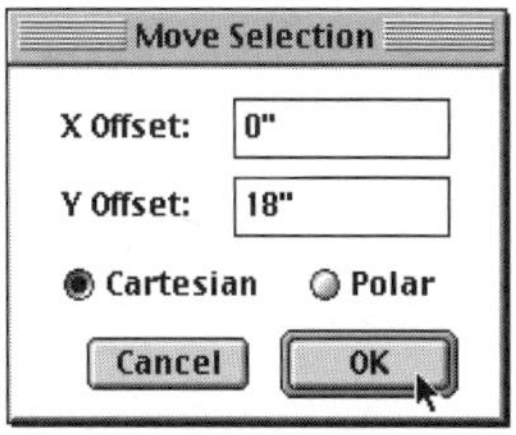

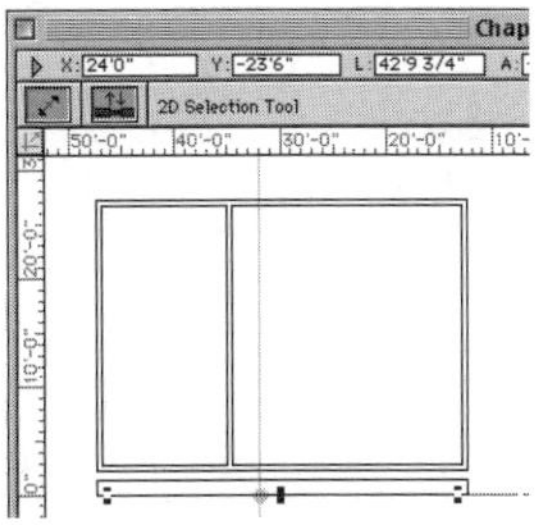

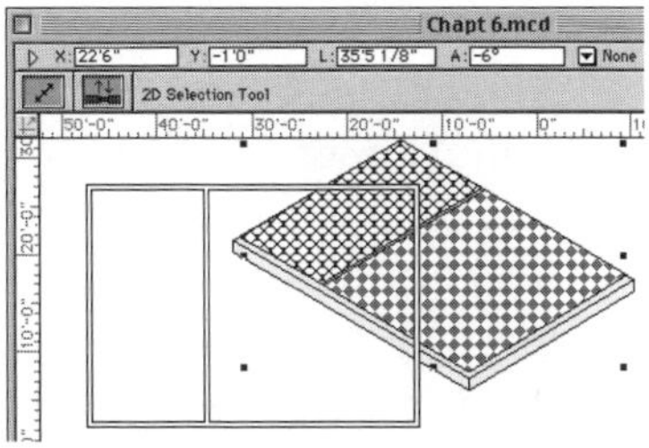

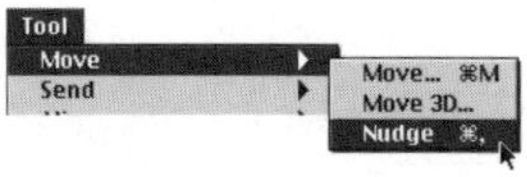

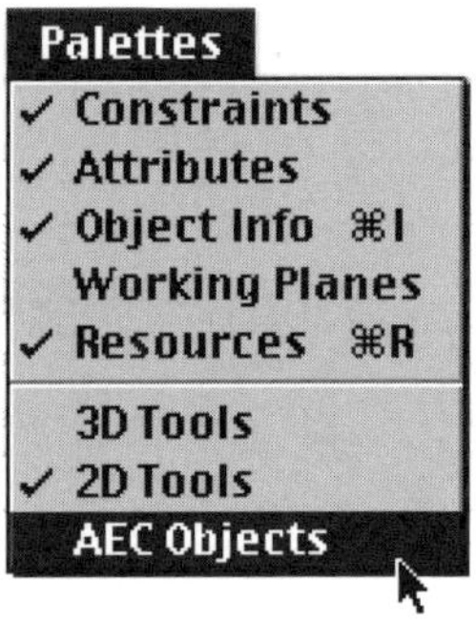

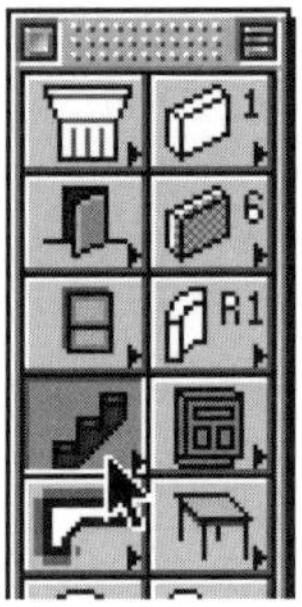

Stairs

There are now several tools to create stairs with depending on whether they are straight, circular, switchback, etc. With *floor* still the active layer, select *ORGANIZE>LAYER OPTIONS> GRAY OTHERS*. Change the default fill color to the same light gray as the walls. We will now create some stairs that lead up to the house. Select the *STRAIGHT STAIR* tool on the *AEC OBJECTS* palette. If you do not see the palette make sure it is open and has a checkmark next to *PALETTES>AEC OBJECTS.*

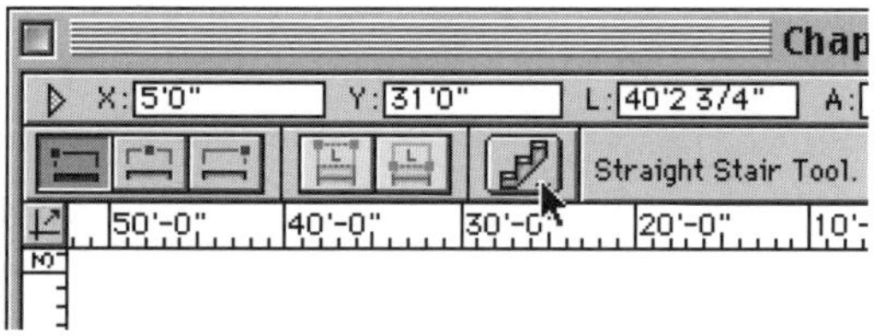

Now click the right most icon to open the *STRAIGHT STAIR PREFERENCES* dialog box.

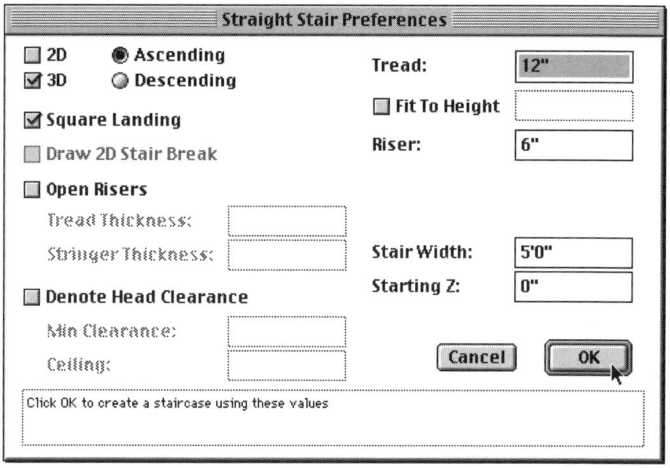

Select the *3D* and the *ASCENDING* buttons to create a stairs going up to the top of the floor. Make sure the *2D* button is not selected since this tool is not a hybrid tool like the *WALL* tool and you do not want to see a 2D stairs in a 3D view. Also select the *SQUARE LANDING* button. For *TREADS* enter 12" (.30m), for *RISER* enter 6" (.15m), *STAIR WIDTH* 5' (1.50m) and for *STARTING Z*

leave it at 0 since you want it to start on the *ground plane*. When you select *OK*, click the second and fourth icons, *ALIGN TOP CENTER OF LANDING*.

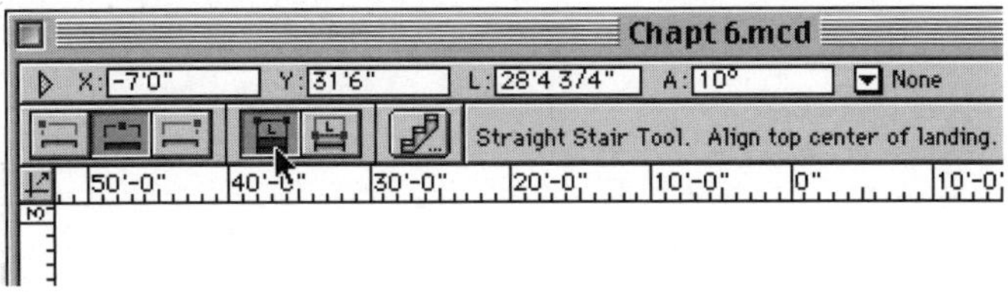

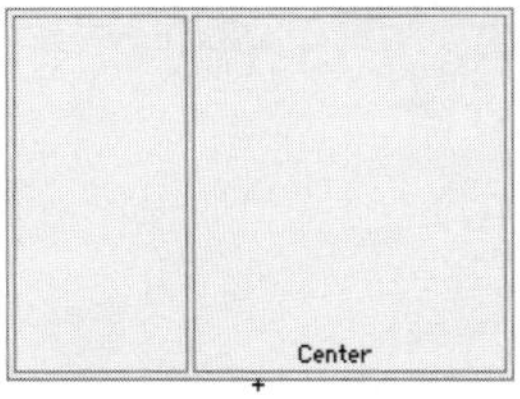

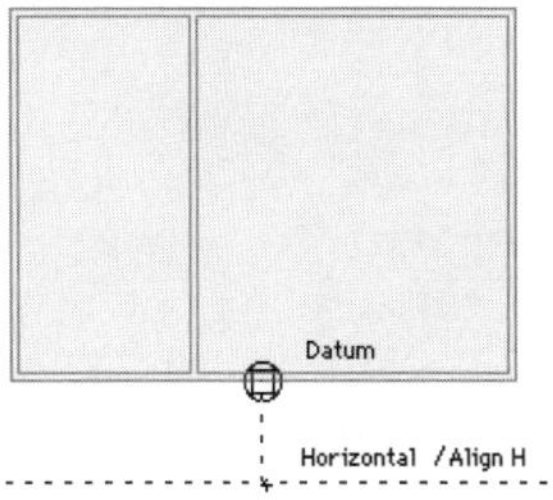

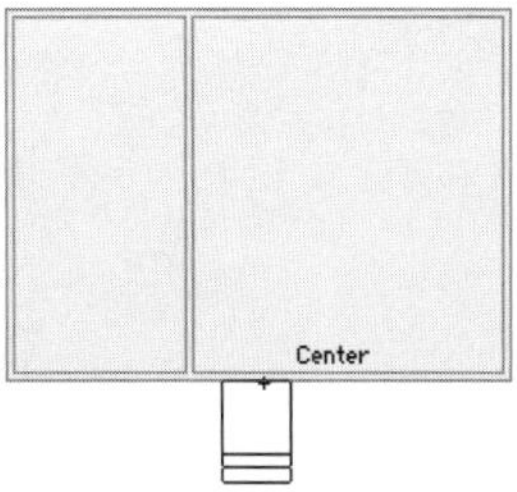

Now place the cursor on the lower center of the floor. When the *center smartcursor cue* appears and the point turns to the floating datum point use the *Tab* and *Return [Enter]* keys to locate a horizontal snapping line for the bottom of the stairs to start 7'-0" (2.10m) away from the wall, -7' (-2.10m) in the *Y* edit box. Move the cursor, to align the datum point with the guide line. The *cue, horizontal/align h* appears.

Press and drag upwards towards the floor from this intersection. When you snap to the floor and see the cue, *center* again, release and click at the same point to create the stairs.

Since a square landing is selected, the stairs will not appear until the cursor is almost at the edge of the floor. Also, it will seem as if an extra tread is created. This is because you are seeing the stairs in *WIREFRAME* and the underside of the structure is visible. When rendered *SOLID*, it will appear as it should along with the flooring patterns. The view will also automatically change to *TOP*. Go back to *WIREFRAME* and *TOP/PLAN*.

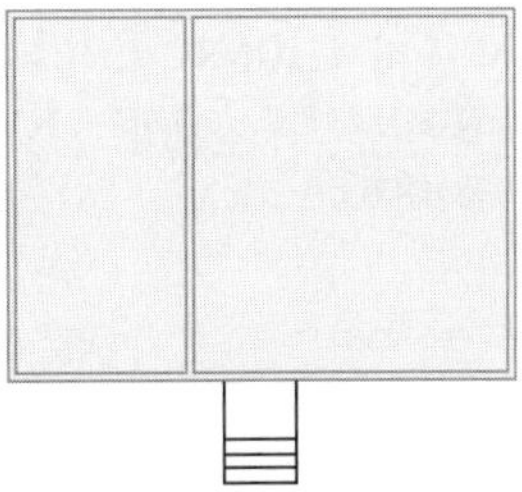

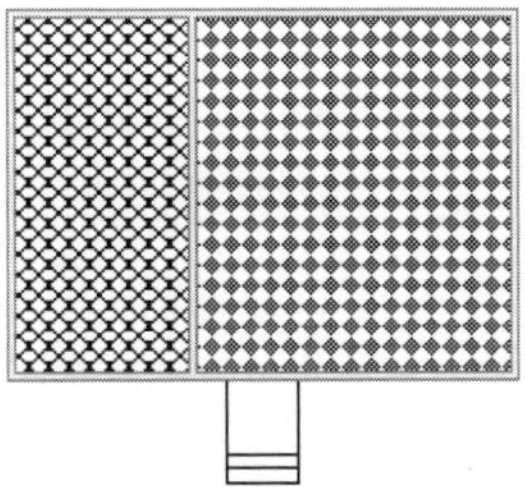

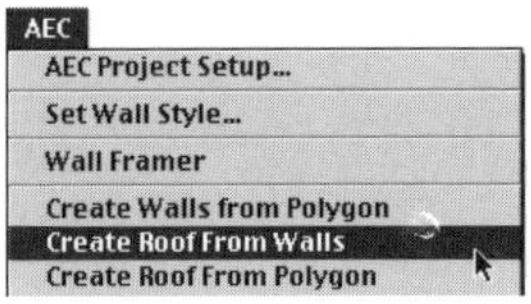

ROOFS

Roofs can be created with several different commands. The new commands, *AEC>Create Roof From Walls* and *Create Roof From Polygon* both create a simple hipped roof with no gables. The *MODEL>Roof Face* command has more flexibility. The roof is a hybrid object similar to the floor. One can either create the roof on a separate layer or in the same layer as the walls. Here we will use a separate layer.

The Roof

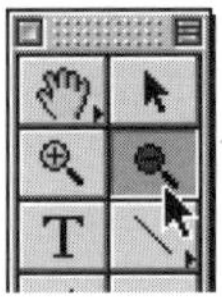

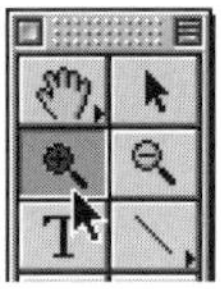

We will create a gable roof with a hip at one end and with a continuous 1' (.30m) overhang. Roofs are made by drawing the roof as individual 2D objects in *Top/Plan* view. As a note, if you can not see the whole building or if there is not enough of a border around it, you may need to zoom further away. Just double-click the *Zoom-Out* tool, then with the *Zoom-In* tool selected, press/drag a marquee around the building leaving a large enough border to work in. The area within the marquee will now fill the screen

Step 1 - the layer

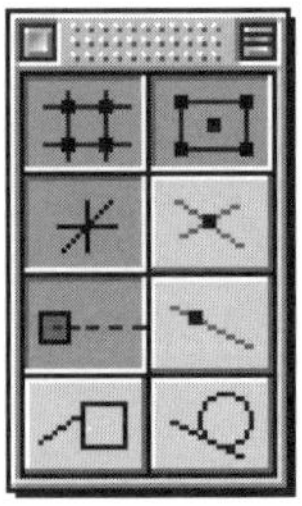

Access the *Layer Setup* dialog box and create a new layer, naming it *roof*. Notice that the scale remains the same as the last entered scale. The new layer should automatically assume a *z* value of 9'-6" (2.85m), which locates the bottom of the *roof* layer right on top of the wall, 18" (.45m) for the floor and 8' (2.40m) for the walls. If not, enter in the *z* value. The Δz *[±z]* value does not matter since the roof command overrides it, so leave it at the value it is set. Also note the order of the layers in the layer list – from the lowest to the highest with the 2D layer on the bottom. Make *roof* the active layer and select *ok*. Go to the *Attributes* palette and change the default *fill* color to a light orange. Also, go to the *Constraints* palette and select the *Constrain Angle* icon.

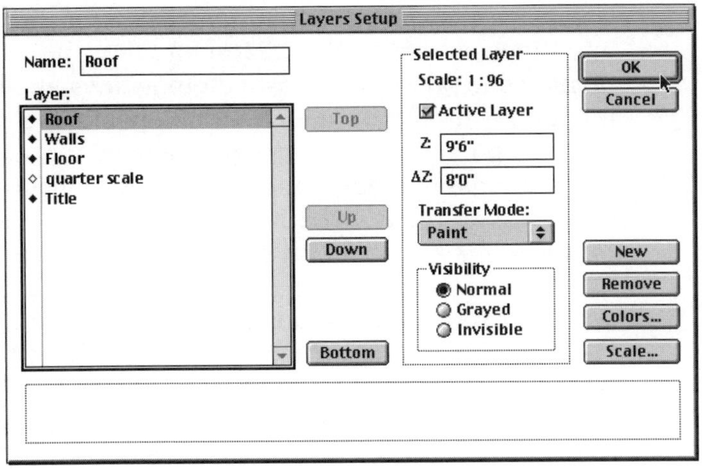

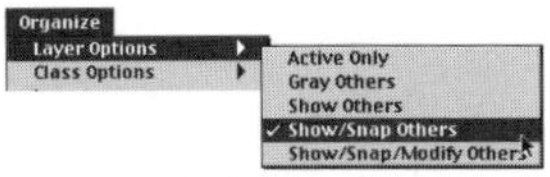

Step 2 - creating guides

ORGANIZE>LAYER OPTIONS>SHOW/SNAP OTHERS should still be selected. Then with the *SINGLE LINE* tool and the *UNCONSTRAINED* modifier icon selected, place a horizontal guide line bisecting the walls that will later be deleted. Make use of the *smartcursor cue, center,* to exactly snap or locate the line to the centerpoints.

With the line still selected, select the *EDIT>GUIDES>MAKE GUIDE* command. The line will change colors and turn from solid to dotted. It is now a guide line that can be snapped to as well.

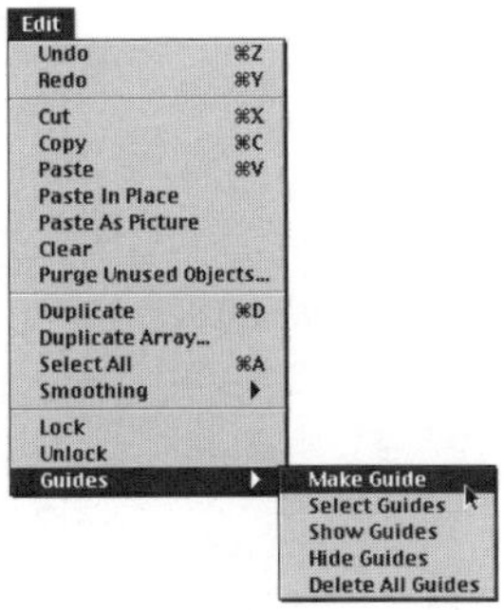

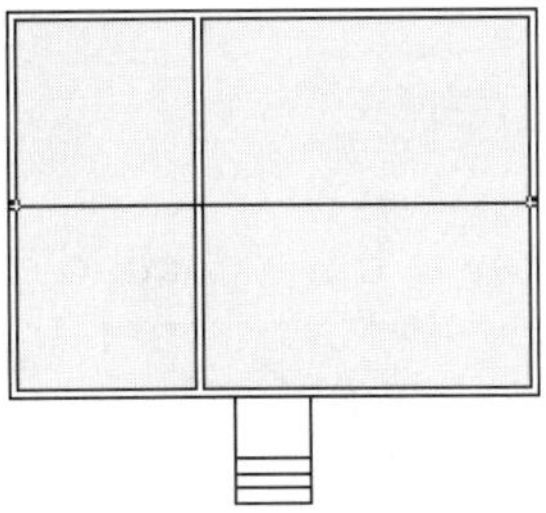

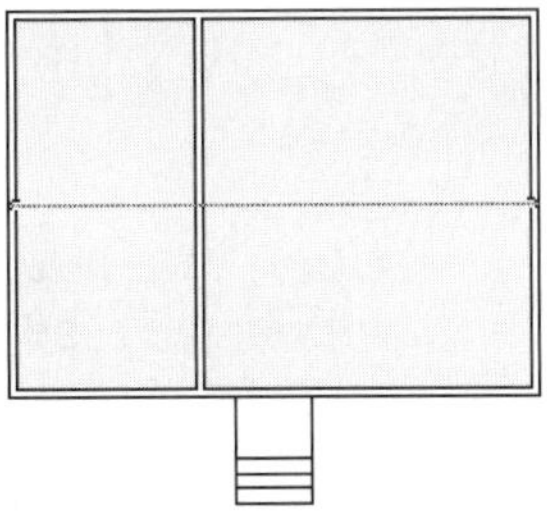

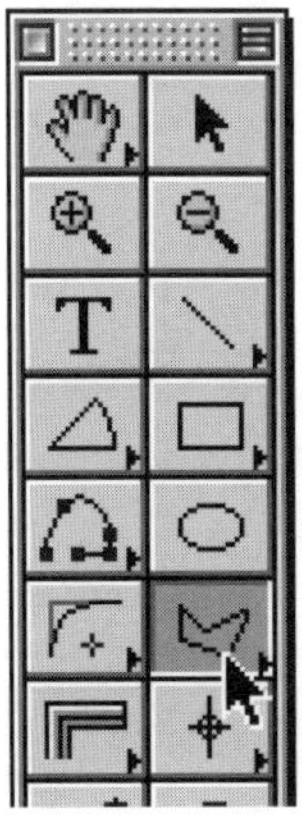

Step 3 - the roof in 2D

Select the *SINGLE-LINE POLYGON* tool. Place the cursor over the upper left exterior corner and move it around a little until that point becomes the new floating datum point.

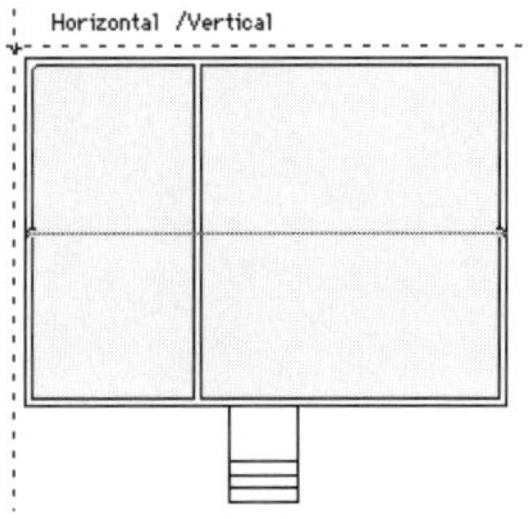

Using the *Tab* and *Return [Enter]* keys enter -1' (-.30m) into the *x* edit box and 1' (.30m) into the *y* box in the *data display bar.* When both dashed guide lines appear move the mouse until the snapping dot appears and click to start the polygon shape that will be used for the first roof plane. Single line polygons are created by clicking each end point no matter whether *CLICK-DRAG DRAWING* in the *VECTORWORKS PREFERENCES* dialog box is selected or not.

Move the mouse to the upper right exterior corner of the building, making use of the *smartcursor*. Note the *Δx [$\pm x$]* dimension in the *data display bar, Tab* to highlight it, then press the *Right Arrow* key to move the cursor to the end of the number in the edit box and enter +1' (+.30m). You can use formulas in the edit boxes and the new number will automatically be calculated.

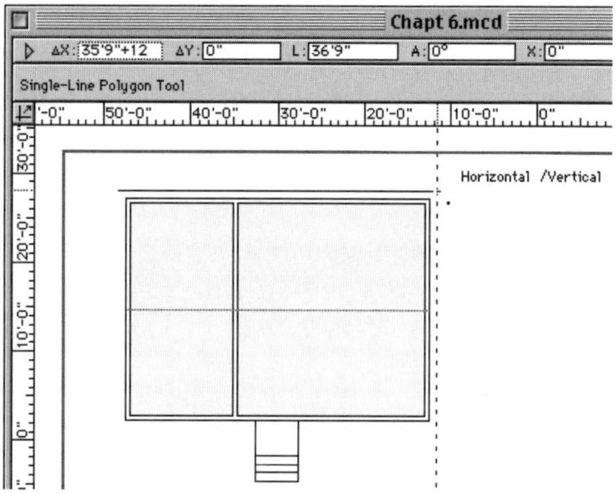

When the *Return [Enter]* key is hit, a dashed guide line appears. Press the *Shift* key and click when the line snaps horizontally to establish the second point.

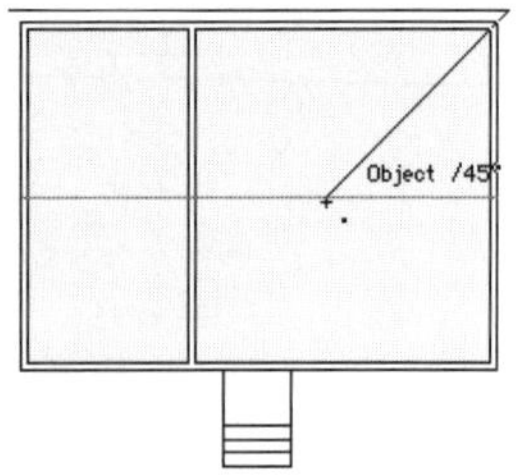

Bring the cursor down to the guide line and when the *cue, object/45°* appears, click. You could have also used the *Tab* key to enter -135° into the *A* edit box in the *data display bar.* This creates basically a 45° angle, but the way

VectorWorks configures it is, 135° from the three o'clock position and the minus sign shows it is moving in a clockwise direction.

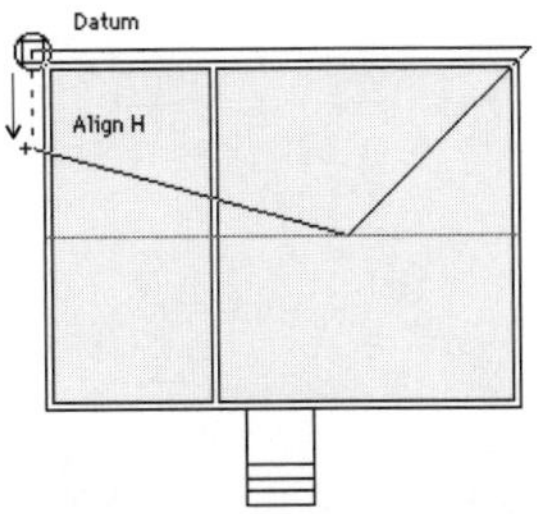

Move the cursor to the starting point and then downwards so a dashed guide line appears. When the *cue, horizontal/align h* or *align h/align v* appears, click again. Move the cursor to the beginning point and click once to end the polygon. The fill color will appear once the polygon is complete.

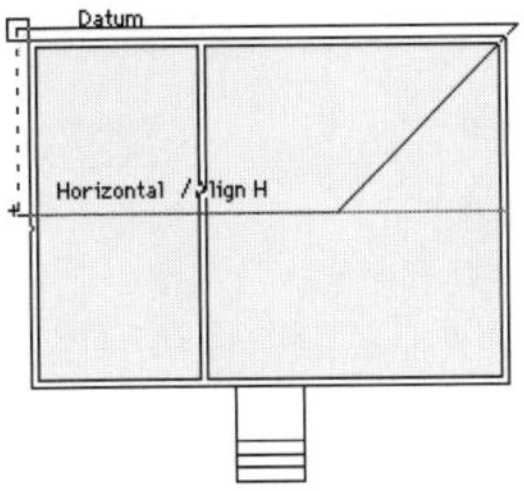

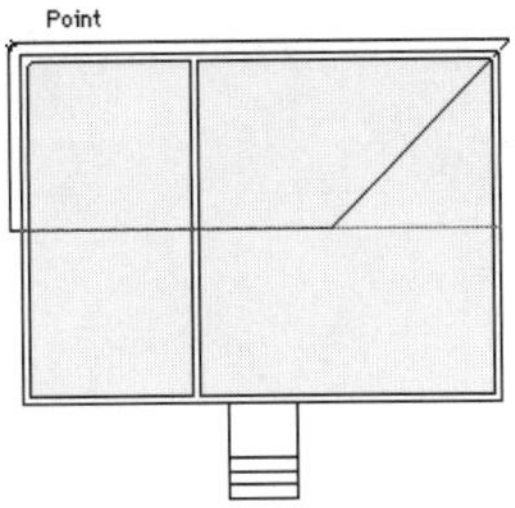

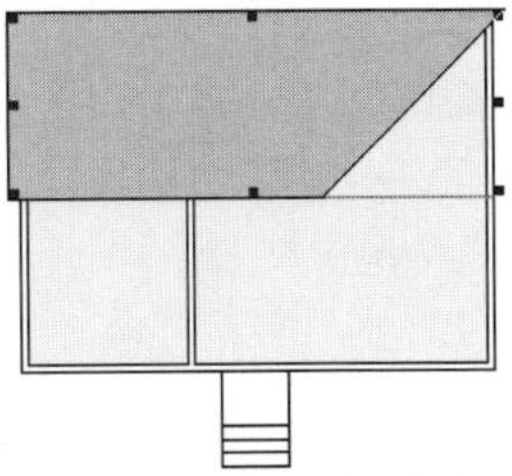

Now for the second plane of the roof. With the SINGLE-LINE POLYGON tool still selected, snap to what will be the rightmost point of the roof peak and when the *smartcursor cue, point* appears, click. Bring the cursor to the top right corner of the first plane (but do not click) and bring it all of the way downwards for a dashed guide line to appear. When the *cue, 45°/align h* appears, click again.

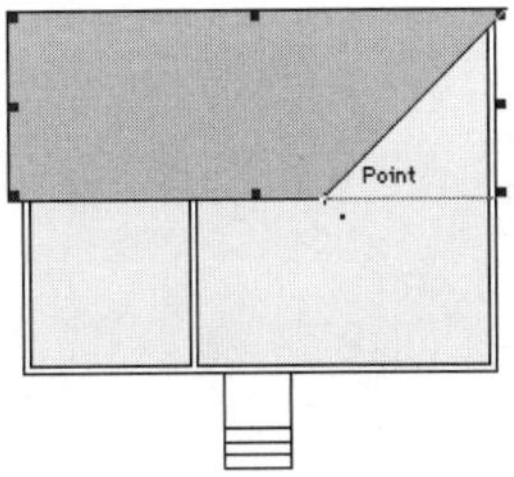

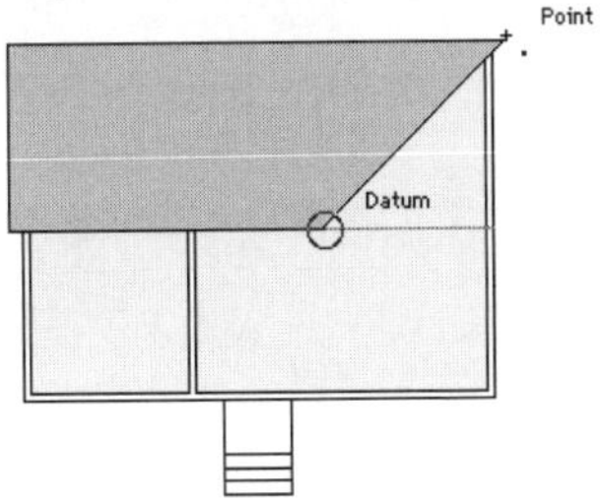

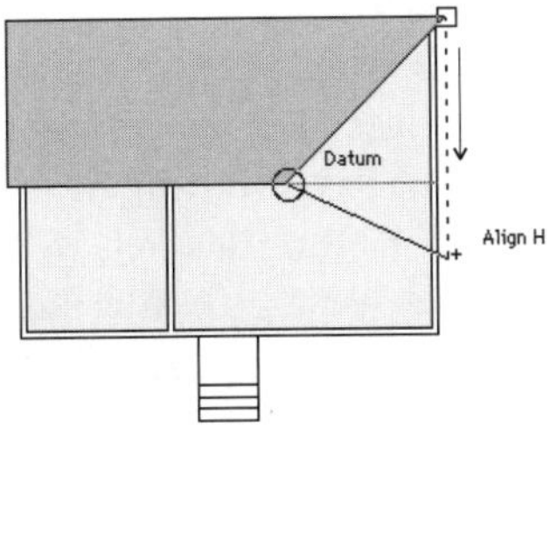

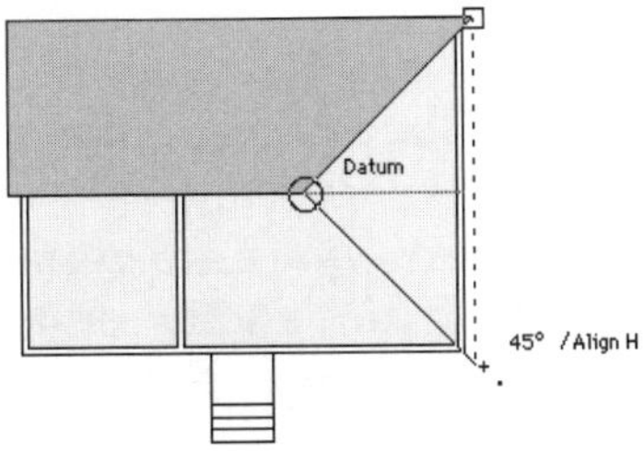

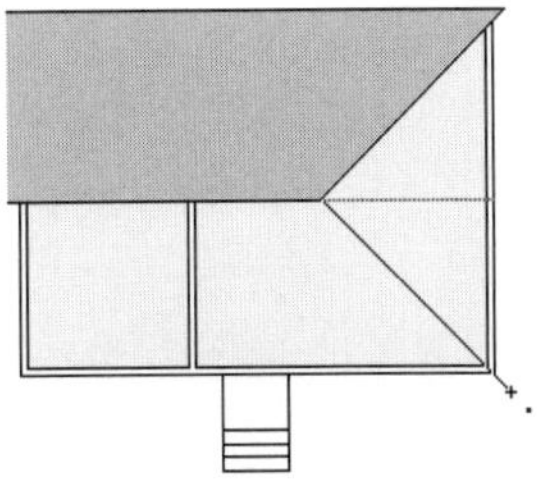

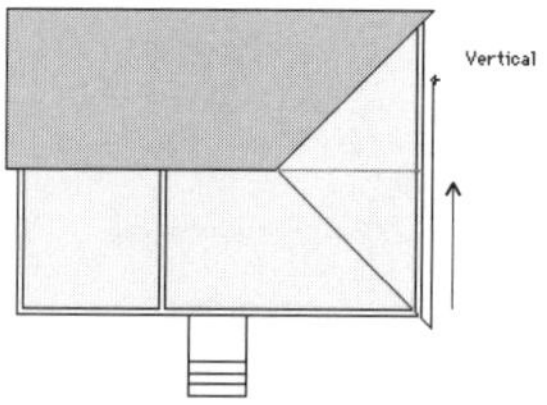

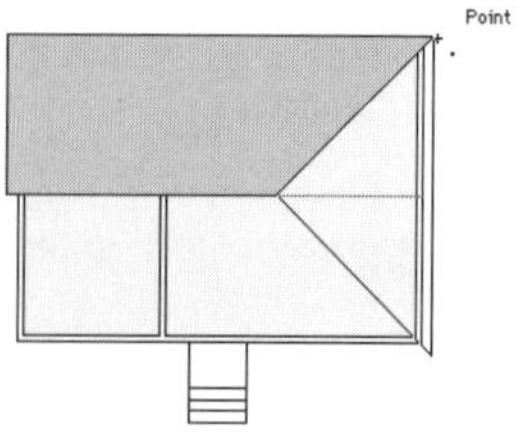

Move the cursor up again to the upper right corner of the roof and click. Then click at the starting point of this roof plane to complete the object. The edge will look as if it has disappeared before you perform this final click. And again, the second roof plane will have the fill color show once the polygon is complete.

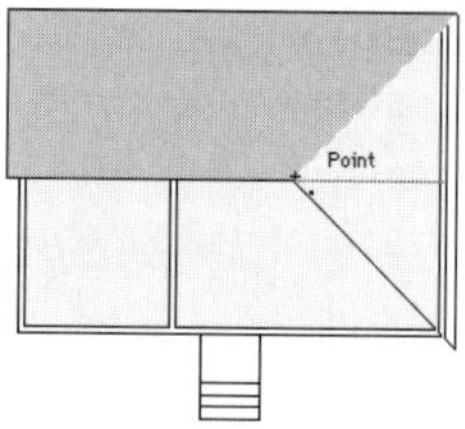

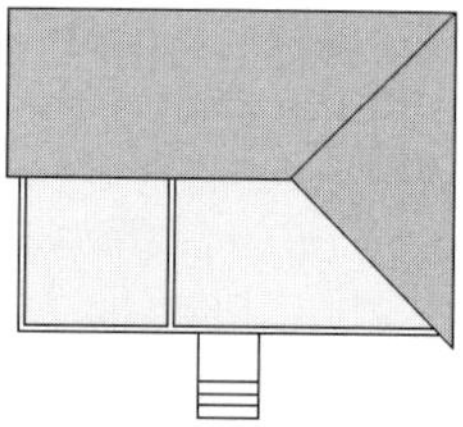

You will not need to draw the third plane since it is identical to the first and it will be duplicated later on.

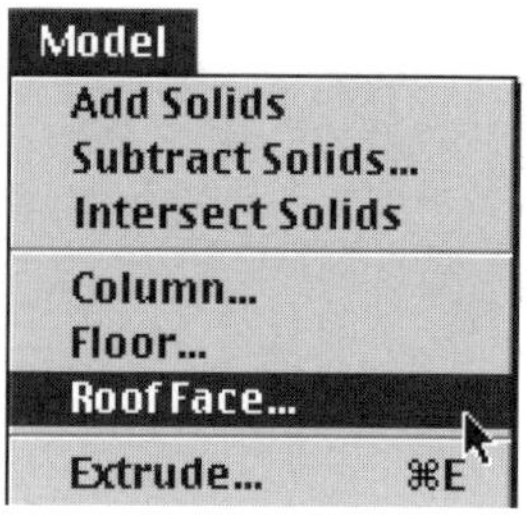

Step 4 - the roof in 3D

Select the top plane of the roof and then the *MODEL> ROOF FACE* command. The *CREATE ROOF FACE* dialog box opens.

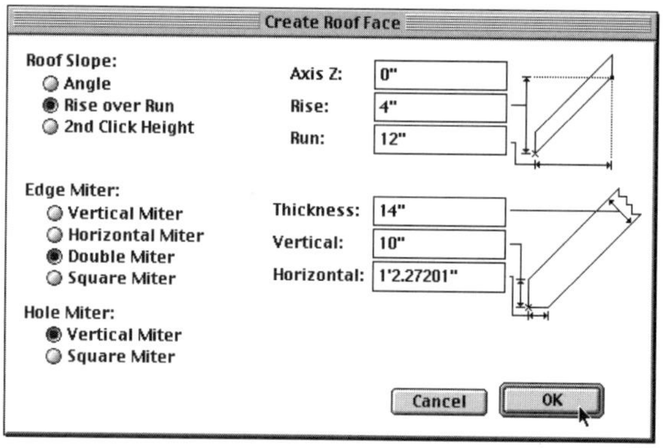

The *AXIS Z* edit box should be left at 0" since we created a separate layer for the roof and set the height above the *ground plane* in that manner. Select the *RISE OVER RUN* button and enter 4 into the *RISE* edit box and 12 into the *RUN* box to create a 4:12 rise.

Under *EDGE MITER* select the *DOUBLE MITER* button. For *THICKNESS* enter the actual dimension of the composite roof including rafters, plywood, roof tile, etc, in this case 14" (.35m). Enter 10 (.25m) in the *VERTICAL* edit box. The *HORIZONTAL* automatically gets calculated. Then select *OK*.

When the dialog box closes the next step is to draw the axis line. In this case it is aligned with the exterior part of the wall. Use the *smartcursor* to find the exterior upper left corner of the building wall. When the *cue, point* appears, press/drag a horizontal axis line that aligns with the exterior of the top wall. Verify that you do not have it snapping to the inside corner instead since both corners will have the same *smartcursor cues*. *ZOOM-IN* closer if you are not sure. The axis line does not have to be drawn the whole length before you release the mouse.

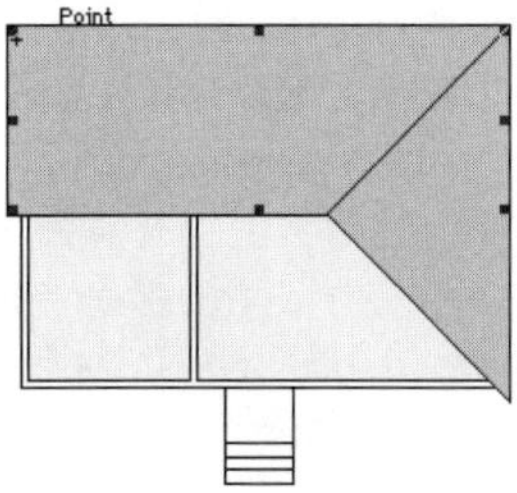

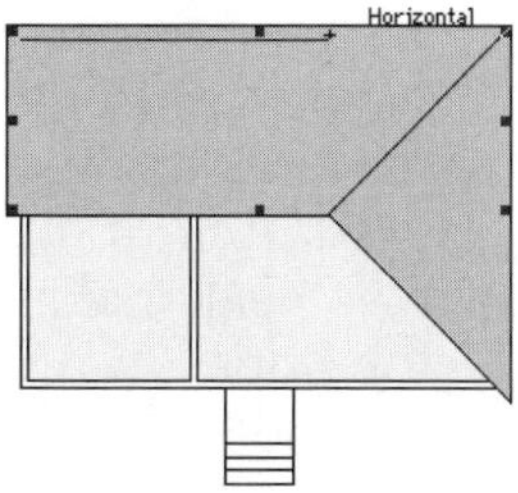

After you press/drag and release, an arrow appears. Move the cursor to the side of the axis line so the arrow is pointing to the roof peak and click.

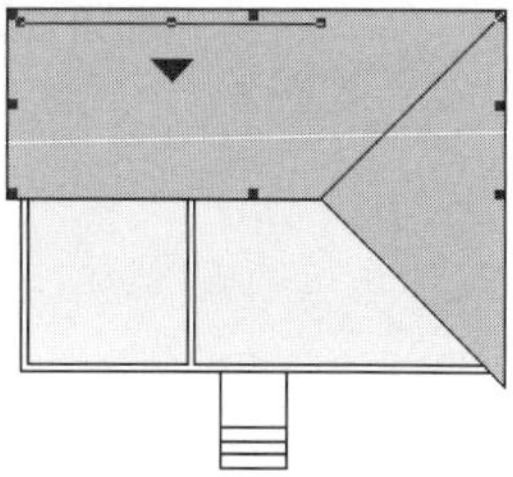

Go through the same steps for the second roof plane. Notice that when you open the *CREATE ROOF* dialog box, it will remember the previous entries so just click *OK*. Then set the axis line and the direction of the upward slope.

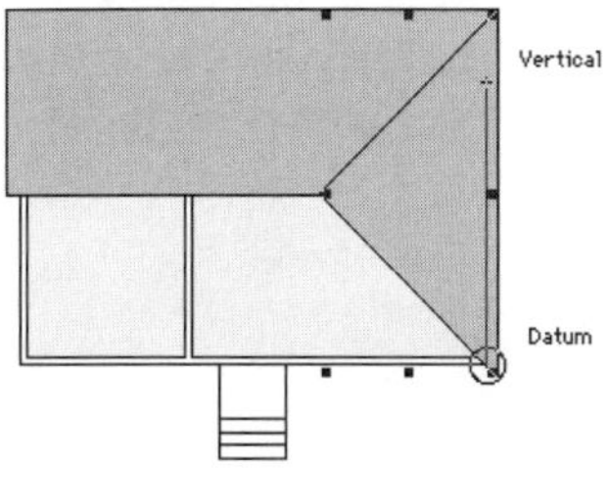

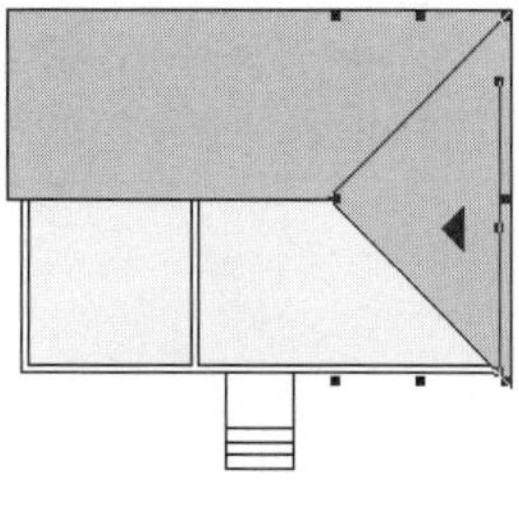

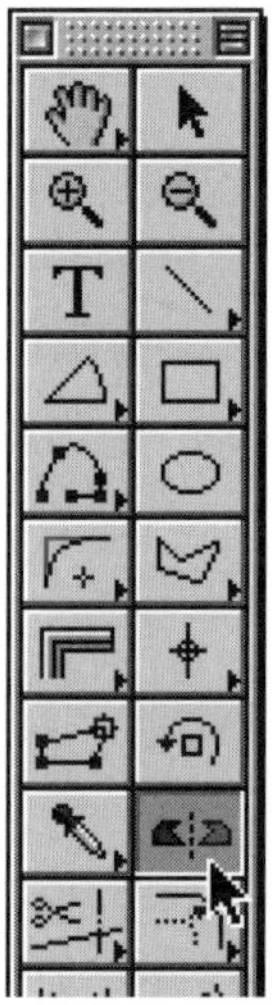

The axis line can really be located anywhere. Some find it easier to locate it on the edge of the overhang rather than directly above the exterior edge of the wall. In that case, though, you would need to calculate the specific height for the edge. You might also find it easier to change the fill for the 2D roof plane to *NONE* before you select the *ROOF FACE* command. This allows you to easily place the axis line and then once the 3D roof is created apply a *SOLID* fill again.

Step 5 - duplicating the roof

In order to not go through all of the previous steps for the third roof plane, you could just duplicate it since it is identical to the first.

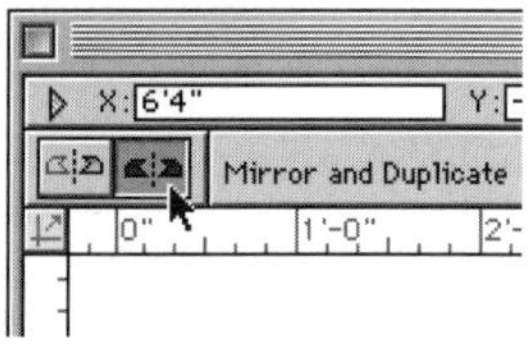

With the first roof plane selected, select the *MIRROR* tool with the *MIRROR AND DUPLICATE* modifier icon. Also, notice whenever you select an object already converted into a roof, the arrow pointing to the peak always appears. It will not print though. Press/drag an axis line along the roof peak making use of the *smartcursor* to exactly locate the ridge. Look for the *cue, horizontal,* before releasing the mouse.

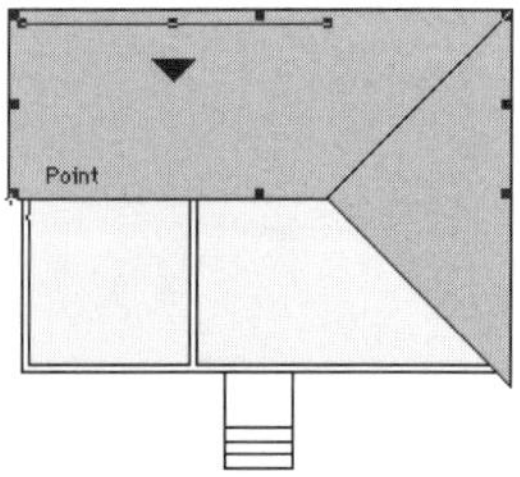

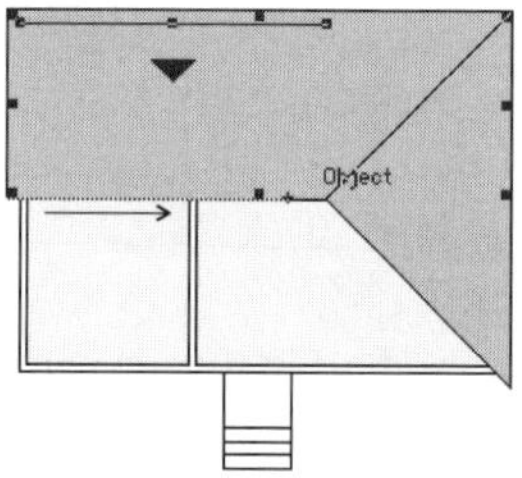

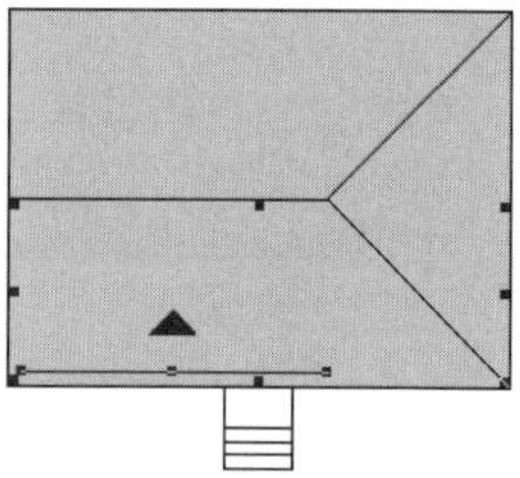

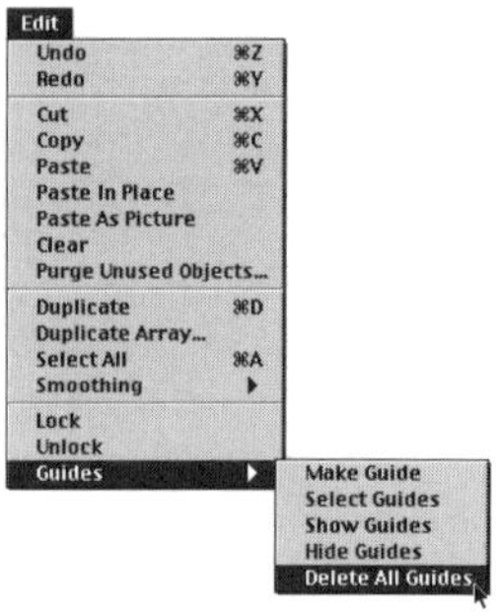

The mirrored plane will mirror itself correctly in 3D space. The roof is now complete and you can delete the guide line by selecting *EDIT>GUIDES>DELETE ALL GUIDES.*

WALLS AND STUFF IN SUMMATION

Change the floor layer to *Top/Plan*, make *title* the active layer, change the default fill to white, and change the *Layer Options* to *Show Others.* Then *Save* and *Quit [Exit].* We have looked at various elements used to create architectural structures. As you can see there are numerous methods to create objects as well as organizing them. Although we have mostly viewed the elements in 2D, they all have 3D components which will be covered in the next chapters.

- In order to project 2D objects into 3D views, the objects will need to be converted into 3D.

- Fill patterns and colors do not show on a 3D object until it actually gets rendered solid.

- In both 2D and 3D layers, one should be aware of the layer stacking order in the *Layers Setup*>LAYER scrolling list. A layer on top will obscure layers below when any of the *Show Others* options are selected under *ORGANIZE>Layer Options*.

- Typically, 2D layers should be on the bottom of the scrolling list and then the 3D layers next, in the order from lowest to highest above the *ground plane*.

- In 3D layers it is best to set up layer heights, Δz [$\pm z$], and the location of the layer above the *ground plane* (z) before you create objects within each layer.

- Remember that the z value in the *Layers Setup* dialog box is only reflected on a linked layer when the *Create Layer Link* command is used. Otherwise the objects within the layer will appear on the *ground plane*. In other words, an object placed at a certain height above the *ground plane* by inserting an amount into the *Layers Setup>z* edit box will not appear at the correct height until the *Create Layer Link* command is used.

NOTES, DOODLES, & OTHER THINGS

Chapter 7

THE 3D DRAWING

LOOKING AT THE DRAWING

In the previous chapter we went through the steps to block out a building with a floor, roof, and walls. After going through all of the trouble of creating the 3D aspect, the question is how do you take advantage of this added information. We will look at how we can view each of these layers individually and as a unit, whether it is an elevation, plan, section, or isometric. We will also look at some of the rendering and projection options.

The tools, commands, constraints, and palettes we will be exploring are;

2D Symbol Insertion Tool
2D Selection Tool
3D Selection Tool
Pan Tool
Walkthrough Tool
Wall Join Tool
Align Layer Views Command
Create Layer Link Command
Cut 3D Section Command
Perspective Command
Projection Command
Rendering Command
Save As Command
Set 3D View Command
Unlock Command
Wide Perspective Command
Constrain Angle Constraint
Attributes Palette
Resources Palette

ALIGNING THE LAYERS

We will need to open an existing file and save it under a different name. Double-click the file, *chapt 6 [chapt 6.mcd]* to open, select the *Save As* command, and name it *chapt 7 [chapt 7.mcd]*, locat-

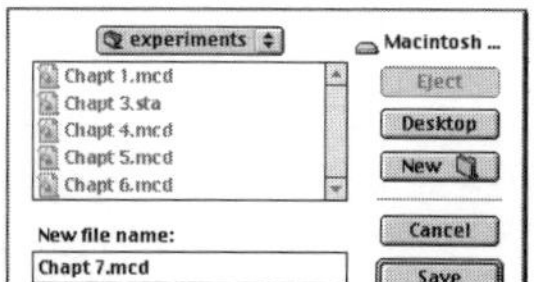

ing it in the *experiments* folder. The original file will remain untouched and the opened copy will then have its name automatically changed to *chapt 7 [chapt 7.mcd]*.

One can change the view of each layer individually by making each one the active layer, then changing the view. If there were numerous layers, this could indeed be a rather tedious task.

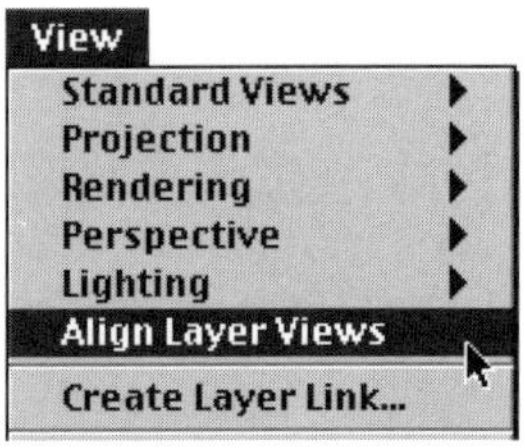

Layers On The Same Ground Plane

If all of the 3D layers created are on the same *ground plane*, in other words, the *z* in the *Layers Setup* dialog box is 0", there is a shortcut. Change the active layer to the desired view and select *VIEW>Align Layer Views*.

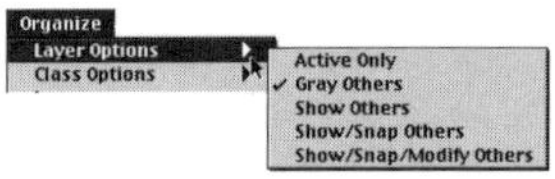

If *ORGANIZE>Layer Options* has one of the *Show Others* or *Gray Others* options selected, then you will see all of the layers changing to the view of this active layer. The *Align Layer Views* command now changes the view of all layers regardless of their visibility, scale, or whether it is a 2D or 3D layer. The other layers, if visible, remain visible, which is a change from earlier versions.

Layers At Different Heights

In the previous file, the *Align Layer Views* really does not help us accomplish viewing the object since each layer was created with a different *z* value or height above the *ground plane*.

To see what happens, make *floor* the active layer and select *ORGANIZE>Layer Options>Show Others*. Change to *Top/Plan* and *Align Layer Views*. The other layers will be visible and will change views. Now change the active layer to *Rendering> Wireframe* and the view to *VIEW>Standard Views>Left Isometric*. Notice that the other three layers still remain in *Top/Plan*. See what happens when *Align Layer Views* is again selected.

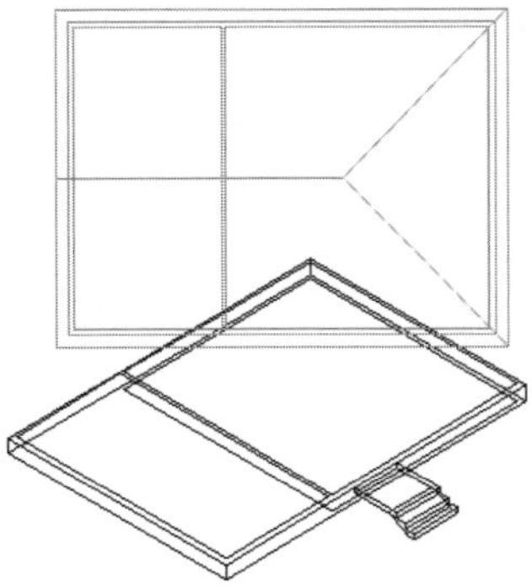

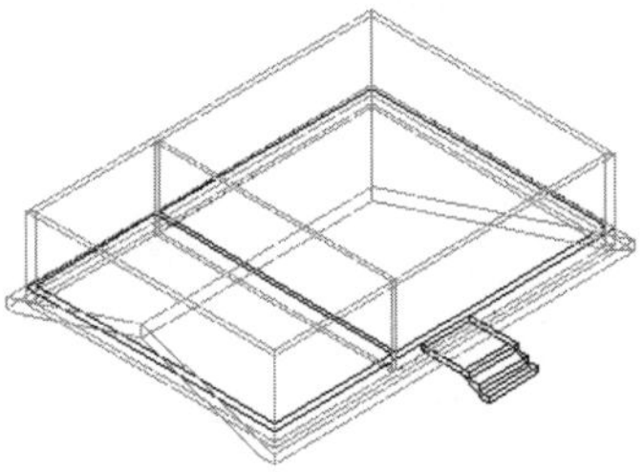

The layers have already changed views and are aligned with the view on the active layer. Unfortunately, each of the layers are not correctly placed above the *ground plane*, so you can not really see how they work together.

LINKED LAYERS

A linked model layer is unique in that any changes, additions, or deletions made to the original or master layers will appear in the linked layer, but any additions actually made on the linked layer will not affect the original layers. In other words, the linking is in one direction. You can select a new view under *STANDARD VIEWS* for the linked layer. All of the layers that were linked will appear correctly while the original layers will remain in whatever view they were in. The view as well as the scale on the original layers are irrelevant to the views and scale on the linked layer.

Creating Linked Layers

What you would need to do is create another new layer for the linked model and link the original layers to it in order to create a 3D model. This layer linking is very handy for many things, but it has to be done with certain care.

Step 1 - linked model layer

The first step is, to go into the *LAYERS SETUP* dialog box, click the *NEW* button, and create another new layer. Name this layer *linked model*. The *z* and Δz *[±z]* of this layer are

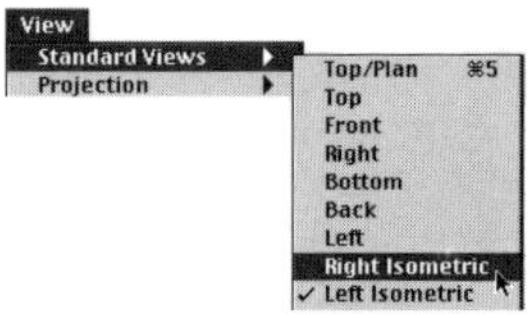

irrelevant. The *ACTIVE LAYER* button is automatically selected for this new layer. Now select *OK*. Go up to *STANDARD VIEWS* and select *RIGHT ISOMETRIC*. Go to *ORGANIZE>LAYER OPTIONS* and select *ACTIVE ONLY*. Everything will disappear from the screen since there is nothing on this layer when *ACTIVE ONLY* is selected.

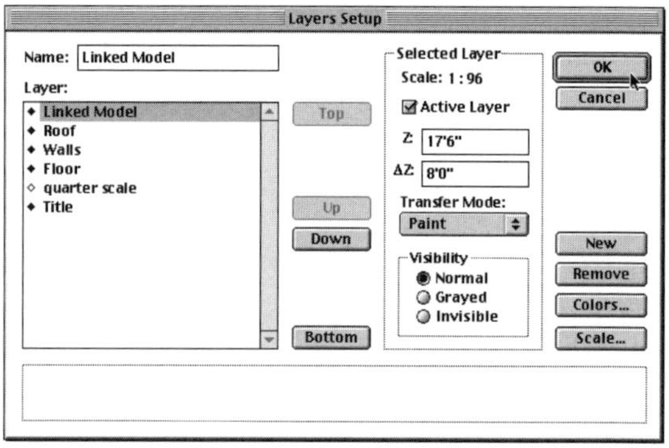

Step 2 - linking

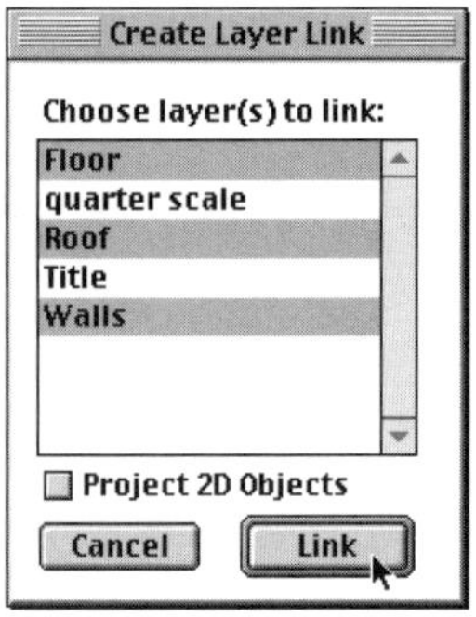

Select the *VIEW>CREATE LAYER LINK* command. The *CREATE LAYER LINK* dialog box opens. *Command*-click [*Control*-click] to select the *floor, roof,* and *walls* layers in the scrolling list leaving the other layers unselected and then click the *LINK* button. When the dialog box closes, the various layers of the building will now be viewed correctly in relationship to each other. You can change the view in this linked model layer and all of the linked elements will change with it. The original layers will not be affected.

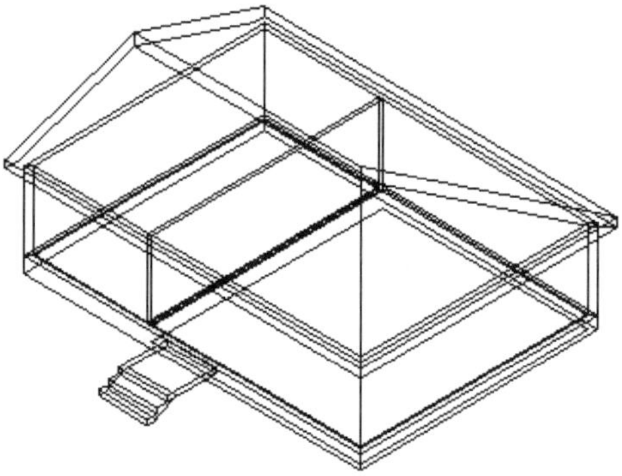

Viewing Linked Model Layers

Once a linked layer is set up and linked, any changes made on the original layers will automatically appear on the linked layer. If it has been rendered, you no longer need to select the appropriate rendering command again in order for the changes to appear.

Step 1 - scale

Open the *Layers Setup* dialog box and with the *linked model* layer selected in the scrolling list, click the *scale* button.

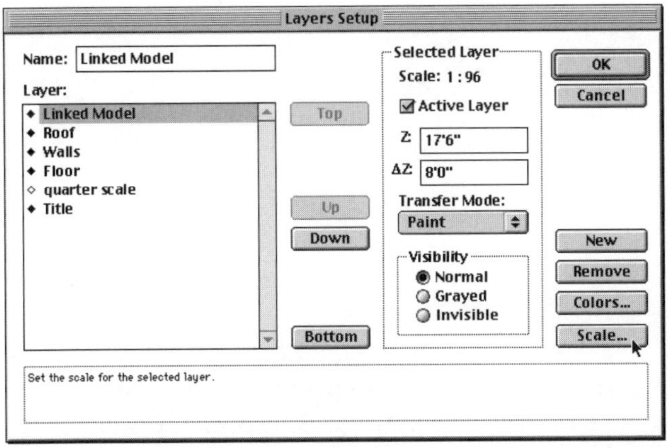

When the *Layer Scale* dialog box opens change the scale to $^1/_{16}$" (1:200) and select *ok* and then *ok* again to exit the *Layers Setup* dialog box. The building will automatically rescale itself.

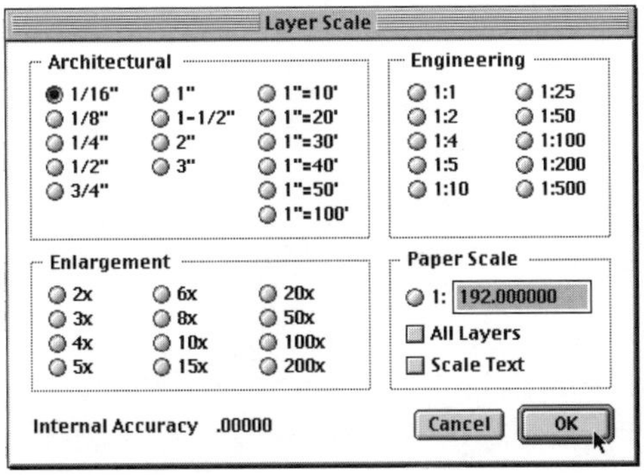

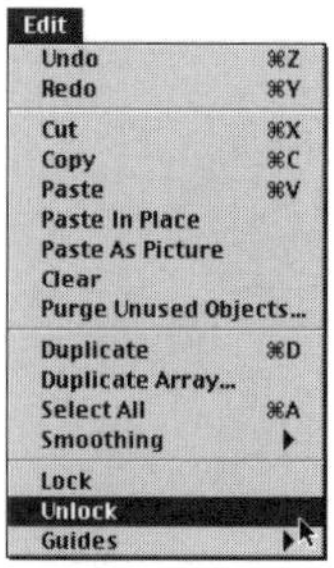

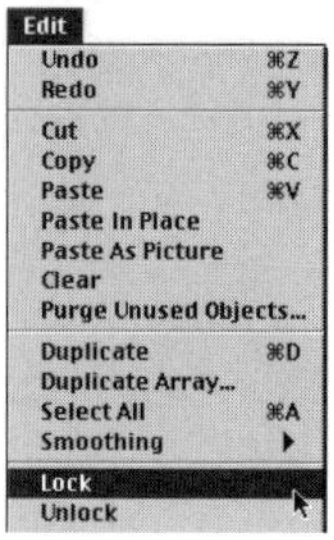

Step 2 - relocating the linked object

The 3D linked model may not be placed exactly on the sheet where you would like it. Also notice when the linked image is selected, the handles are gray meaning it is locked. With it still selected go to *EDIT>UNLOCK*. The handles turn black. Press/drag the selected objects and place it centered on the sheet taking into account the title block. You may want to temporarily change the *LAYER OPTIONS* to *SHOW OTHERS* to see the title block. Then use the *EDIT>LOCK* command.

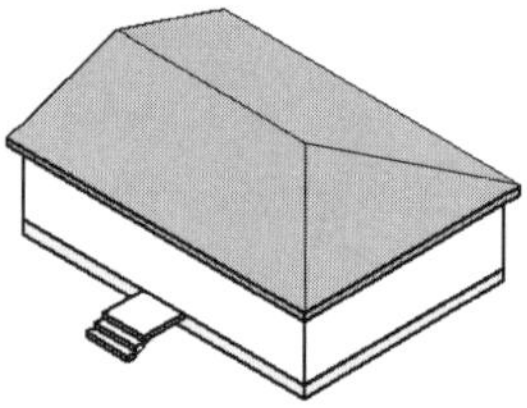

Step 3 - rendering

Select *VIEW>RENDERING>SOLID*. If there is already a check mark next to it, a dialog box opens asking if you want to re-render everything. Select *OK*. The building will change from appearing transparent (*WIREFRAME*) to *SOLID*.

Try selecting *VIEW>RENDERING>SHADED SOLID*. The building will be rendered in different shades.

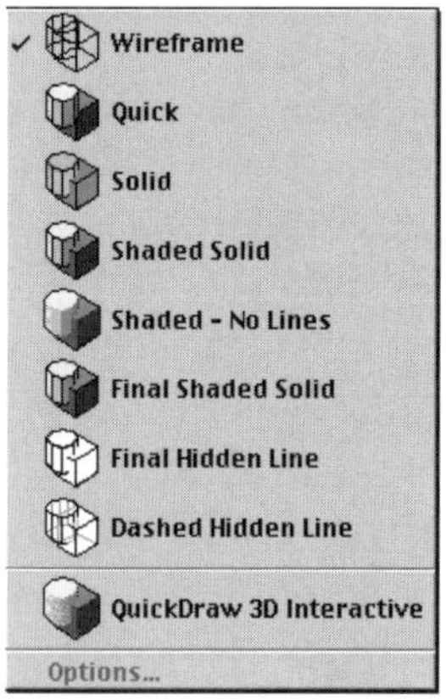

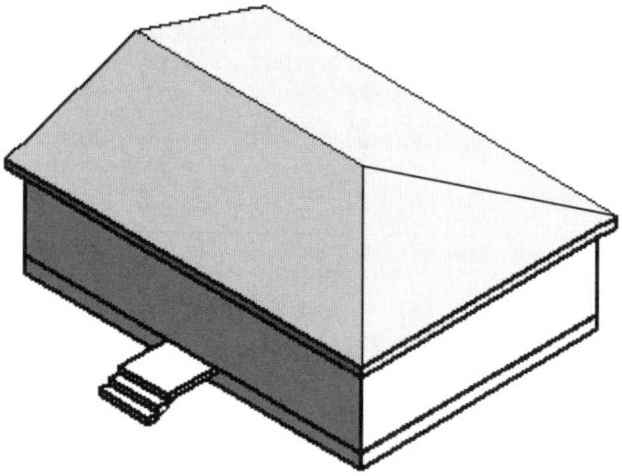

Step 4- revisions

Go back to the *roof* layer and use the *Command 5 [Control 5]* keys to change to *TOP/PLAN* if necessary. With one plane of the roof selected, notice that the *ATTRIBUTES* palette shows *NONE* for the fill although the object appears with a fill color. In order to actually change the fill to *NONE* on the roof plane, you would need to choose the *ORGANIZE>EDIT GROUP* command to get back to the original 2D object, then change the fill to *NONE* with the *ATTRIBUTES* palette, and finally click the *DONE* button to exit the group in the upper right.

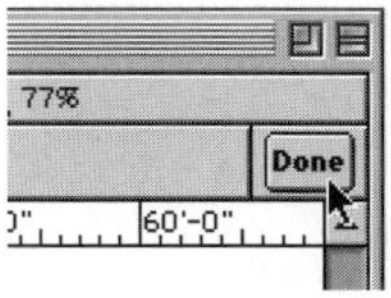

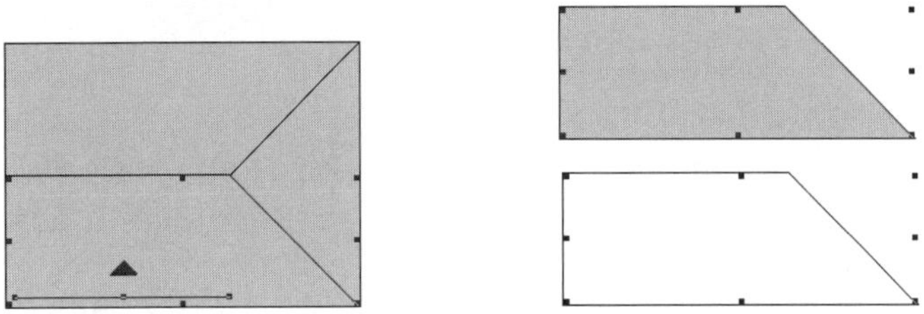

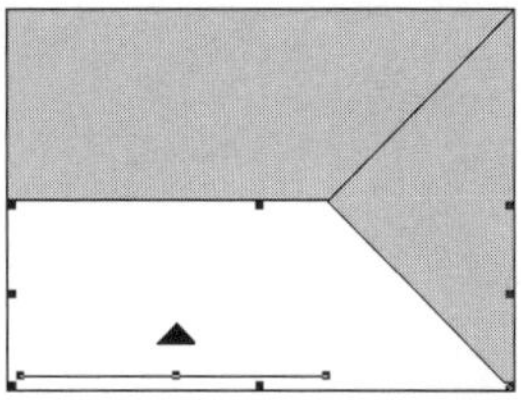

Go to the *walls* layer and change it to *TOP/PLAN*. Add another interior wall, making use of the *WALL JOIN* tool with the first icon in the mode bar, for both wall ends. Change the new wall to the same light gray *FILL* color you have been using on the walls.

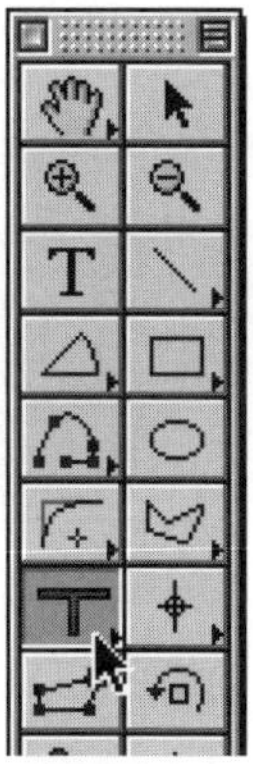

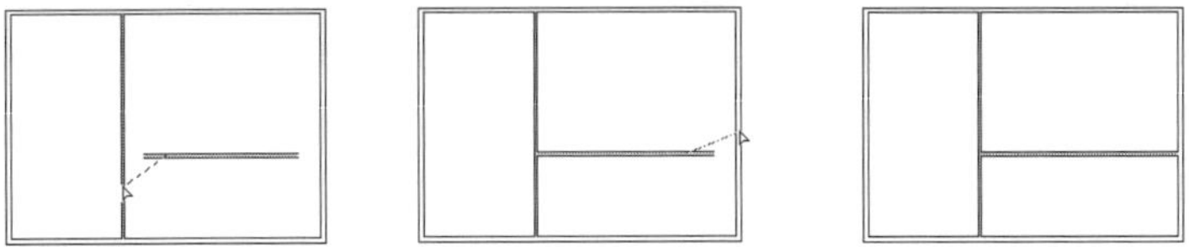

Make the *linked model* layer active again. You will now be able to see through the roof plane that is transparent and if the new interior wall was placed under this part of the roof, it will be visible as well. Notice that the interior walls also get shaded. As a note, the changes are now immediately apparent and it is not necessary to re-render the *linked model* layer. Previously the changes were only immediate if rendered in *WIREFRAME*.

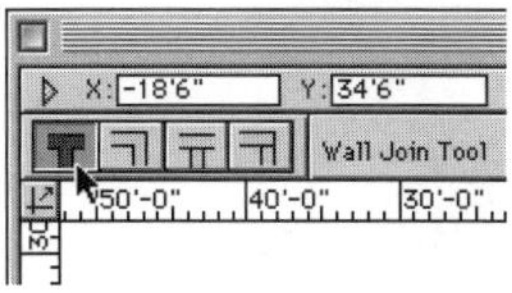

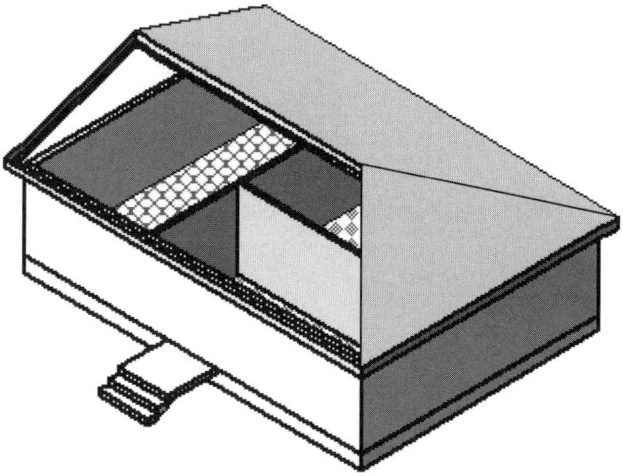

Step 5 - fill patterns

Make the *walls* layer active and *Shift*-select all of the exterior walls. With the *Attributes* palette, press/drag the fill button down to *Pattern.* Then when the pattern style button appears press/drag to one of the patterns that looks like stucco.

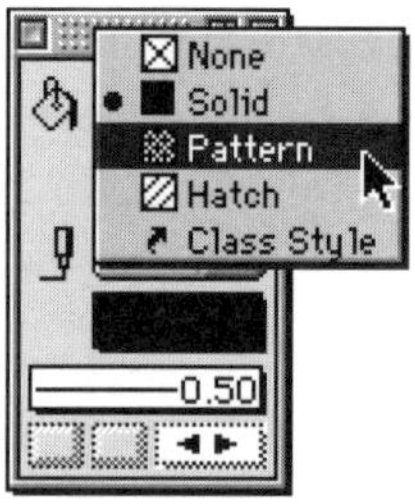

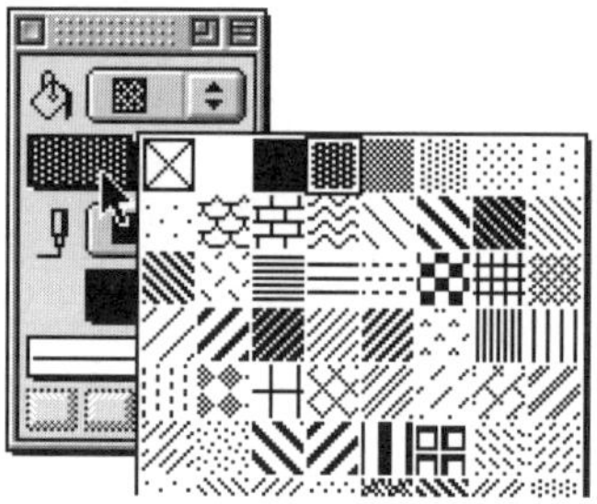

Make the *floor* layer active and change to *Top/Plan*. Select the stairs and select *Pattern* from the fill pop-out menu. Then press/drag to one of the fill patterns that looks like tile. The *Pattern* will not appear on the stairs until rendered.

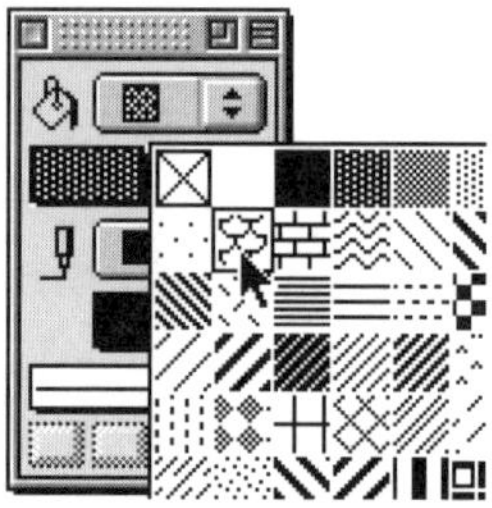

Now, make the *roof* layer active. Select the three roof planes and give them a fill *Pattern* that looks like Spanish tile. The plane that previously had *None* selected for the fill would need to be selected by clicking the edge of the plane, since it does not have a surface, or you could just press/drag a marquee around all three planes. Go to the *linked model* layer, select FRONT view.

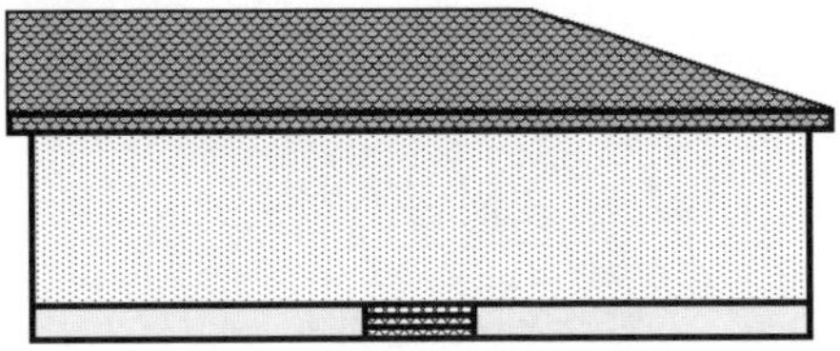

Change the view to RIGHT ISOMETRIC and note how the fill PATTERN appears on the roof and stairs. The pattern covers the object, but appears flat to the screen and does not project along with each plane of the object. This is just the way it is, so if you use a fill PATTERN take that "design feature" into account.

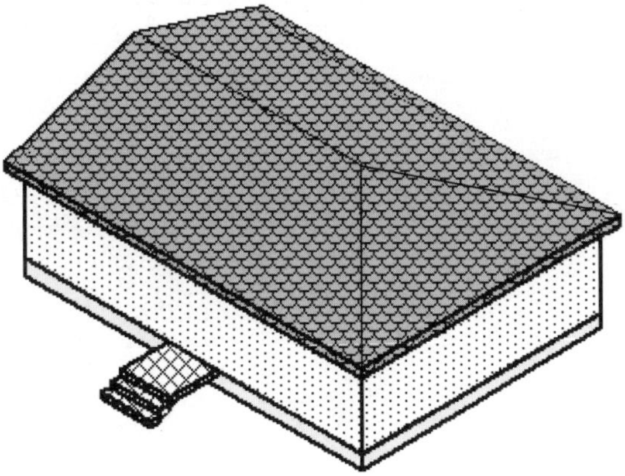

Step 6 - colors

Go back to the *floor* layer and select the floor patterns. Verify that you are selecting the grouped 3D polygons, rather then the floor, with the OBJECT INFO palette. It will say GROUP rather than FLOOR. Notice in the ATTRIBUTES palette that there are two buttons for color as well as the PATTERN selection button on the left. This is because a PATTERN is made up of two components, the background color which

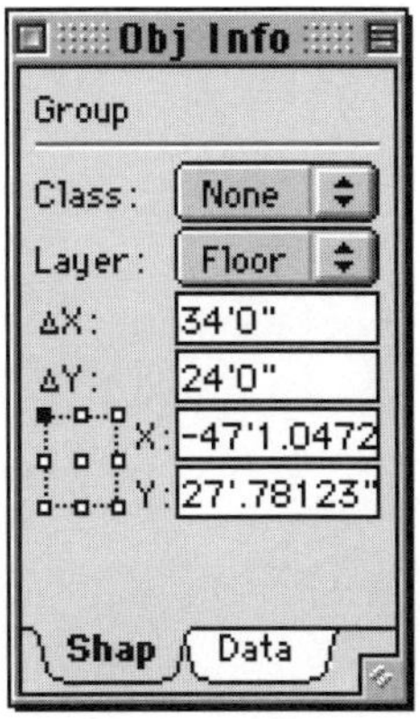

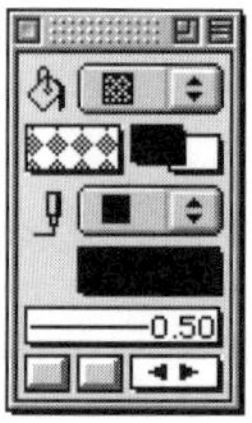

defaults to white and the foreground color which defaults to black. Change the background color of the object with the white button and the foreground color with the black button. The color you pick for each button corresponds to the black and white of the pattern itself. Although the colors will appear in the pattern button, you can not see it on the object until it is rendered *Solid*.

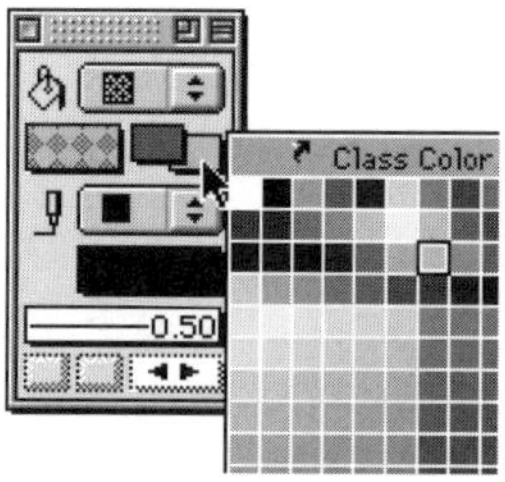

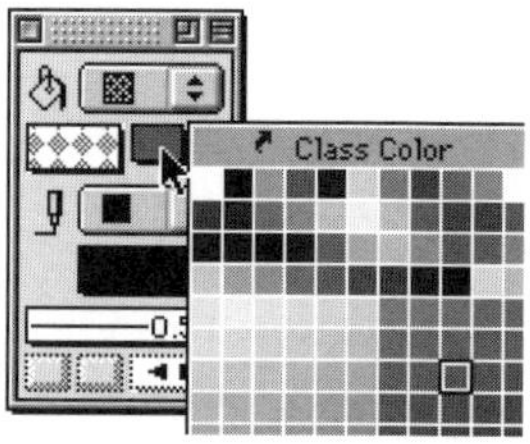

Now select the stairs and go through the same steps with the *Attributes* palette. Again, no changes will be seen on the object until it is rendered because it is 3D only, not hybrid, although you can see the selected colors on the *Attributes* palette if the object is selected.

Change this layer to *Left Isometric* view and select *Rendering>Solid*. Notice how the color appears on both objects.

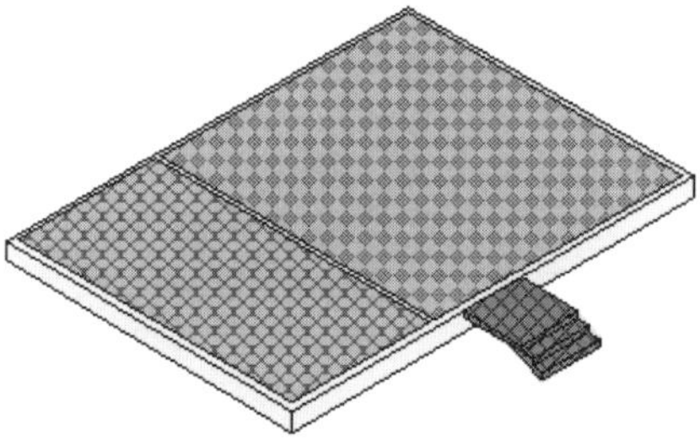

Go to each of the layers and change the colors of the objects. Then go to the *linked model* layer and look at the drawing. Select *Rendering>Solid* and then *Shaded Solid*.

Now try selecting *Rendering>Shaded No Lines*. This *Rendering* option works well if you have a color selected for the fill although the shading does change the colors.

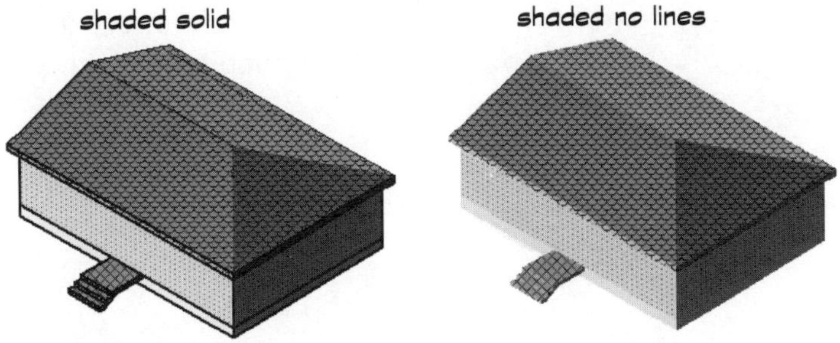

Symbols In Walls

When symbols are placed in one of the original layers, they will automatically be seen in the *linked model* layer. We will import and place some of the symbols previously created.

Step 1 - importing symbols

Select *PALETTES>RESOURCES* to have the *RESOURCES* palette open if it is not already checked. Navigate in the palette's scrolling list to the *chapt 5 [chapt 5.mcd]* file. This should be located in the *experiments* folder. Select the file name in the scrolling list and then the *ENTER* button or you can just double-click the name. If the buttons are not visible, click the second top button to expand the palette.

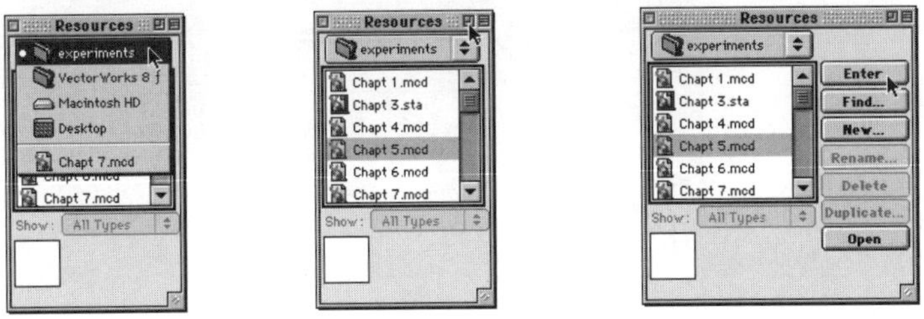

The different symbols and resources that were created in this file, *chapt 5 [chapt 5.mcd]*, are listed in the scrolling list. Click the hybrid symbol, *door 36x84 (door 90x200)*, press the *Command [Control]* key, click *window dh30x48 (window 75x120)*, to select both and then the *IMPORT* button.

Navigate to the bottom of the pop-out list to the active file, *chapt 7 [chapt 7.mcd]*. Notice that these symbols are now residing in this file as well. Any changes made to the symbols here will not be reflected back to the symbols in the original file.

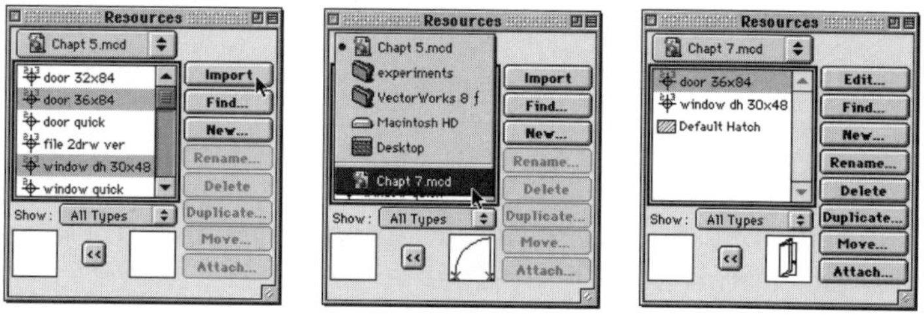

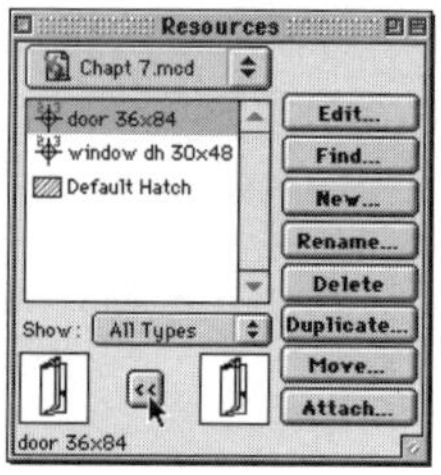

Step 2 - placing and viewing symbols

In the *Resources* palette click the door symbol name in the scrolling list and click the arrow button to move it from the preview window to the selected symbol window. Double-clicking the symbol name in the scrolling list does the same thing. Make *walls* the active layer and the view *Top/Plan*. Select the *2d Symbol Insertion* tool.

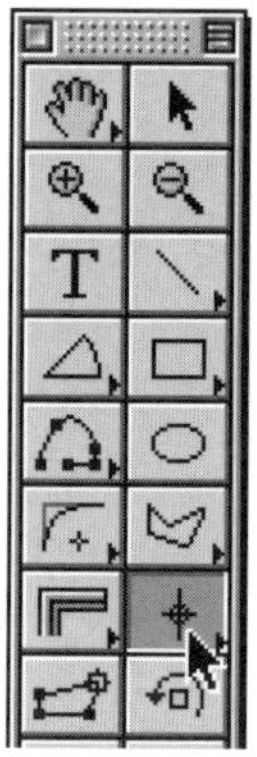

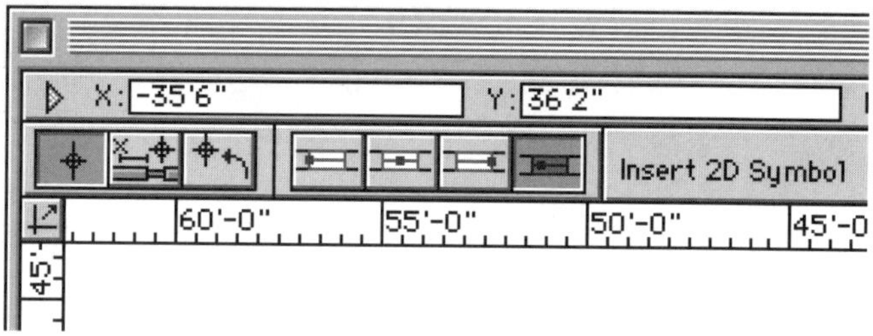

Notice the new icons in the mode bar. The first icon is the default for placing a symbol with a mouse click. The second icon is for placing a symbol an exact distance from a point within a wall, and the third is for selecting a symbol. The second group of icons shifts the insertion point for a selected symbol within a wall. The last icon of this group uses the default insertion point when the symbol was created.

Place a few doors by clicking on the walls. Notice how the wall gets cut. Place several more doors, but instead of clicking, press/drag the mouse around the insertion point. Notice that a dashed outline of the symbol appears and the symbol revolves around its insertion point. If you can not see the outline, *Zoom-In* closer.

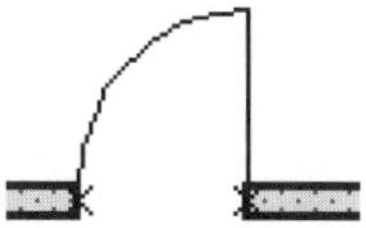

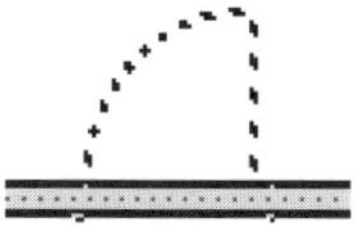

Also place a door on the drawing but not on a wall. With the *2D Selection* tool, try press/dragging the symbol onto the wall with the second modifier icon in the mode bar selected and then with it not selected. Use the *I* key to toggle it on and off or just click. With this last example the dragged symbol will not cut the wall unless the second icon is selected, and it will be placed on top instead.

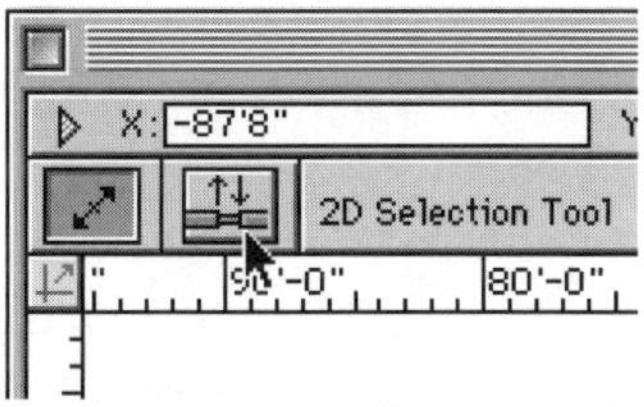

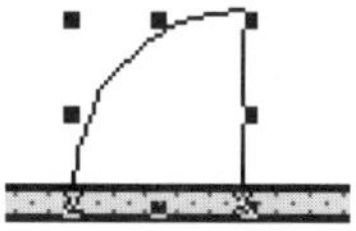

Step 3 - exactly placing symbols with cues

In order to place the door so that it will be centered on the lower wall and landing, first select the *2D Symbol Insertion* tool. Use the *I* key to toggle to the *center insertion point* in the mode bar. Then move the cursor along the lower wall and when the *smartcursor cue, center* appears, press to place the door and drag to either side of the door and wall to set the direction and side of the door swing. Release the mouse when the symbol is placed with the door opening inwards. Before deselecting the tool, cycle back to the last icon with the *I* key so that the original insertion point is now selected. This lower wall will have at least three points where the *cue center* appears. Make sure it is the center for the whole wall segment.

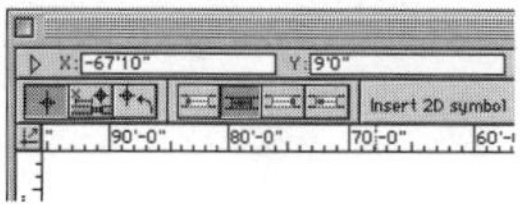

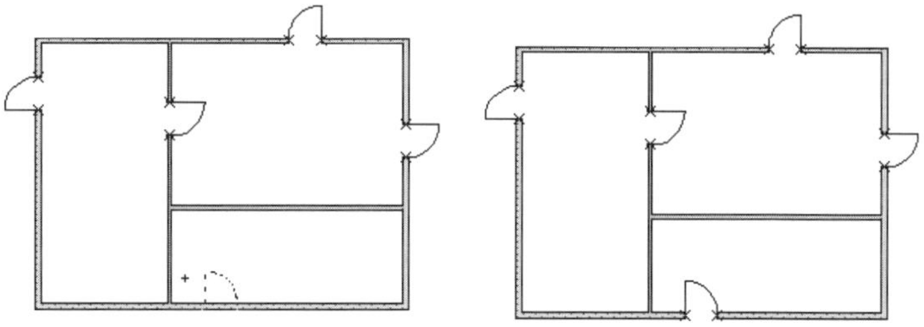

Step 4 - exactly placing symbols with references

Double-click the window symbol in the *Resources* palette and select the *2d Symbol Insertion* tool. We will place two windows so that they are 4'-0" (1.20m) on-center and centered on the space to the right of the door we just placed using the new *set reference point* icon. Use the *U* key to cycle to this second icon. You may need to click the drawing to make the drawing window active instead of the *Resources* palette.

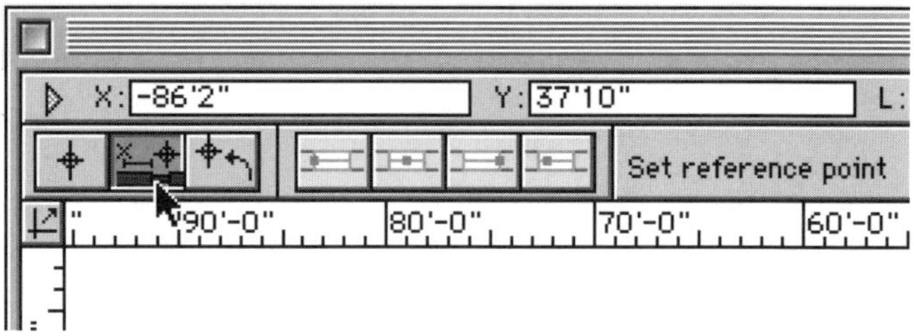

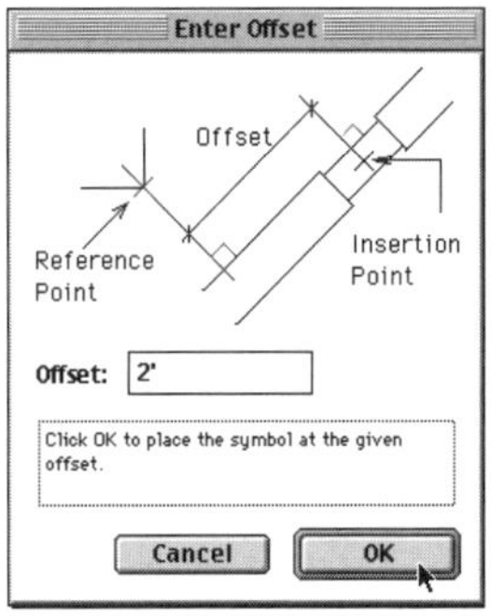

Making use of *smartcursor cues*, snap to the center of the wall segment to the right of the door. Notice that the *smartcursor* recognizes a different center for the interior and exterior side since each face has a different length. Snap to *center* on the exterior face, press at this point to set the reference point, drag towards the side you want to place the window and release, and then click to open the *Enter Offset* dialog box. Enter 2'-0" (.60m) into the *offset* edit box and click *ok*. The location of the symbol adjusts to the distance entered from the reference point. So basically, you press/drag from a specific point, release, and click. The amount you drag is not important - only the direction.

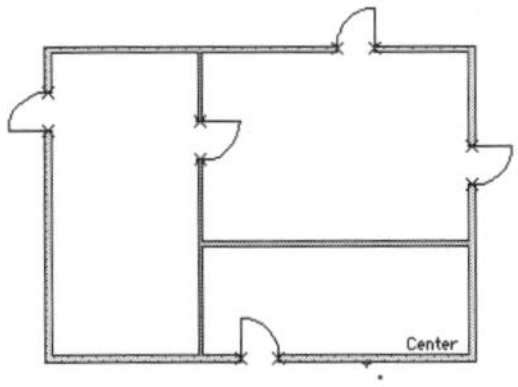

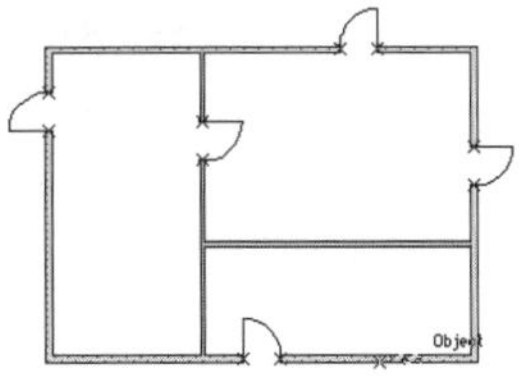

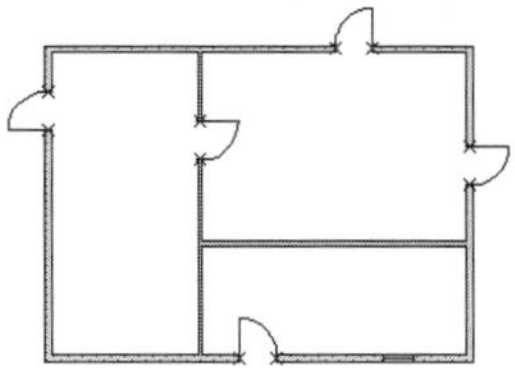

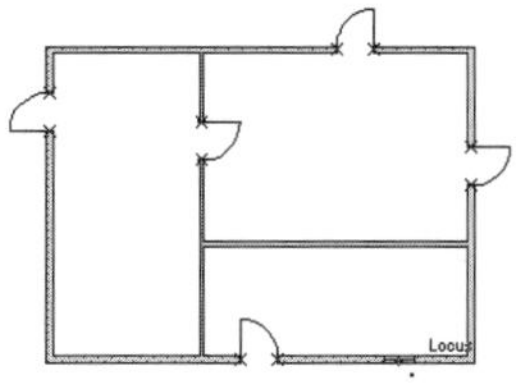

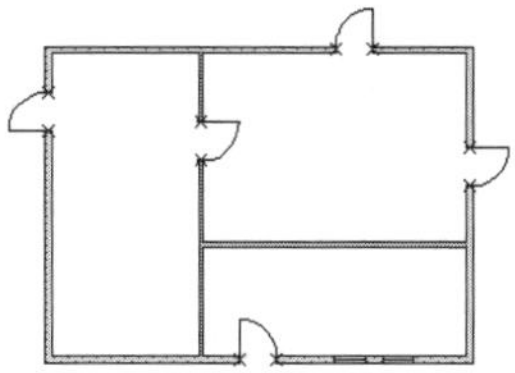

For the next window, snap to the center of the first window. The *cue* will be *locus*. Press/drag to the left and click. When the ENTER OFFSET box opens enter 4'-0" (1.20m) and click OK. It is not necessary to enter a minus sign since you set the direction when you press/dragged - use the minus sign if you need to reverse the direction. Now both windows are centered on this wall segment and are 4'-0" (1.20m) on-center with each other.

As a note, the *smartcursor cues* for a wall recognize the overall center for each wall length. Once a symbol is placed in a wall or another wall joins this wall length, you can also find the center for each segment.

Place a few more windows on the building. Now go back to the *linked model* layer and select *VIEW>RENDERING>SOLID*. You can see how the symbols automatically cut the wall.

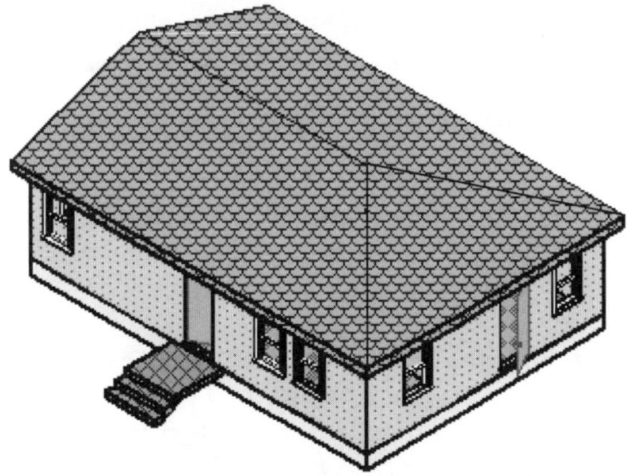

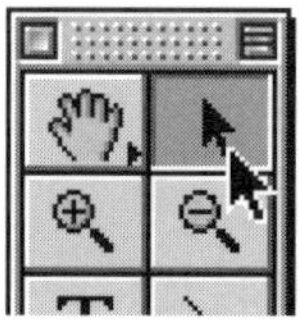

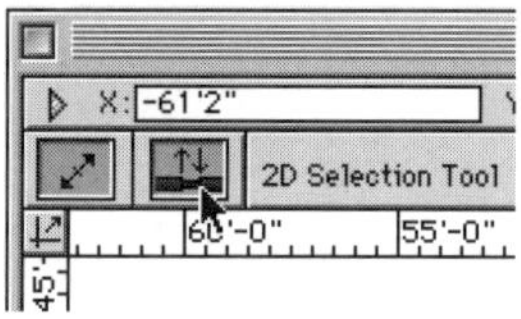

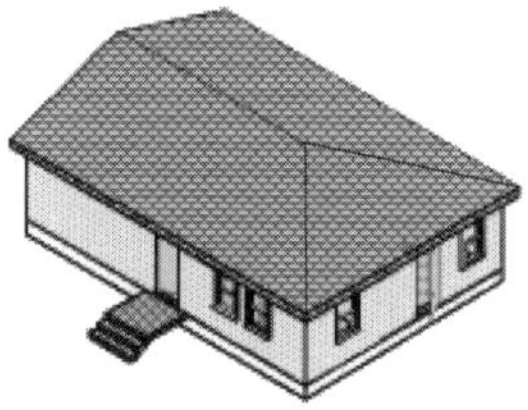

Step 5 - removing symbols

Go back to the *walls* layer. With the *2D Selection* tool and its second modifier icon selected, press/drag a symbol away from a wall in *Top/Plan* view to see how the wall gets automatically healed. If this icon is selected, a symbol can now be deleted from a wall without first press/dragging it away.

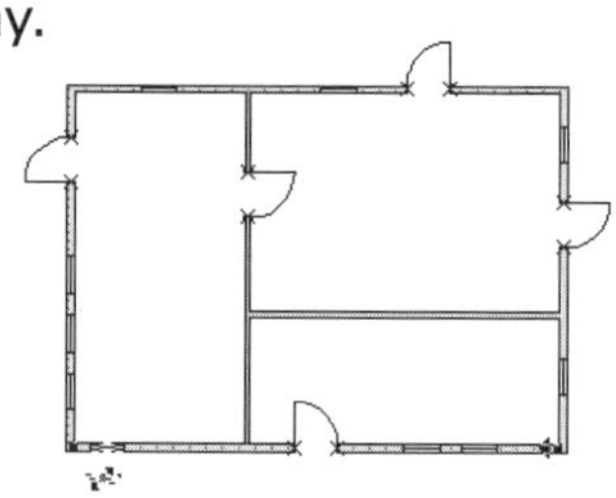

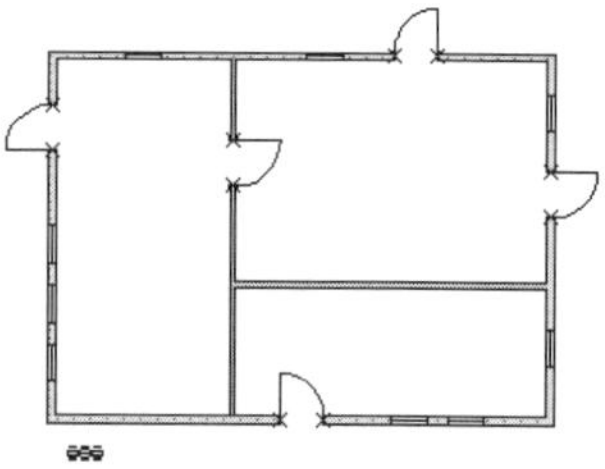

Notice that the *2D Selection* tool has two different icons. Symbols respond differently depending on whether the second icon is selected or not. If the icon is deselected, the symbol gets locked within the wall and press/dragging only changes its location. Also note that the cursor is the *resize* cursor when dragging a symbol within a wall, not the *press/drag* cursor.

Step 6 - selecting a symbol

Now before going back to the *linked model* layer we will quickly place one more door. Just select the *2D Symbol Insertion* tool, cycle with the *U* key so that the third icon, *pick up symbol*, is selected, and click on a door. This changes the selected symbol in the *Resources* palette.

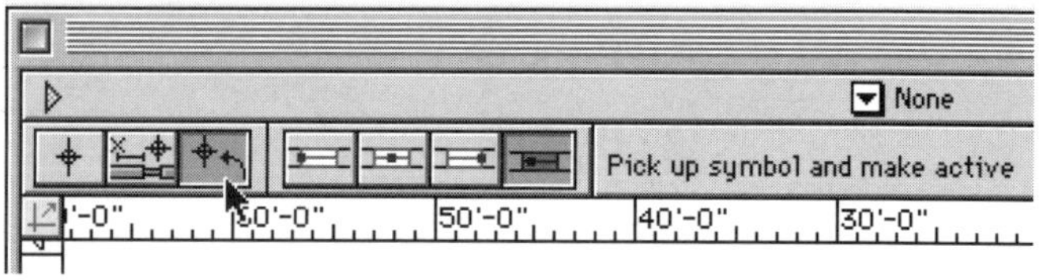

Place a door 4" (.10m) away from a wall intersection either using the *smartcursor* and the first icon or using the *set reference point* mode - in fact it is a good idea to try both. Go back to the *linked model* layer to see how the model changes as well.

Creating Perspectives

Once a 3D drawing is created, it is easy to show a perspective view.

Step 1 - bird's eye view

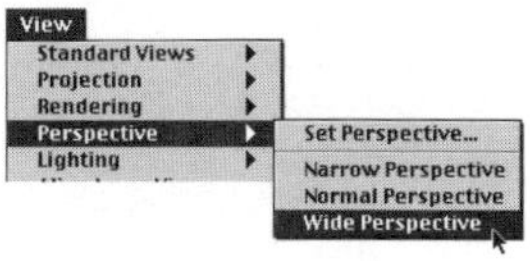

With the *linked model* layer active change the view to *TOP* and *VIEW>PERSPECTIVE>WIDE PERSPECTIVE.* The view will change to a bird's eye perspective. If you want to see inside of the building, the *RENDERING* needs to be in *WIRE-FRAME*, otherwise you would have to go back to the *roof* layer and change the roof fill to *NONE*. Be aware that the location of the model on the sheet affects the perspective, since the vanishing point is in the middle of the sheet.

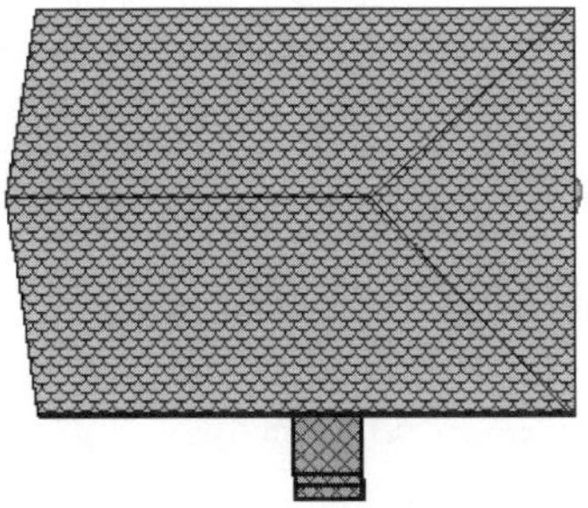

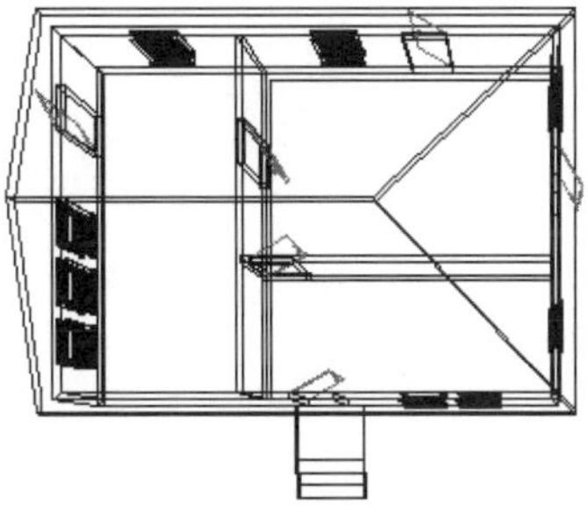

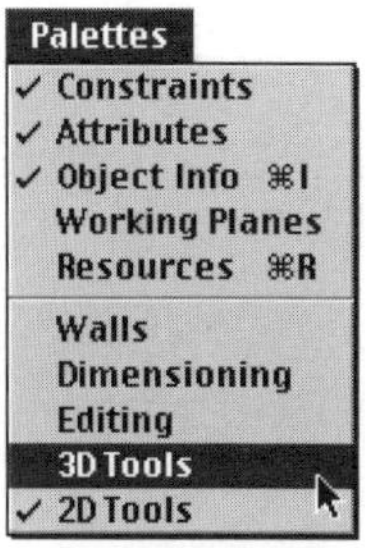

Step 2 - other perspective views

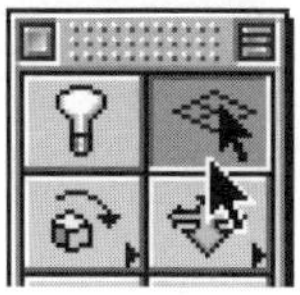

If you select the *3D SELECTION* tool in the *3D TOOLS* palette, you will see five icons in the mode bar. If the palette is not opened go to *PALETTES>3D TOOLS*. Clicking each one will change the view from *TOP* to *FRONT* to *RIGHT* side and to the two front isometric views. The images will differ depending on whether the *PROJECTION* is *PERSPECTIVE* or *ORTHOGONAL*.

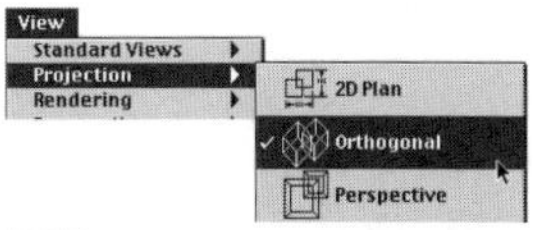

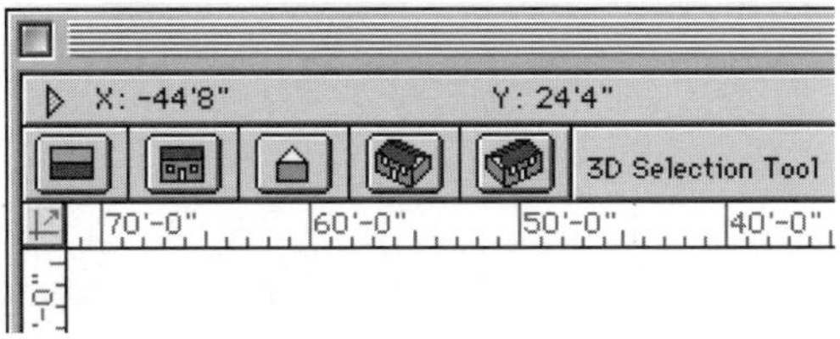

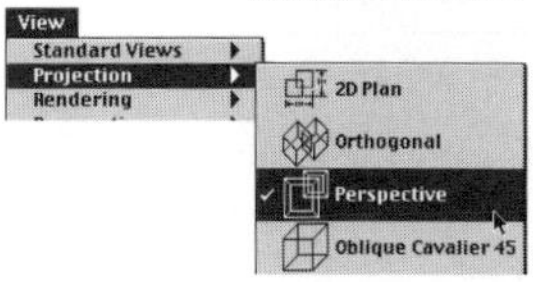

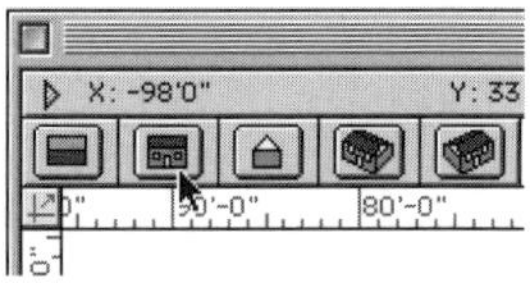
X: -98'0"
Y: 33
90'-0"
80'-0"

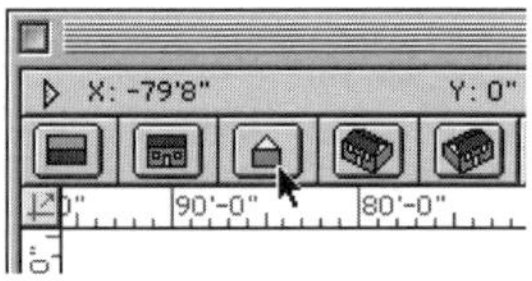
X: -79'8"
Y: 0"
90'-0"
80'-0"

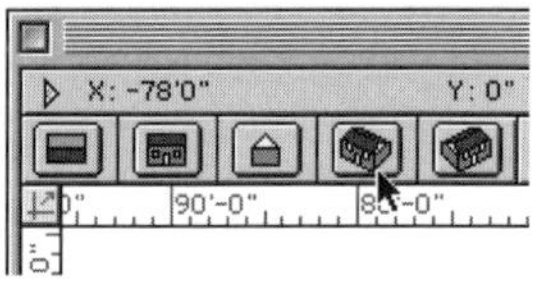
X: -78'0"
Y: 0"
90'-0"

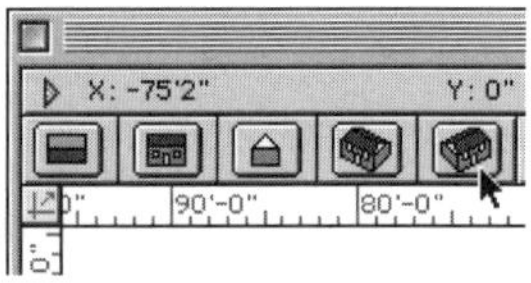
X: -75'2"
Y: 0"
90'-0"
80'-0"

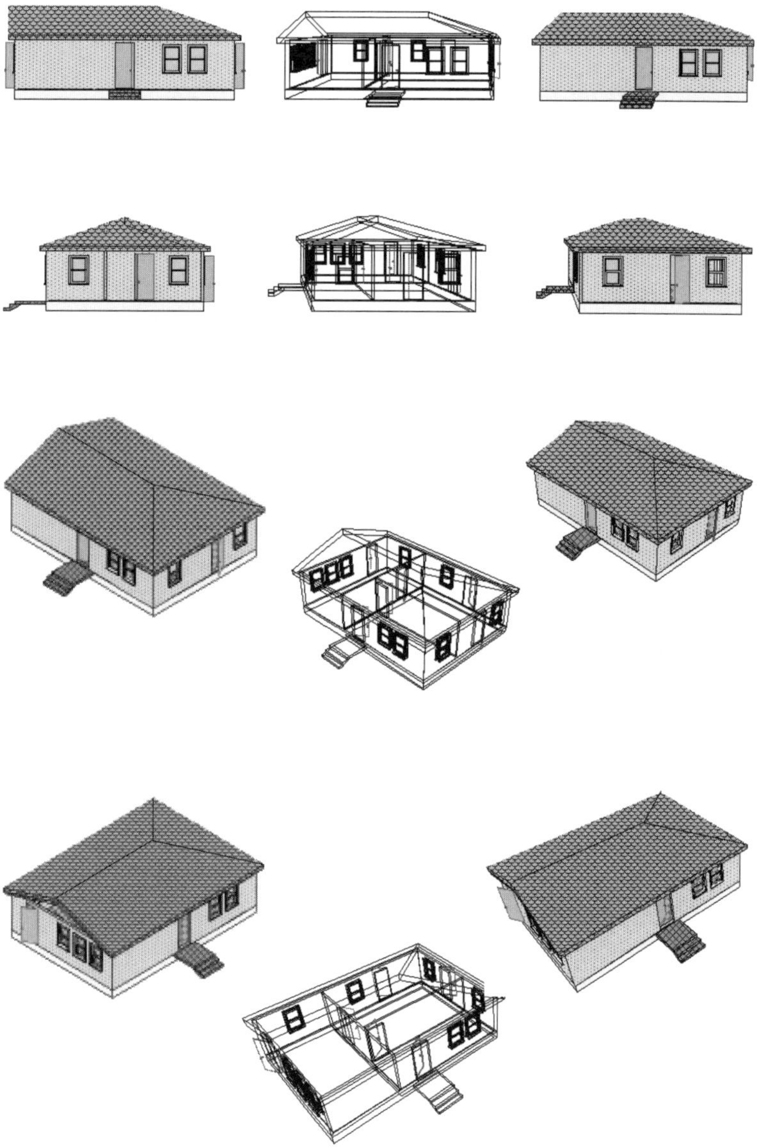
Orthogonal - Solid
Perspective - Wireframe
Perspective - Solid

Creating A Custom Perspective

You can also set up your own perspective with specific station points and horizon lines.

Step 1 - locating the station point

Go back to *Top/Plan* in the *linked model* layer. Select *VIEW>Set 3D View*. Now press/drag from the desired station point or place where the viewer is located towards the view point.

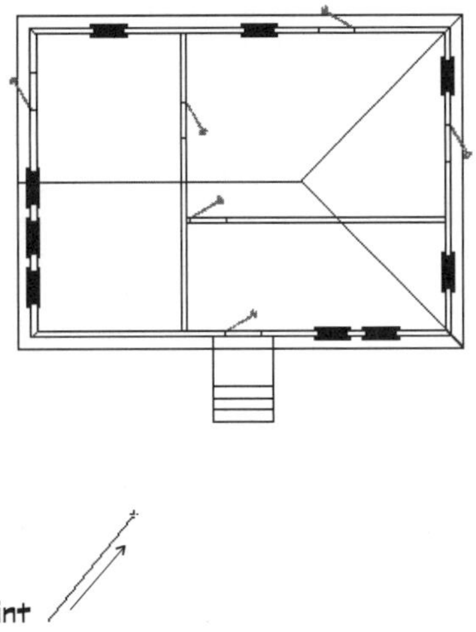

Step 2 - viewer height and cone of vision

The *Set 3D View* dialog box opens. Enter 5'-0" (1.50m) for *VIEWER HEIGHT* and 4$^1/_2$' (1.30m) for *LOOK TOWARD HEIGHT*. Select *NORMAL* for *PERSPECTIVE* which sets the cone of vision, and then click *OK*.

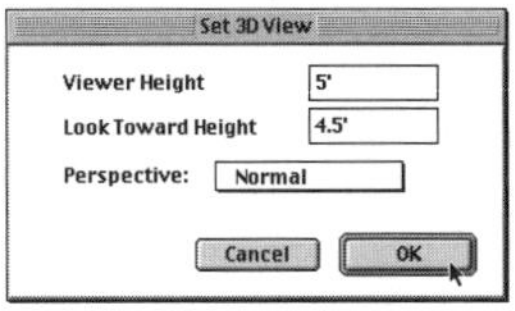

Step 3 - viewing the perspective

Depending on many variants, you may be able to see all or just part of the 3D view. Press/drag the *clipping frame* corners to view more of the perspective. Do note, that if you want to print the image, it has to be within the printable area demarcated by the *printable boundary* rectangle. If it extends beyond that edge you would need to use the *Walkthrough* tool to move further back.

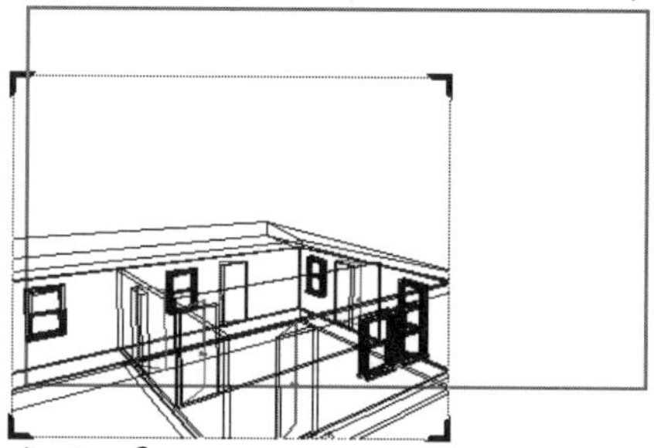

Step 4 - walking through the perspective

Select *VIEW>RENDERING>SOLID* and the *WALKTHROUGH* tool and place the cursor in the middle of the drawing window, which may be different than the middle of the *clipping frame*.

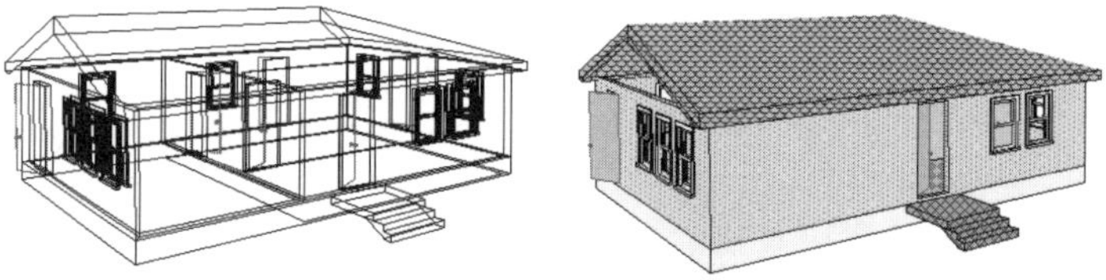

Now to move closer in, very slowly press/drag the cursor upwards. The higher the cursor is above center, the quicker the movement. Notice that the space is in *WIREFRAME* when moving, but when the mouse is released, it will re-render. Also notice the *clipping frame*. Press/drag the corners to resize the viewable area.

To move back from the building, press/drag downwards below the center of the drawing. To move left, slowly drag the cursor to the left of center, and to move right, drag it towards the right. You can even move through the walls and into the building and change your viewing direction within the rooms.

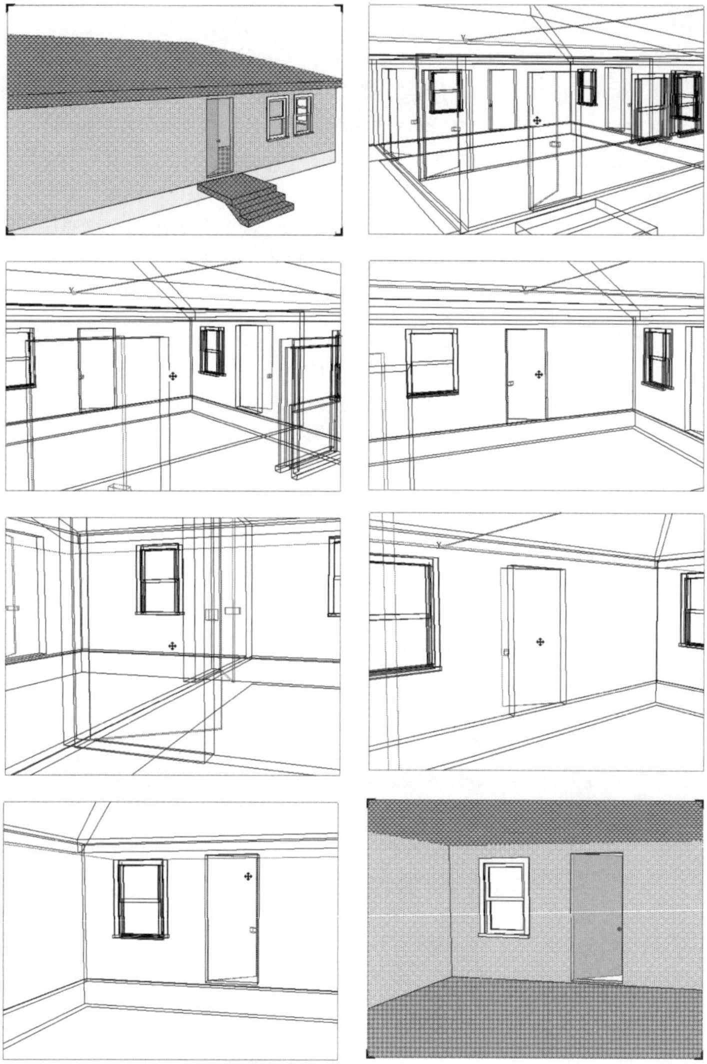

If you want to move the *VIEWER HEIGHT* upwards, press the *Option [Control]* key and press/drag upwards. To change the viewer's *LOOK TOWARD HEIGHT* upwards, press the *Option [Control]* key and press/drag towards the left of center. And of course, pressing the *Option [Control]* key and moving the mouse in the opposite direction moves the *VIEWER HEIGHT* and viewer's *LOOK TOWARDS HEIGHT* in reverse.

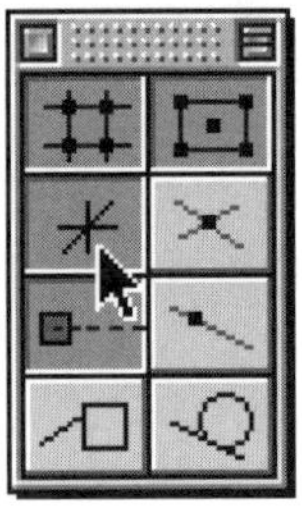

SECTIONS

Once you have a 3D drawing, a section can easily be generated. The section is actually a 3D duplicate of part of the original object which can also be viewed and revised separately. If the drawing is created on several layers, you would take the section on the *linked model* layer. If all of the information is on one layer than take the section on that one layer. Sections are not linked, so any changes to the original layers will not be reflected in the section.

Cutting A 3D Section

In the drawing we are working in, make the *linked model* layer the active layer, the view to either *Top/Plan* or *Top*, and the *Projection* to *2D Plan*. Sections can be taken in other views as well.

Step 1 - creating a section

Select the *MODEL>Cut 3D Section* command. Now with the mouse, press/drag a cut line where you want the building sectioned, using the *S* key to toggle the *Constrain Angle* constraint on. When you release the mouse an arrow appears, similarly to when the roof was created. This time click on the side of the cut line to determine which side is to be the sectioned piece.

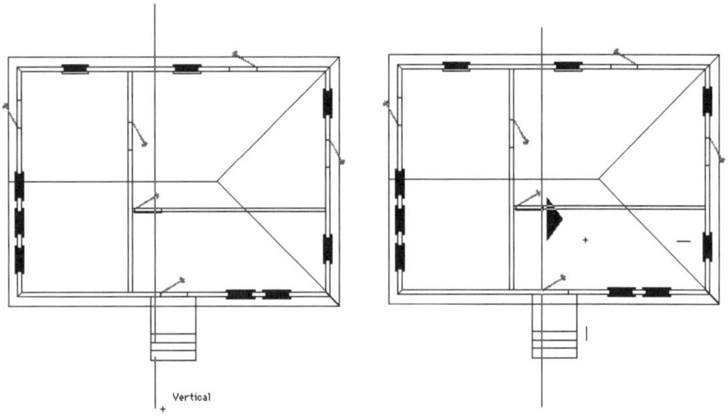

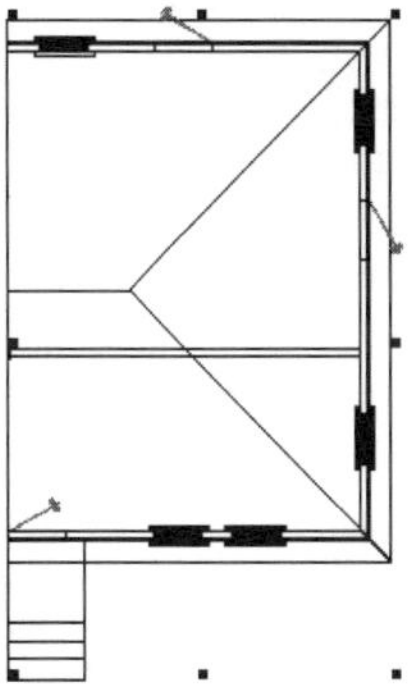

Step 2 - working with the section

When the *Cut 3D Section* command is used, it will automatically create a new layer, in this case *layer-1*, and make it active. The new layer will also be in the same view as the original layer. The *Cut 3D Section* command automatically decomposes both walls and symbols into 3D polygons and it creates a grouped object which can be modified with the *Edit Group* command. This is a 3D section, though, and can be shown in any of the other views or rendering options as well as perspective. Remember that the section is not linked, so any changes made to the original layers will not be reflected.

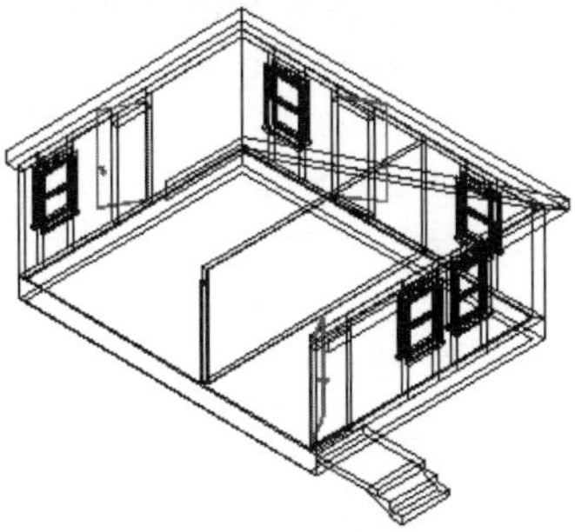

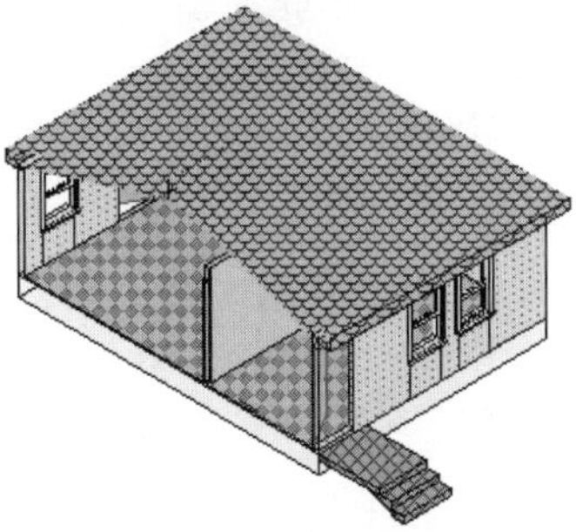

You can relocate the section onto another layer by using *Cut* and *Paste*. For now, leave it on the new layer. Go into the *Layers Setup* dialog box, select *layer-1*, use the *Tab* key to highlight the *name* edit box, and rename the layer *section*

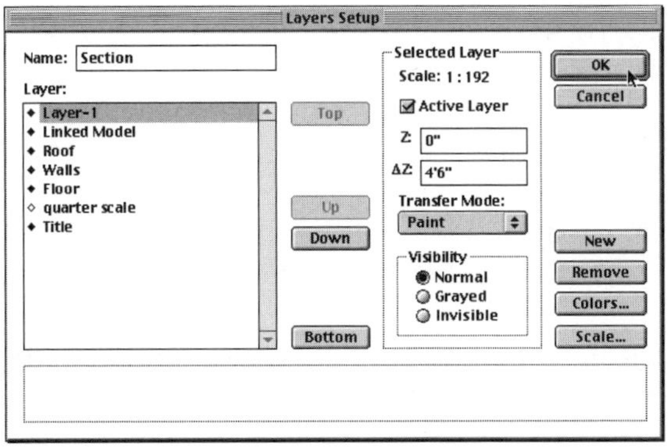

If you were cutting and pasting, you would remove this new layer **after** you relocate the section with the *REMOVE* button in the *LAYERS SETUP* dialog box. Remember that whatever linked layer you are pasting it into, the 3D section will be in the same view. *SAVE* and *QUIT [EXIT]* the file you have been working with.

THE 3D DRAWING IN SUMMATION

The great advantage to working with computers is that once the plan is drawn, you do not need to redraw each elevation, section, etc. In my opinion, aside from the *smartcursor*, *CREATE LAYER LINK* happens to be one of the more powerful features in VectorWorks. As you can see, once the different elements of a drawing are created, there are many options for viewing each element. The ability to add color and textures to an object is quite helpful even if you do not have a color printer and even if the texturing and rendering capabilities are somewhat minimal.

- When using the *ALIGN LAYER VIEWS* command, be aware of the different *z* values in the *LAYERS SETUP* dialog box.

- The *z* value in the *LAYERS SETUP* dialog box only comes into play when using linked model layers.

- Objects that do not have a surface, or have a fill with *NONE* selected, or are rendered in *WIREFRAME* (transparent), can only be selected by clicking the edge or marquee selecting.

- 3D objects that are in *WIREFRAME* will not show their fill patterns or color until rendered *SOLID*.

- The *STRAIGHT STAIR* tool makes 2D, or 3D, or both 2D and 3D objects, but it is not considered a hybrid tool. If you want the stairs to appear appropriately for both 2D and the 3D views, create both objects and with both selected make a symbol. The symbol will be hybrid.

- Symbols can be rotated when placed by press/dragging rather than clicking.

- The location of the insertion point in a symbol can be changed with the *I* key before it is placed.

- Symbols can now be press/dragged onto a wall and have it cut the wall if the second icon is selected with the *2D SELECTION* tool.

- Symbols can be set so that only their position can be changed within a wall if the second icon of the *2D SELECTION* tool is not selected.

- Symbols can be placed exactly within a wall either with the *smartcursor* or by selecting the *SET REFERENCE POINT* icon.

- A symbol can be made active in the *RESOURCES* palette by clicking on an already placed symbol on the drawing with the *PICK UP SYMBOL AND MAKE ACTIVE* icon of the *2D SYMBOL INSERTION* tool.

- 3D sections are not dynamically linked to the original layers. Any changes to the original plans will therefor not be reflected in the section.

- In *TOP/PLAN* view, roof, walls, and floors will not need to be rendered for the fill color or *PATTERN* to appear, but stairs made with the *STRAIGHT STAIR* tool will. The roof, floor, and walls are hybrid objects, having both a 2D and a 3D component. The stairs we created were 3D only. 3D objects need to be rendered *SOLID* in order to see fills, whether color or *PATTERN*.

NOTES, DOODLES, & OTHER THINGS

Chapter 8

WORKING WITH MULTIPLE VIEWS

WHY MULTIPLE VIEWS

There are times when you might want to show the plan, an elevation or two, an isometric, and a section all on the same sheet and all at the same time. You would naturally want to take advantage of the computer and not have to redraw each view or even have to cut and paste copies of the different views. This would be done similarly to creating a linked layer but taking it one step further.

The tools, commands, constraints, and palettes we will be exploring are;

Constrained Linear Dimension Tool
Round Wall Tool
Add Surface Command
Create Layer Link Command
Lock Command
Reference Marker Command
Unlock Command
Wide Perspective Command
Snap To Edge Constraint
Object Info Palette

SETTING UP THE MULTI-VIEW SHEET

We will need to open the previous file we were working with and save it under another name. Double-click the *chapt 7 [chapt 7.mcd]* file. Then create a new document by selecting the *Save As* command and name it *chapt 8 [chapt 8.mcd]*. The *chapt 7 [chapt 7.mcd]* file will automatically close and be replaced with the new file.

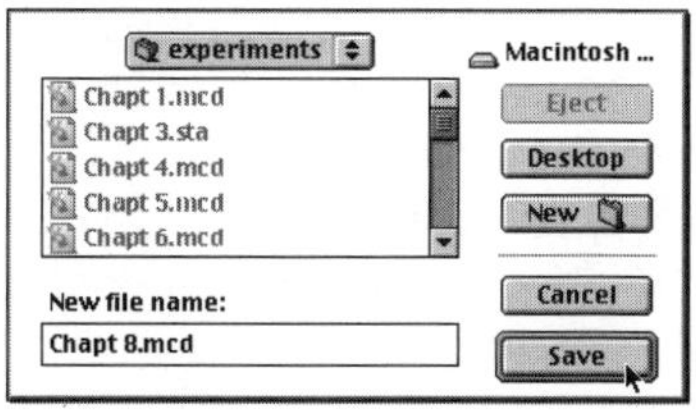

Creating Multiple Views

Basically we will be creating several linked layers, same as in the previous file, and linking them back to the original layers. The difference is, we will create a linked layer for each view we wish to see.

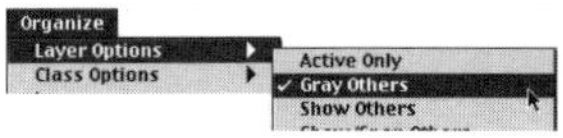

Step 1 - creating the layers

Change the *LAYER OPTIONS* to *GRAY OTHERS* and the *RENDERING* to *WIREFRAME*. Open the *LAYERS SETUP* dialog box and create 5 new layers all in $^1/_{16}$" (1:200) scale and with *z* and Δ*z [±z]* heights equaling 0 naming them; *ll plan, ll front, ll left, ll isometric,* and *ll perspective*. *ll* is short for linked layer.

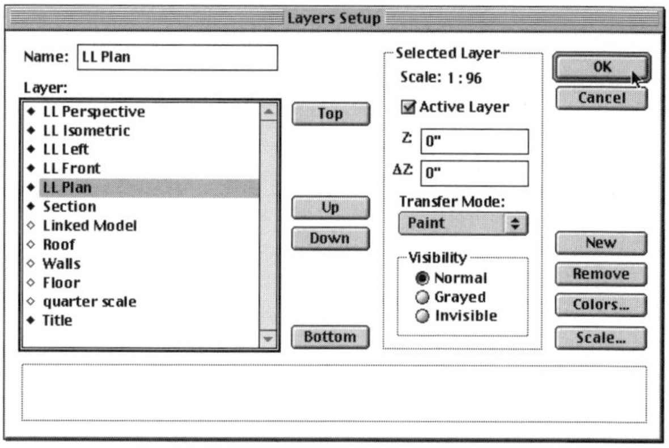

Notice that if you create the first new layer and change the *LAYER SCALE*, then each of the following layers will use the same scale. Make sure that the *SCALE TEXT* box is not checked in this dialog box.The *z* and sometimes the Δ*z [±z]* values are automatically calculated and need to be changed. By using the word linked, or the letters ll, or something else to clue you into the fact that these are linked model layers helps avoid linking a linked model layer to another linked layer.This is not as big an issue as earlier versions of the program, but do note, if a linked layer is linked to another linked layer, it will not render unless you are using *WIREFRAME* or *QD3D*. Make the layer *linked model, floor, roof,* and *walls* layers *INVISIBLE* before you select *OK*.

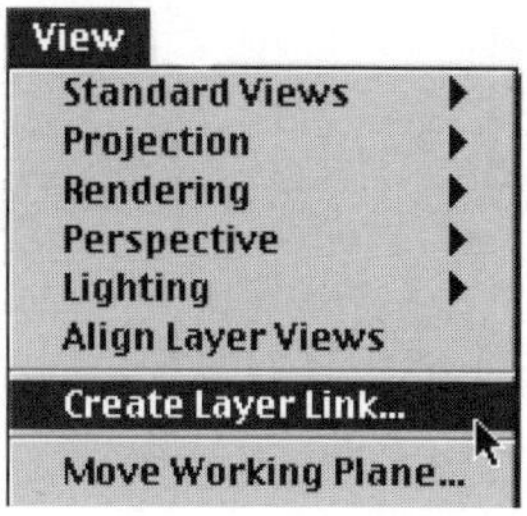

Step 2 - linking the multiple layers

With *II plan* the active layer, select *VIEW>CREATE LAYER LINK* and *Command*-select [*Control*-select] the *floor, walls, and roof* layers. You will need to scroll through the list to find the other layers. Also select the *PROJECT 2D OBJECTS* box and then the *LINK* button.

Change the view to *Top/PLAN*. Notice that there is a text object for the scale designation floating around somewhere to the right that was originally included in the template. Go back to the *floor* layer, locate the text object, and delete it. It is automatically deleted from the model layer.

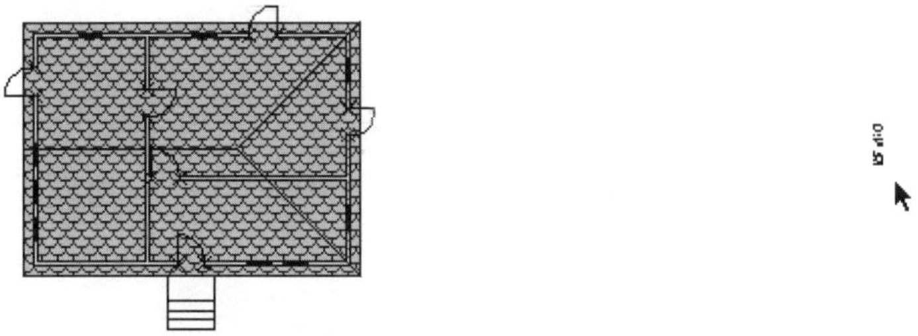

With *II front* the active layer, use the *CREATE LAYER LINK* command and again link the *floor, walls*, and *roof* layers. The *PROJECT 2D OBJECTS* box should not be checked on this layer nor on any of the following linked model layers. Change the view to *FRONT*.

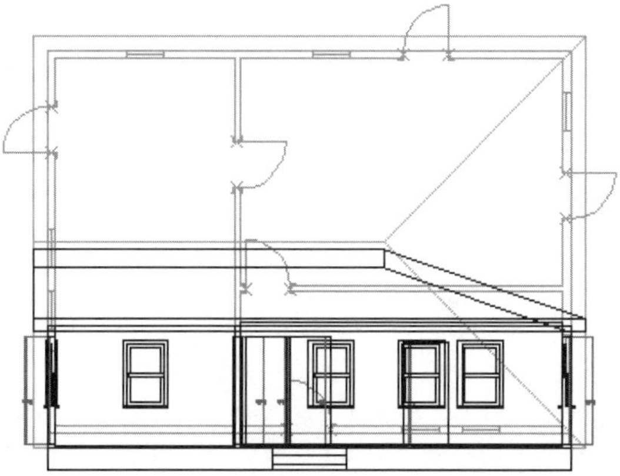

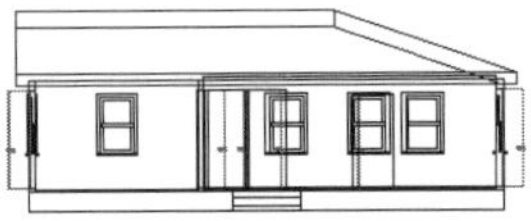

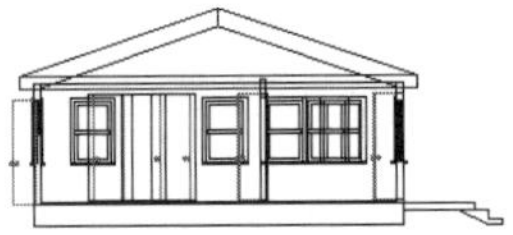

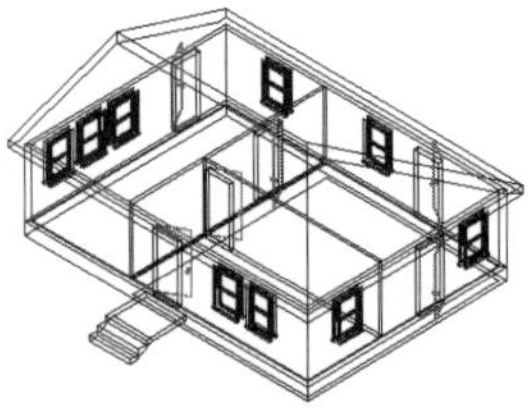

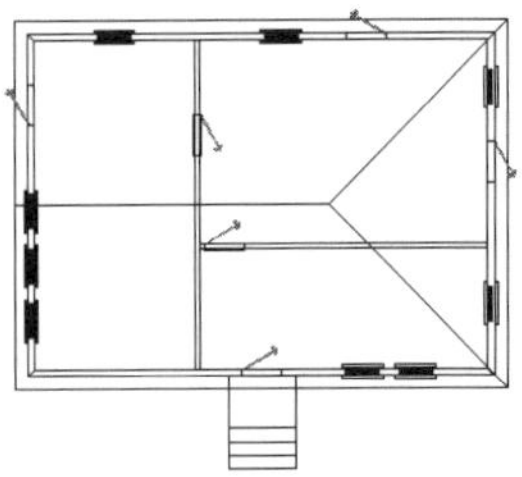

Notice that each of these linked layers are placed one on top of another. For right now do not worry about this, although you can change the *Layer Options* to *Active Only* if it really does bother you.

With *// left* the active layer, change the view to *Left* then link the same *floor, walls,* and *roof* layers.

With *// isometric* active, link the same three layers and change the view to *Right Isometric.*

And finally, with *// perspective*, link the *floor, walls*, and *roof* layers again, changing the view to *Top*.

All of the linked model layers appear in *Wireframe* except for the *// plan* layer which seems as if it is rendered *Solid.* Since the walls, roof, floor and the particular symbols we had used are hybrid objects, the 2D aspect does show with fill colors and *patterns* in *Top/Plan* even though it is not rendered. The stairs and floor pattern, though, do not appear with a fill in *Top/Plan*, because they are 3D objects only, without any 2D counterpart. Change *Layer Options* to *Active Only*. Notice the difference in how the hybrid door symbols appear in *Top* versus *Top/Plan.*

When we linked these layers on the linked model layers with the *CREATE LAYER LINK* command, we selected only the original or master layers and did not link any that had the word linked or *ll* in the name in the scrolling list. That is why we use the word linked or *ll*, or something else, because you should be aware of the limitations of a linked layer being linked to another linked layer.

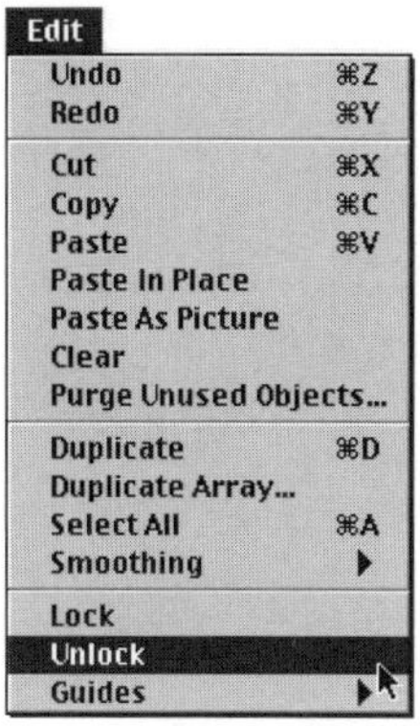

Step 3 - unlinking a layer

There are times you may want to change which of the original layers were actually linked. For instance, in the case of the *ll plan* layer you might want to see a floor plan rather than a roof plan.

With *ll plan* the active layer, *Option [Control]* press/drag through the building to select all of the objects, and then choose *EDIT>UNLOCK*. Use the *Option [Control]* key while press/dragging since some of the handles may be beyond the object itself so you might miss something.

Notice that the selection handles change from gray to black once the *UNLOCK* command was used. Click on the drawing to deselect and then select just the roof, which gets selected as one object rather than the 3 planes, and *Delete*. This deletes the link to the *roof* layer. Then choose *SELECT ALL* and *EDIT>LOCK*. This will only get rid of the link to that particular layer and does not delete or interfere in any way with the original or master layer. You could also *SELECT ALL* and use the command *UNLOCK*, then *Delete [Backspace]* to get rid of all of the linking on the model layer. This way you can start the linking process over. You may need to double-click the *PAN* tool to force a screen redraw.

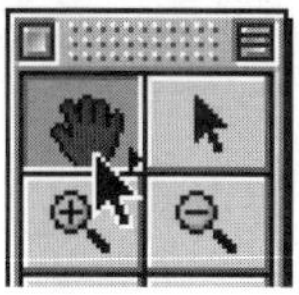

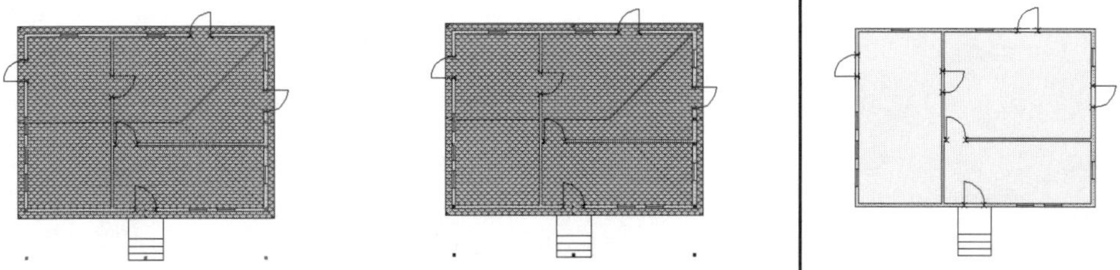

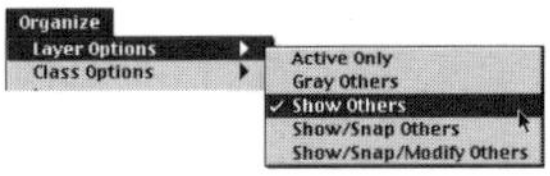

Step 4 - viewing multiple layers

Go to the *Layers Setup* dialog box and change the scale for the *// plan* layer to 1/8"=1'-0" [1:100] and select *ok*. Select *ORGANIZE>Layer Options>Show Others*. Notice that each of the linked model views are placed one on top of another.

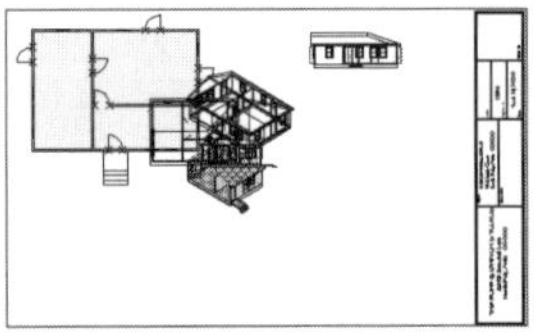

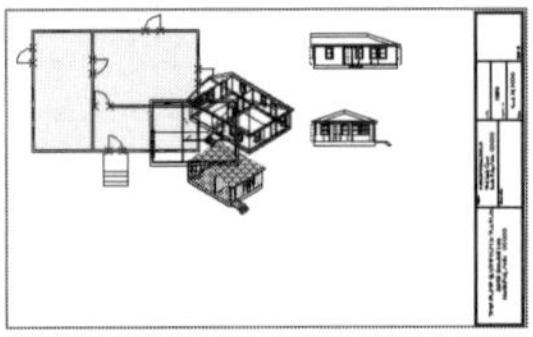

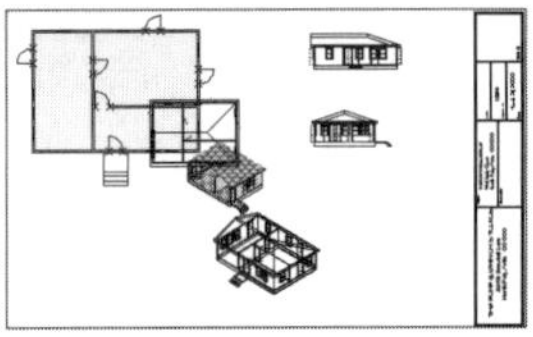

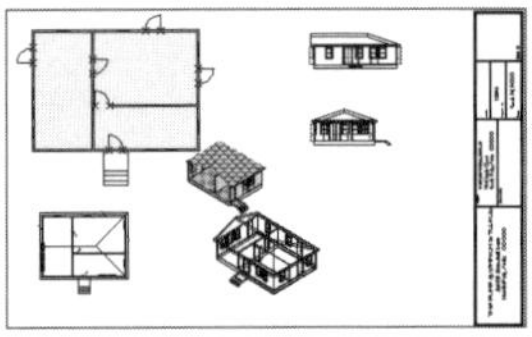

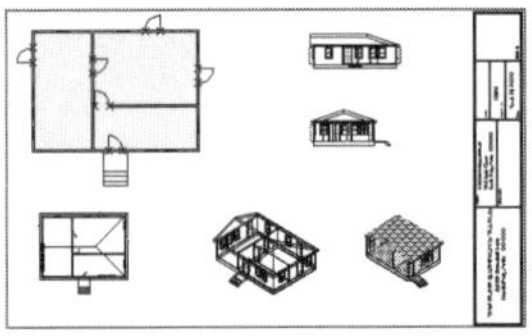

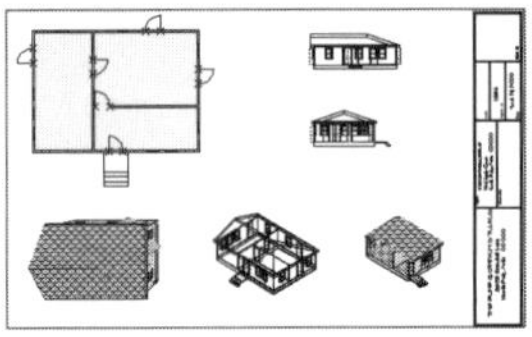

With *// plan* the active layer, do a *Select All* and choose the *Unlock* command. Press/drag the object moving it to the upper left corner of your sheet and with it still selected choose *Lock*.

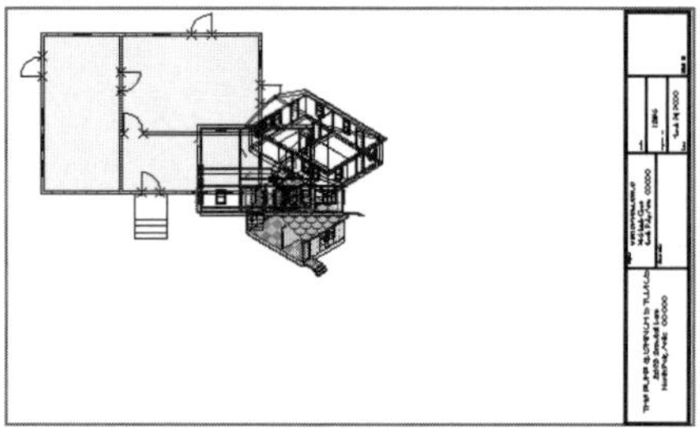

Do the same for each of the linked layers, by making each one the active layer, selecting and unlocking, moving to a new location, and relocking. Finally, make the *section* layer active and relocate the section. It is not necessary to *Lock* and *Unlock* it.

This way all of the linked layers are visible at the same time without blocking each other. The *title* and *section* layers are also visible even though they are not linked. Notice that this multiple viewing of linked layers allows objects at different scales to be visible at the same time.

With the *// perspective* layer active, use the *VIEW>Perspective>Wide Perspective* command to create a bird's eye view of the roof. If the perspective goes outside of the printable boundary, you may need to go back to *Orthogonal* projection, *Unlock* it, move the image, *Lock*, and reselect *Wide Perspective*. You may also want to use the *Walkthrough* tool to adjust its placement as well. Render this layer *Solid*.

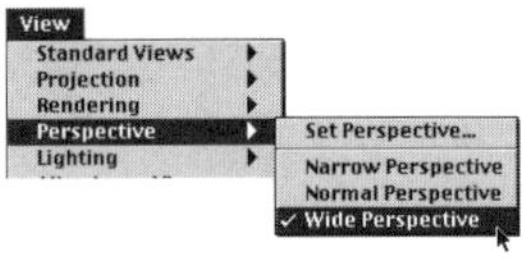

Step 5 - creating detail titles

We will want to place a title and scale for each individual image. Select *AEC>Create Markers>Reference Marker* to individually label each of these views on their respective layers.

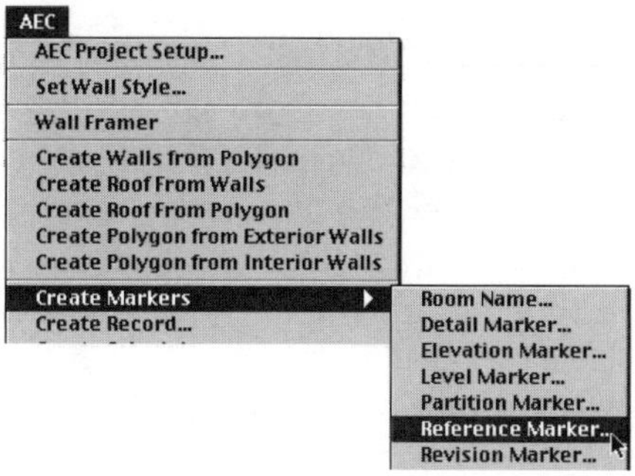

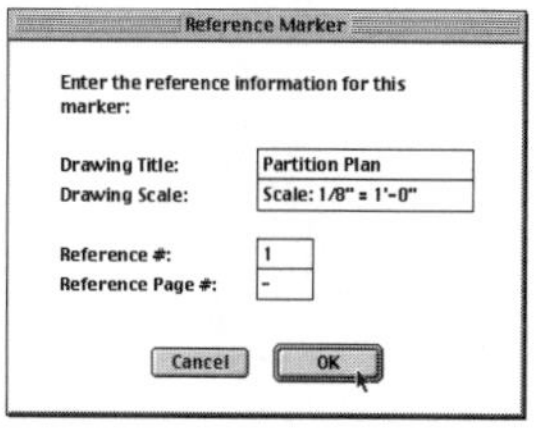

The command is smart enough to sense the scale for the active layer and insert it into the correct edit box in the *Reference Marker* dialog box that opens. When you enter the rest of the information and click *ok*, the dialog box closes and the *bulls eye* cursor appears. Click to place the left side of the title string. Now when you view the sheet, you can see a multitude of views, scales, and rendering options each clearly marked. If you need to change a marker, just select it and *Edit Group*.

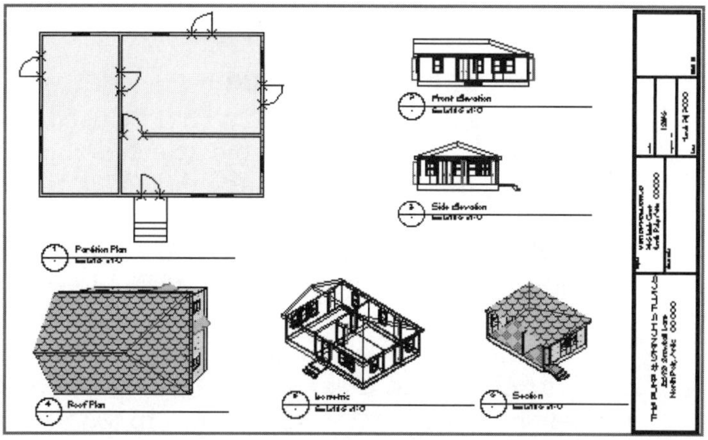

Using Multiple Layers

Now that this system is set up, let us see what we have. Change the LAYER OPTIONS to ACTIVE ONLY. Go back to the original layer, *floor*, and change the default line weight to the thinnest weight. Also change the view to TOP/PLAN.

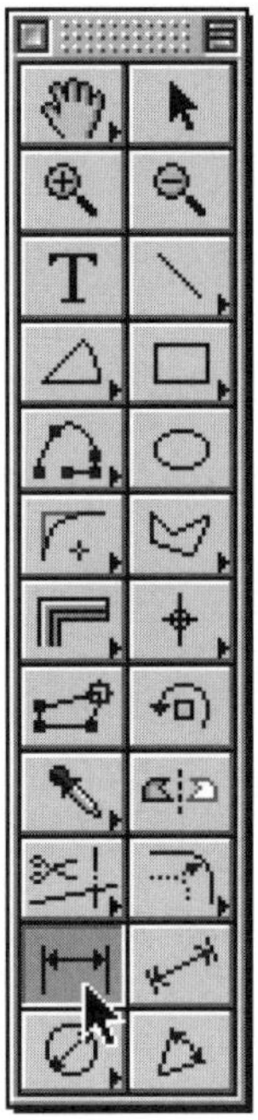

Step 1 - creating a dimension

The rectangle for the floor should be selected. Select the CONSTRAINED LINEAR DIMENSION tool and the right-most icon, SELECTED OBJECT(S) DIMENSION. Now click exactly where you want the dimension line located. The dimension line appears with the correct dimension. Easy!

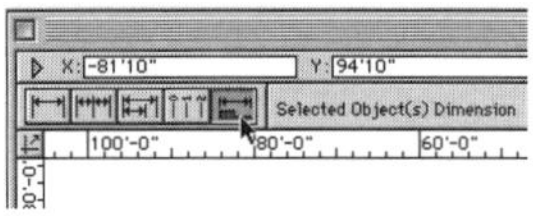

Follow the same steps, but click on the right for the vertical dimension. This particular modifier icon allows you to automatically dimension selected objects with a click.

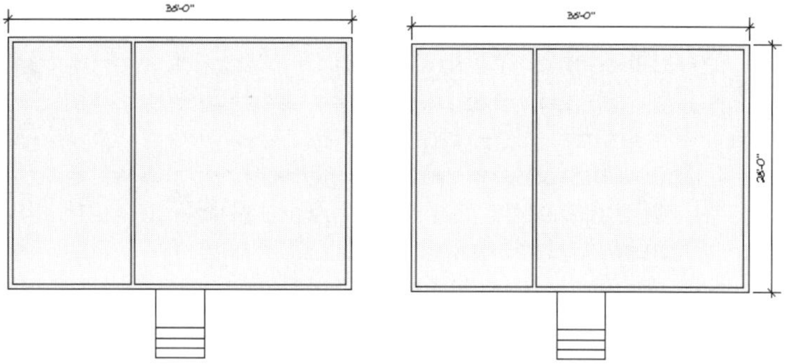

Step 2 - wall dimensioning

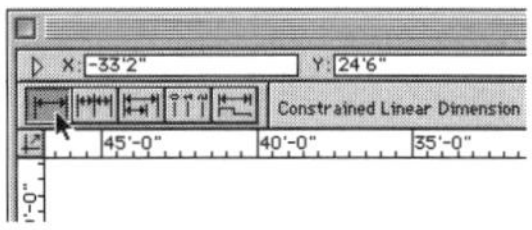

The previous modifier icon can not be used to dimension pieces of walls, only the whole selected object. Instead, select the first icon and change the active layer to *walls*.

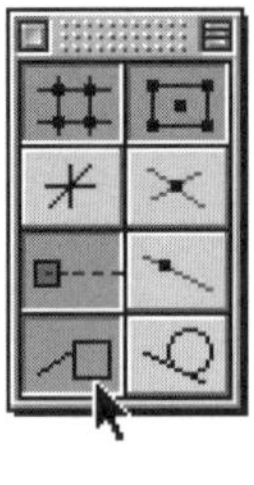

In order to locate a door opening off of a wall, press on a wall surface, drag to one corner of the door opening, and release, then click to establish the dimension line location. Be careful that you are snapping to the wall face and not its centerline. Make use of the SNAP TO EDGE constraint to align it perfectly using the *F* key to toggle it on and off.

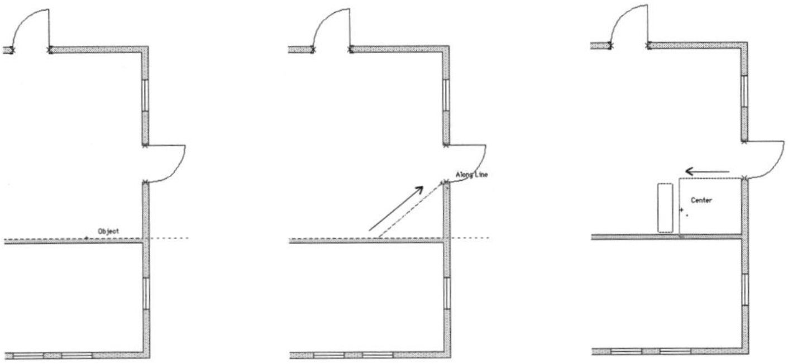

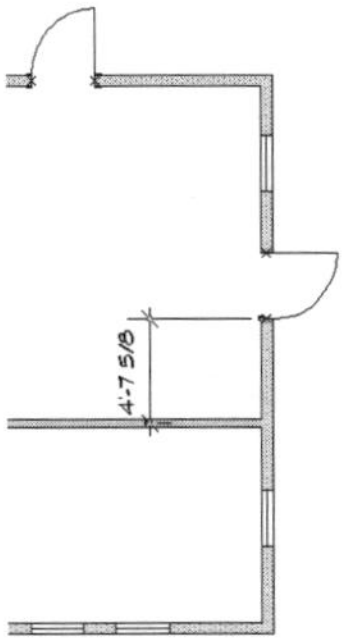

Step 3 - dimensions without witness lines

There are times you may only want dimension lines and markers without any witness lines. With the *Single Line* tool and the *constrained* modifier icon, place a line between two interior walls making use of the *Snap To Edge* constraint. The length of this line is what gets converted into the dimension so it is very important to place it exactly. The constraint can be toggled on an off with the *F* key. Since the *Snap To Edge* constraint does not always readily recognize an edge of a wall, use the *T* key to set the edge lock on the wall surface. With the line selected, choose the dimension line style in the *Attributes* palette. The selected line will convert to a dimension line.

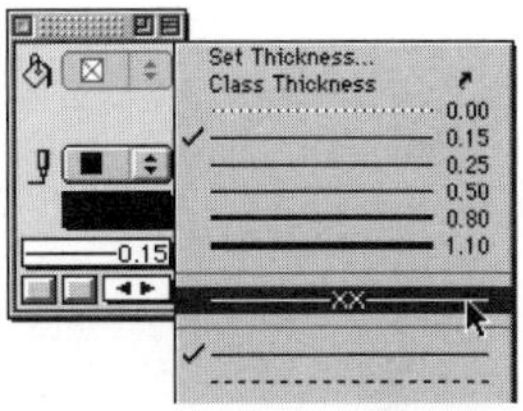

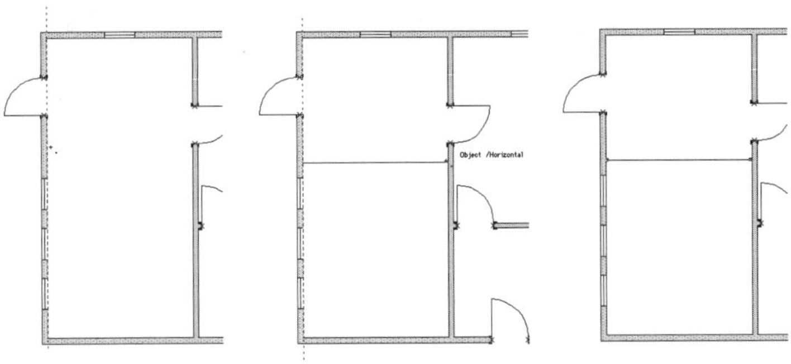

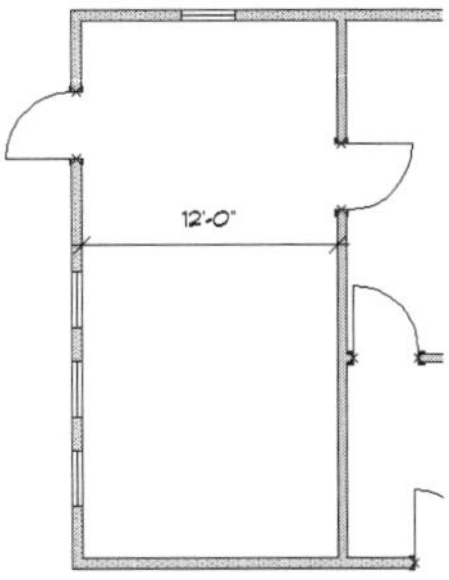

Step 4 - viewing the dimensions

Make the *ll plan* layer active and change to *Layer Options>Show Others*. Notice that the dimensions only show in the plan view. This is due to the *Create Layer Link>project 2d objects* box which was checked only in this layer when linked.

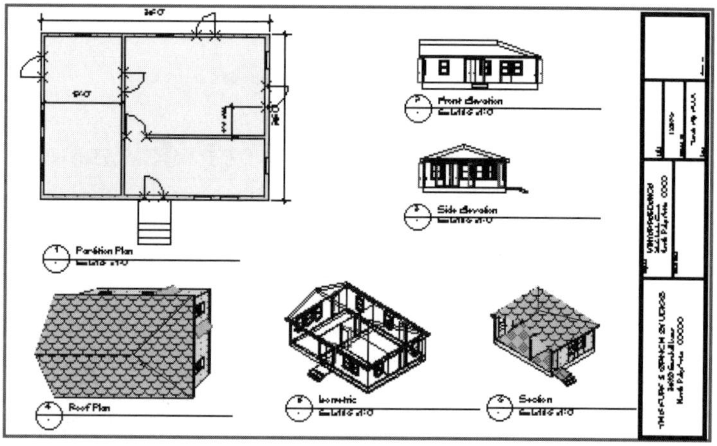

For those familiar with previous versions of the program, notice that all of the dimensions do rotate to be aligned with the dimension line in the linked layer. Dimensions do now project correctly in linked layers for *Top/Plan*, *Top*, *Bottom*, and isometric views if in *Projection>Orthogonal* or *Projection>2d Plan*. The dimensions will not project correctly for any of the elevation views, *Perspective*, or *Oblique* projections. For these, you can always place the dimension directly on the linked layer instead of the master or original layers.

Adding To The Building

At this point you may want to add another element to the building, such as a patio. Make the *floor* layer active, change the *Layer Options* to *Active Only*, and change to *Top/Plan* view. Also change the default line weight to .25.

Step 1 - the patio floor

We will create a patio with a rounded corner. Use the *Rectangle* tool to create a rectangle snapping to the lower left corner of the building and the bottom of the stairs. Use the *Quarter Arc* tool and press/drag from the lower right of the rectangle. Enter -4'-0" (1.2m) into the *Y* edit box and to keeping it constrained to a quarter of a circle by either hitting the *S* key to select the *Constrain Angle* icon or pressing the *Shift* key. Create another rectangle snapping to the lower left of the first rectangle and the lower left of the arc. *Shift*-select the three objects and use the *TOOL>Add Surface* command to combine them into one object. Then use the *MODEL>Floor* command and set the *thickness* to 18" (.45m).

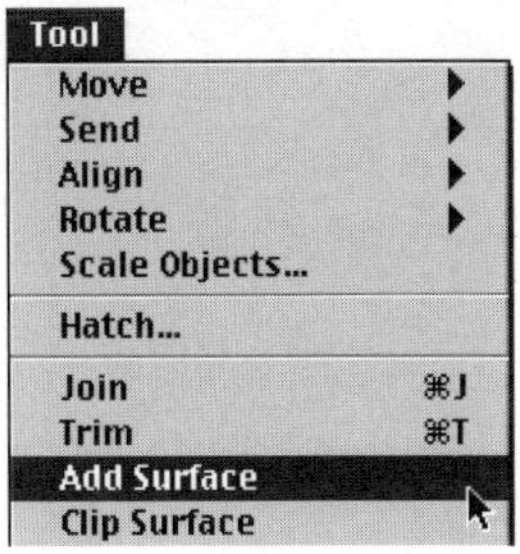

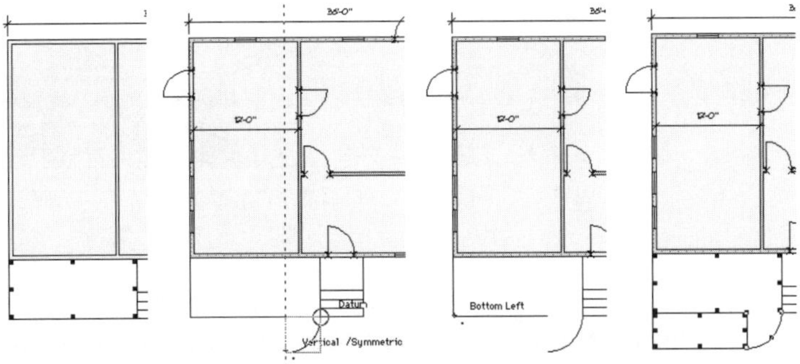

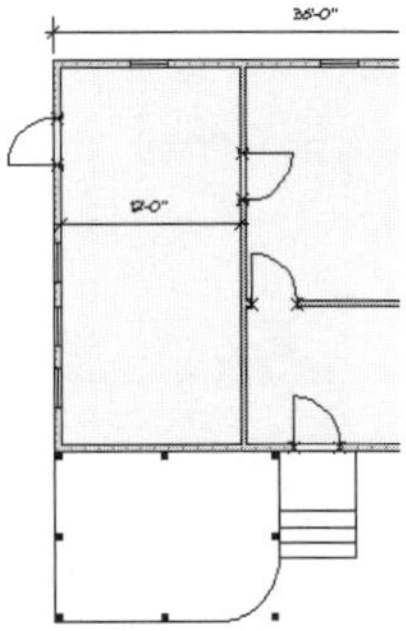

Step 2 - the railing

Open the *Layers Setup* dialog box and make *walls, floor,* and *title* the only layers that are *normal* - the rest should be changed to *invisible*. Change the active layer to *walls* and select *Layer Options>Show/Snap Others*.

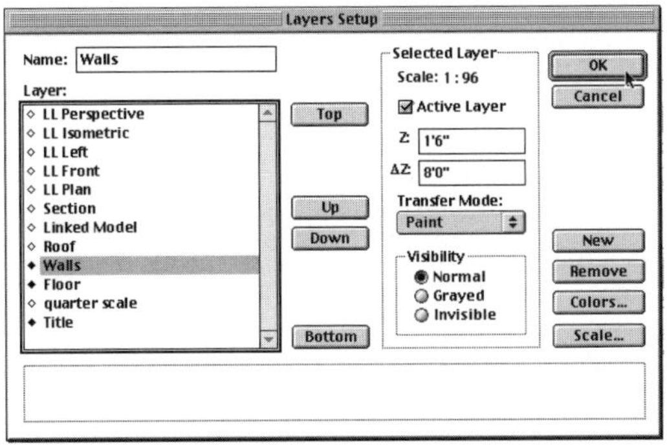

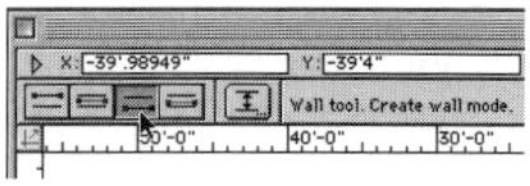

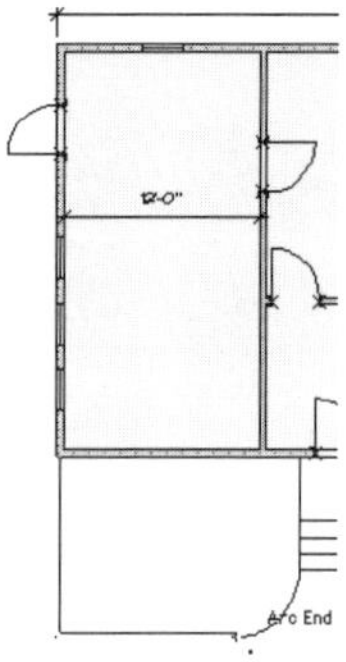

We will create a railing using the *WALL* tool. Select the tool and the right-most button to open the *WALL PREFERENCES* dialog box. Change the *SEPARATION* to 3" (.075m). With the third icon selected, snap to the lower left of the building and click, then click at the lower left of the patio, and double-click to end when the *smartcursor* snaps to the spring point of the curve with the *cue* saying *arc end*.

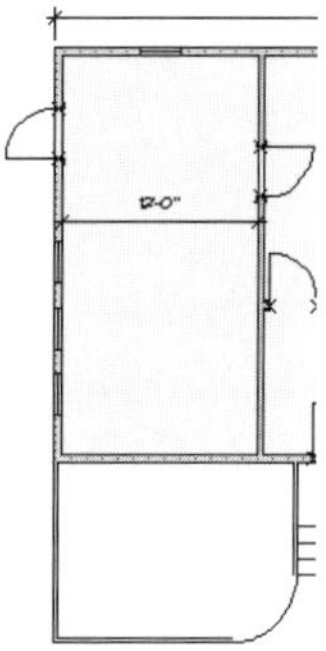

Make another segment of wall on the right side of the patio snapping to the lower left of the stairs and the top right of the patio. The *cues* will be *corner* for both points.

Now select the *ROUND WALL* tool and the third icon. Also select the icon second from the right, *ARC BY TWO POINTS AND CENTER*.

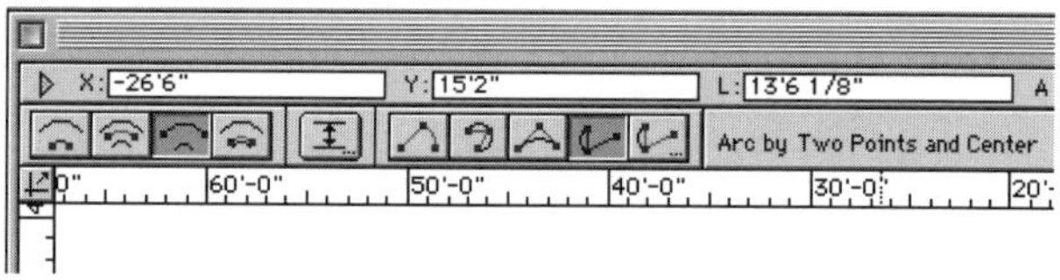

Snap to the lower end of the horizontal wall and press, then drag to the lower outside point of the right wall and release the mouse button. Use the *smartcursor* to line the center point with the two straight wall ends and click.

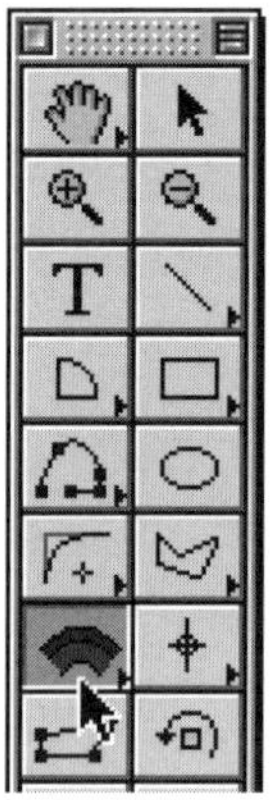

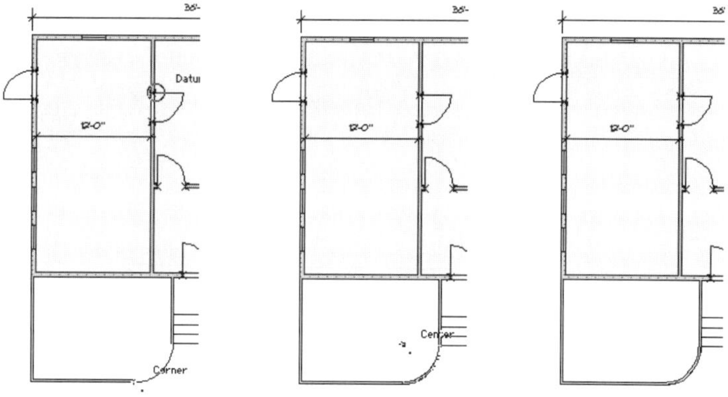

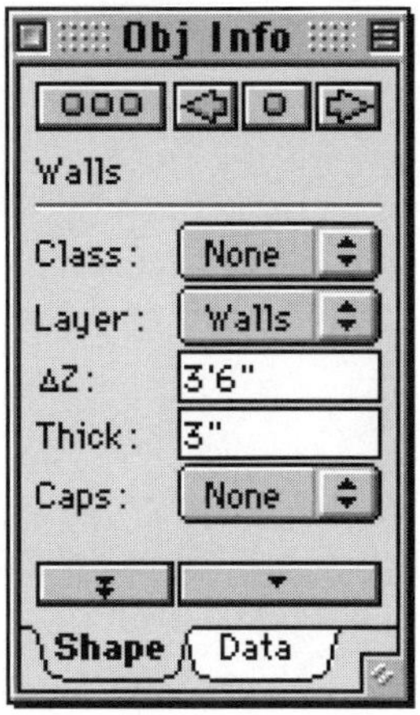

Now to adjust the wall height, *Shift*-select the four wall segments. In the *OBJECT INFO* palette enter 3'-6" (1.05m) in the *Δz (±z)* edit box. The height of these wall segments will automatically adjust.

Step 3 - viewing the addition

In order to view the changes and make any adjustments, if necessary, open the *LAYERS SETUP* dialog box. Make the *walls* and *floor* layer *INVISIBLE*, and change all of the layers beginning with *//* and the *section* layer back to *NORMAL*. Make *// plan* the active layer. When you click *OK* notice how the patio now appears on all of the views.

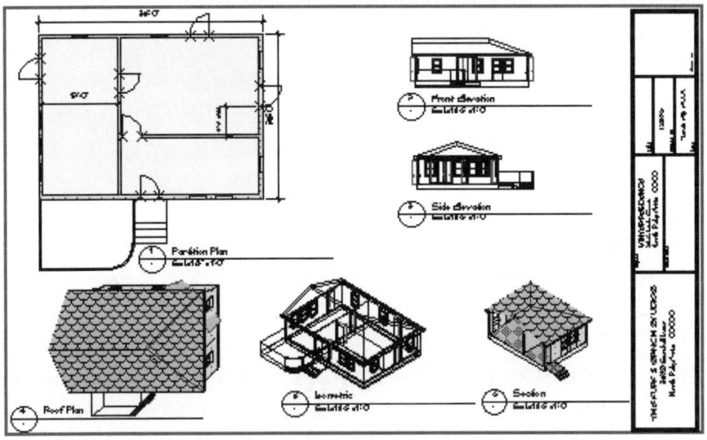

MULTIPLE VIEWS IN SUMMATION

SAVE the document and *QUIT [EXIT]* the program. Multiple viewing of an object is another advantage to working with computers. Once the different elements of a drawing are created, there are many options for viewing the drawing as a whole or as individual parts or elements. Different scales and views can be visible all at the same time and with all views linked back to the original or master layers.

- 2D objects and the 2D aspect of hybrid objects will appear with a fill color and *PATTERN* if one was designated in the *ATTRIBUTES* palette, even if not rendered.

• If you need to view several objects at different scales all at the same time, set up a multiple view document.

• Changes made on an original or master layer show in the linked layer, but changes or additions made on linked layer do not affect the original. In other words, it is a dynamic one-way connection.

• Sections are static and have no connection or link to any of the other layers. Changes made on other layers will not appear on the section and changes on the section will not appear in the original.

• An original or master layer can be linked to many different linked model layers.

• Be aware that linking a layer to another linked layer does not work with most rendering options.

• Changes made to a master or original layer will not appear on a rendered linked layer until that layer becomes active. When the linked layer becomes active, it will automatically rerender and the changes will appear.

• In order to see dimensions or other 2D objects in an isometric view, check the *PROJECT 2D OBJECTS* box in the *CREATE LAYER LINK* dialog box.

Chapter 9

MORE WALLS AND OTHER STUFF

SOME MORE STUFF

In the previous chapters we went through the steps to block out a 3-dimensional building with a floor, roof, and walls. We are going to now be looking at creating a variety of objects you might have outside or on the building as well as fine tuning what you already have.

The tools, commands, constraints, and palettes we will be exploring are;

- *2D Symbol Insertion* Tool
- *Align Plane* Tool
- *Double-Line Polygon* Tool
- *Eye Dropper* Tool
- *Fillet* Tool
- *Hemisphere* Tool
- *Mirror* Tool
- *Set Working Plane* Tool
- *Classes* Command
- *Clip Surface* Command
- *Create Roof From Walls* Command
- *Cut 3D Section* Command
- *Edit Group* Command
- *Flip Vertical* Command
- *Lock* Command
- *Move* Command
- *Paste In Place* Command
- *Rendering* Command
- *Unlock* Command
- *Snap To Edge* Constraint
- *3D Tools* Palette
- *Object Info* Palette
- *Resources* Palette

Chapt 8.mcd

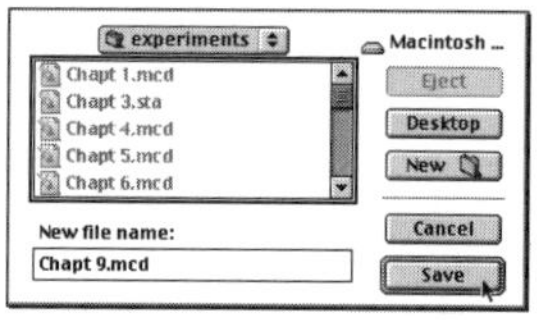

MORE CLASSES

Open up the *chapt 8 [chapt 8.mcd]* file for the building you just created and do a *Save As* naming it *chapt 9 [chapt 9.mcd]*. To make things less confusing go into the *Layers Setup* dialog box, *Shift*-select each layer that has *ll* in its name designating a linked layer and the *section* layer and click the *invisible* button. Select the original or master layers *walls, floor,* and *roof* and change them to *normal*. The *title* layer always remains *normal* or visible. Make *roof* the *active layer*.

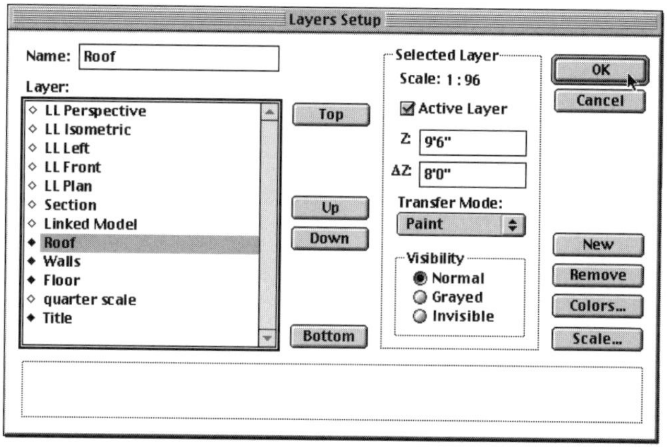

There are times you may want to see an object or part of an object in one view but not in another. What you would need to do is to create a new separate class. With this release of Vector-Works, classes have much of the flexibility of layers, but with some noted differences.

Creating Classes

We will create a series of classes for different uses. We have previously looked at using a class to subdivide an object, such as a door and its hardware. Some tools, such as the dimensioning tools, and commands, such as the *Create Guides* command, place the objects created, automatically into a separate class. Another typical use of classes might be to look at different schemes for early design phases of a project or at ways of subdividing the different aspects within a project.

Step 1 - classes

Either go to *ORGANIZE>CLASSES* or to the arrow on the *data display bar* that designates class and select *CLASSES*. A dialog box opens called, oddly enough, *CLASSES*. Select the *dimension* class and click in the *INVISIBLE* column with the open diamond. All of the dimensions we had created will be invisible, unless the *dimension* class is active. This class is a default class and should not be changed. Also notice there is a class called *guides* that was automatically created when we had previously used the command.

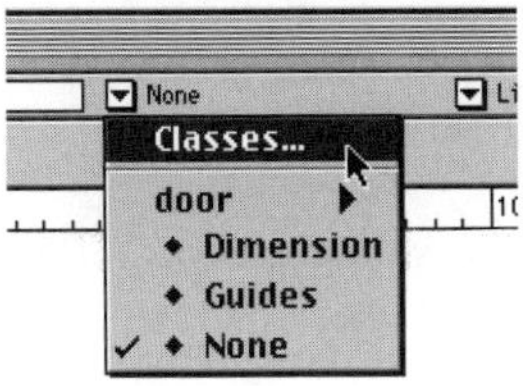

Step 2 - classes for design schemes

We will look at some different roof types and place each in its own class. Select the *NEW* button and enter *roof-scheme a* in the *NAME* edit box when the *CLASS OPTIONS* dialog box opens. Make sure the *CREATE NEW CLASS* button is selected and click *OK*. Create another new class called *roof-scheme b.* Remember to place the hyphen without any spaces.

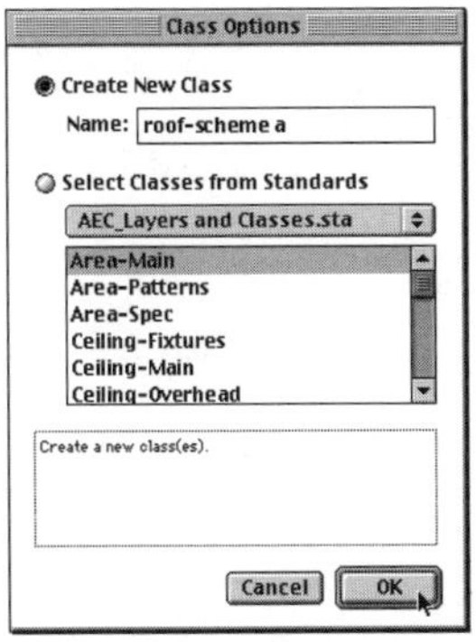

Step 3 - classes to subdivide a project

We also will be looking at some landscape elements. Create two new classes now called, *landscape-hardscape* and *landscape-softscape*. Once the classes are created, exit the dialog box.

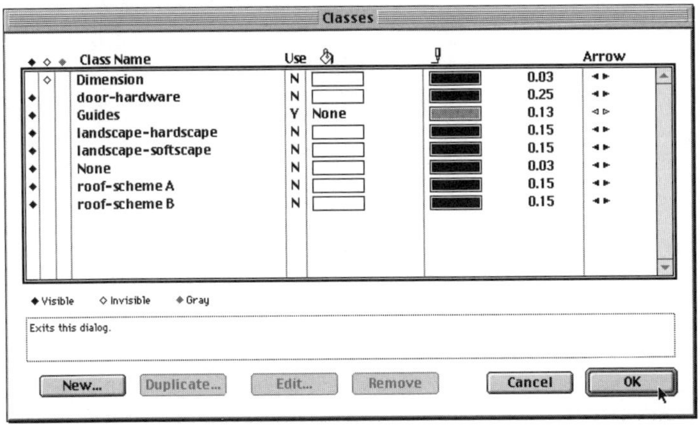

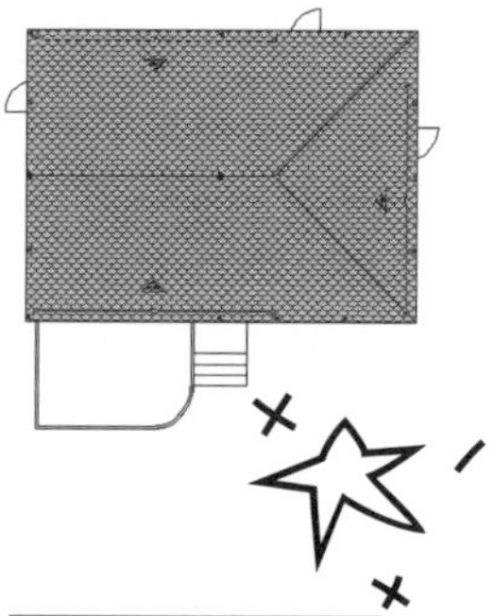

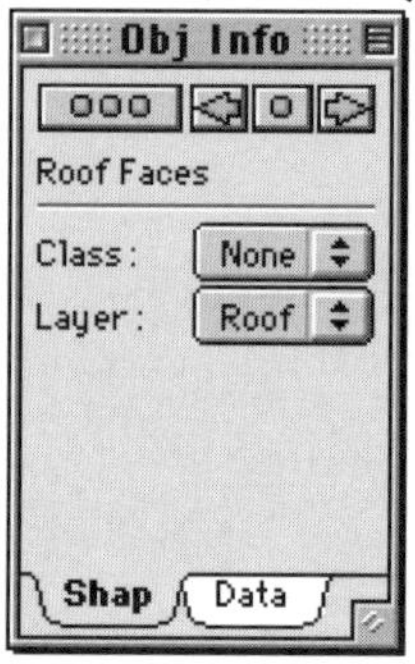

Step 4 - changing a class of an existing object

We will want to place the first roof we created into the *roof-scheme a* class. With *roof* the active layer, *Shift*-select the three pieces. You will know they are selected if you see three arrows on the roof. Using the OBJECT INFO palette, change the pop-out at the top from *none* to *roof-scheme a*. This is the method you now use to change a class of an object.

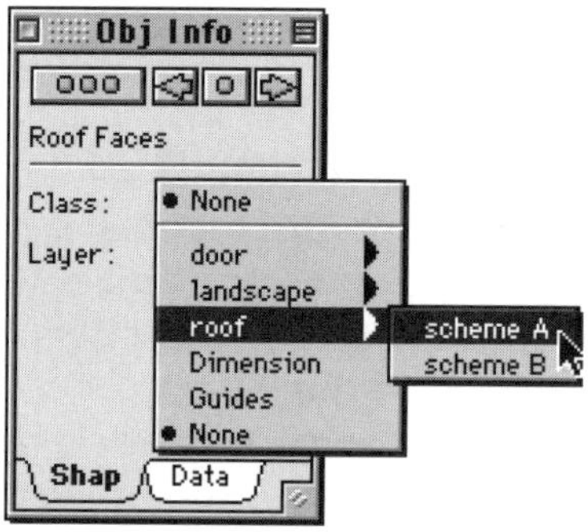

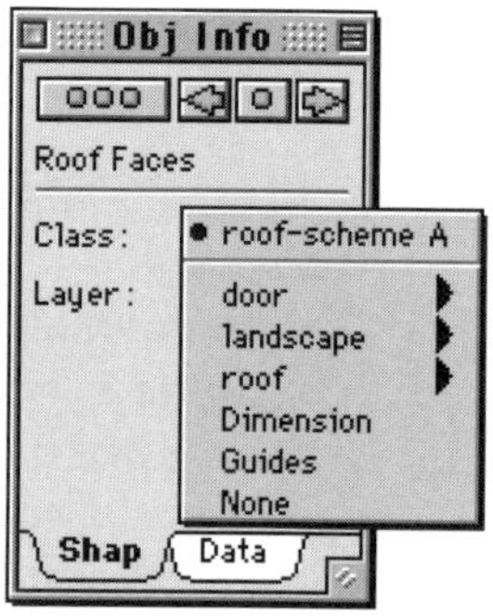

MORE WALLS

Select LAYER OPTIONS>ACTIVE ONLY, change the layer to *linked model,* and the view to LEFT ISOMETRIC with RENDERING>SOLID. You will notice that the one wall under the gable needs to be revised so that it meets the underside of the roof.

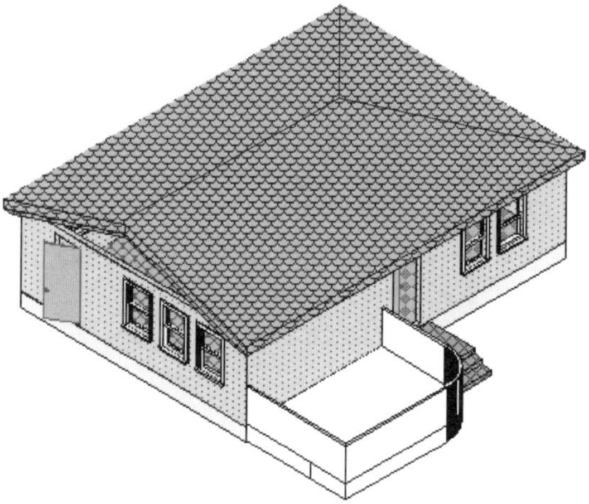

Adding A Gable End Wall

Since we had created the roof in its own layer and changed its class, the new triangular gable end wall will be added in the same layer and class as well. Make both the *roof* layer and the *roof-scheme a* class active. Change the default line weight to the third line weight and the *FILL* color to white.

Step 1 - creating the end wall

Change the view to *TOP/PLAN* and select the top and bottom roof planes changing the fill to *NONE* with the *ATTRIBUTES* palette. Change the *ORGANIZE>LAYER OPTIONS* to *SHOW/SNAP OTHERS.* This allows you to easily see where to place the wall.

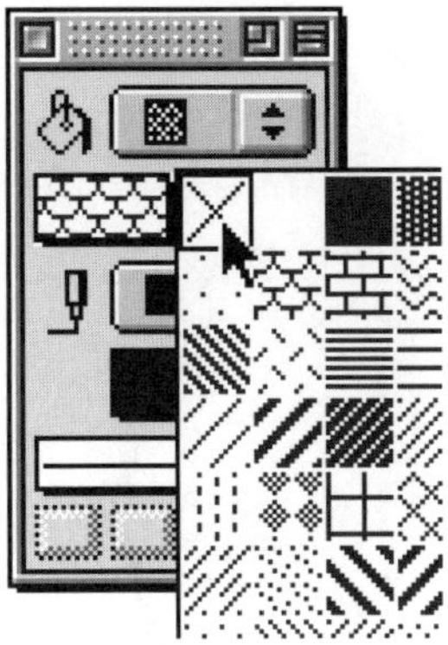

Use the *ZOOM-IN* tool to magnify the left side of the building where the wall peak needs to be added. Select the *WALL* tool and this time select the third modifier icon which has the control line on the bottom.

Open the *WALL PREFERENCES* dialog box by clicking the rightmost icon and change the *SEPARATION* to 6" (.15m). Place the cursor on the top part of the wall using the *smartcursor* to snap to the outside corner in order to align with the existing wall and click once when the *cue, point* appears. Double-click to end this wall segment on the lower left of the existing wall when the *smartcursor* snaps to the outside corner. Notice while drawing that the edges of the new wall obscure the edges of the wall below as if it were erased.

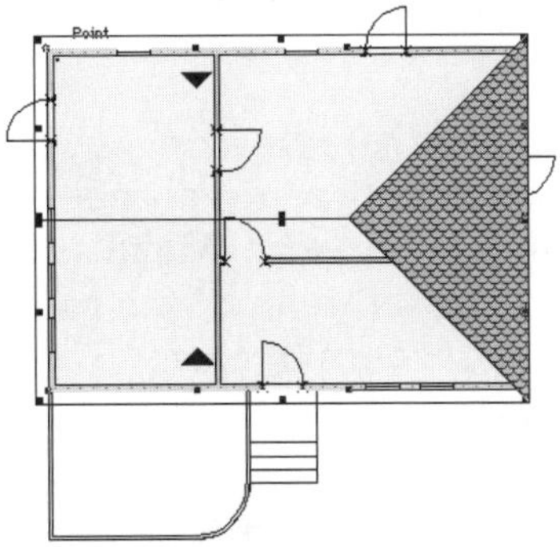

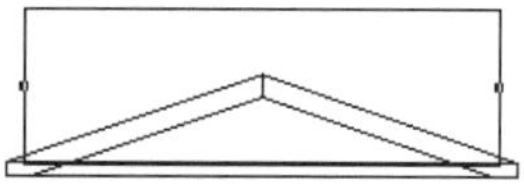

Change to *Layer Options>Active Only*. Now with this new wall segment still selected, change the view to *Left* and *Zoom-In* closer. When we initially created the roof, the roof starting height, or *axis z,* was set at the edge of the walls, not the edge of the overhang, which is why the roof sticks beyond and below this new wall.

Step 2 - adding the peak

Since we did not assign a particular Δz *[±z]* value to this layer, the wall was created either with no height or some undesignated height. The first thing to do is give it some arbitrary height. Select the *PALETTES>Object Info* command to open the *Object Info* palette. With the wall selected, enter 6' (1.80m) into the Δz *[±z]* box. When you hit either the *Tab* or *Return* [*Enter*] keys, the wall reshapes to the new height.

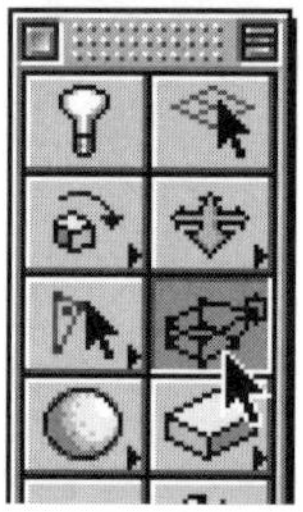

Change to the *3d Tools* palette either by clicking the *3d Tools* palette or if it is not opened, choose *PALETTES>3d Tools*. Select the *3d Reshape* tool and the first icon.

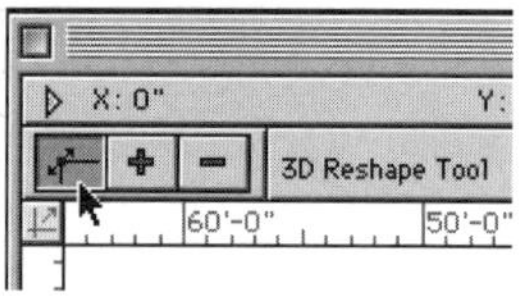

Press/drag from one of the upper corners of the wall down to the bottom of the wall. Look at the *data display bar* and when *top* reads 0, or the *smartcursor* snaps to the bottom, release the mouse.

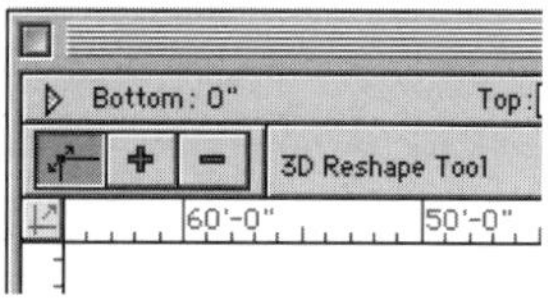

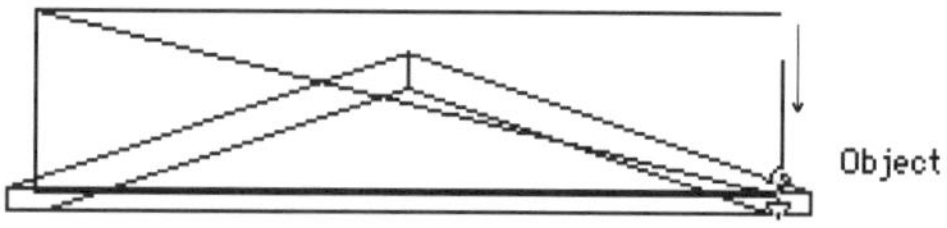

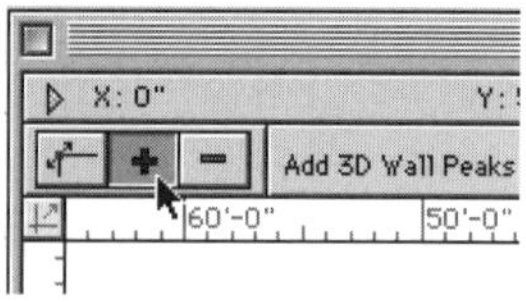

Change to the middle icon, *add 3d wall peaks* and press/drag from the other top corner of the wall, to the middle of the peak of the roof. Make sure you are not snapping to the outside corners of the roof but to the middle. You may need to zoom-in closer. This adds a new point or vertex to the top of the wall.

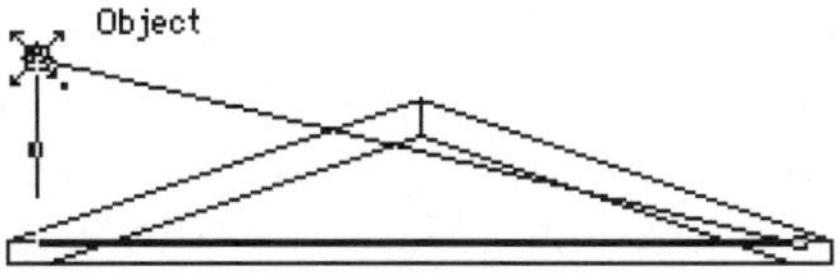

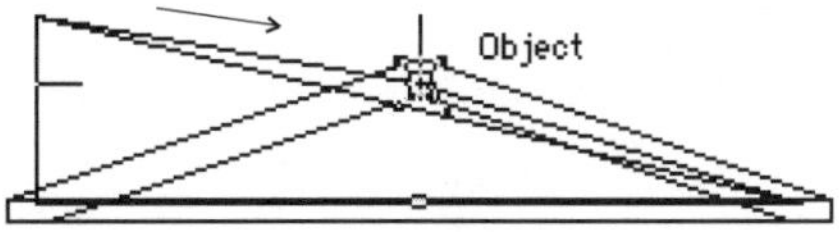

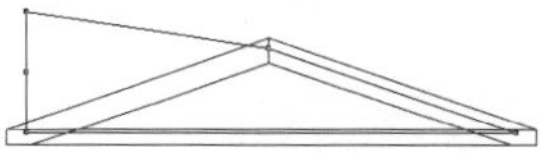

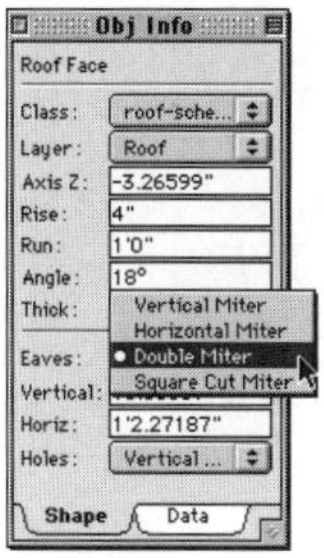

As a note, when the roof was originally created, the miter type selected, affects the placement, or *AXIS Z* location of the roof and its relationship to the walls. When it is a *VERTICAL MITER* or *SQUARE MITER*, the *AXIS Z* location is at the underside of the roof. A *HORIZONTAL MITER* places the *AXIS Z* on the top side of the roof, and a *DOUBLE MITER* places it in between. The *VERTICAL, SQUARE,* and *HORIZONTAL MITERS* can both easily be changed with the *OBJECT INFO* palette with the *EAVES* pop-out menu, but the *DOUBLE MITER* will not go back to the original values once changed. Some kind of bug. You can always use the *UNDO* command.

Now, change back to the first icon, which is now called *RESHAPE 3D WALLS*, and press/drag the last upper corner down to the lower corner, again verifying *TOP* in the *data display bar*, or making use of the *smartcursor*.

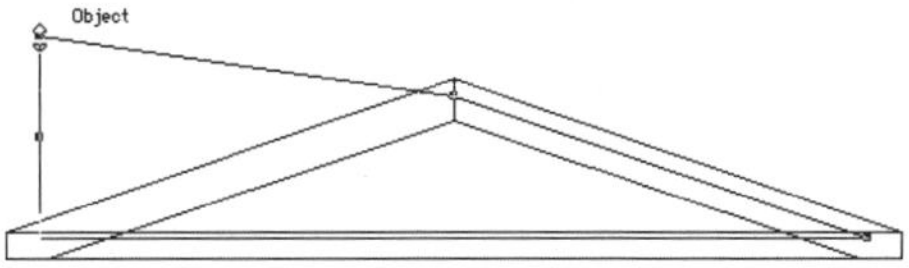

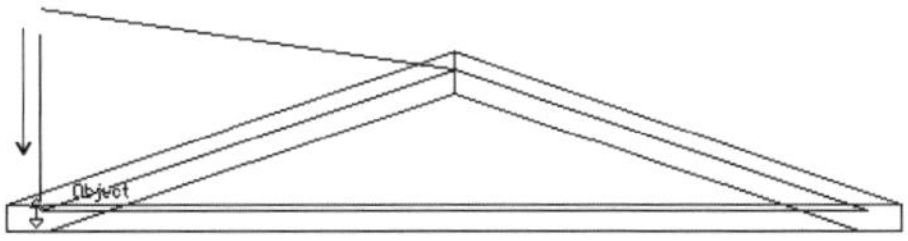

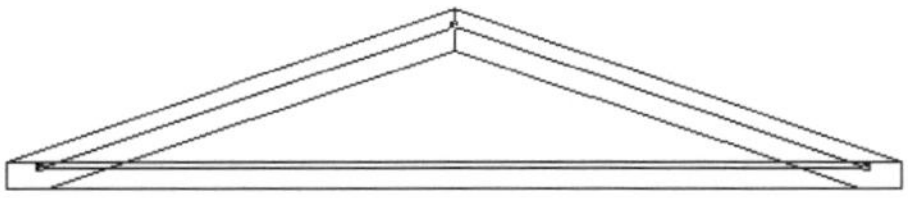

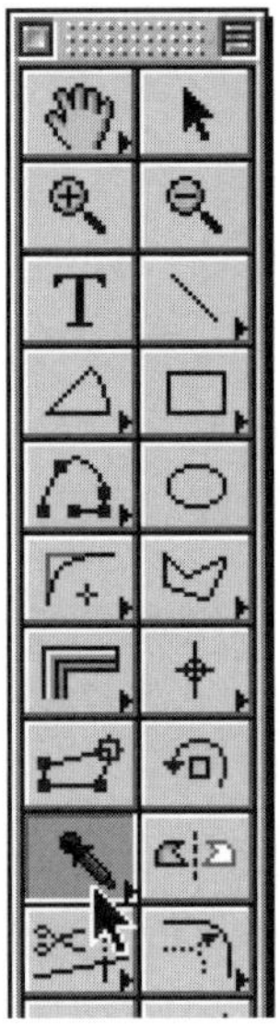

Step 3 - gable end wall attributes

We will want the gable end wall to have the same attributes of color and pattern as the other exterior walls. In order to easily do this, make the *walls* layer active, select the *Eye Dropper* tool and the right most icon to open the *Pick Up/Put Down Filter* dialog box. Select the boxes as shown below.

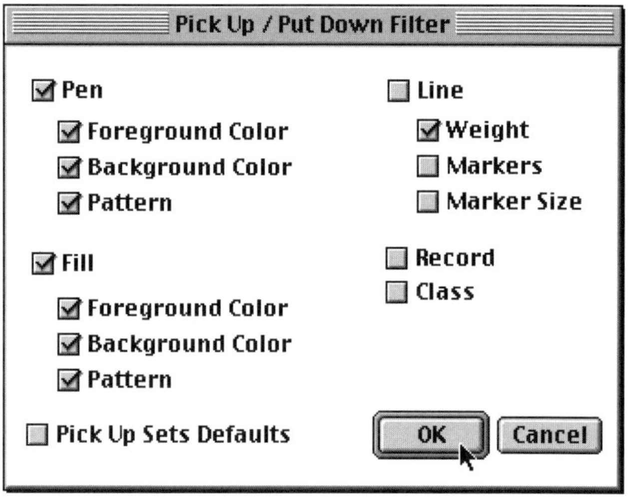

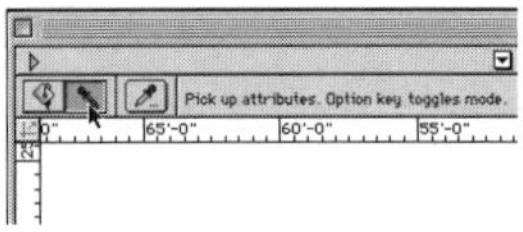

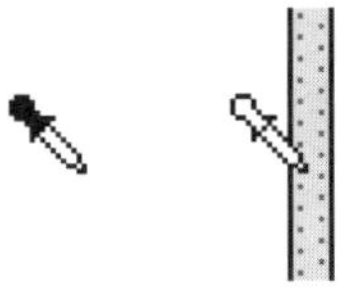

With the *pick up attributes* icon selected, click on one of the exterior walls. Make the *roof* layer active, and change the icon to the *put down attributes* icon. Click on the gable end wall, not the roof. The fill will not appear since this layer has *Rendering>Wireframe* selected and it is in a 3D view.

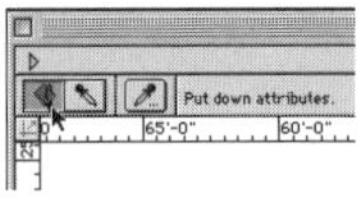

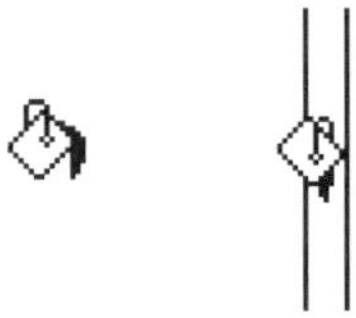

This is one of the tools that has some entertaining noises if you have the sound turned on in your operating system. The cursors changes as well. A programmer was probably having a long week when this tool was developed.

Step 4 - viewing the gable end wall

Make the *linked model* layer active. The view should still be *Left Isometric*. The image will automatically re-render reflecting the changes. Once redrawn, you can see the opening being filled by the new triangular wall placed on top of the existing wall. Notice, that although the selected fill *PATTERN* for the roof planes is *NONE*, the edges are still visible.

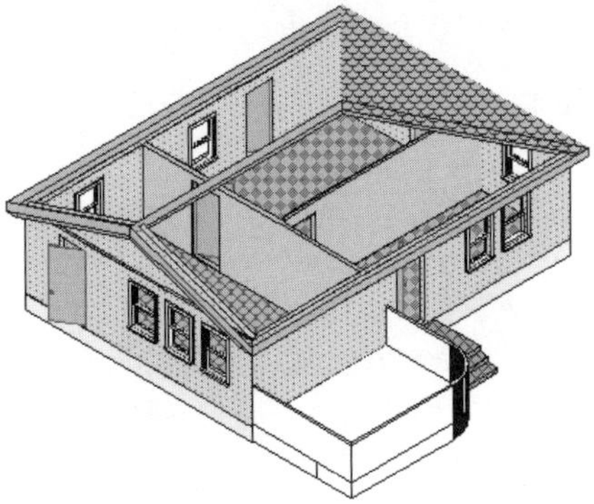

You can see by placing the roof in its own layer that there is a horizontal line dividing the upper and lower wall segments under the gable. If this is something that you can not live with, you can either mask it with a 3D polygon, or by placing the roof in the *walls* layer you can modify the existing wall to give it a peak. Basically you would just select the wall you want to add a peak to, select the *3D RESHAPE* tool with the *ADD 3D WALL PEAKS* icon, and press/drag a peak one of the top corners of the wall.

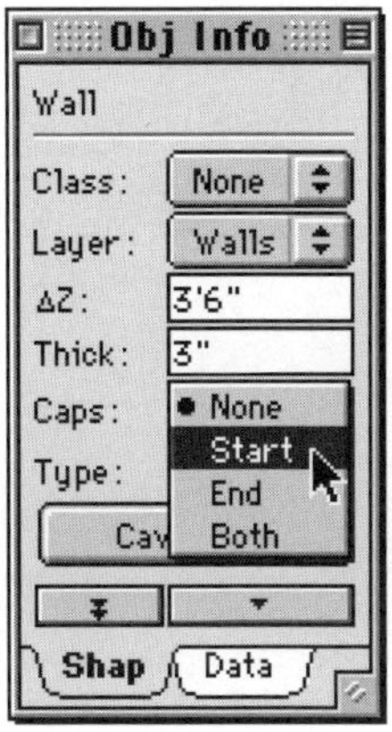

Step 5 - one more thing

Make the *walls* layer active and the view *TOP/PLAN*. Notice where the patio railings hit the full height wall. It looks as if the walls are joined rather than butting. What you would need to do is to select a railing and then a cap, whether *START* or *END*. When the patio wall segment is selected, look for the arrow on the wall to see which end is the starting side and with the *OBJECT INFO* palette make the appropriate *CAPS* selection.

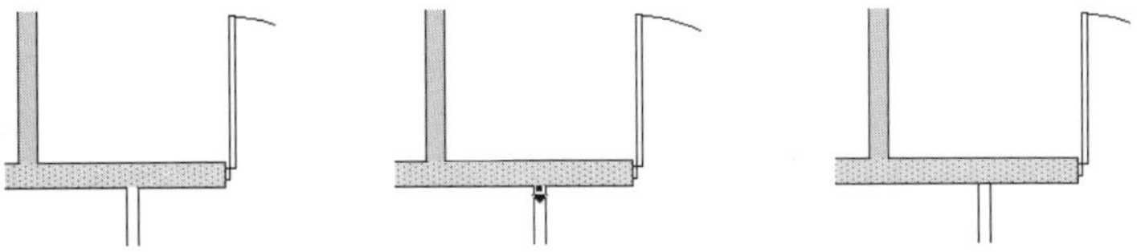

MORE ROOFS

By placing the previous roof and wall end gable in its own class, we can make this class, *roof-scheme a,* invisible and have a look at another roof plan.

Another Roof

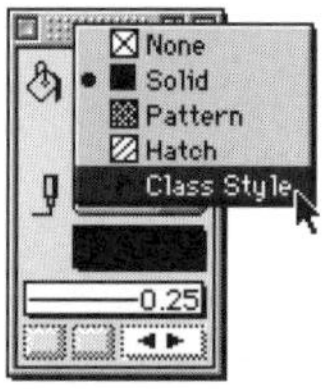

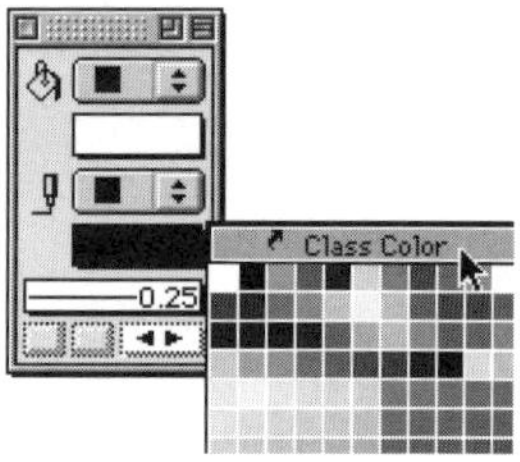

Open the *Classes* dialog box and click in the *invisible* column next to *roof-scheme a.* You can now set default attributes of pen, fill, line, and arrow heads for a class. Double-click the *roof-scheme b* class to open the *Edit Class* dialog box. This dialog box allows you to set attributes for objects within a class. These attributes can be used when the object is actually created if *use at creation is selected.* This will not affect existing objects already in the class. It is not global. If the box is not checked you can still access these attributes with the *Attributes* palette by selecting an object and then *class color* or *class style.*

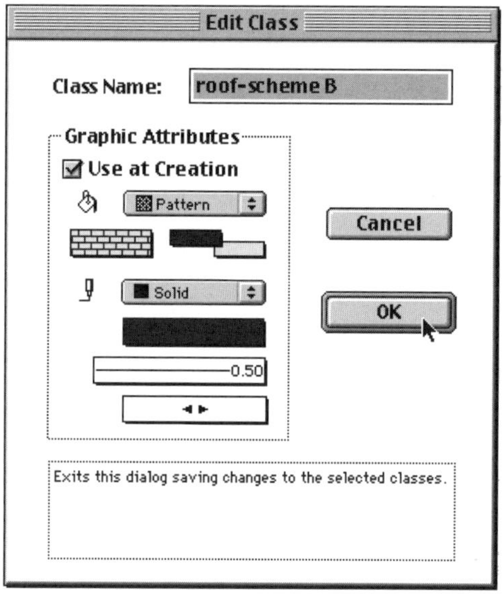

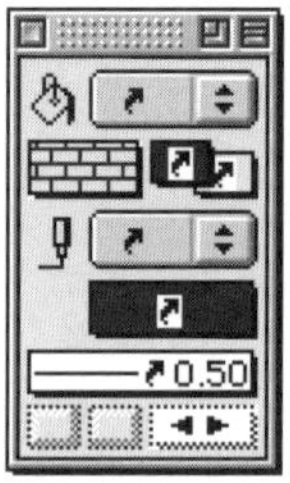

Make the selections to match the choices above. When this class is active, the *Attributes* palette will have arrows in the boxes designating a class attribute. Click the *ok* button to exit both of the dialog boxes.

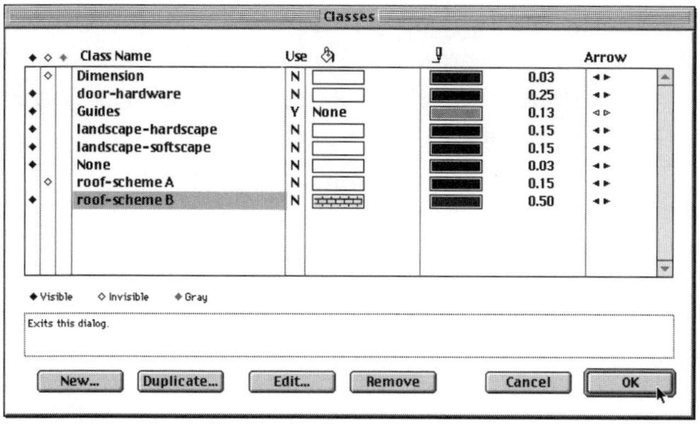

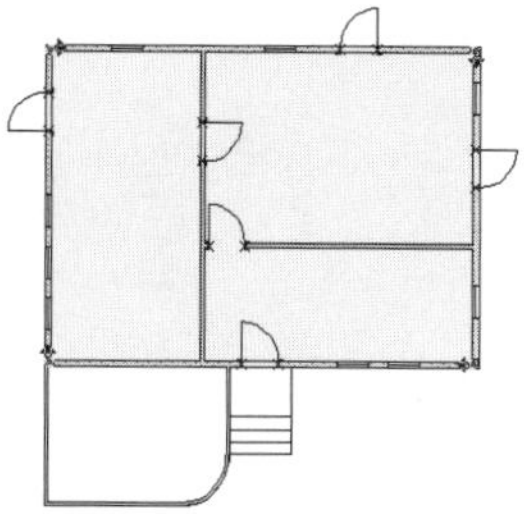

Step 1 - the roof itself

Layer Options and *Class Options* should both be *Show/Snap/Modify Others*. With the *roof* layer and the *roof-scheme b* class active, change the view to *Top/Plan*, and *Shift*-select the four exterior walls of the building. To make a simple hipped roof, just select *AEC> Create Roof From Walls*.

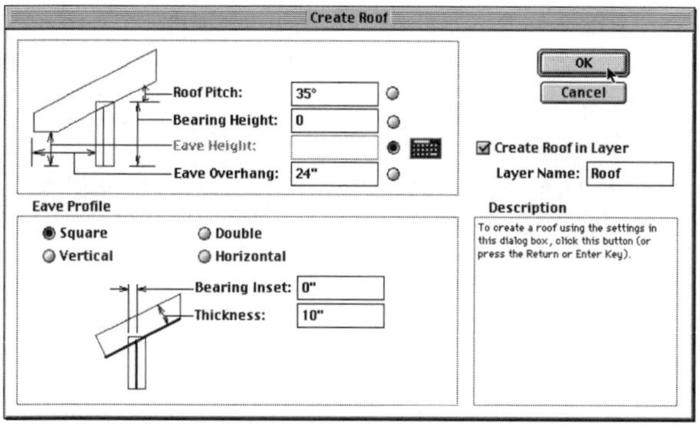

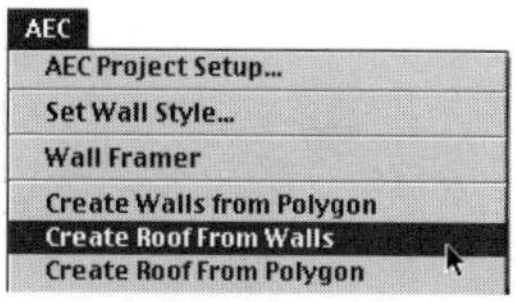

When the *Create Roof* dialog box opens enter 35° for *roof pitch* or you can enter 7:20 for the rise over run using a colon. Leave *bearing height* 0 since we set the height by the layer height. The *eave overhang* should be 24" (.60m). The *eave profile* should be *square*, *bearing inset* 0, and *thickness* 10" (.25m). Click the *create roof in layer* box, verify that the *layer name* is the same as in your document, and click *ok*. The hipped roof is automatically created in the *roof* layer, and in the active class, *roof-scheme b*.

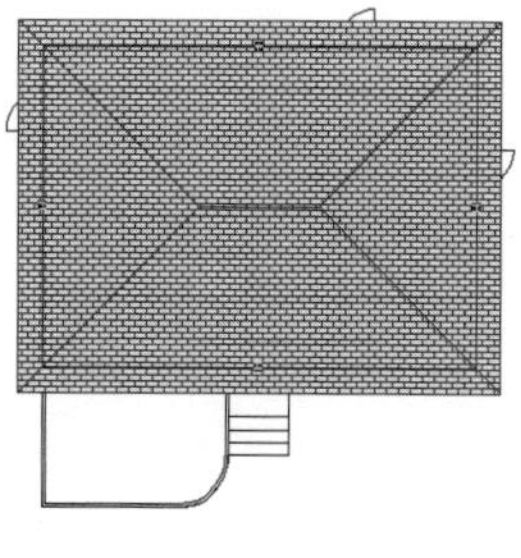

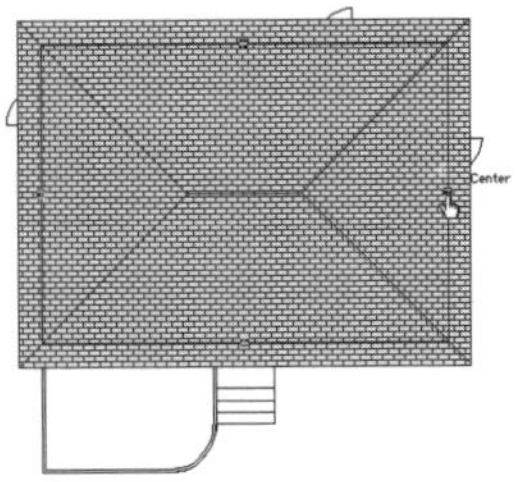

Step 2 - revising the roof

If you wanted to revise the roof, just click on one of the handles when the *pick* cursor appears. The *EDIT ROOF SETTINGS* dialog box opens.

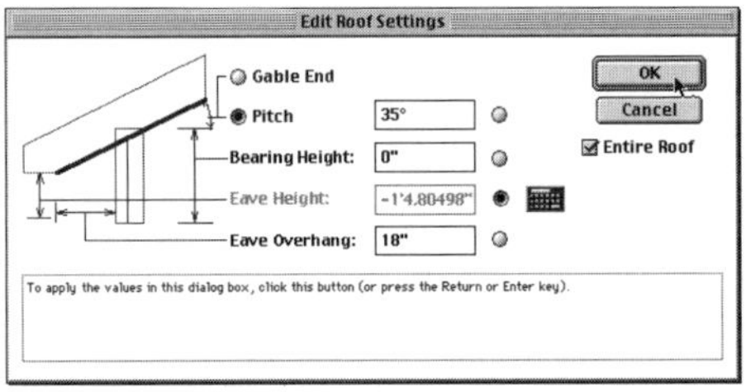

You can use this dialog box to make changes to individual faces of the roof depending on which roof face you clicked with the *pick* cursor, or you can select the *ENTIRE ROOF* box to make changes to all of the faces. Change the *EAVE OVERHANG* to 18" (.45m) and click the *ENTIRE ROOF* box. When you click *OK* the roof changes.

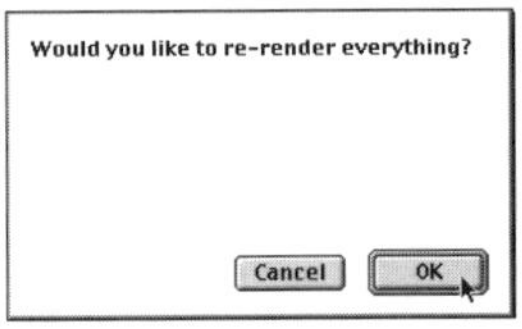

Step 3 - more roof changes

Look at the *linked model* layer to view this roof and change *LAYER OPTIONS* to *ACTIVE ONLY*. Since it still shows the scheme a roof, you will need to reselect the *RENDER>SOLID* command. An alert box will open asking if you wish to re-render. Just click *OK*.

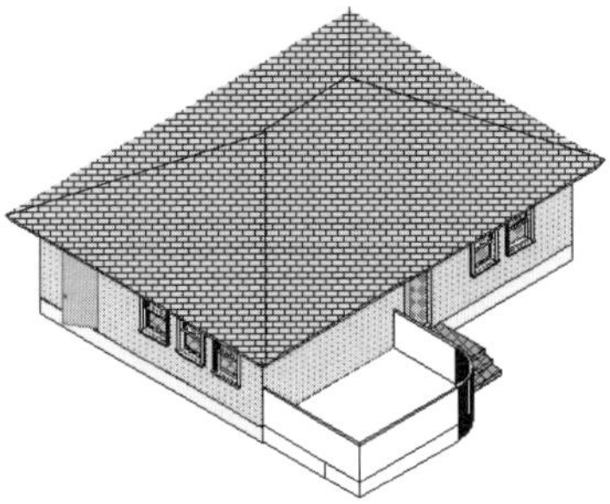

You can use the *EDIT ROOF SETTINGS* dialog box to create a gable end wall as well. Go back to the *roof* layer and click the left roof face with the *pick* cursor. When the dialog box opens click the *GABLE END* button and then *OK*. The roof will reform. Change the view to *LEFT ISOMETRIC* and then

Solid rendering. Notice how the class attributes are applied to the gable wall end. This unfortunately can not be changed unless you *Ungroup* the object. Also notice how the gable end wall does not exactly match the underside of the roof. This is a bug that will hopefully be corrected in future releases.

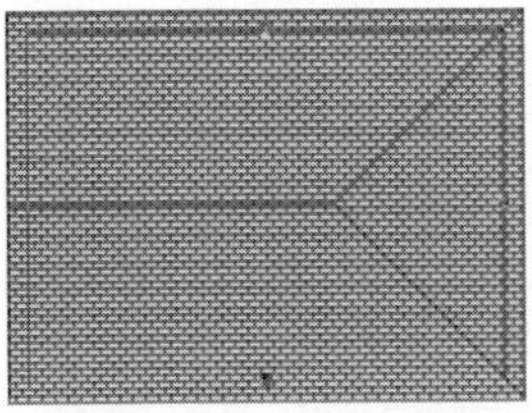

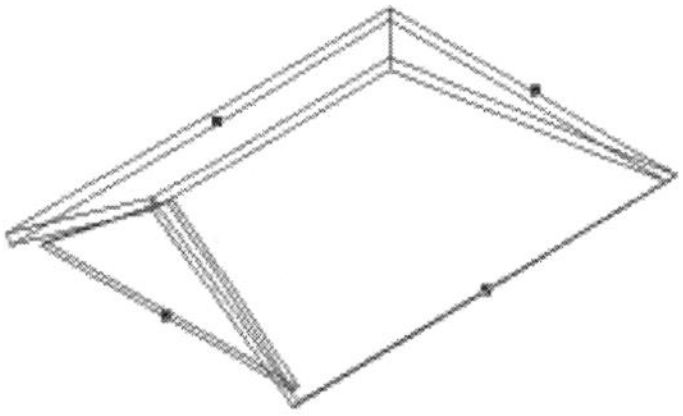

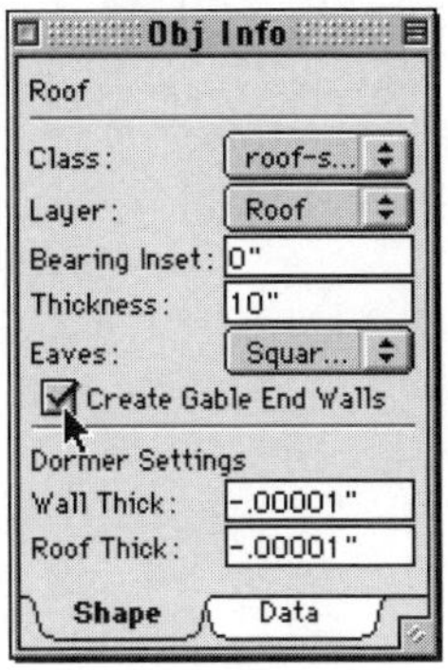

You can delete this gable end wall by selecting the roof object and unchecking the *create gable end walls* box in the *Object Info* palette. If you do not see the box when the roof is selected, close and reopen the *Object Info* palette to force a redaw.

For right now we will delete the gable entirely. In the 3D view, place the cursor on the selection handle at the center bottom of the wall. Click when the *pick* cursor appears. The *Edit Roof Settings* dialog box opens again. Click *pitch* and enter the original settings. You will need to re-select *Solid* for the changes to appear. If we were in *Wireframe* the changes would be immediately apparent. Also go into the *Classes* dialog box and make the *roof-scheme b* class *invisible*.

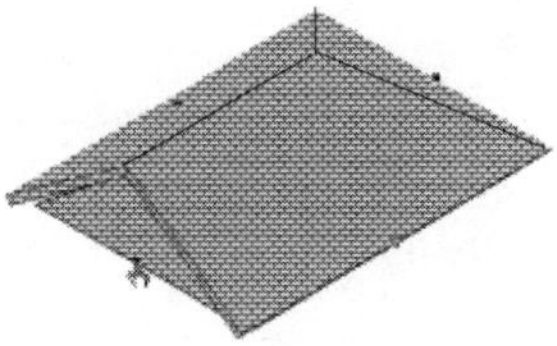

MORE SYMBOLS

VectorWorks includes a library of symbol resources which is basically a collection of symbols saved in various documents. While all of the symbols may not be to your liking, it is usually easier to modify an existing object then to create one from scratch. So, you can either use the existing symbols, modify them, or create your own. They can be imported from other files, saved in a template file, or created in the current file or any combination of the above.

Finding And Importing Symbols

Once symbols are created and saved, the main question is, how do you locate and bring them into the active document. We will locate and import several different symbols and symbol folders from the existing resources into this document. All of the symbols are located somewhere within the *toolkit* folder.

Step 1 - navigating to a symbol

Make sure the RESOURCES palette is open. If not go to *PALETTES>RESOURCES* to select. Navigate from the *VectorWorks 8 ƒ* folder, to the *toolkit* folder, to the *architectural* folder, to the *symbols* folder. When you double-click this folder you will see icons, each one representing a file with different symbols.

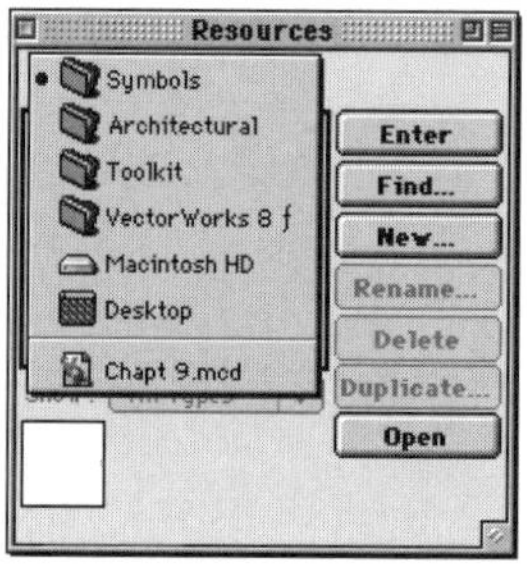

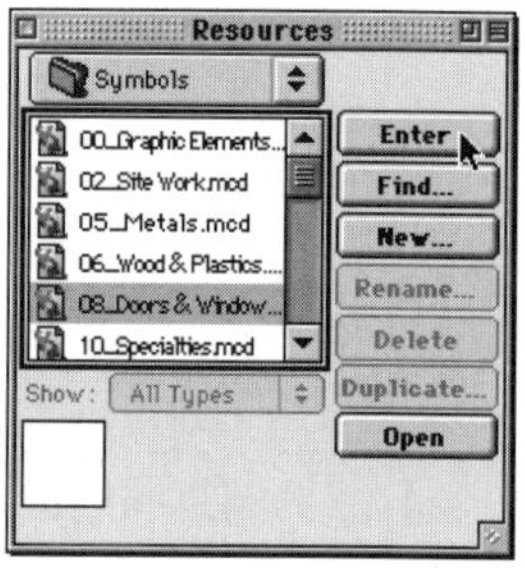

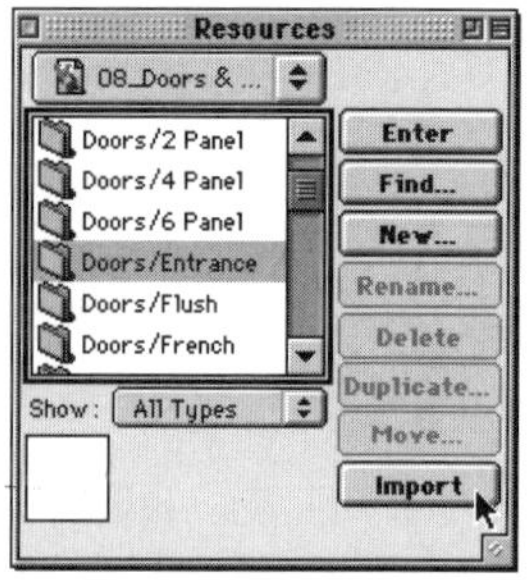

You can either OPEN or ENTER the file. It is not necessary to OPEN a file, unless you need to actually view the document to see the symbols. Go down to *08._doors & windows.mcd* folder, click the ENTER button, then select *doors/entrance,* then the IMPORT button. What we have been doing is importing a whole folder of symbols rather than just an individual symbol.

Navigate back to the active document, *chapt 9 [chapt 9.mcd],* which is at the bottom of the navigational listing. As a note, all open VectorWorks documents will appear below the line in this pop-out menu. Notice that the imported symbol folder is now located in the RESOURCES palette for this current document along with the other previous symbols.

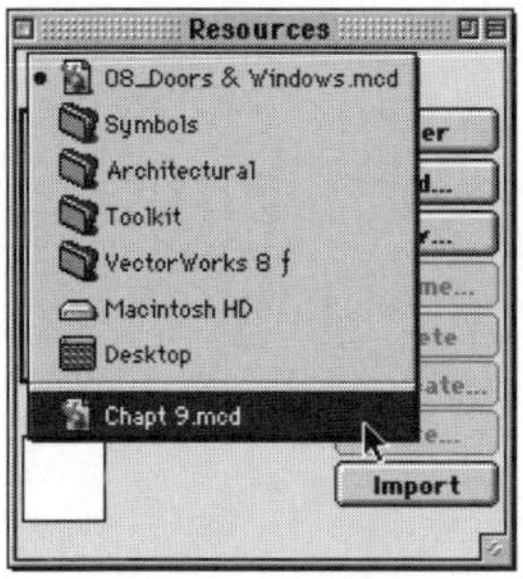

Step 2 - finding more symbols

We will want to bring into this file a few tree symbols. Since we are viewing the file in 3D, the symbols should be hybrid rather than the 2D plan or 2D elevation symbols. Finding an existing symbol should be easy using the *FIND* button on the *RESOURCES* palette but you do need to know where it is located.

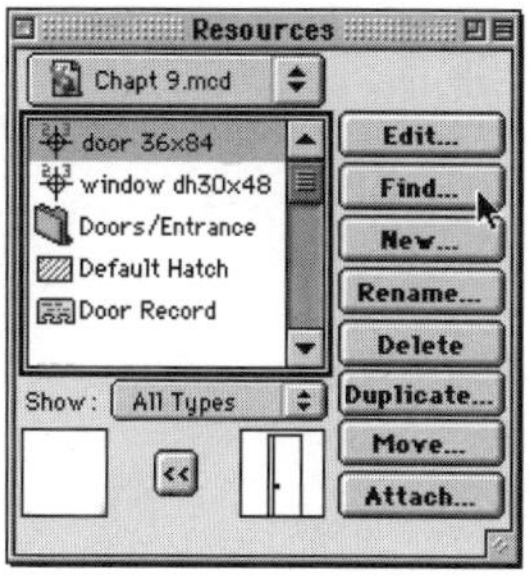

Click the *FIND* button. When the *FIND RESOURCE* dialog box opens, type *bush 2* in the *NAME* edit box and click the *SET WHERE [BROWSE]* button to tell VectorWorks where to look for the symbol. Navigate from the *VectorWorks 8f>toolkit> specialties>landscape design>symbols* folder. Double-click the *symbols* folder and click the *SELECT CURRENT* button.

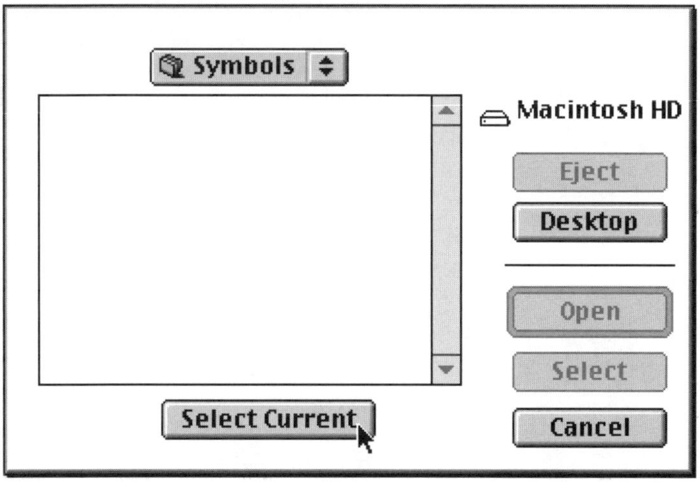

When the *FIND RESOURCE* dialog box appears click the *FIND* button. The symbol will be found and selected. Just click the *IMPORT* button to bring it into the active file. With the *FIND* button you need to actually locate the folder containing the file for the resource you want. You can not have the file buried within several folders.

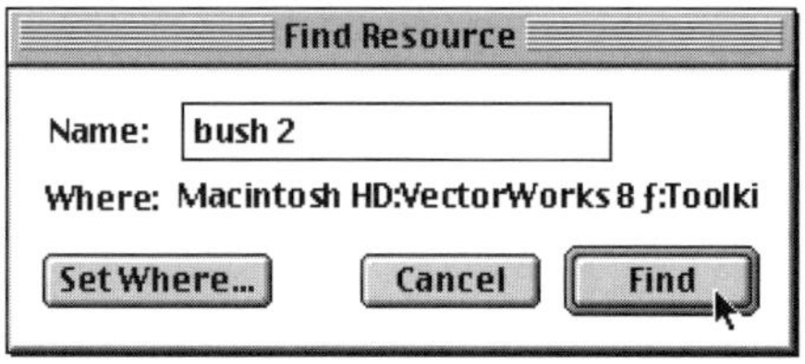

Click the *FIND* button again to find another symbol. This time the symbol is located in the same file, so we do not have to set its location. Type in the symbol name *shr1_3d* and click the *FIND NEXT* button. When the symbol is found you may need to scroll down in the list to actually see it selected. Click the *IMPORT* button.

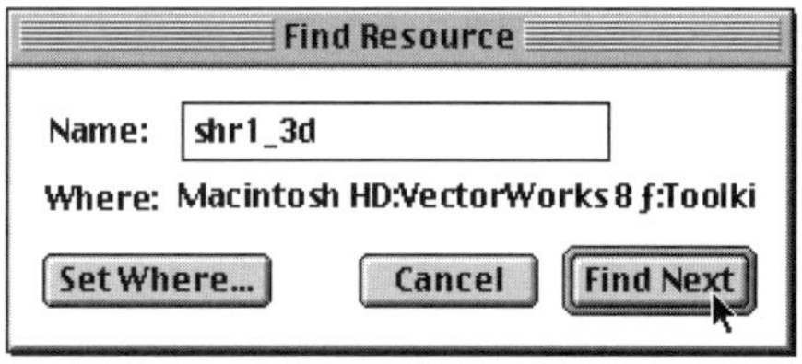

In the *RESOURCES* palette, press/drag down to the active file at the bottom of the pop out menu. Both symbols are now located in this file.

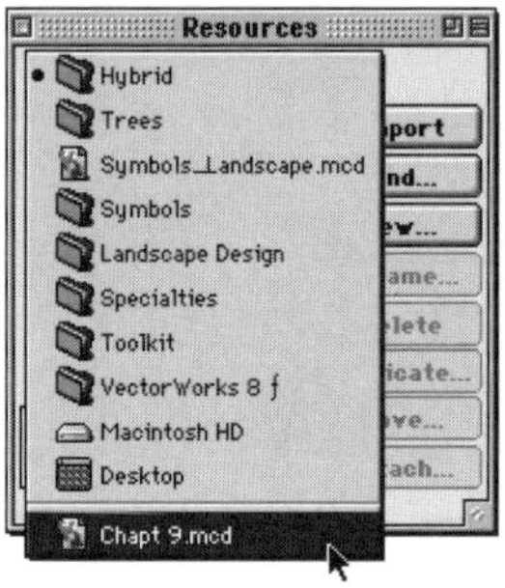

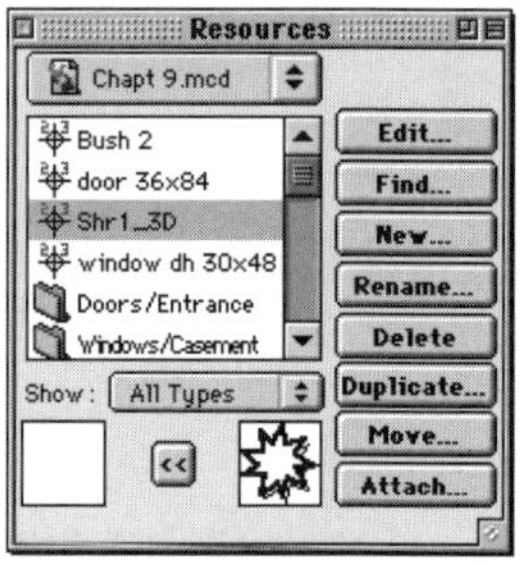

Click the *FIND* button again and then the *SET WHERE [BROWSE]* button. Navigate *VectorWorks 8f>toolkit>architectural>symbols* and double-click *symbols* then click *SELECT CURRENT*. We will be looking for several symbols. Type in the symbol name, click *FIND* in the *FIND RESOURCE* dialog box, and then *IMPORT* in the *RESOURCES* palette when found, then the *FIND* button again for each of the following symbols; *sofa7, coff_tab, chaise, chair2*. It is not necessary to change the *SET WHERE [BROWSE]* for these symbols since they are all located in the same place and note that the button will be *FIND NEXT* not *FIND* in this dialog box. Navigate back to *chapt 9 [chapt 9.mcd]*.

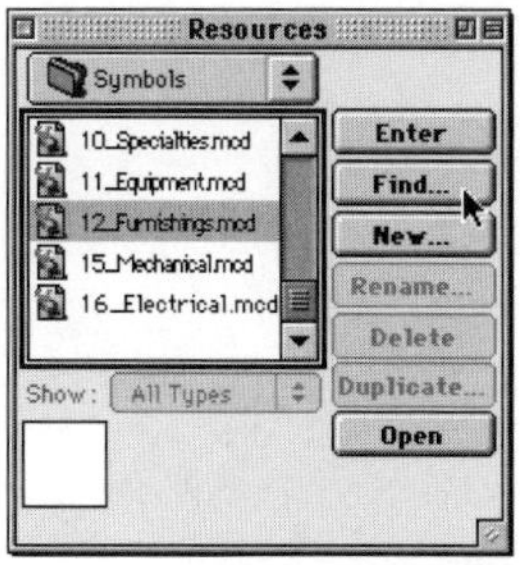

Working With Symbols

Once the symbols are imported you place them in the same manner we have been using. You can also edit these imported symbols which will not affect the original symbols located in the *toolkit*. Make the *walls* layer and the *none* class active and change to *TOP/PLAN*.

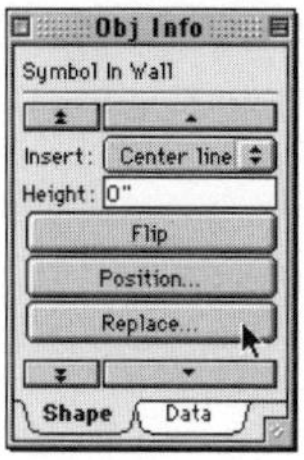

Step 1 - replacing a symbol

If you want to replace a symbol already located on the drawing, select the symbol, in this case any door but the one on the lower wall. In the *OBJECT INFO* palette click the *REPLACE* button. In the *SYMBOL REPLACE* dialog box, navigate to the *doors/entrance* folder and select *entr7*. With the new symbol selected, click *REPLACE*. One thing to note when replacing symbols – you can not modify the insertion point location.

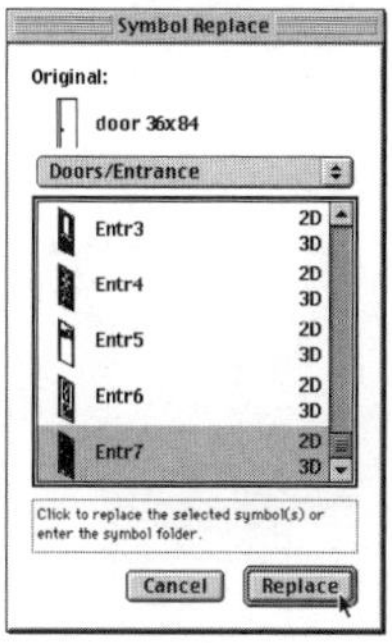

Step 2 - removing a symbol resource

In order to remove a symbol resource, just select its name in the *RESOURCES* palette and then the *DELETE* button. As an example, place a few copies of *doors/entrance>entr5* on the drawing. Then select the symbol's name in the *RESOURCES* palette and the *DELETE* button. An alert box will open asking if you really do want to delete the resource. If any of the symbols were already placed on the drawing

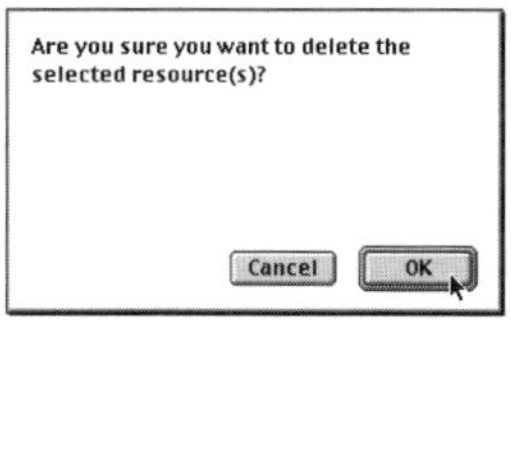

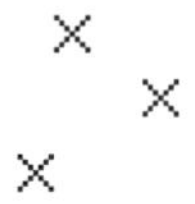

they would disappear as well, but a locus point would remain showing its original insertion point. Select and delete the locus points that remain like any other object.

Step 3 - removing a symbol instance

In order to remove just an instance of a symbol already placed in a wall, you no longer need to press/drag it away from a wall before you delete it. Select the centered door on the lower wall and with the *2D Selection* tool and the second icon selected, delete it.

Step 4 - placing symbols

One thing to be aware of is the symbol's insertion point. Most, if not all of the symbols included with the program have their insertion point centered. This is not always the best location for certain object types and at one point you might want to develop your own system and revise the existing symbols.

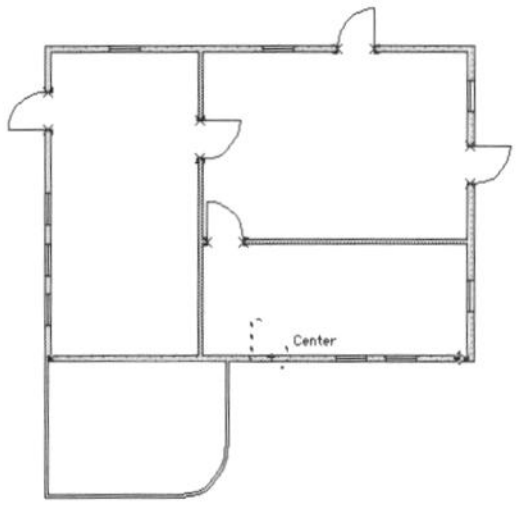

Select the *2D Symbol Insertion* tool and the *entr7* symbol. Hit the */* key until the center insertion icon is selected. Snap to the center of the lower wall and press when the *smartcursor cue, center,* appears and drag the cursor to the inside of the building so that the door opens inward. It should now be centered on the landing and wall. Make sure you are snapping to the wall center and not the center between two symbols or another wall that intersects this wall. If you had dragged and released to the exterior side, the door would have opened outwards.

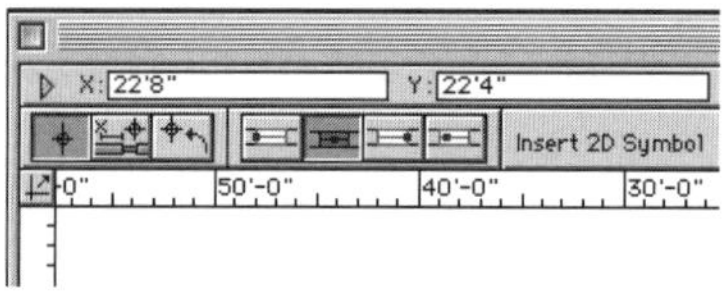

As a note, the door symbols included with VectorWorks have the insertion point centered on the door. The door symbols we created, place the insertion point at the hinge. There are advantages and disadvantages for each.

By having the insertion point centered, you always know where it is. Its location can always be changed by hitting the *I* key when the *2D SYMBOL INSERTION* tool is selected.

On the other hand, particularly with doors, it easier to locate a door on a drawing off of its hinge side rather than its centerpoint, but this becomes a personal preference. To see which method you like, try placing a door that comes with VectorWorks and the one that we created, locating it exactly 6" (.15m) away from the end of a wall. You can use the *smartcursor* and the *data display bar* or use the new *SET REFERENCE POINT* icon for the *2D SYMBOL INSERTION* tool. If the *data display* boxes do not highlight with the *Tab* key or the mode bar icons do not change with the *U* key, click the drawing window to make it active rather than the *RESOURCES* palette.

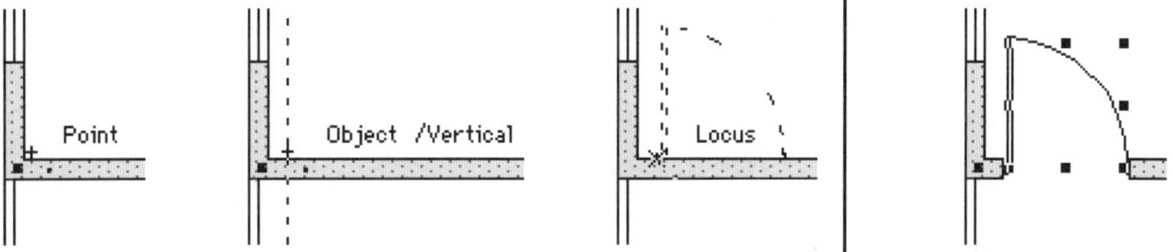

Step 5 - more symbols

Place instances of the furniture on the *walls* layer and *none* class, and instances of the plants on the *floor* layer and *landscape-softscape* class. Go back to the *linked model* layer and view the object in *WIREFRAME* and *SOLID*. Change the active class to *roof-scheme b* and again view it in *WIREFRAME* and *SOLID*.

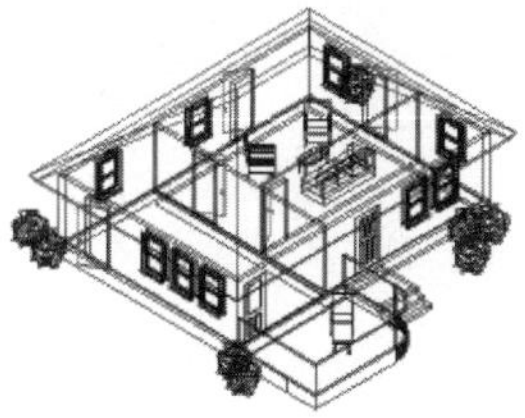

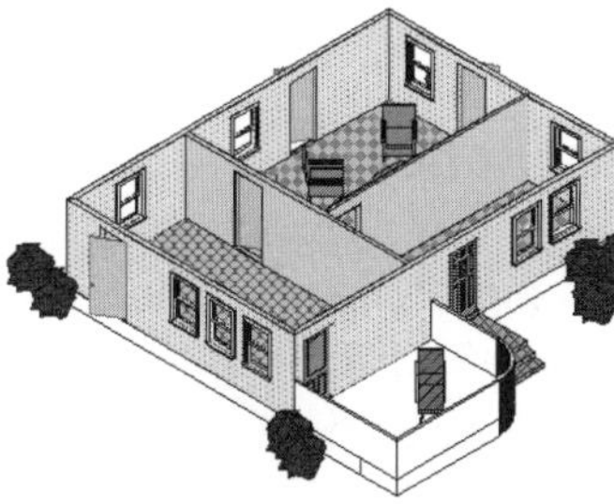

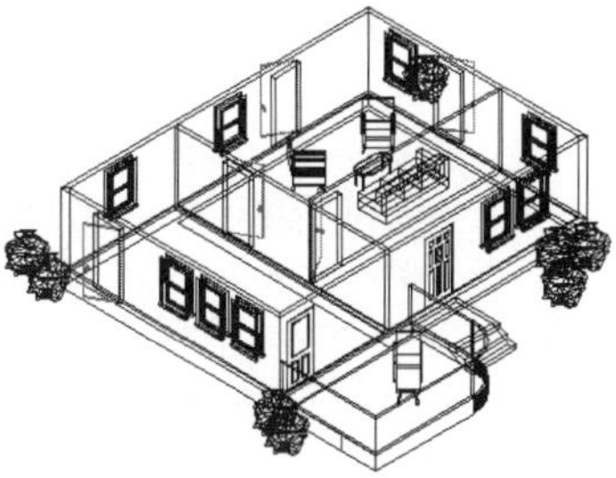

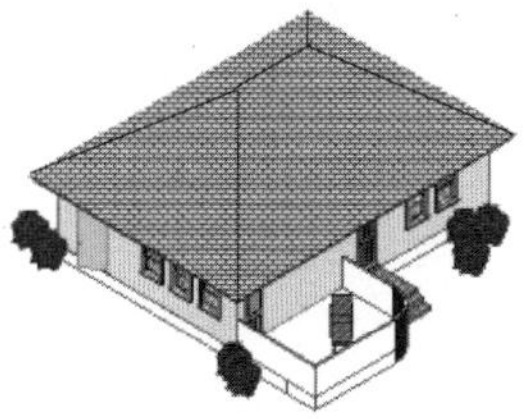

ROOF STUFF

Many times you may need to place different objects in a roof such as a chimney or skylight. The method you would use depends on whether the roof was made with the *Roof Face* command or the *Create Roof From Walls* or the *Create Roof From Polygon* commands. The first command, previously known just as the *Roof* command, creates a hybrid object, which we used in our *roof-scheme a*. The second two commands are new, and create a special high level *roof object* which allows you to make changes via a dialog box, our *roof-scheme b*. Each method of creating a roof has its own ease as well as limitations.

Quick Chimney

A chimney can be created by just extruding a rectangle and placing it on the roof for either method of roof creation. This works fine for creating a quick chimney since the roof when rendered, automatically hides the lower section of the chimney with most of the rendering selections. The limitation is that you do not see a seam where the chimney joins the roof.

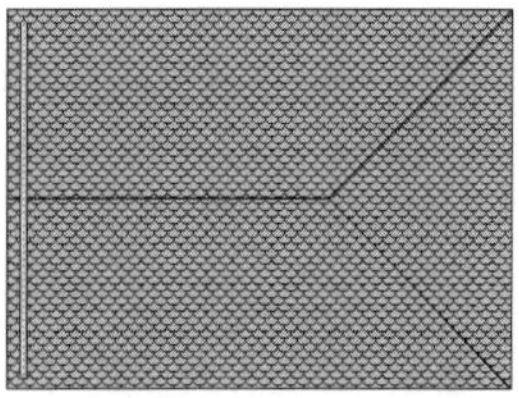

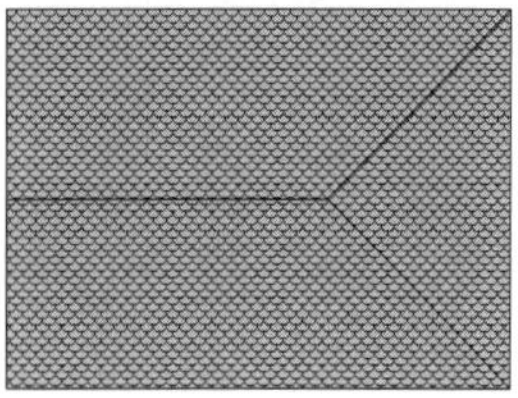

Step 1 - making the chimney

Make the *roof* layer and the *roof-scheme a* class active in *Top/Plan* view. Use the *Eye Dropper* tool to change the *none* fill on the two planes to match the attributes of the third filled roof plane. Since they do not have a fill, the *Eye Dropper* tool will only recognize the edge. With just the wall selected, use *TOOL> Send>Send To Back,* so that the triangular wall is hidden by the roof. Even though both the wall and the roof are hybrid objects since the wall was drawn after the roof, the 2D portion was placed on top. Create a rectangle 3'x2' (.90m x .60m) and use the *Extrude* command. Enter 6' (1.80m) for the *extrusion* and select *ok*.

Step 2 - placing the chimney

Now, with the chimney selected, press/drag it to place it correctly at the location and change views to place it at the appropriate height. Either press the *Shift* key or hit the *S* key to select the *Constrain Angle* constraint.

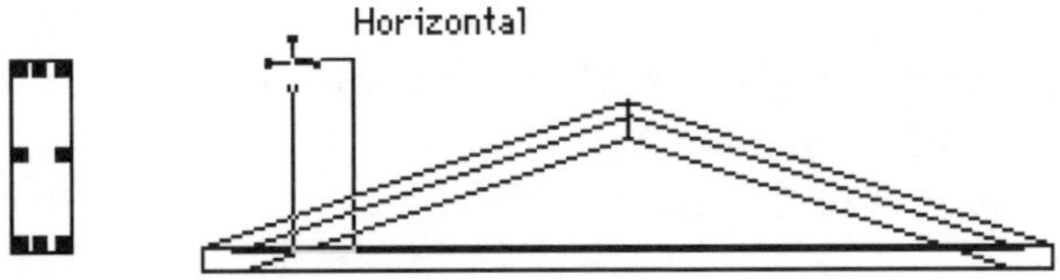

Step 3 - viewing the chimney

Change the view to *Right Isometric*. Select *VIEW> Rendering>Shaded Solid*. Notice how the chimney does not have any lines where it intersects the roof.

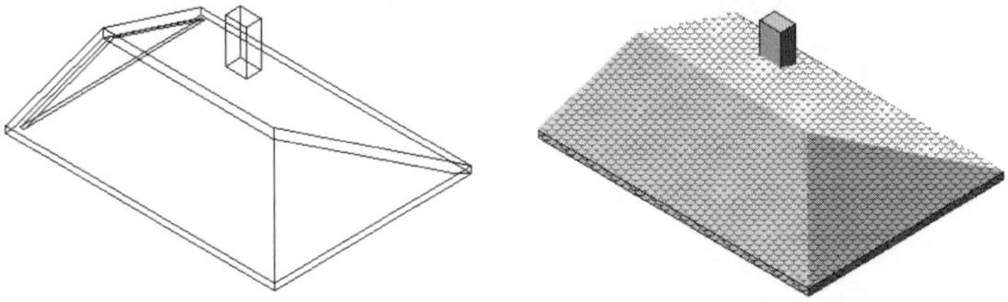

Un-quick Chimney

If you need to actually see a line where the chimney hits the roof, you would either need to cut the chimney and get rid of the hidden part or cut a hole in the roof. We will look at the option of cutting the chimney for *roof-scheme a* and for cutting a hole for *roof-scheme b*.

Step 1 - making the chimney

With *roof-scheme a* the active class, change the view to *Left*, rendering to *Wireframe*, and select the first chimney. Make a duplicate and place it on the opposite plane of the roof.

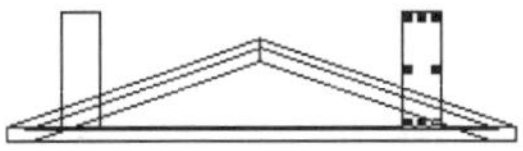

Step 2 - cutting a 3D object

Select *MODEL>Cut 3D Section*. Press/drag a cutting line along the top edge of the roof plane snapping to the two corners, making use of the *smartcursor cues*.

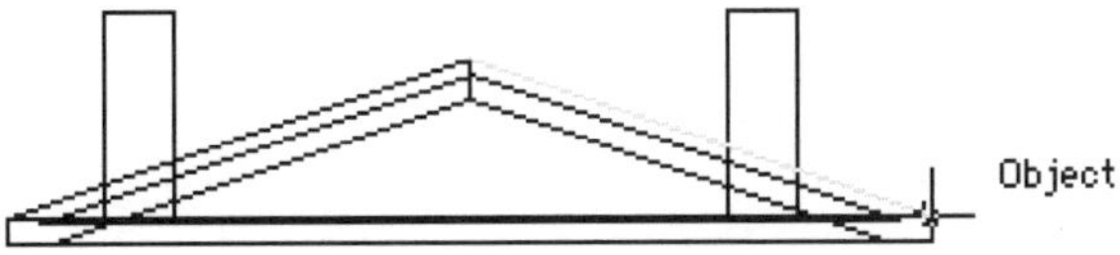

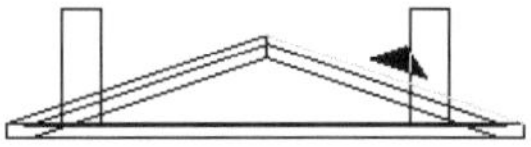

When you release the mouse, an arrow appears similarly to when you created the roof. Click on the side of the chimney you want to keep (not on the side you want to be cut away).

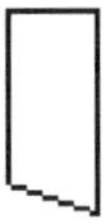

Step 3 - placing the chimney

The original chimney remains and a duplicated 3-dimensional piece is placed on a new layer automatically created, called *layer-1*. Select the new chimney and with the *Object Info* palette, change the class to *roof-scheme a* and the layer to *roof*. Now make *roof* the active layer.

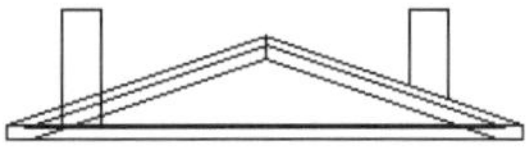

You should have three chimneys on the roof. Select and delete the second chimney. For that matter you can also delete the layer that was automatically created for the 3D section by going to the *Layers Setup* dialog box, selecting the new layer called *layer-1,* and click the *remove* button. A dialog box appears asking if you really want to delete the layer. Select *yes* and then *ok*.

QuickDraw 3D Interactive

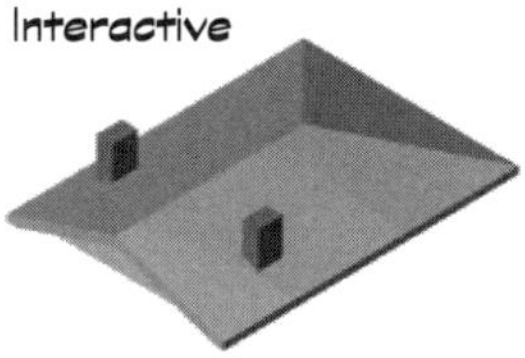

Step 4 - viewing the chimneys

Change the view to one of the isometric views and compare *Final Hidden Line* to the other *Rendering* choices including the *Dashed Hidden Line* rendering style.

Dashed Hidden Line

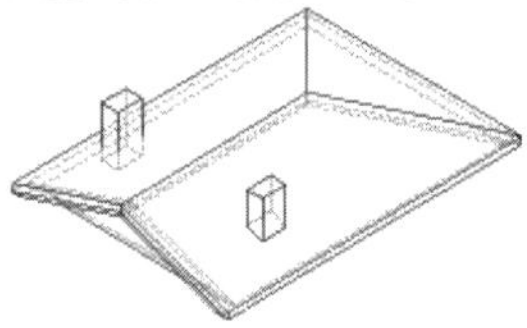

Wireframe

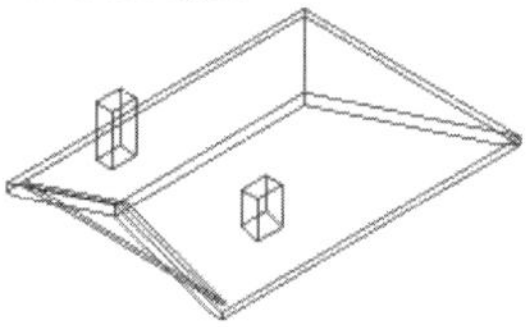

Final Hidden Line

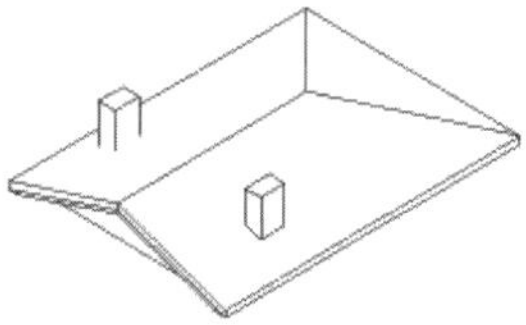

Solid

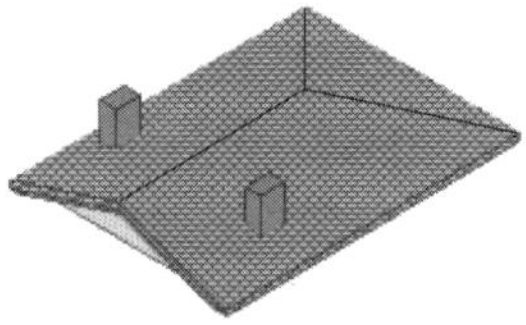

Shaded Solid

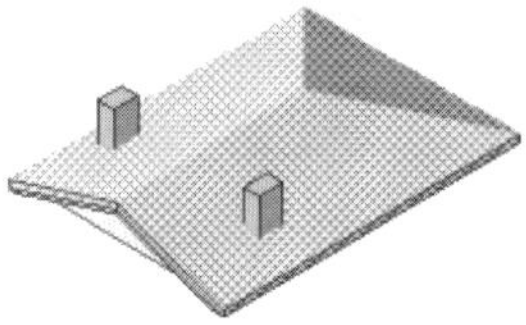

Shaded - No Lines

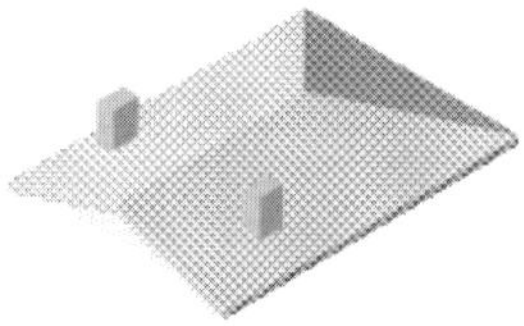

Step 5- another chimney

We are going to make a hole in the roof object made with the new roof commands. Change the active class to *roof-scheme b* and the view to *Top/Plan*. Select the roof object and then *Edit Group*. Draw a 3'x2' (.90m x .60m) rectangle, locating it where the chimney goes, to create a hole in the roof. With the rectangle selected, select the *Copy* command and then *Exit Group*. The hole is visible once you exit. Do a *EDIT>Paste In Place* and then extrude this rectangle to 6' (1.80m). A chimney is now placed in the hole in the roof.

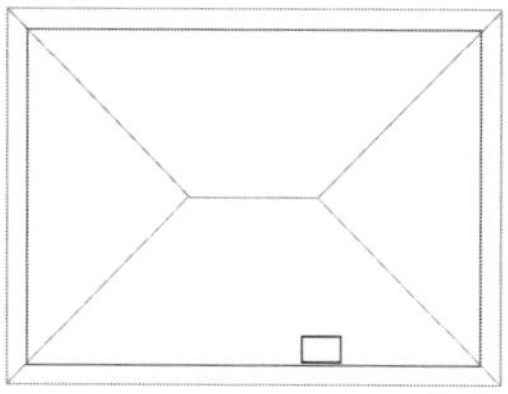

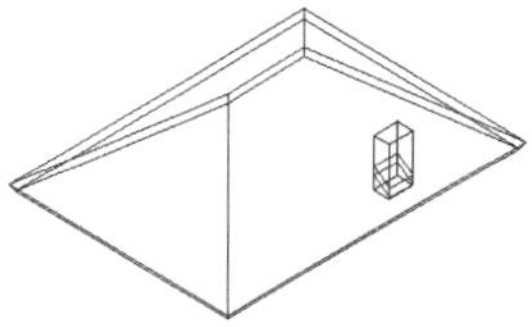

You can use this method to create holes in this type of roof object - just place a 2D object in the *edit roof mode*. The previous roof face of *scheme a* can also have a hole but it is a little more involved. One thing to be aware of – if you want to create a round or curved hole, it will not work with the *roof object* and you will have to use the roof face method. This is a bug with version 8.0 and will hopefully be fixed with later releases.

Roof Object Skylight

Placing skylights on roofs depend on how the roof was created, whether it was a roof face or a roof object. We will look at an example for each. How the skylight appears depends on the rendering option as well.

Make roof the active layer, *roof-scheme b* the active class, and *Layer Options* to *Active Only*. In order to place a skylight on a roof object, the skylight has to be a 3D symbol, not a hybrid. The location of the symbol from the insertion point controls whether the roof gets a vertical or a square miter. Creating a symbol to be used as a skylight is not intuitive at all, in terms of its positioning within views. So be prepared for up-side-down and inside-out and do not try and make sense - just follow the steps.

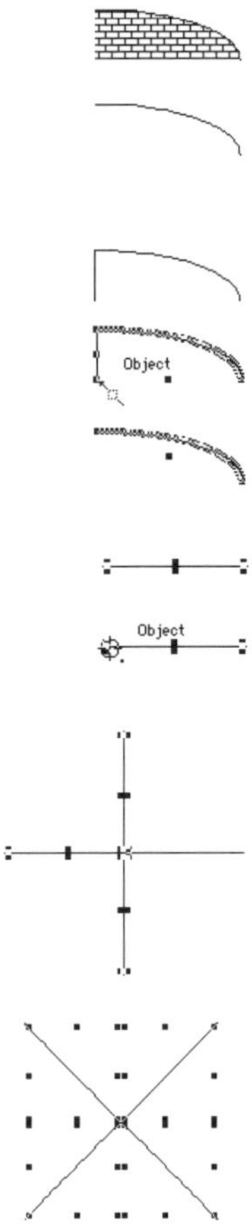

Step 1 - creating the skylight

Change the view to *Top*. With the *Quarter Arc* tool draw a quarter ellipse measuring 18" x 6" (.45m x .15m) and change the fill to *none* and the line weight to .25 with the *Attributes* palette.

Select the arc and the *MODEL>Convert To 3d Polys* command. Use the *2d Reshape* tool with the *delete a vertex* icon to get rid of the radius that appears after the object was converted. Change the view to *Front*, and with the object selected use the *Duplicate Array* command.

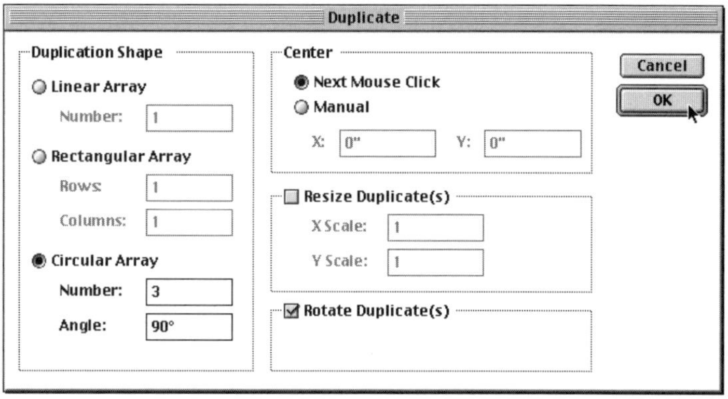

When the dialog box opens, select *circular array*, enter 3 for *number* and 90° for *angle*, and select *rotate duplicate(s)* and the *next mouse click* button, then *ok*. When the dialog box closes click on the left side of the object. The duplicates will appear. Select the four pieces, *Group* them, and then *Rotate* them 45°.

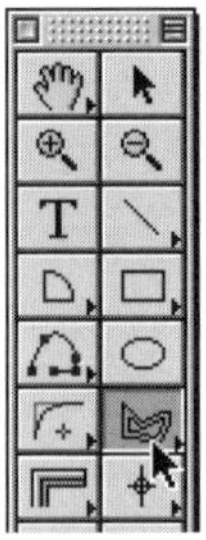

Select the *Double Line Polygon* tool and click the right icon to open the *Double Line Preferences* dialog box. Enter 1 1/2" (.03m) for *separation* and select *create polygon*. With the third icon selected for the control line, click at the top left corner and then each following corner in a clockwise direction. You only need to do a single click to end. With the object selected, change the fill to *solid* and the line weight to .25 in the *Attributes* palette and then *Extrude* this object to 4" (.10m).

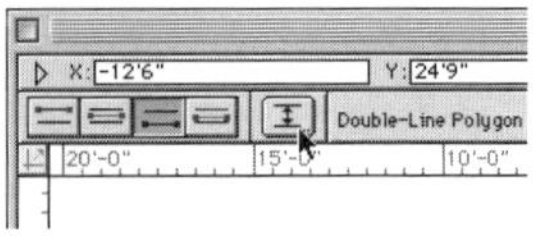

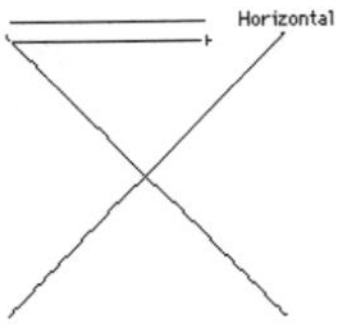

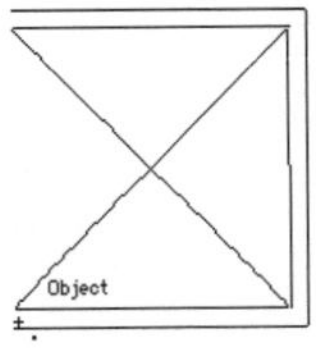

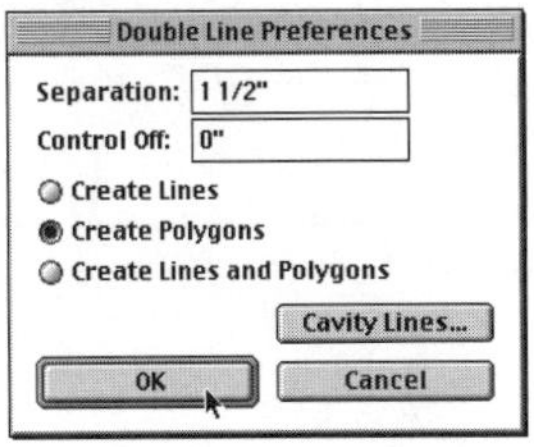

Change to *Top* view and press/drag to align the top of the framing with the bottom of the glass keeping the object constrained with the *Shift* key. Also, when using the *2D Selection* tool to move the object, deselect the first icon with the *U* key so that you do not inadvertently get the *resize* cursor.

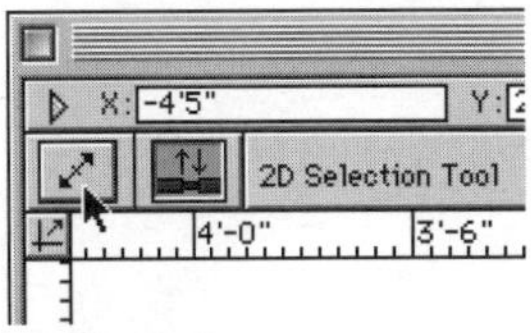

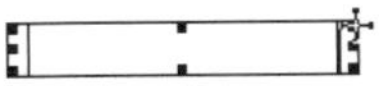

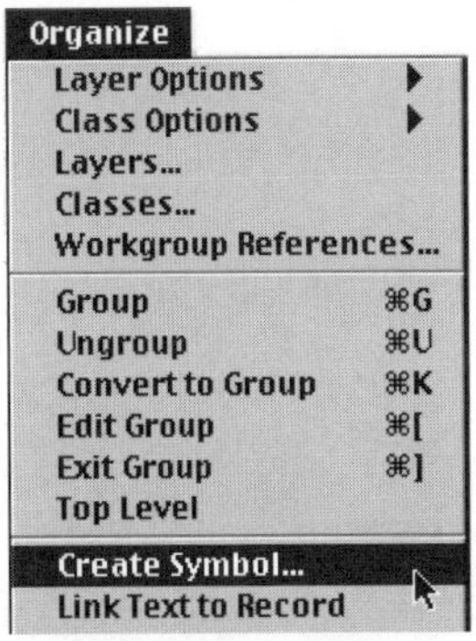

Change to *Front* view and select the glass and framing and then the *ORGANIZE>Create Symbol* command. When the dialog box opens, click the *options* button and choose *on edge*, then *ok*. Name the symbol *skylight 36x36 ver (skylight .9x.9 ver)*, select *next mouse click*, and then click *ok*. When the dialog box closes, the *Move Symbol* dialog box opens so that you can locate the symbol within an existing folder. Just click *ok* to exit without putting it in a folder and then click the object's center. This way the symbol is left in the *Resources* palette rather than filed in a folder within the palette.

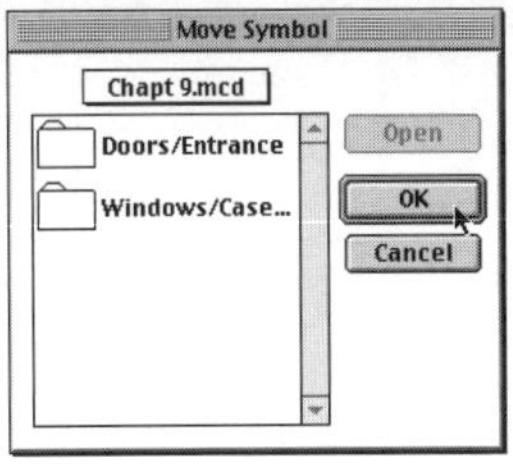

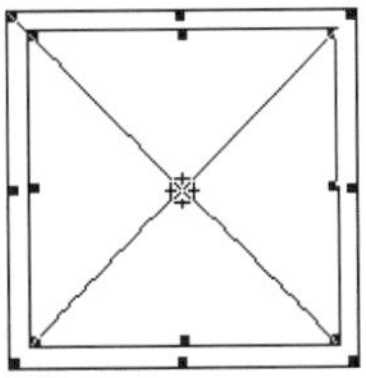

Select the object in the *Resources* palette and the *edit* button. When the *Edit Symbol* dialog box opens, select *3D component* and then click *edit*. The view should be *Front*.

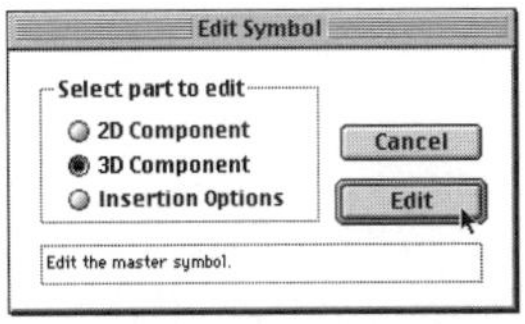

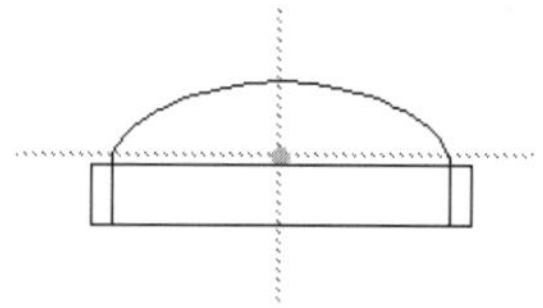

Change it to *Top*. With both objects selected, use the *Rotate>Flip Vertical* command and move the object so that the bottom of the frame sits on the insertion point. The whole thing is now upside down.

top

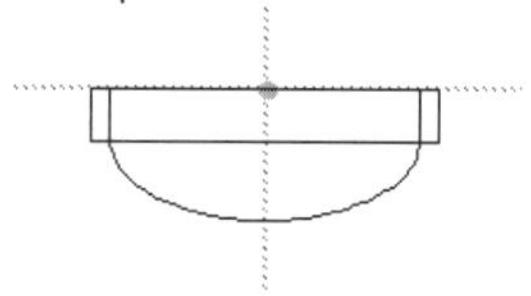

Change the view to *Front* and then to *Left* to verify the insertion point location, then click *exit symbol* .

front

left

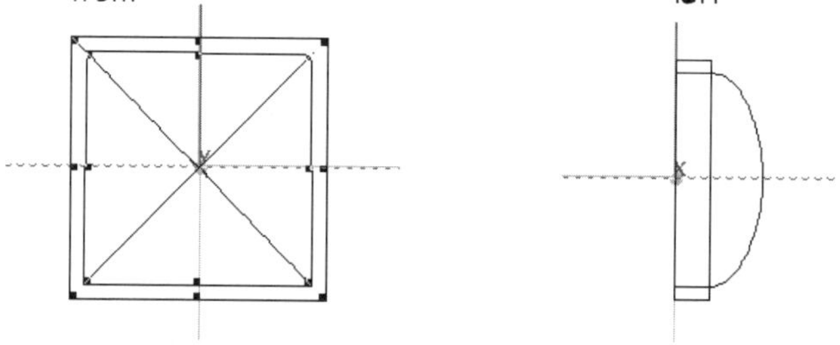

Step 2 - placing the skylight in a roof object

This new symbol should be selected in the *Resources* palette. Change to *Topl/Plan* and select the *2d Symbol Insertion* tool and click on the roof object where the symbol should be located. The *Edit Roof Element* dialog box opens. Click the *edit skylight* button on the upper right. The options change in the dialog box. Adjust the location with the *offset* edit boxes and then click *ok*.

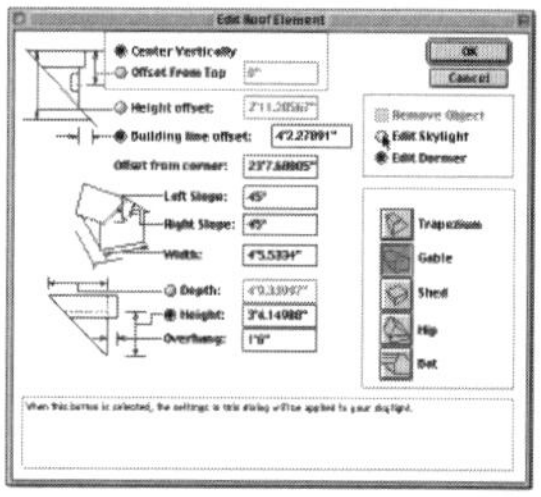

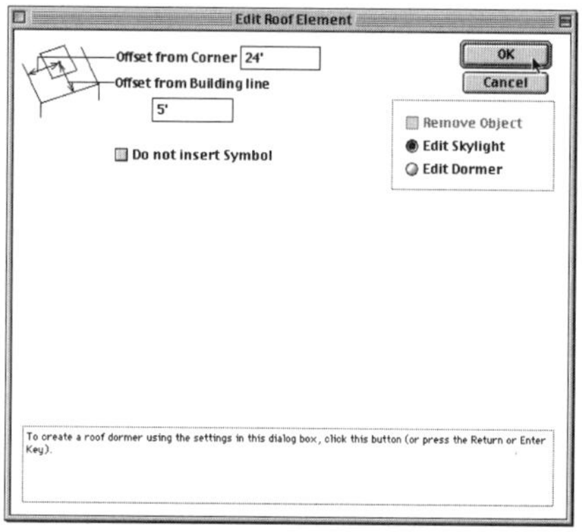

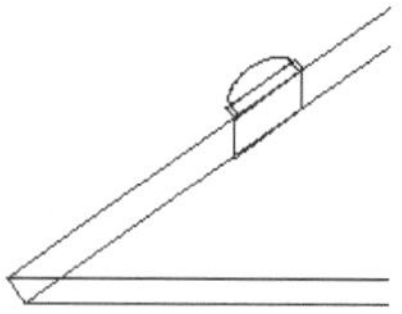

You can view this skylight in different views. Notice that it is flush to the roof top and that the miter within the roof is vertical.

Step 3 - square miter skylights

You may want the miter on the roof object to be square rather than vertical. We will make a duplicate of this symbol and adjust the duplicate for a square miter. Select the skylight *36x36 ver (skylight .9x.9 ver)* and the *DUPLICATE* button in the *RESOURCES* palette. When the *ASSIGN NAME* dialog box opens, name it *skylight 36x36 sq (skylight .9x.9 sq).*

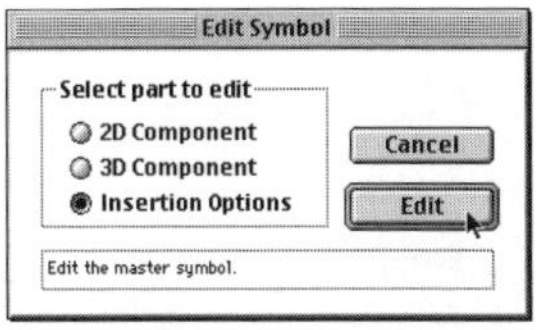

Select the new symbol and the *EDIT* button. When the *EDIT SYMBOL* dialog box opens, click *INSERTION OPTIONS* and then the *EDIT* button. When the *INSERTION OPTIONS* dialog box opens, change the *INSERT IN WALLS* to *ON CENTERLINE* and then click *OK*. With the symbol selected, again click the *EDIT* button in the *RESOURCES* palette and then the *3D COMPONENT* button. You will need to make the view *TOP* and then use the *MOVE* command to move the bottom of the frame a distance away from the insertion point. This distance should be the overall roof thickness, which in this case is 10" (.25m). When done, change to *TOP/PLAN* and place an instance of this symbol on the roof object and compare to the previous skylight.

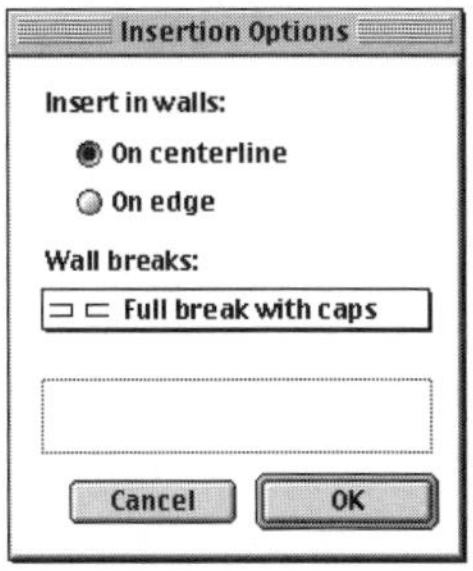

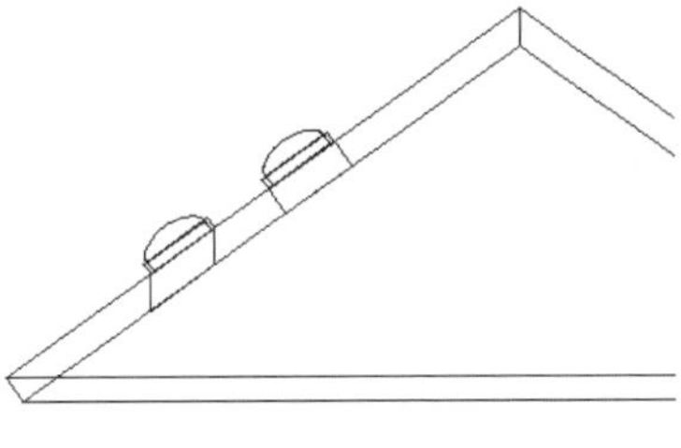

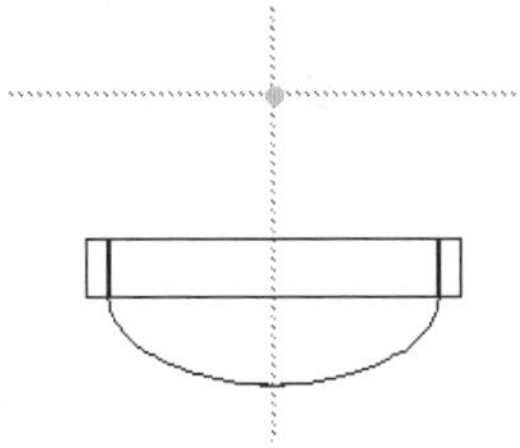

As a note, the outside of the frame is what controls the opening size. There is no way to circumvent this since 3D loci do not override the cut area in a *roof object* the same way they do in walls. One other thing, with both of these symbols, there really is no object for the glass. What we created was a line that shows the ribs or the hip edges. This looks fine in *WIREFRAME* or any of the rendering options that show lines but if you are using another rendering program or even *QD3D* it will appear as if there is nothing above the framing.

Roof Face Skylight

You can not place a round or domed skylight onto a roof object. This is a bug with version 8.0 and hopefully will be fixed in later releases, but until then, you would need to use the *roof face* instead. You can either start with a roof made with the *Roof Face* command, or you can add all of the other items, chimney, holes, etc, to the *roof object* and then use the *Ungroup* command. This will change the *roof object* into individual *roof faces*.

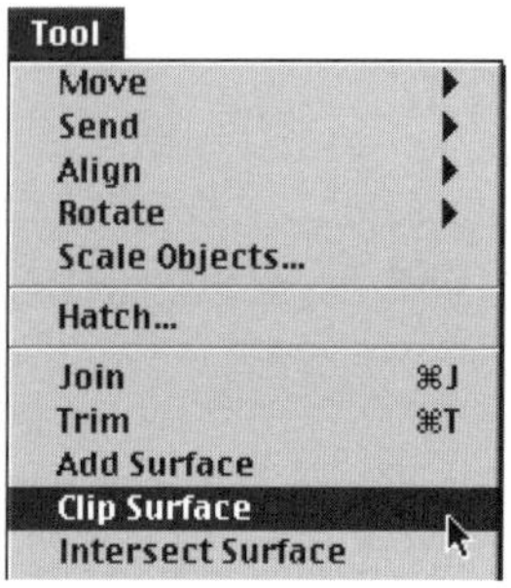

Step 1 - making a hole

Make *roof-scheme a* active and change to *Top/Plan* view. Select one of the roof faces and then the *Edit Group* command. This brings you back to the original 2D object. With the *Ellipse* tool and the *circle by diameter* icon selected, draw a circle with a 2'-0" (.60m) diameter. Select the circle and the roof face and then the *TOOL>Clip Surface* command. Once you use the command, a hole is cut and the circle used as the cutting object then needs to be deleted. Click *done*.

Step 2 - change the miter

You now have a choice as to the miter configuration at the hole edge. Select the *roof face* and then look in the *Object Info* palette. Scroll down if necessary using the double downwards pointing arrows to get to the bottom of the palette. In the *holes* pop-out menu change to *square cut miter*.

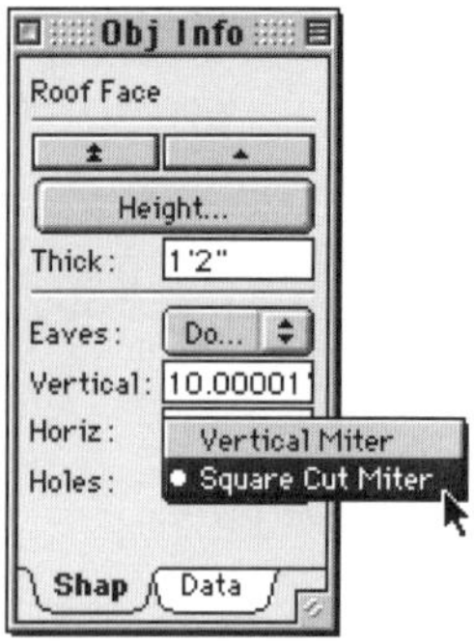

Step 3 - making the skylight dome

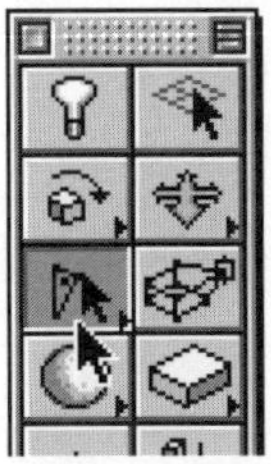

We will now change the *working plane* to match the roof face. Change the view to *Top* and the rendering to *Solid*. With the *Set Working Plane* tool, click on the *roof face* where the hole is cut.

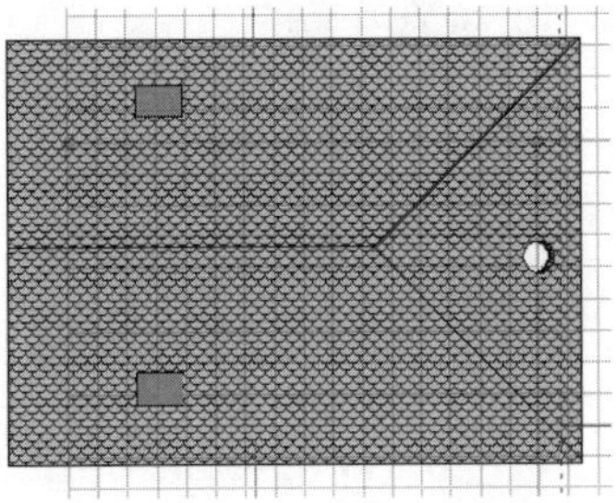

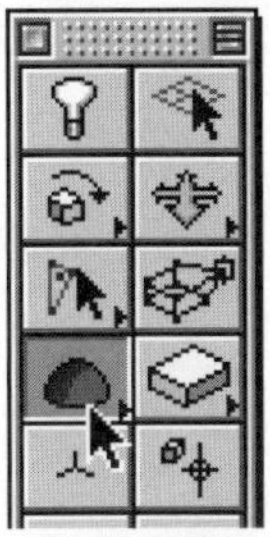

Select the *Hemisphere* tool and the *by diameter* icon. Press/drag to create the object, snapping to the hole edges. When the hemisphere is created, change the fill to *none* and line weight to the thinnest weight.

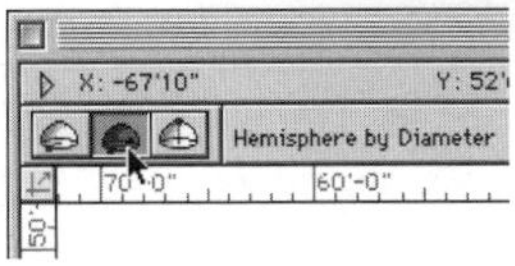

By changing the *working plane,* a 3D object is aligned with this plane while being created rather than located on the *ground plane*. Look at the roof in other views.

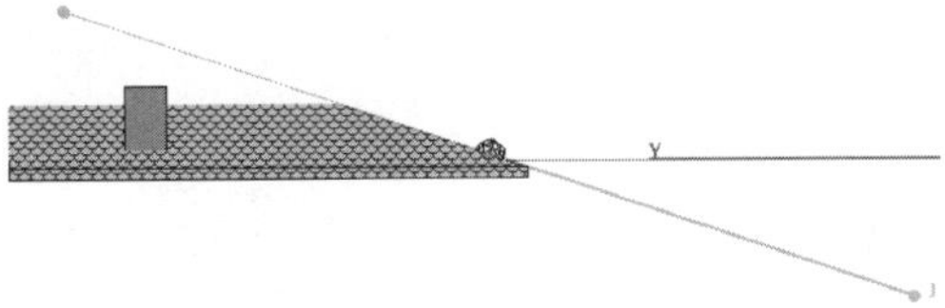

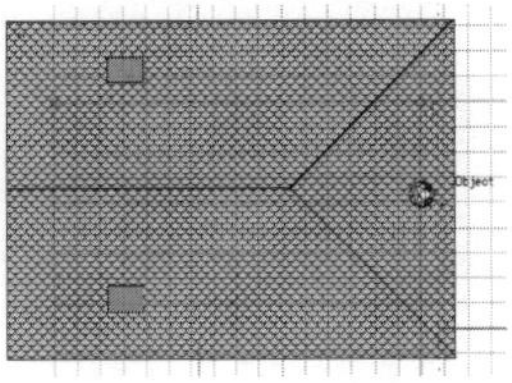

With the *Set Working Plane* tool, click anywhere on the blank drawing to have it aligned with the *ground plane* again. Notice that the pink grid for the *working plane,* disappears.

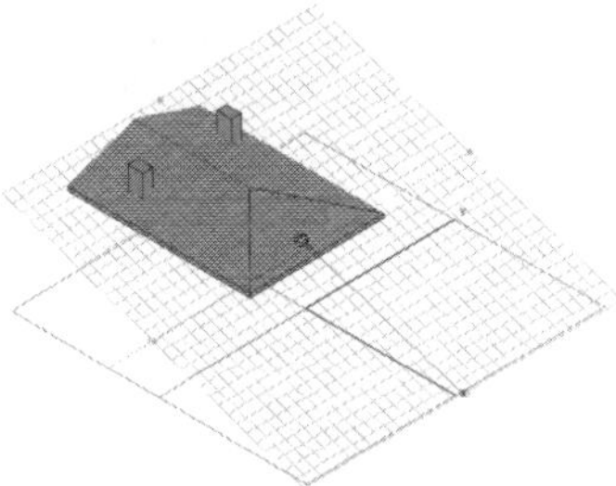

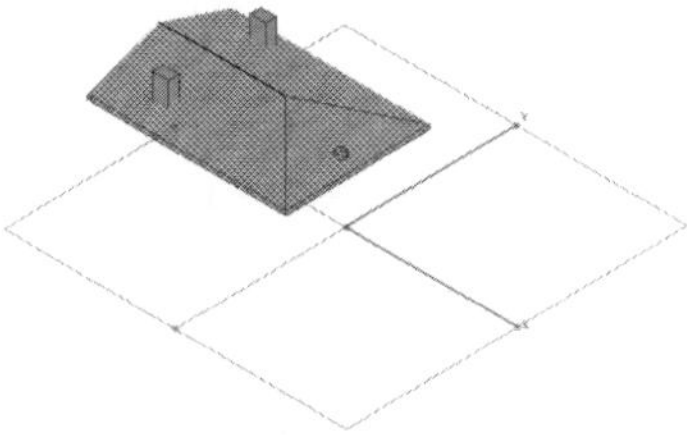

SITE STUFF

There are a variety of elements that go on a site plan. What you need to keep in mind is whether or not you also want these elements to project into a 3D space for a 3-dimensional drawing and whether they need to be a solid object so that it can receive a fill color or pattern. You can always convert a 2D object into 3D if necessary, or if you are using a linked layer you can project 2D objects, but with some limitations.

Property Lines

When showing a building there are times when it is appropriate to show property lines and sometimes it would be nice if it can project in 3D. Typically though, 2D objects such as a line will not project, nor will a dashed line style, but there is a work-around.

Step 1 - creating the property line

With *floor* the active layer and *none* the active class, in *Top/Plan*, create a rectangle that is 50'x75' (15.00m x 22.50m). Select the rectangle and change the fill to *none*, the line weight to .8 and place it around the building. Now change the line style to an appropriate dot and dash style for a property line by pressing on the line style button in the *Attributes* palette.

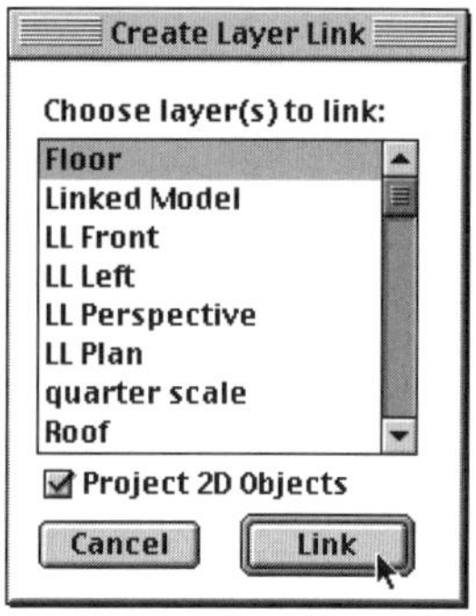

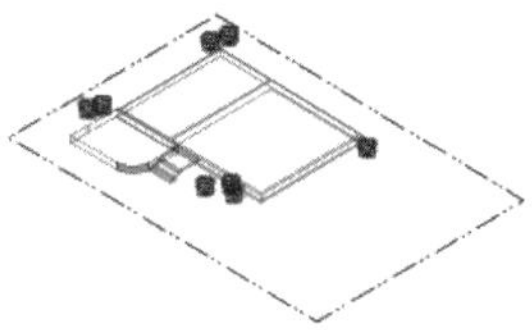

Step 2 - projecting the property line

Go back to the *ll isometric* layer, change to *Rendering>Wireframe*, and select *View>Create Layer Link*. Select the *floor* layer in the scrolling list and click to select the *project 2D objects* button before you choose *link*.

Just the *floor* layer will appear in the center of the sheet. Even though you had already linked this layer, linking it again will not cause any problems. Select *Create Layer Link* again and this time select *walls* and *roof* then *link*, but do not select the *project 2D objects* box.

Notice now we have two separate linked objects. This is because we unlocked and moved the first linked element earlier. Select the first one, *Unlock* and *Delete* it. Select the one with the property line, *Unlock* and relocate it, then re-*Lock* it.

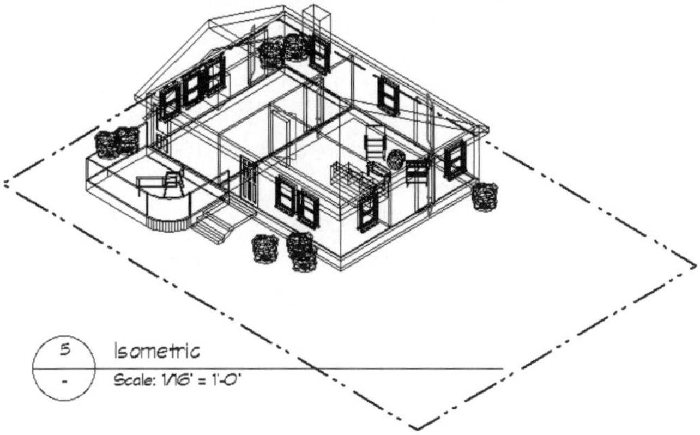

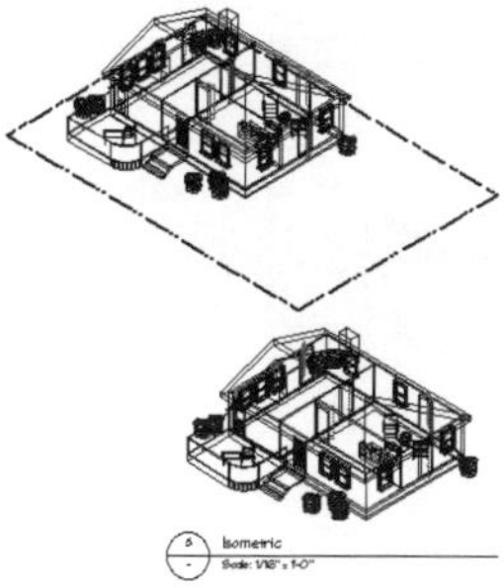

Choosing *Project 2D objects* allows you to not only project a 2D object but also to give it a line style other than solid. Normally, dashed line styles will not appear on 3D objects, which is why we did not create a 3D polygon from the rectangle instead.

Step 3 - viewing the property line

There are times you might want to see the property line in one view, but not in another. Go back to the *floor* layer. What you would do is, create another class called *landscape-site info* and click the *invisible* button in the *Classes* dialog box. Notice that there are a multitude of new classes automatically created when we imported the symbols. Exit and select the property line and using the *Object Info* palette, change its class to the one we just created. The selected object automatically moves to the new class and in this case will disappear since the class is not visible. If you look at the *II isometric* layer, the property line appears if *landscape-site info* is active and it will disappear if *none* becomes the active class. You may need to force a screen redraw by double-clicking the *Pan* tool.

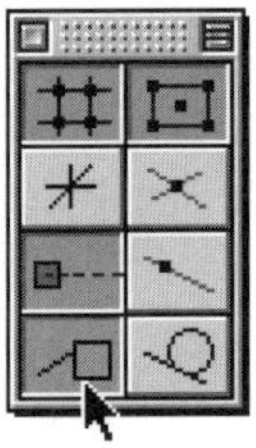

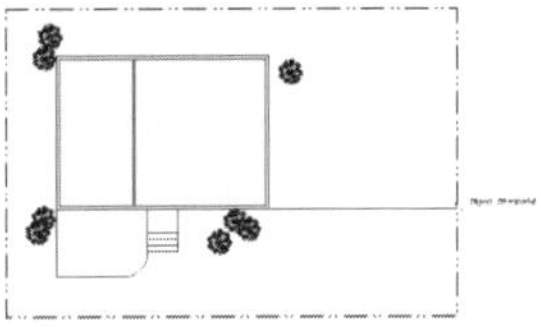

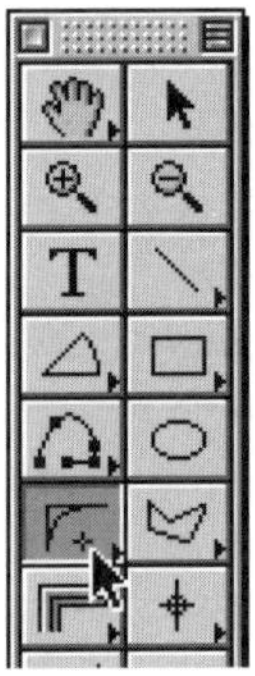

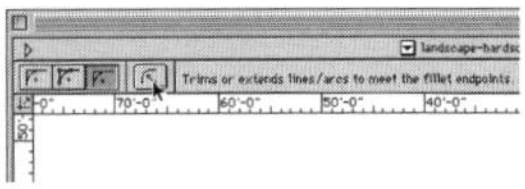

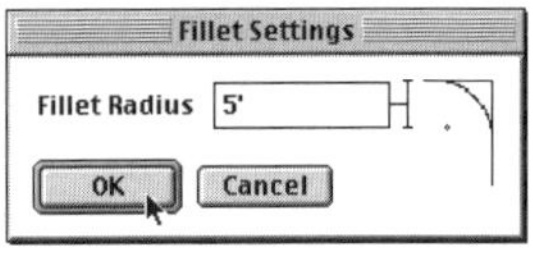

Driveway

The next item you might want to create is a driveway that is radiused at the property line. Make *floor* the active layer, *landscape-hardscape* the active class, and select the *Snap To Edge* constraint. You will also need to make the *landscape-site info* *visible* in the *Classes* dialog box.

Step 1 - creating a driveway edge

Select the *Single Line* tool with the *constrained* modifier icon and draw a line from the building edge over towards the property line for one side of the driveway. Make use of the *smartcursor* and make sure you are snapping to the actual edge of the building and the property line.

Step 2 - creating the radius

Select the *Fillet* tool with the *trims or extends lines/arcs to meet the fillet endpoints* modifier icon. Then click the right most icon to open the *Fillet Settings* dialog box. Enter 4' (1.20m) and select *ok*.

Now press/drag anywhere on the driveway edge and release on the property line. The side you release on should be towards the centerpoint of the arc.

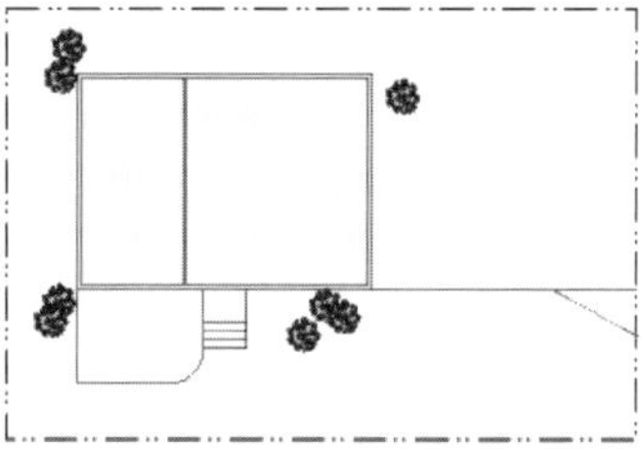

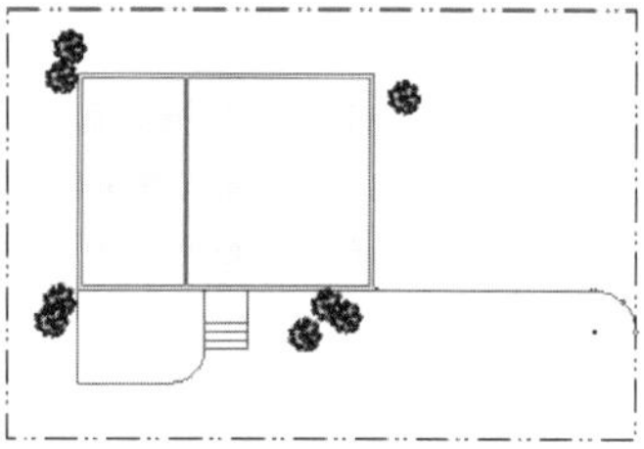

Step 3 - finishing the driveway

The modifier icon used with the *Fillet* tool automatically creates the radius portion and trims the line at the spring point of the arc. You have two objects, the arc or fillet and the line. Select both and *Group*. With the grouped object selected use the *Mirror* tool with the *mirror and duplicate* modifier icon. Press/drag an axis line 4'-0" (1.20m) over

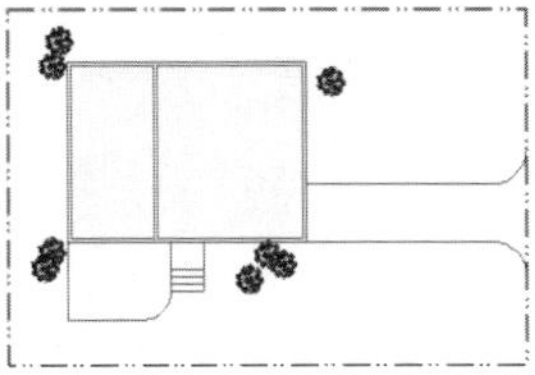

making use of the floating datum point and entering the dimensions into the *data display bar* (half the width of the driveway). Use the *Shift* key to keep it constrained. When you release the mouse, the other edge is created. Select both edges and *GROUP* to keep them from getting inadvertently misaligned and change its line weight to .25.

The driveway is also visible in *// isometric* since the *PROJECT 2D OBJECTS* box was selected.

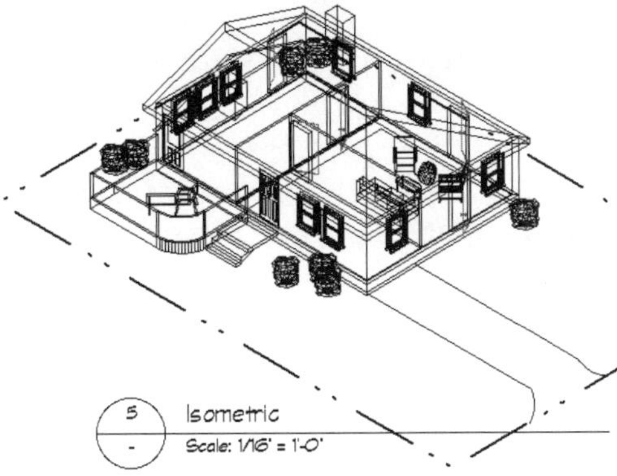

OTHER STUFF IN SUMMATION

SAVE the document and *QUIT [EXIT]*. As you can see there are many ways to get to the same point when drawing with VectorWorks. The little things and the fine tuning are the time consuming elements. Although you will find there are certain tools you will use most of the time, the other tools do become quite valuable when doing that odd and infrequent little task.

- How to organize a drawing depends on the type of projects you do as well as how you want it to appear. The roof is just one example of a decision of choosing between a layer or class for organization.

- One way to think of a class for organization is as a method to subdivide a layer.

- The location of the insertion point for symbols is important and a system should be developed to remember just where it is located.

- Depending on the 3D object to cut, use either the *Cut 3D Section* command or the *Edit Group* command and cut the original 2D object.

- Using the *Cut 3D Section* on a symbol or wall changes the object into a grouped object.

- 2D elements can be projected into 3D, but with some drawbacks, so be aware of how you use it.

- Only solid lines appear in 3D views. If you want to project a 2D object with a dashed line style use the *Layer Link* command.

- If you want a 3D object with a line style, select a pen *pattern* on the *Attributes* palette instead.

Chapter 10

USING VECTORWORKS

CREATING A NEW TEMPLATE

We have gone through many steps to learn how to create and organize objects. What we will do next is look at how to organize a drawing. There are many ways this can be done depending on the type of work you produce as well as your office standards. What we will do is look at one type of template with a more sophisticated level of information integral within it.

The following tools, commands, constraints, and other items will be explored;

- *Linear Dimension* Tool
- *Text Insertion* Tool
- *Wall* Tool
- *Classes* Command
- *Custom Tool/Attribute* Command
- *Date Stamp* Command
- *Document Preferences* Command
- *Guides* Command
- *Drawing Size* Command
- *Save As Template* Command
- *Save Sheet* Command
- *Set Origin* Command
- *Set Wall Style* Command
- *Purge Unused Objects* Command
- *Snap To Distance* Constraint
- *Snap To Intersection* Constraint
- *Resources* Palette
- *Worksheet*
- *View Bar*

SETTING UP THE ENVIRONMENT

We will create a new template with typical elements you might use on a one-story residential project. First we will set up a file and once all of the information is entered, we will then save it as a template file to be used as a basis for future projects. It will

VectorWorks 8.5.1

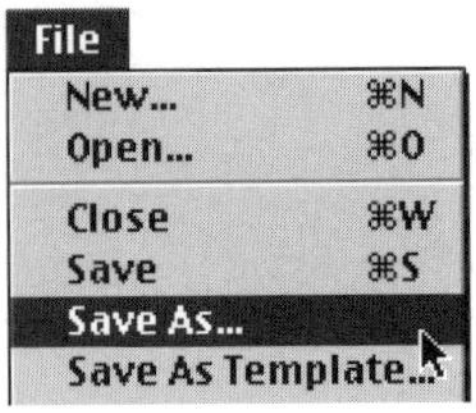

include a typical sheet size, layers and class setups, title block, and other things. To start, double-click the *VectorWorks 8* icon or select *FILE>NEW* if already opened. Do a *FILE>SAVE As* and give the untitled document the name *Resid C1 [Resid C1.mcd]*, locating it in the *VectorWorks 8 ƒ* folder. This naming differentiates the project types (residential, commercial....), various sizes (C, D...), and number of stories. Change to *WORKSPACES>AEC (STREAMLINED)*.

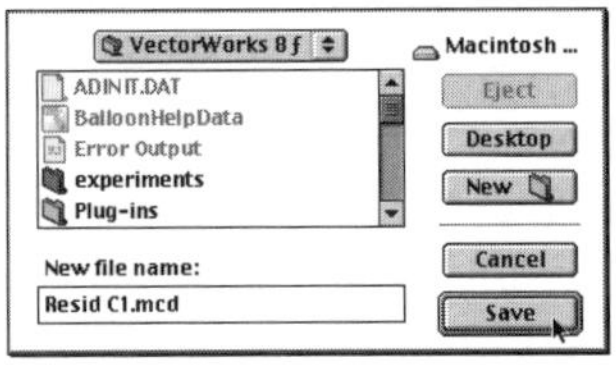

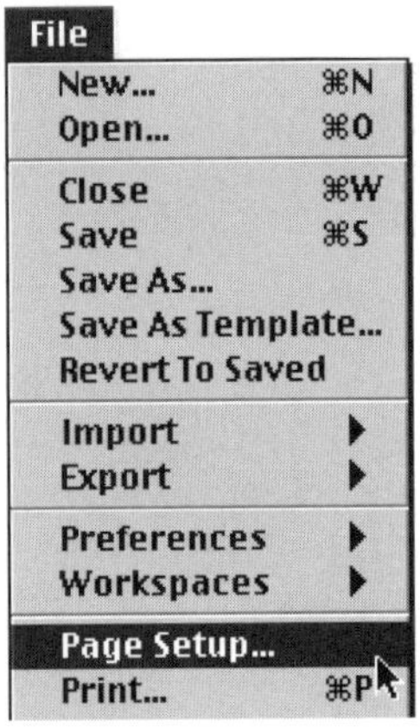

Sheet Size

We will set up a template using a "C" (A2) size sheet which is 18"x24" (.42m x .59m). If your printer only has the options for letter and legal (A4 or B4) you might want to consider tiling the pages.

Step 1 - choosing the sheet size

First go to *FILE>PAGE SETUP [PRINT SETUP]* and select "C" (A2) size with *LANDSCAPE*. If your printer or plotter does not have that capacity choose *LEDGER* (A3) with *PORTRAIT*. And last, if you only have *LETTER* or *LEGAL* size available, select the larger of the two (A4 or B4) with *PORTRAIT*. Check the *HI-RESOLUTION PRINTING* box and *LARGER PRINT AREA* if these options are available. Many of the printer drivers have the different choices located in pop out menus or under an *OPTIONS* button. Make sure your printer has the capability to print the size sheet you selected.

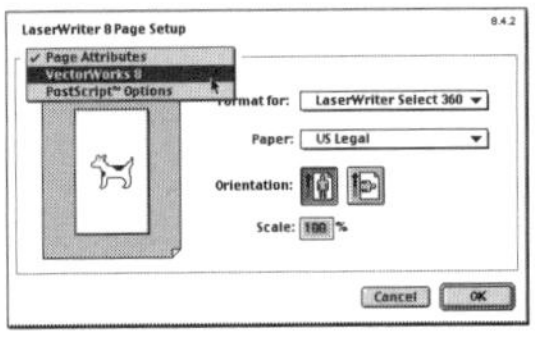

Step 2 - tiling

If your printer has the capacity to print a "C" (A2) size sheet you will not need to tile the sheets and can skip the rest of this step.

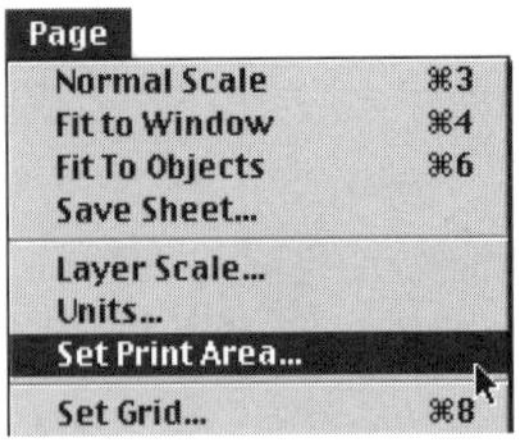

If you do not have the option of directly printing a "C" (A2) size, go to *PAGE>SET PRINT AREA* to open the *SET PRINT AREA* dialog box. Press/drag down to *US ARCH C* (*ISO A2*) under *SIZE*. Notice that it will automatically show the *WIDTH*

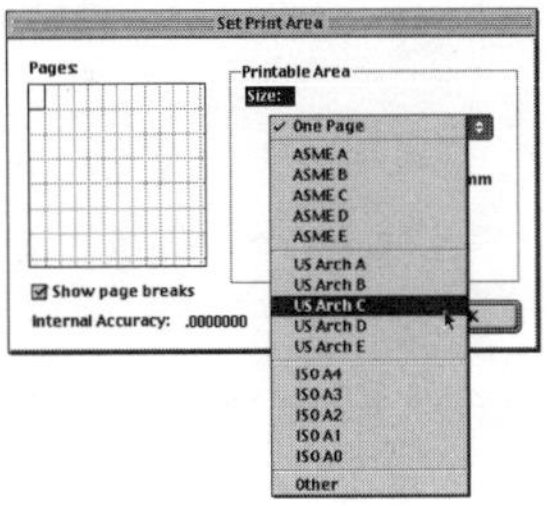

and *HEIGHT* under *PRINTABLE AREA* in the appropriate dimensioning system as well as calculate the correct number of sheets under *PAGES*, based on the *PAPER* selected in the *PAGE SETUP* [*PRINT SETUP*] dialog box. It will also recognize whether *PORTRAIT* or *LANDSCAPE* was selected. Select the *SHOW PAGE BREAKS* box and *OK*.

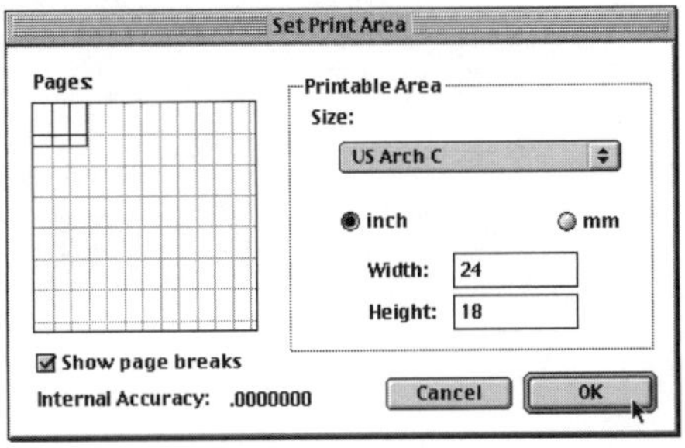

When the dialog box closes, the drawing window also shows the outline for the printable area for each sheet. You could have also selected the number of whole sheets to be printed under *PAGES* by clicking in the page boxes. The *SIZE* under *PRINTABLE AREA* will then reflect the actual printing size taking into account the margins.

Measurement System

Select the *UNIT NAME* in the measurement system you will use by selecting *PAGE>UNITS* to open the *SET UNITS* dialog box. Select the amount of precision you want VectorWorks to show (*DISPLAY PRECISION*).

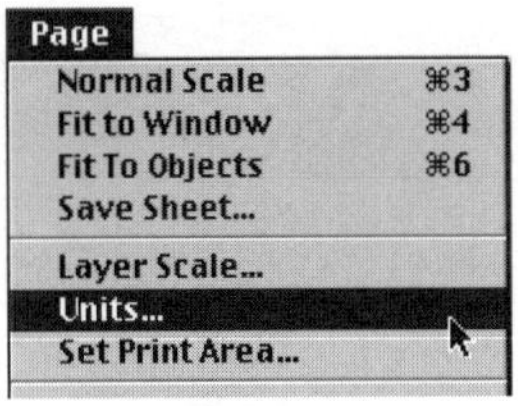

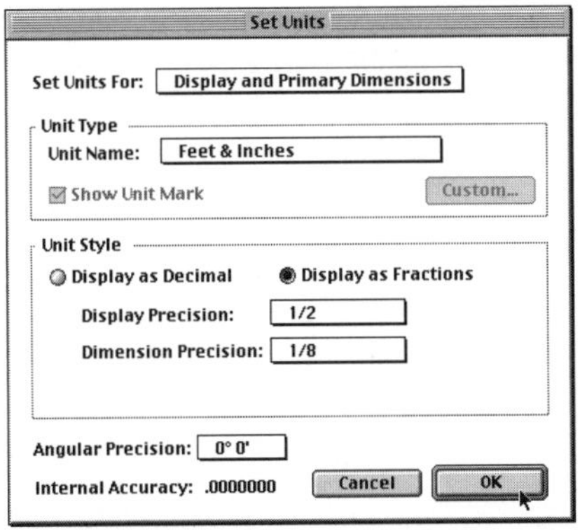

Grids

Go to *PAGE>SET GRID* or double-click the *SNAP TO GRID* icon to open the *SET GRID* dialog box and enter the *REFERENCE GRID* and *SNAP GRID* that would initially be most helpful.

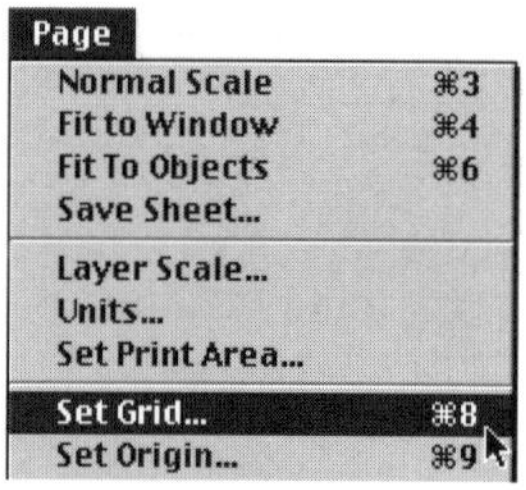

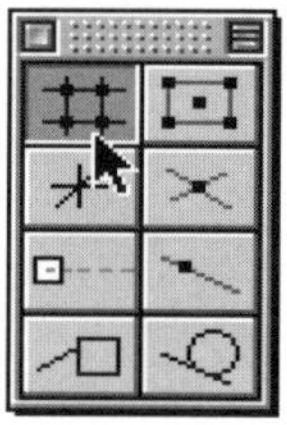

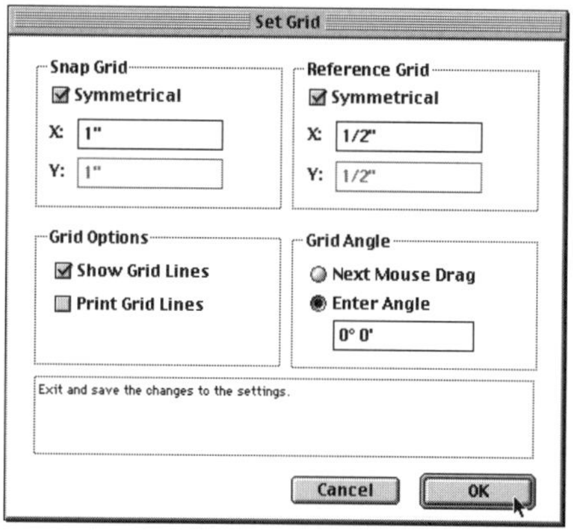

Origin Point

We will change the location of the origin point to the lower left corner so that we are only dealing with the positive XY quadrant, same as the quadrants you learned (and of course remember) in geometry. Right now the origin point should be located in the center of your printable area.

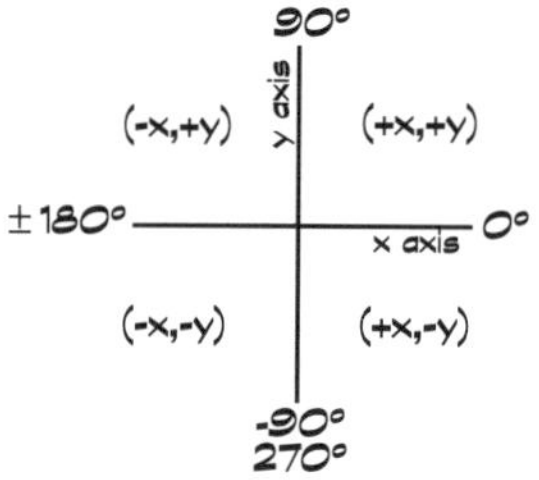

Step 1 - changing the origin point

Use the *ZOOM-IN* tool to get closer to the lower left corner of your printable area. You might need to first use *PAGE> FIT TO WINDOW* in order to find the corner where you need a closer look. Once you are close enough to clearly see that corner, select *PAGE>SET ORIGIN*. The *SET ORIGIN* dialog box opens.

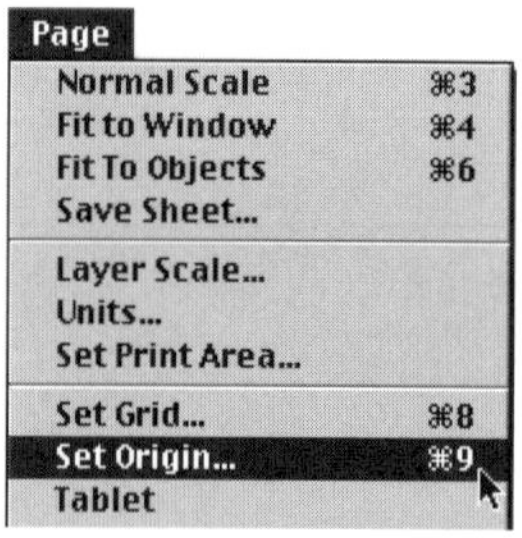

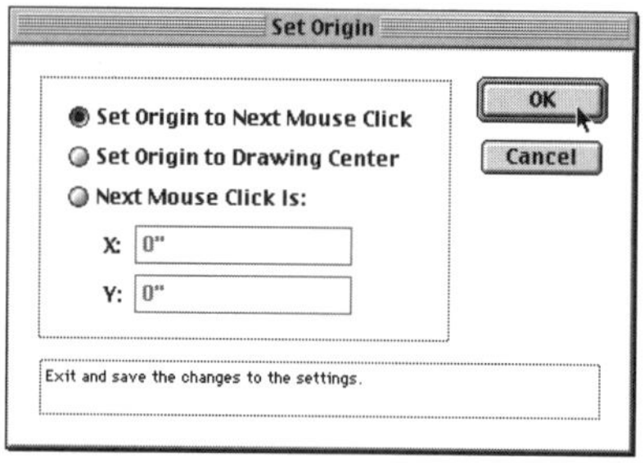

This dialog box now allows you to place an origin point off of the drawing area which is useful when importing some documents. Select *SET ORIGIN TO NEXT MOUSE CLICK* and *OK*. Place the *bulls eye* cursor on that lower left corner of the printable edge and click. Notice that the coordinates for this point have now changed to (0,0) in the *data display bar* as well as on the rulers. If you can not align the cursor exactly with the corner, then deselect the *SNAP TO GRID* constraint either by clicking it or hitting the *A* key, then do *SET ORIGIN* again.

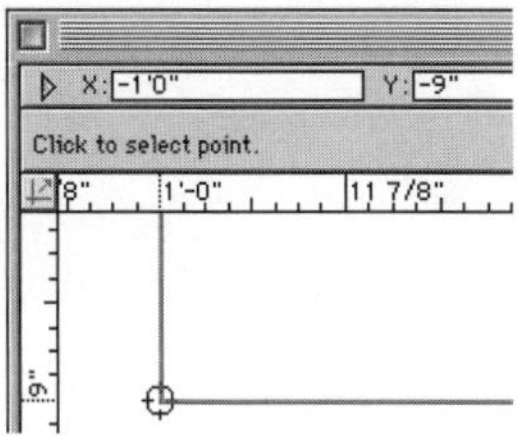

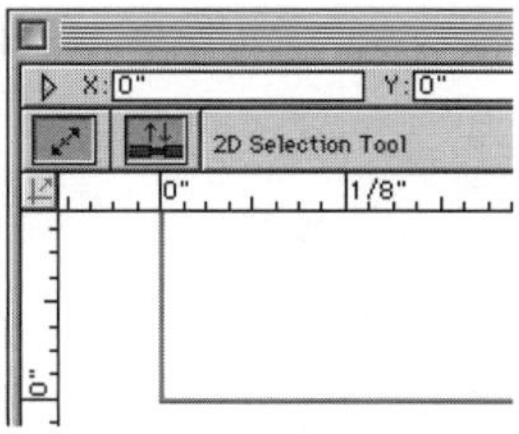

Other Default Items

Verify that the *CONSTRAINTS* palette has the three default icons selected. Double-click the *SNAP POINTS* icon and in the *SMART POINTS* dialog box check both the *HORIZONTAL/VERTICAL EXTENSIONS* and *USE FLOATING DATUM* boxes, then *OK*. Double-click the *CONSTRAIN ANGLE* icon to verify that only the *30,60* and *45* boxes are checked in the *ANGLE SNAPS* dialog box. Double-click the *SNAP TO EDGE* constraint and select *USE 2ND VECTOR*, *USE FLOATING EDGE*, and *SNAP TO EXTENSION LINES* in the *EDGE SNAPS* dialog box. The middle line weight is helpful to be selected as the default weight in the *ATTRIBUTES* palette.The default *TEXT>FONT* and *SIZE* should also be selected.

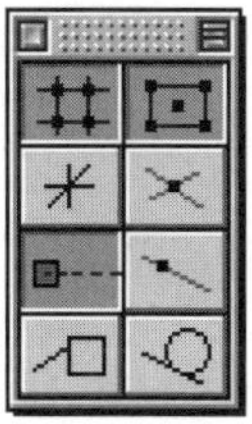

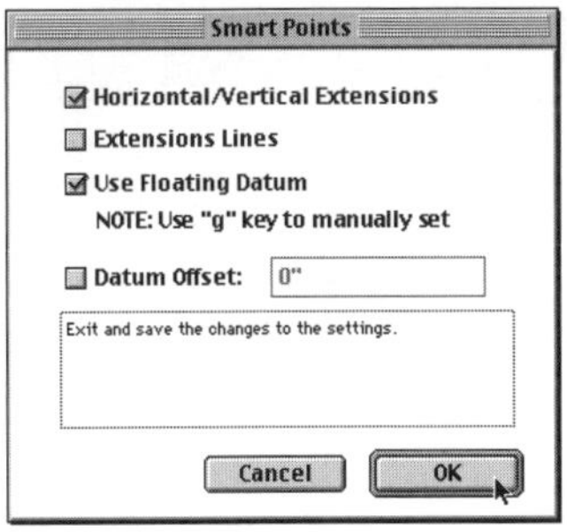

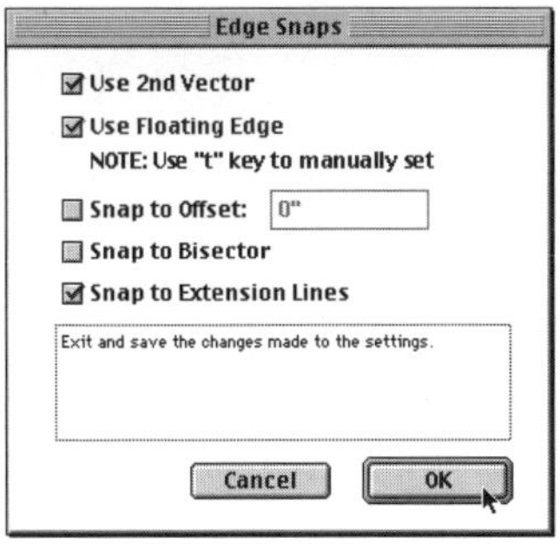

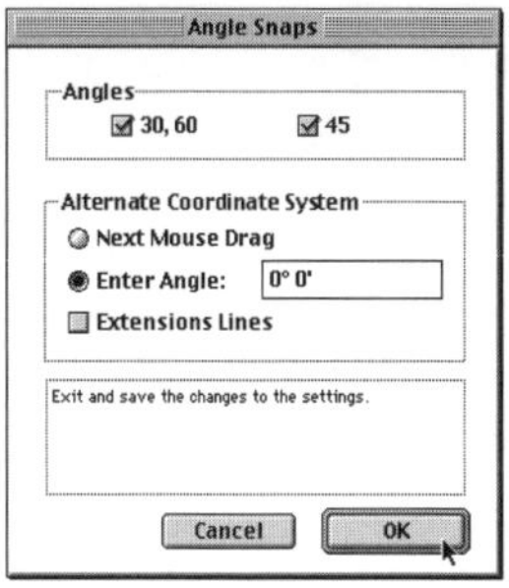

ORGANIZING INFORMATION

Our new template will include a series of layers and classes, and a group of commands which control the visibility settings of these layers and classes. Understanding how you put together a set of drawings is critical to making this work well.

The first issue to analyze is what type of information gets reused on different printed sheets versus what is unique to one sheet. Careful planning will prevent the need to redraw items and save time later on. The other issue is knowing where objects should be located – on which layers and classes. This should be intuitive and easy to remember whatever method you use to separate information.

The Drawing Matrix

To start with, I generally look at the end point, the individual printed sheets necessary for a set. These sheet names will be made into commands. When activated, each command will make visible the correct combination of layers and classes for that particular sheet. For this example, we will create a set that has thirteen sheets.

Title Sheet
Site Plan
Demolition Plan
Partition Plan
Roof Plan
Reflected Ceiling Plan
Telephone & Electrical Plan
Floor Finish Plan
Furniture Plan
Cabinetry Plan
Exterior Elevations
Details
3D View

The next thing to determine is the layers necessary to divide information up. Layers are being used for items at different heights z and Δz $[\pm z]$ values, different scales, and for linked layers. Classes are used to subdivide the layers further. To think this through you would need a good understanding of how VectorWorks works. In this example we will be setting up 13 layers and 35 classes (which includes *none* and *dimension*) for the 13 sheets.

It is easier to arrange the combination of sheets, layers, and classes if we arrange all the information in a matrix. For this example, all the layers and classes are on the left side of the matrix and the sheet names/commands are on the top. The visibility settings for each sheet are marked with an ✘ for visible and active, ✓ for visible, ❍ for grey, or just left empty for invisible.

	Sheet Names/Commands	Title Sheet	Site Plan	Demolition Plan	Partition Plan	Roof Plan	Refl Ceiling Plan	Tele & Elec Plan	Flr Finish Plan	Furniture Plan	Cabinetry Plan	Exterior Elev	Details	3D View	master layers	all on
Layers																
Title		✗	✓	✓	✓	✓	✓	✓	✓	✓	✓	✓	✓	✓		✗
Foundation Floor				✓	✓	○		✓	✗	✓	✓				✗	✓
First Floor				✗	✗		✓	✗	✓	✗	✗				✓	✓
First Flr Ceiling							✗	○			○				✓	✓
Roof						✗									✓	✓
LL Grade			✗											✗		✓
LL Front												✗				✓
LL Left												✓				✓
LL Right												✓				✓
LL Back												✓				✓
Details 1/2													✓			✓
Detail 1 1/2													✗			✓
Detail 3													✓			✓
Classes																
None		✓	✓	✓	✓	✓	✓	✓	✓	✓	✓	✓	✓	✓	✗	✗
Dimension			✓		✓	✓	✓	✓	✓		✓	✓	✓			✓
title-block		✓	✓	✓	✓	✓	✓	✓	✓	✓	✓	✓	✓	✓		✓
-info		✗														✓
landscape-bldg			✓											✓		✓
-plantg			✓											✓		✓
-hardscape			✓											✓		✓
-info			✗													✓
floor-layout				✓	✓	○		✓	✓	✓	✓	✓		✓	✓	✓
-patterns									✓							✓
-info									✗							✓
walls-new					✓		✓	✓	✓	✓	✓	✓		✓	✓	✓
-existg				✓	✓		✓	✓	✓	✓	✓	✓		✓	✓	✓
-info					✗											✓
roof-layout			✓			✓						✓		✓	✓	✓
-info						✗										✓
doors-layout				✓	✓			✓	✓	✓	✓	✓		✓	✓	✓
-refl clg							✓									✓
windows-layout				✓	✓			✓	✓	✓	✓	✓		✓	✓	✓
-refl clg							✓									✓
lighting-layout							✓	○			○				✓	✓
-info							✗									✓
electrical-switchg								✓								✓
-devices								✓							✓	✓
-info								✗								✓
cabinetry-layout							○	○			✓				✓	✓
-info											✗					✓
furniture-layout										✓					✓	✓
-info										✗						✓
fixtures-plumbg					✓						✓				✓	✓
-appliances											✓				✓	✓
demolition info				✗												✓
elevation info												✗				✓
details info													✗			✓
3D info														✗		✓

A ✓ or an ✗ or a ❍ in a column shows which layers and classes need to be visible for a sheet. The ✗ also denotes which class should have information specific for that sheet and designates which layer and class are active. Other layers and classes without any mark should be *INVISIBLE*. In addition the *dimension* class usually is *NORMAL* or visible, but you may need to move the dimension objects to another class in certain instances. Also note that we created two sheets, *master layers* and *all on*, which are handy for working with the file but do not actually get printed.

So for example, if we look at the matrix for the *partition plan* sheet, you will notice in the column that the *title, foundation,* and *first floor* layers are visible with *first floor* being the active layer. The *none, dimension, title block, floor-layout, walls-new, walls-existg, walls-info, doors-layout, windows-layout,* and *fixtures-plumbg* classes are visible with *walls-info* being the active class. Any information specific for the *partition plan* sheet that does not show on any of the other sheets, goes onto the *walls-info* class. The basic difference between this sheet and the *demolition plan* sheet, for instance, is that the *walls-new* and *walls-info* classes are invisible and the *demolition info* class is visible and active. (We are also not showing *fixtures-plumbg* or *dimensions* on the *demolition plan*.) So any information specific to the *demolition plan* sheet, and not appearing anywhere else, goes into the *demolition info* class.

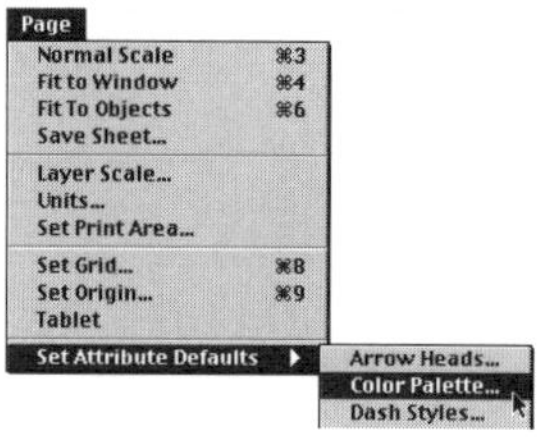

Once a matrix is developed for a template, it is handy to keep a hard copy to use for any future revisions. It also gives a quick overview of where to locate items on the drawing.

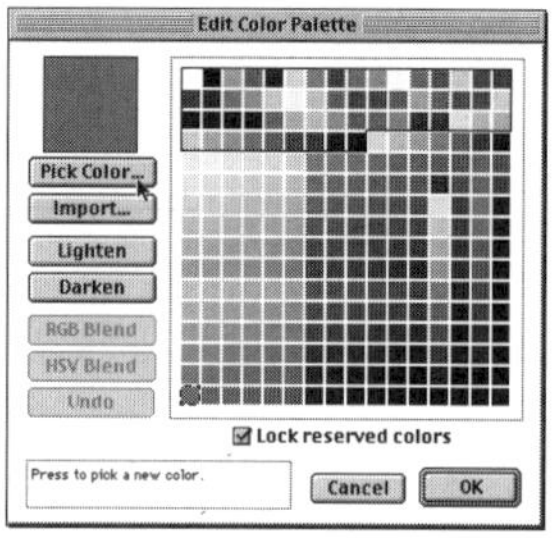

Layers

You will need to set up a bunch of new layers with a specific scale and *z* and Δz *[±z]* values for each. We will also assign a *FILL BACKGROUND* color and a *PEN FOREGROUND* color so that it will be easy to locate which layer an object is located on. If you plan on customizing the colors, do that now by going to *PAGE>SET ATTRIBUTE DEFAULTS>COLOR PALETTE* and make your modification in the *EDIT COLOR PALETTE* dialog box that opens.

Step 1 - setting up the first layer

Open the *Layers Setup* dialog box, rename the existing layer and change the information as follows.

name

With *layer-1* highlighted under *name*, type in *title*.

scale

The *scale* will default to full scale or *1:1*. Change it to 1/4"=1'-0" (1:50), one of the more common scales, rather than leaving it at full scale. This way there is no problem with the automatic dimension precision if you are using a wide variety of scales. Make sure the *scale text* box is not selected.

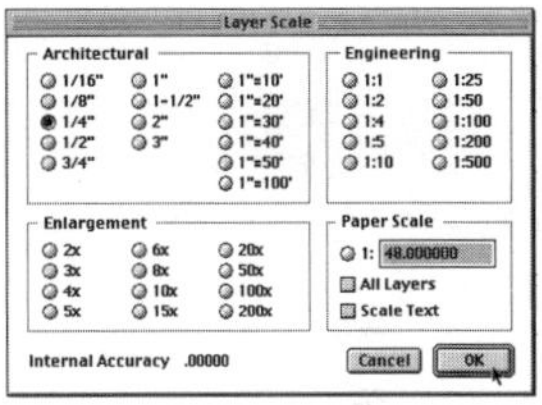

colors

Click the *colors* button to open the *Layer Colors/Color* dialog box in order to designate a color for this layer. I typically select a distinct dark color for the *pen foreground* and a lighter shade of that color for the *fill background*. Generally, it is not necessary to select a custom color for the other two options unless using a color printer.

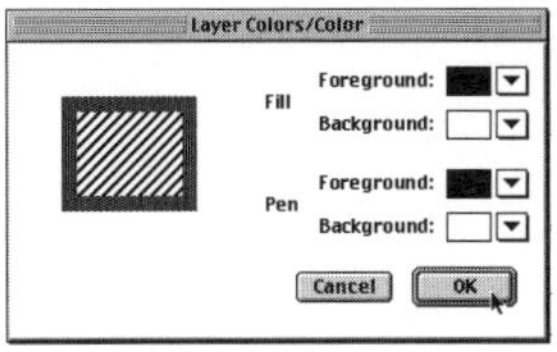

z & Δz [±z]

The *z* and *Δz [±z]* remain at 0 since the *title* layer is 2D and does not need any height above the *ground plane*, *z*, nor does it have any layer height or layer thickness, *Δz [±z]*.

Step 2 - setting up the other layers

Create new layers and enter the appropriate information as listed on the following page. Enter a color choice for each as well. The first five layers, or master layers, (*title, foundation floor, first floor, first flr ceiling,* and *roof*) should have their visibility set to *normal* and the rest of the layers to *invisible*. (As a note *LL* is short for linked layer).

NAME	SCALE	Z	Δz [±z]
Title	1/4"=1'-0"	0	0
Foundation Floor	1/8"=1'-0"	0	1'-6"
First Floor	1/8"=1'-0"	1'-6"	8'-0"
First Flr Clg	1/8"=1'-0"	9'-6"	6"
Roof	1/8"=1'-0"	9'-6"	3'-0"
LL Grade	1/16"=1'-0"	0	3'-0"
LL Front	1/4"=1'-0"	0	0
LL Left	1/4"=1'-0"	0	0
LL Right	1/4"=1'-0"	0	0
LL Back	1/4"=1'-0"	0	0
Details 1/2	1/2"=1'-0"	0	0
Details 1-1/2	1 1/2"=1'-0"	0	0
Details 3	3"=1'-0"	0	0

If using metric, it should read as follows;

NAME	SCALE	Z	Δz [±z]
Title	1:1	0	0
Foundation Floor	1:100	0	.45m
First Floor	1:100	.45m	2.40m
First Flr Clg	1:100	2.85m	.15m
Roof	1:100	2.85m	1.00m
LL Grade	1:200	0	1.00m
LL Front	1:50	0	0
LL Left	1:50	0	0
LL Right	1:50	0	0
LL Back	1:50	0	0
Details 25	1:25	0	0
Details 10	1:10	0	0
Details 5	1:5	0	0

name

Click the *NEW* button to create another layer and enter the names as outlined above. Each time you create a layer it is easier to enter the layer information as well.

scale

VectorWorks will automatically select the previous scale, so if you are not changing the *SCALE*, then this button does not have to be selected.

colors

Designate a new color with the *COLORS* button for each layer to easily locate an object.

z & Δz [±z]

VectorWorks will automatically calculate the *z* and *Δz [±z]* values, but this is not always correct. It also depends on the order the layers are created in. The text boxes can always be changed by highlighting and typing in the correct values. Remember, VectorWorks assumes inches unless you show the foot marker ('), that is if *FEET & INCHES* is selected under *PAGE>UNITS> SET UNITS.*

Step 3 - ordering the layers

As a rule, you want the 2D layers on the bottom so that they are not obstructing the layers above. Therefor, move the detail layers by selecting each one individually in the scrolling list and clicking the *DOWN* or *BOTTOM* button so that they appear at the end. Make *title* the bottommost layer since it is 2D and always visible then click *OK*.

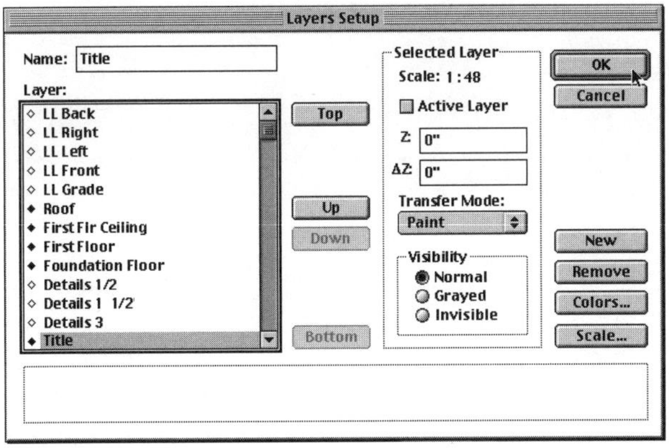

Colors For Organization

What we would like to do for this template is to be able to designate one color per layer, rather than a multitude of colors, in order to locate and visually organize objects. We

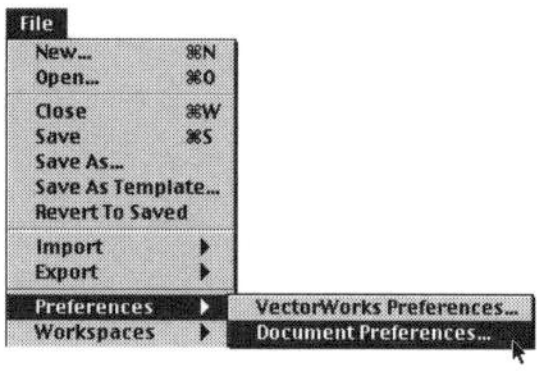

have already selected the colors for each layer in the *LAYERS SETUP* dialog box. In order to limit a color per layer go to *FILE>PREFERENCE>DOCUMENT PREFERENCES.* When the *DOCUMENT PREFERENCES* dialog box opens, select the *DISPLAY>USE LAYER COLORS* box. As a note, if you want to *PRINT* in black and white, select the *BLACK AND WHITE ONLY* box just before you print. VectorWorks will remember the colors once this box is deselected after printing.

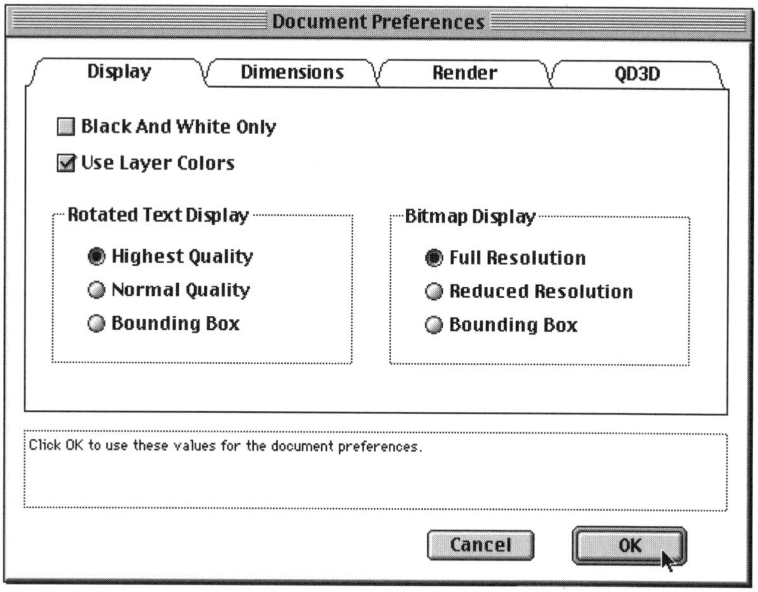

Classes

Classes are handy for adding another level of organization allowing you to manipulate the environment even further. Basically you would use a class to further subdivide a layer. Each class can now have default attributes and objects created in a class can automatically have these attributes applied. Classes also have an increased capacity for visibility settings. Typically two classes are automatically created, *none* and *dimension.* We will set up more classes in order to allow you to organize the drawing even further.

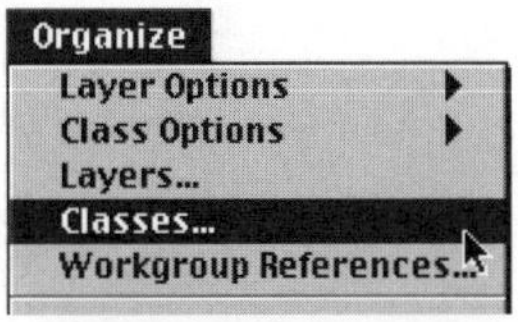

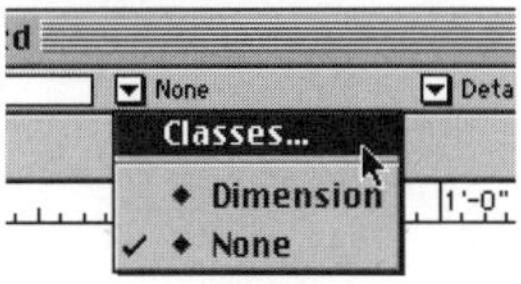

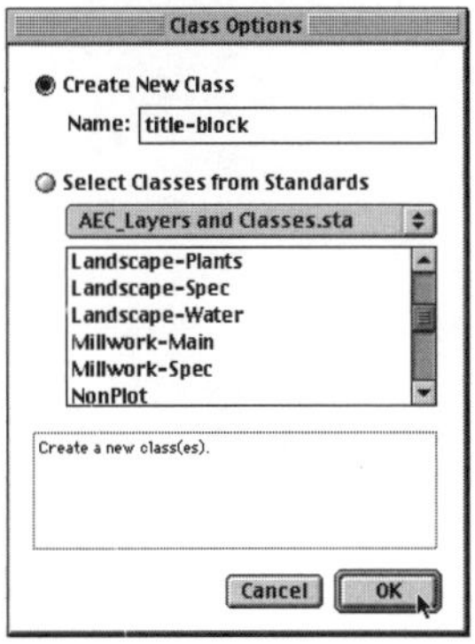

Step 1 - creating classes

Access the *Classes* dialog box by either going to *ORGANIZE>Classes* or accessing it on the pop-out menu in the *data display bar*. Click the *new* button and when the *Class Options* dialog box opens enter the new name in the *name* edit box, then click *ok*. Make sure the *create new class* button is selected. Go through this process for each new class.

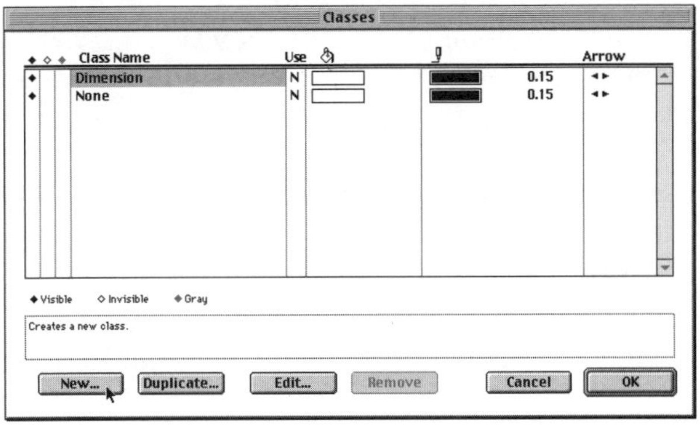

Create the following 33 classes in addition to *none* and *dimension* which generally should never be changed. The order does not matter since classes automatically get alphabetized in the pop-out menu. Also, it seems as if we are creating a ton of classes – which we are, but the hyphen allows the formation of submenus which somewhat abbreviates the long list in the pop-out menu.

title-block
-info
landscape-bldg
-plantg
-hardscape
-info
floor-layout
-patterns
-info
walls-new
-existg
-info

roof-layout
-info
doors-layout
-refl clg
windows-layout
-refl clg
lighting-layout
-info
electrical-switchg
-devices
-info

cabinetry-layout
-info
furniture-layout
-info
fixtures-plumbg
-appliances
demolition info
elevation info
details info
3D info

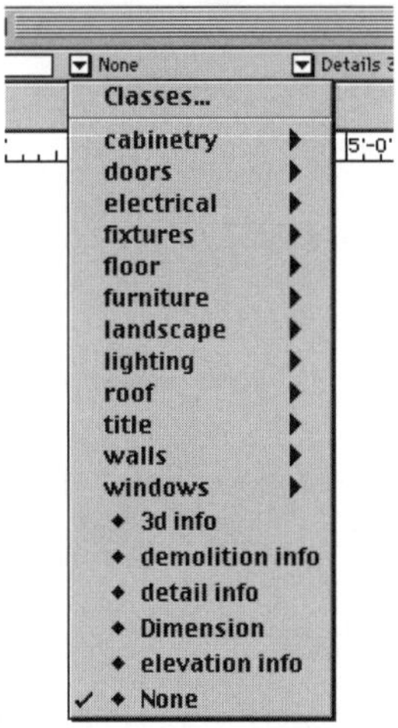

Notice that all of the classes with *info* in their name also have the ✘ in the matrix. These classes are visible only one per sheet. So information which is sheet specific goes into these classes whereas other classes may be visible for several different sheets.

In addition, the *dimension* class is usually visible, but you may need to move the dimensions for the partitions to the *walls-info* class if you only want them to show on the *partition plan,* otherwise they will appear on all of the plan sheets. Same thing goes with dimensions that are specific to a plan such as the *cabinetry* or *tele & elec plan.* They would need to be relocated to the appropriate info class so that they would not appear on the other plans.

Step 2 - designating class attributes

Once you have created the classes, all you would need to do is to double-click the class name to open the *Edit Class* dialog box. Double-click the *demolition info* name so that some default attributes can be set.

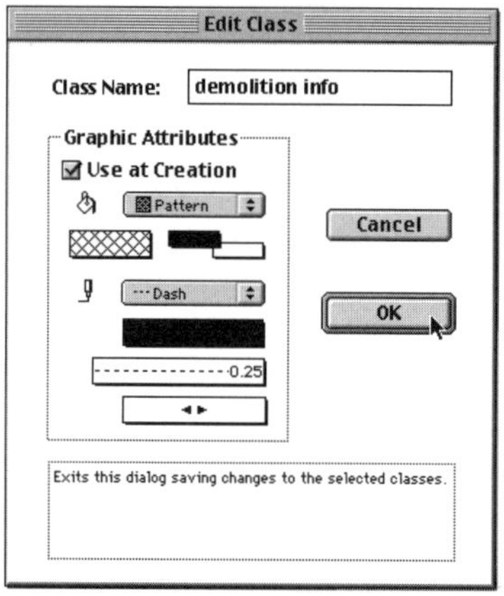

Notice the different pop-outs for fill and pen. Basically these are the same as in the *Attributes* palette. If you check the *use at creation* box, any items drawn in this class will have these attributes unless they were already existing. Changes to this dialog box do not affect items al-

ready drawn - it is not global. If this box is not checked, the objects created in this class will get the normal default attributes, although you can easily select *CLASS STYLE, CLASS COLOR,* or *CLASS THICKNESS* and apply them like any other attribute. This just makes it easier to standardize. When an object is selected, look for the arrows in the *ATTRIBUTES* palette signifying a class attribute. Set the typical attributes for some of the other classes as well.

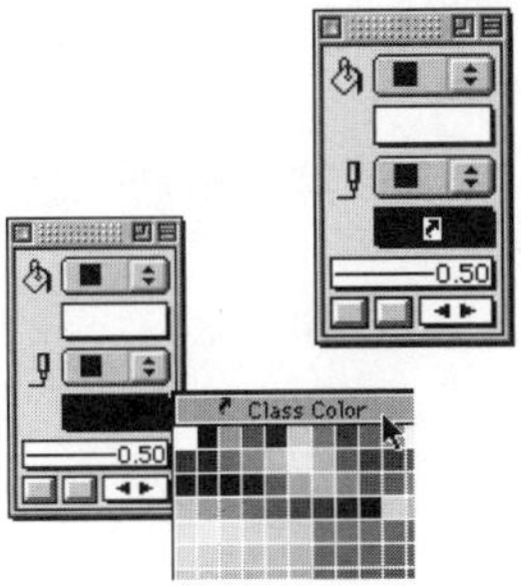

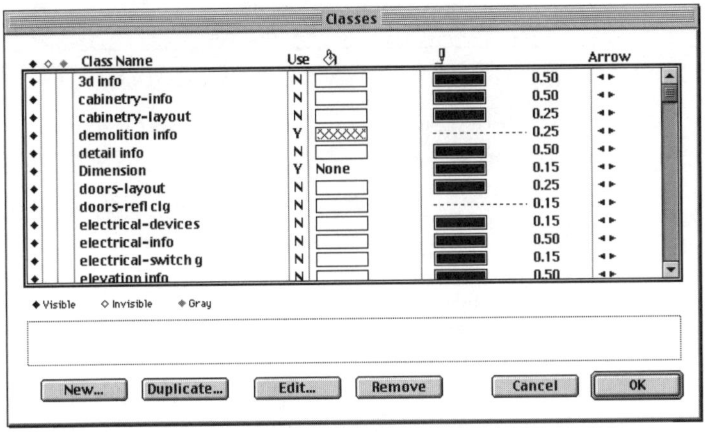

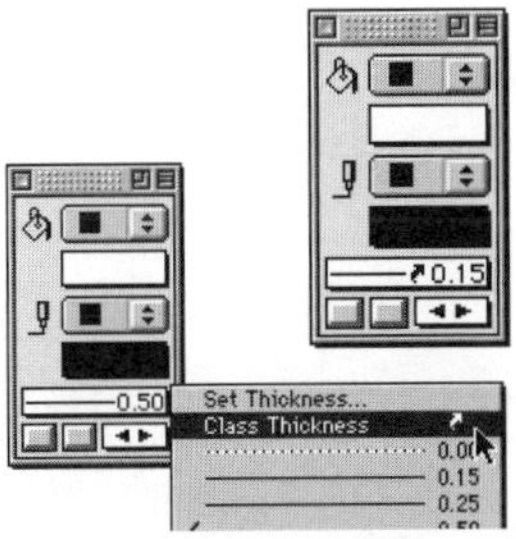

Visibility Settings

Once all of these layers and classes are created, the last thing you would want to do is to go into the dialog boxes and change the visibility settings each time you need to print a sheet. You will need to initially save the visibility combinations, but what we will do is create a script for each sheet that will automatically change the settings when selected. Fortunately there is a command which makes this much easier. It also allows you to designate the active class, the active layer, the view, and the *CLASS* and *LAYER OPTIONS*.

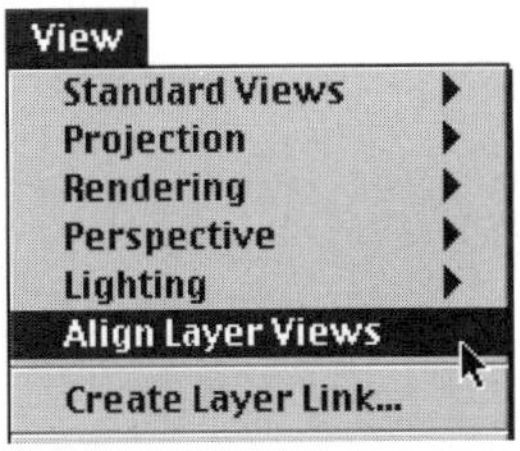

Before we start, change the *STANDARD VIEWS* to *TOP/PLAN* and then select *VIEW>ALIGN LAYER VIEWS*. Then change the linked layers to their appropriate view; *ll grade* to *TOP*, *ll front* to *FRONT*, *ll left* to *LEFT*, *ll right* to *RIGHT*, and *ll back* to *BACK*. Once you have been working with a drawing you may need to

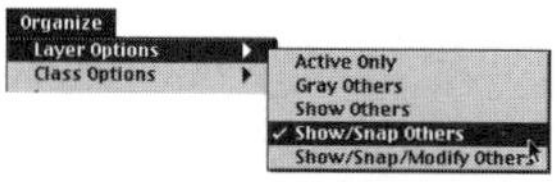

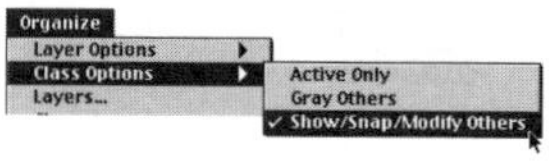

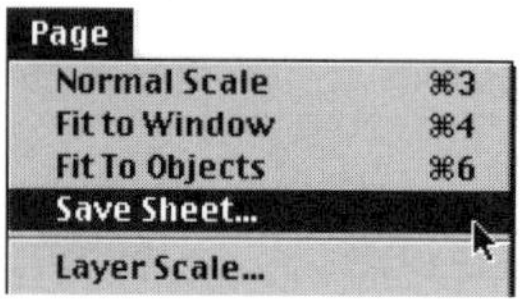

change the views for the *// grade* and the *// 3D view*. Also change the *ORGANIZE>LAYER OPTIONS* to *SHOW OTHERS* and the *CLASS OPTIONS* to *SHOW/SNAP/MODIFY OTHERS*.

With the active layer *title block* in *TOP/PLAN* view, open the *SAVE SHEET* dialog box by going to *PAGE>SAVE SHEET*. Now using the matrix we had set up, we will create the different commands for the drawing sheets.

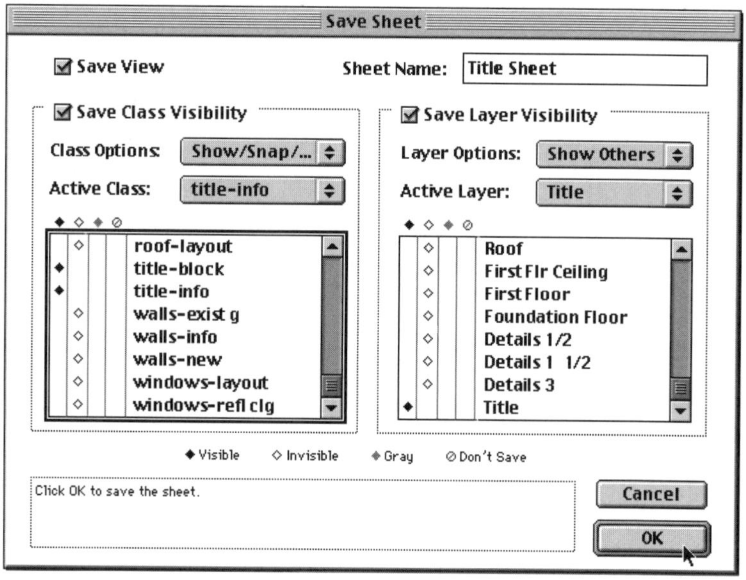

Step 1 - setting up the title sheet

Under *SHEET NAME* enter *title sheet*. Make all the classes *INVISIBLE* except for *none, title-block,* and *title-info* and all the layers *INVISIBLE* except for *title* by clicking in the appropriate column. Make sure you scroll through the lists so that all of the classes and layers are set up appropriately. Select the *SAVE VIEW* box so that this sheet remains in *TOP/PLAN*. Check the *SAVE CLASS VISIBILITY* box and make sure the *ACTIVE CLASS* pop-out has *title-info* selected. The *SAVE LAYER VISIBILITY* box should be selected. The *LAYER OPTIONS* should be *SHOW OTHERS* and the *ACTIVE LAYER* pop-out should have *title* selected. Select *OK*.

Basically what we just did is to use the matrix for the class and layer visibility settings. Those with a ✓ or an ✘ are visible, those with a ❍ are gray and the rest are invisible. The class and layer with the ✘ are active.

Step 2 - setting up the other sheets

We will go through the same process with the other sheets. The *none, title block,* and *dimension* classes and the *title* layer should be visible for each of the following sheets unless noted otherwise. The *LAYER OPTIONS* should have *SHOW OTHERS* selected and the *CLASS OPTIONS* should be *SHOW/SNAP/MODIFY OTHERS* unless instructed otherwise. You can only create one sheet at a time, so select *OK* after each sheet is set up and then reselect the *Save Sheet* command.

site plan

The four *landscape* classes and *roof-layout* should be visible with *landscape-info* being active. The *ll grade* layer should be visible and active. At this point you may also want to link the *ll grade* layer to the *foundation floor, first floor,* and *roof* layers. Depending on where you locate exterior stairs, the *floor-layout* class might need to be visible as well. As a note, although we do not need to see items on the *first floor* master layer on the *site plan,* the reason we are linking this master layer is that the *ll grade* linked layer will be used in the *3D view* sheet as well and in that sheet we will see those items. What we see will be controlled by the visibility of the classes.

demolition plan

The classes *floor-layout, walls-existg, doors-layout, windows-layout,* and *demolition info* should be visible with the latter being active. It is not necessary to have the *dimensions* class visible. If you do have a few dimensions that you want part of the *demolition plan,* then create the dimensions and move them to the *demolition info* class. *Foundation floor* and *first floor* should be visible with the latter being the active layer.

partition plan

The classes *floor-layout, walls-existg, walls-new, walls-info, fixtures-plumbg, doors-layout,* and *windows-layout* should be visible with *walls-info* being the active class. The *foundation floor* and *first floor* layers should be visible with the latter being active.

roof plan

The classes *roof-layout* and *roof-info* should be visible with the latter being active. The *floor-layout* class and the *foundation floor* layer should both be gray, particularly if exterior stairs from the building are located here. The *roof* layer should be active and visible.

reflected ceiling plan

The classes *walls-new, walls-existg, doors-refl clg, windows-refl clg, lighting-layout,* and *lighting-info* should be visible with the latter being active. *Cabinetry-layout* should be gray. The visible layers should be *first floor* and *first flr ceiling* with the latter active.

For this set up, when you create symbols for doors and windows, the symbols should have a separate component for the reflected ceiling view. This is why we have a *doors-layout* and a *doors-refl clg* class. The 2D part of the symbol will have two components, the typical plan view going into the *layout* class and the typical ceiling view going into the *refl clg* class. The 3D component goes into the *layout* class. The same is true for windows.

telephone & electrical plan

The classes *floor-layout, walls-new, walls-existg, doors-layout, windows-layout, electrical-switchg, electrical-devices,* and *electrical-info* should be visible with the latter active. Also, *lighting-layout* and *cabinetry layout* classes and *first flr ceiling* layer should be gray. *Foundation floor* and *first floor* should be visible and the latter the active layer.

floor finish plan

The classes *floor-layout, floor-patterns, floor-info, walls-new, walls-existg, doors-layout,* and *windows-layout* should be the visible classes. *Floor-info* should be active. *First floor* and *foundation floor* should be visible and the latter the active layer.

furniture plan

The classes *floor-layout, walls-new, walls-existg, doors-layout, windows-layout, furniture-layout,* and *furniture-info* should be visible with the latter active. The *dimension* class should be invisible with this sheet. *Foundation floor* and *first floor* should be visible and the latter active. Since we are placing furniture on the same layer as walls, make sure that any furniture placed adjacent to walls have the *INSERTION OPTIONS* set to *ON EDGE* and *NO BREAK.*

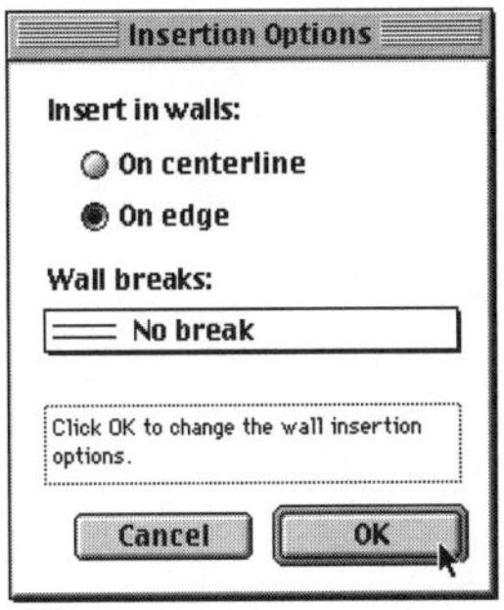

cabinetry plan

The classes *floor-layout, walls-new, walls-existg, doors-layout, windows-layout, fixtures-plumbg, fixtures-appliance, cabinetry-layout,* and *cabinetry-info* should be visible with the latter active. *Lighting-layout* should be gray. *Foundation floor* and *first floor* layer should be visible and the latter active. *First flr ceiling* should be gray. Like the furniture, make sure any symbols placed against a wall have the *INSERTION OPTIONS* set to *ON EDGE* and *NO BREAK.* You could also set *CLASS OPTIONS* to *GRAY OTHERS.* This allows you to see the walls but not snap to them, hence the symbols will not cut the walls.

exterior elevations

The classes *floor-layout, walls-new, walls-existg, roof-layout, doors-layout, windows-layout,* and *elevation info* should be visible and the latter active. The layers *ll back, ll right, ll left,* and *ll front* should be visible with the latter active. All layers should be in the correct view before using the *Save Sheet* command.

At this point you may also want to link each of the four elevation layers to the master layers of *foundation floor, first floor,* and *roof.* Do not select the *Project 2D objects* box in the *Create Layer Link* dialog box.

details

The only class that should be visible in addition to the three classes always visible is, *details info,* and this should be active as well. *Details 1/2, details 1 1/2,* and *details 3* should be the visible layers with *details 1 1/2* the active, all in *Top/Plan* view.

3D view

The classes *landscape-buildg, landscape-plantg, landscape-hardscape, floor-layout, walls-new, walls-exist g, roof-layout, doors-layout, windows-layout,* and *3D info,* should be visible with the latter active. The class, *floor-layout* does not need to be visible if there are no stairs or other elements on the outside of the building. The active layer should be *ll grade* but the view should be *Right Isometric. Dimensions* should be invisible. Verify that the view is correct before you select the *Save Sheet* command since this can not be modified within the dialog box.

You are using the same linked layer as you used for the *site plan* sheet but with a different visibility setting for the classes and view. So, any information that is specific for the *3D view* should go on the *3D info* class.

master layers

It is handy to also make a script that will make the four master or original layers visible even though you are not going to print them. Make the *foundation floor, first floor, first flr ceiling,* and *roof* layers visible with *foundation floor* active. LAYER OPTIONS should be set to ACTIVE ONLY. Make the classes, *none, floor-layout, walls-new, walls-existg, roof-layout, doors-layout, windows-layout, lighting-layout, electrical-devices, cabinetry-layout, furniture-layout, fixtures-plumbg,* and *fixtures-appliance* visible and the class *none* active. The *title layer* and the *dimension* and *title block* class should be invisible.

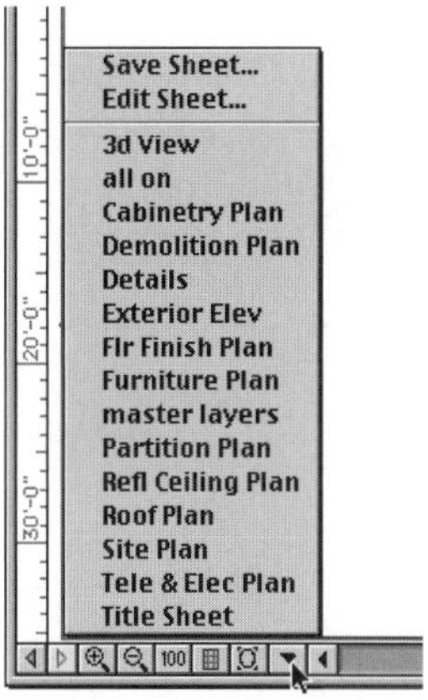

all on

It is also handy to have a script that makes all layers and classes visible in case you need to find an object. In this case, it does not matter which class or layer is active, but it is helpful to have the LAYER OPTIONS set to SHOW/SNAP/MODIFY OTHERS.

Using The Sheets

Once these scripts have been created, they are very easy to use to get from one drawing sheet to another. Just select the appropriate script and all of the classes and layers will change their visibility and options according to how the script was saved.

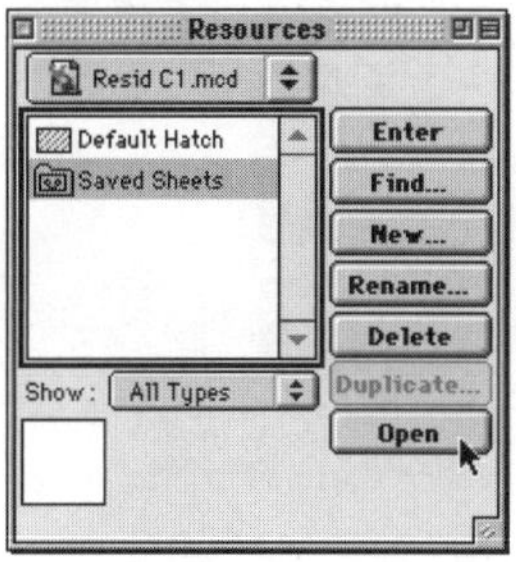

Views Bar Pop-Out

If you have SCROLL BARS selected in VECTORWORKS PREFERENCES>DISPLAY, then the *views bar* will be visible on the lower left of the drawing. If you press on the *sheets pop-up* shortcut menu, which is the arrow, second from the right, you can press/drag to the desired sheet.

Floating Palette Scripts

If you prefer a floating palette, go to the RESOURCES palette and navigate to the current file. You will see a command folder called *saved sheets*. Select it and the OPEN button. A floating palette opens called *saved sheets*. Just double-click one of the names to get the desired sheet.

SETTING UP SHORTCUT SCRIPTS

There are some aspects of drawing that require a rather tedious method of changing preferences, attributes, or default settings. Some of these can be done rather easily by creating a custom command, or script, that can either change the settings without changing the default settings, or change the default settings only. Some of the more obvious ones would be to make a variety of different default settings for the *Attributes* palette, or to have a dimensioning command that would automatically change the line weight and select the tool, or one that changes the text parameters, or one that changes the separation for double lines. We will go through the steps necessary to create these.

Attribute Scripts

If there are several default settings you use for fills, pens, and line styles you might consider creating scripts so that they can automatically be selected. We will set up several of these for various uses.

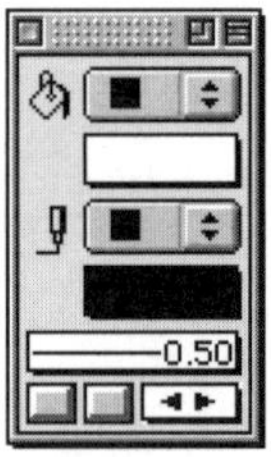

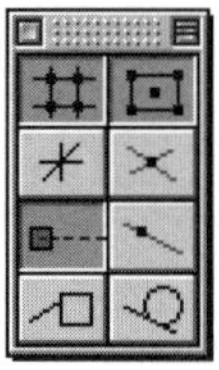

Step 1 - creating the normal default

The first script we will create will be for the most often used set of attributes. With nothing selected, change the *Attributes* palette so that the *fill* is *solid* and white, the *pen* is *solid* and black, the line weight is .50, and the markers are the arrow shaped. Also make sure that you have the three constraint icons selected of *Snap To Grid*, *Snap To Object*, and *Snap Points*. Select *ORGANIZE>Custom Tool/ Attribute*. The *Custom Tools* dialog box opens.

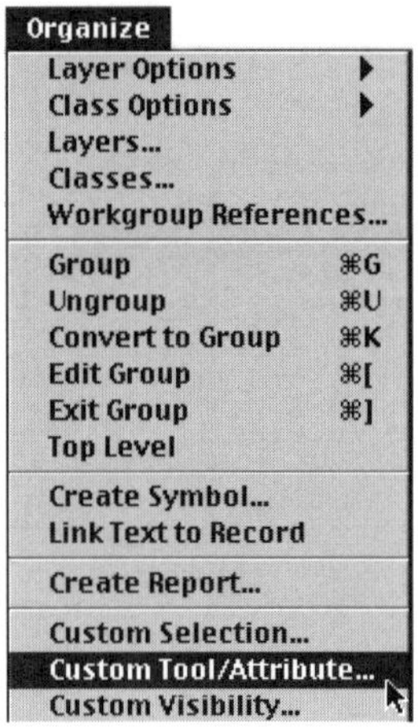

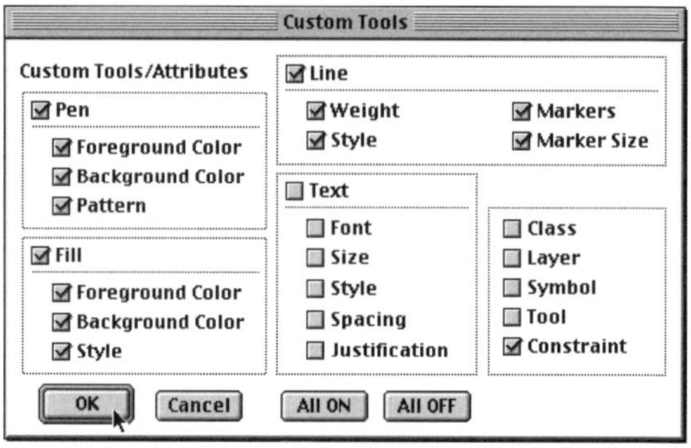

Select the *PEN, FILL,* and *LINE* boxes which automatically selects each of the boxes within their respective groups. Also select *CONSTRAINT* on the lower right so that this script remembers the three selected icons on the *CONSTRAINTS* palette. When you select *OK*, the *ASSIGN NAME* dialog box opens.

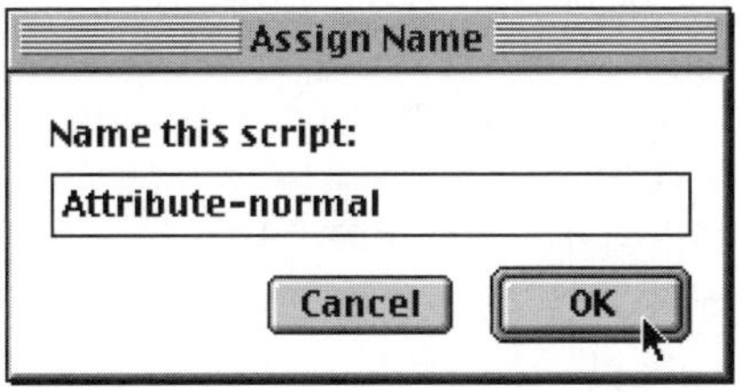

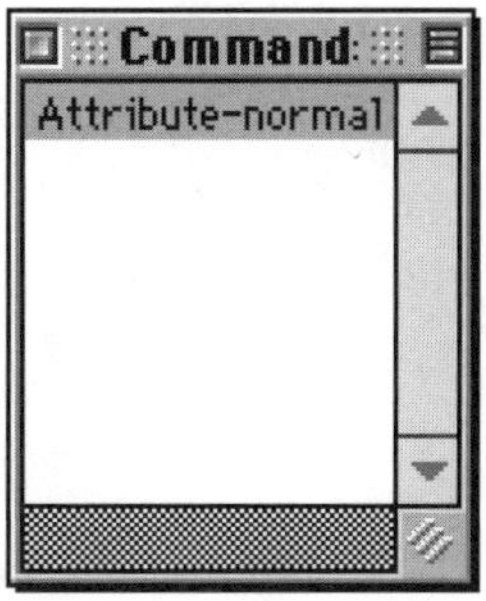

Enter *attribute-normal* and then select *OK*. A floating script palette will automatically open called *commands* and this new script will automatically be placed there.

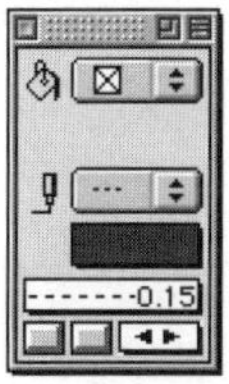

Step 2 - creating other attribute sets

Select a different set of attributes, such as the thinnest line weight, a *fill* of *NONE*, a dashed line style, and a *pen* color of red. And go through the same steps naming this script *attribute-demo*.

Create a variety of combinations, but remember that how you name these scripts should easily recall what the set is comprised of, or what its use is for. You may want a script as simple as a heavy solid line, or green color, or something for a more particular purpose such as property line, or new object. You can also use it to create a custom line weight, with *SET THICKNESS*, so that you do not have to access the *SET THICKNESS* dialog box every time you want to use this custom weight.

Step 3 - using an attribute script

To see why you have gone through all of these steps, take a break and try out these new commands. To change back to the normal attributes, just double-click that script name in the floating palette. See how the defaults change when you double-click any of the script names.

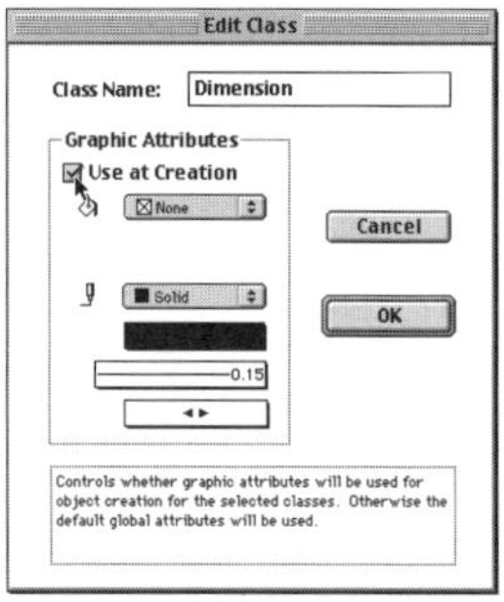

Dimension Script

Many times when you create a dimension, you want the text to be a certain size and font, and the line weight to be a certain thickness. This of course means changing all of the attribute defaults every time you want to create a dimension. Since any object made with the dimensioning tools automatically goes into the *dimension* class, you could set up the default attributes by setting a class attribute and selecting *Use at Creation* in the *Edit Class* dialog box. This, though, will not select the text. In this case it would also be a good idea to create a script.

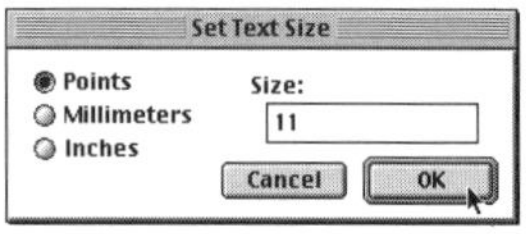

Step 1 - creating a dimension script

With only the *Selection* tool selected, change to the lightest line weight and the *solid* line style. Change the text to 11 *points* in the *Set Text Size* dialog box under *TEXT>Size> Set Size* and select a *Font* for the text in the dimension. Then select the *Constrained Linear Dimension* tool. Select the *Custom Tool/Attribute* command and click the *pen> foreground color, fill>style, weight, markers, marker size, font, size, tool,* and *constraint* buttons. Name this script, *dimension line.*

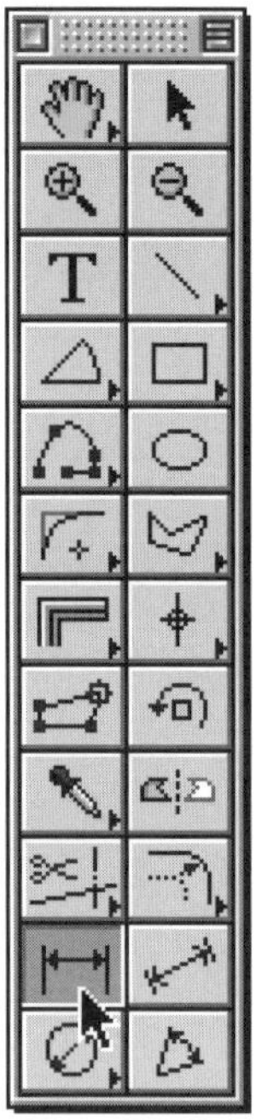

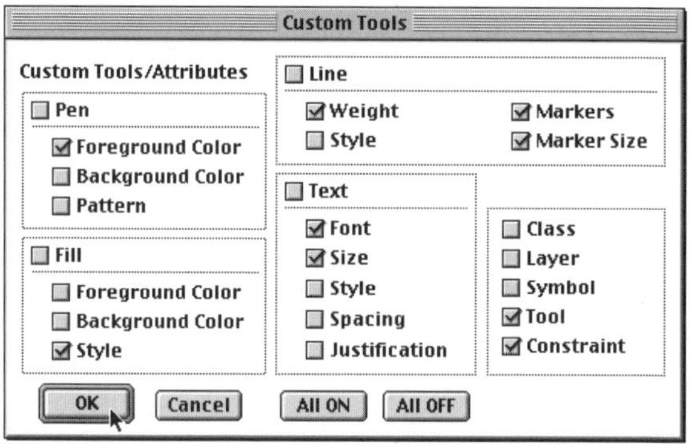

Step 2 - using a dimension script

For each instance of creating a constrained dimension line, just double-click this script. The time saving element for dimensioning is, you do not have to change the defaults for line weights and font styles, then select the tool, and change the defaults back once done. All of this is done with one simple double-click. Be aware that scripts use the last modifier icon that was selected in the *data display bar*. Also notice, that once the script is used, the last selected tool is still selected. The dimensions will automatically be placed in the *dimension* class.

Text Scripts

Generally on a drawing, the text might have 3 different sizes, styles or even another font entirely. By creating and using a script, every time you need to create a block of text, rather than changing each of the settings and then selecting the *Text Insertion* tool, all you would have to do is double-click the appropriate script. With the *Text Insertion* tool it is important to remember two things in order to change the defaults. No object should be selected, and the *2D Selection* tool should be the selected tool. The *Text Insertion* tool could be selected, but you can not have started a text block - in other words, you can not have already clicked the drawing with this tool.

Step 1 - creating text scripts

First, select the *Font*, the *Size* such as a 12 pt, and then the *Text Insertion* tool. Make sure the default is for *Left* justification. Select the *Custom Tool/Attribute* command and click to select the *pen>foreground color, fill>style,* and *text* boxes in the *Custom Tools* dialog box. Select *ok* and name the command, *text-typ*. You will not be able to select the *tool* box.

Now, with the *2D Selection tool*, change the default *Size* to *18* pt, the *Style* to *Bold*, and the spacing to *1-½ Space*, then select the *Text Insertion* tool. Go through the same steps naming this script, *text-sub title*.

Finally, change the default *Size* to *24* pt, the *Style* to *Bold* and *Underline*, the spacing to *Double Space*, and select the *Text Insertion* tool and create the script naming it *text-title*.

Step 2 - using text commands

Scripts made with this tool do not work as cleanly as scripts made with other tools. You would need to manually select the *Text Insertion* tool first before you double-click the script itself. Once the *Text Insertion* tool is selected, just double-click each of the scripts to change the settings. These scripts do change the defaults for *TEXT*, unlike other scripts that have *tool* selected, which just change the one instance.

Misc Object Scripts

You can also create scripts for objects, such as a red rectangle, or blue line, or double lines with the script remembering the *separation*. When the script is double-clicked, the tool will automatically be selected and the object can be drawn with these specified values. Once the object is created the tool and the attributes default back to the previous settings. The exception is the *separation*, which changes the value in the *Double Line Preferences* dialog box.

Step 1 - red rectangle script

Change the default values in the *Attributes* palette so that the color for the *pen* is red and the fill is *none*. Select the *Rectangle* tool and then the *Custom Tool/Attribute* command. When the *Custom Tools* dialog box opens, select the appropriate boxes along with the *tool* box and save the script as *red box*.

Step 2 - blue line script

Change the default values in the *Attributes* palette so that the *pen* color is blue and the line weight is the middle weight. Select the *Constrain Angle* icon and the *Single Line* tool, then select the *Custom Tool/Attribute* command. This time when the *Custom Tools* dialog box opens, select along with the appropriate boxes, the *tool* and *constraint* boxes, and name this script as *blue line*.

Step 3 - 4" double line

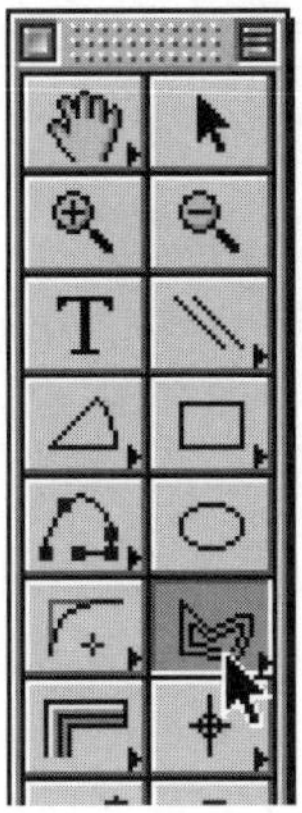

Change the default line weight to .15, select the *Double-Line Polygon* tool and click the right most button to open the *Double Line Preferences* dialog box. Change the *separation* to 4" and check *create lines*. Also select the *Constrain Angle* constraint before you select the *Custom Tool/Attribute* command. Select the *line>weight, line>style, tool,* and *constraint* boxes, and name this script *double line-4"*. Because you are using the *Double-Line Polygon* tool and *create lines,* you would click at each point and double-click to end the object unless you are at the starting point, in which case it would be a single click. The object created is actually a series of individual lines even though it is made with the *Double-Line Polygon* tool.

Symbol Selection Scripts

A script can be created so that the *2D Symbol Insertion* tool is selected along with a designated symbol. If you have several common symbols you are using continually on a drawing, creating a script for each allows you to avoid going to the *Resources* palette to select symbols.

Step 1 - creating symbol selection scripts

At this point we do not have any symbols imported into this document. After you do import some of the more commonly used symbols, just select the desired symbol in the *Resources* palette and then select the *2D Symbol Insertion* tool. When you select the *Custom Tool/Attribute* command, select just *symbol* and *tool*. Name the script with *sym-"symbol name."*

Wall Scripts Or Wall Styles

It is no longer necessary to use this command to make wall scripts. There is a new command, *AEC>Set Wall Style*, that allows you to set the defaults for up to ten straight and five radiused wall styles. When you select the command, the *Current Wall Style Settings* dialog box opens.

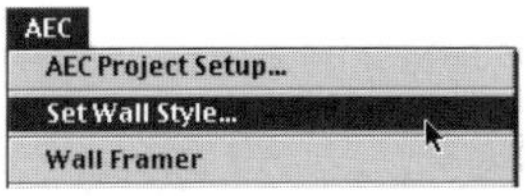

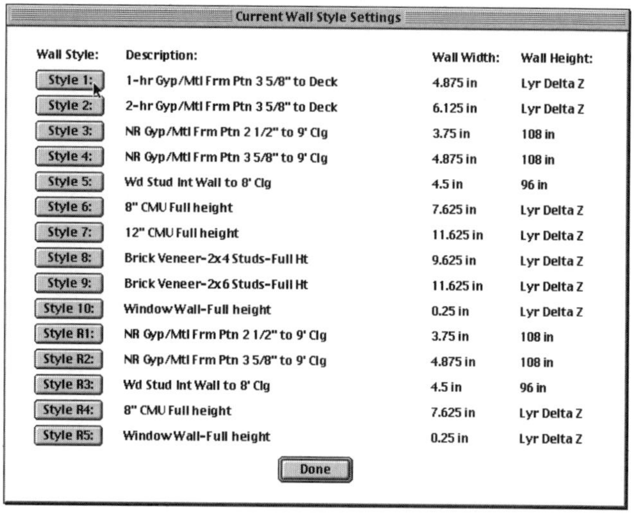

Click the *STYLE 1* button to open the *WALL STYLE 1* dialog box which allows you to change the name and settings for this wall type.

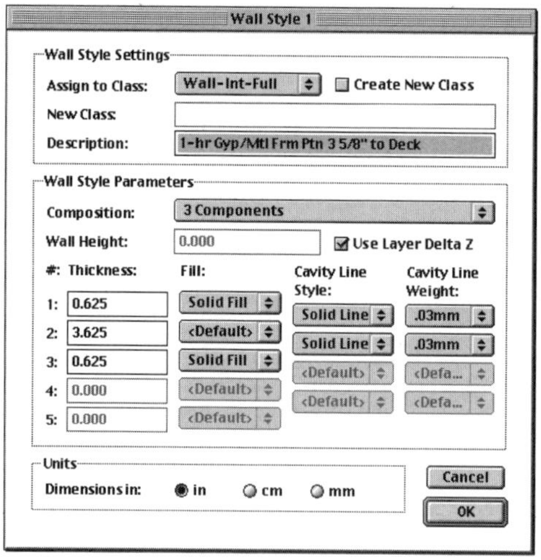

Wall Style Settings

If you want the wall to go into a specific class, check the *CREATE NEW CLASS* box and enter the class name exactly as it is spelt in the *CLASSES* dialog box. So in the case of this file, it would either be *walls-new, walls-existg*, or *demoli-*

tion info. What you enter for *description* will be entered in the same manner to the *Current Wall Style Settings* dialog box.

Wall Style Parameters

Typically, you would select the *use layer delta z* box unless you are creating a low partition, in which case, fill in the *wall height* edit box. The *composition* pop out allows you to select up to five components. *Components* are similar to cavity lines and cavity fills in the *Wall Preferences>Cavity Setup* dialog box. The difference is that for *fill* you can not pick a *pattern*, only a *hatch*, and you would need to know which number the dashes are in the *Attributes* palette in order to pick the *cavity line style*. The *Cavity Setup* dialog box is more visual. One other thing to note, unlike the *Cavity Setup* dialog box, is that you do not set the overall width of the wall thickness. Instead, it automatically adds up the amounts for each of the *components* under *thickness,* although you will not see the total.

Using A Wall Style

Once you have set up the wall styles, they are very easy to use. Look on the *AEC Objects* palette. The top three icons on the right are the tools for using these wall styles and each pops out for five different styles. Use these like any other tool. The only thing is, you have to remember which number designates which style.

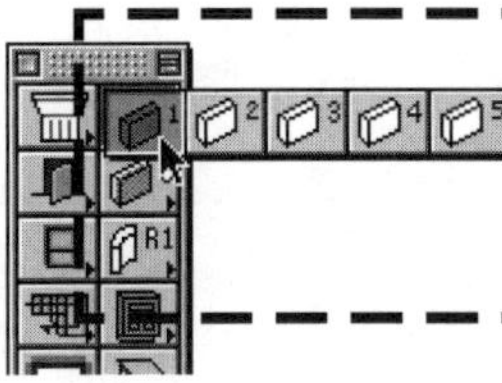

As a note, if you apply a fill *pattern* to a wall using the *Attributes* palette, when you use *Rendering>Solid* the fill *pattern* will appear in a 3D view as well. On the other hand, a *fill, pattern* or *hatch,* designated either in this dialog box or the *Cavity Setup* dialog box, appears only in *Top/Plan* and appears solid in a 3D view.

Organizing And Accessing Scripts

All of the scripts we have created are located in a palette called commands. We can rename the palette by selecting it in the *Resources* palette and clicking the *rename* button. When

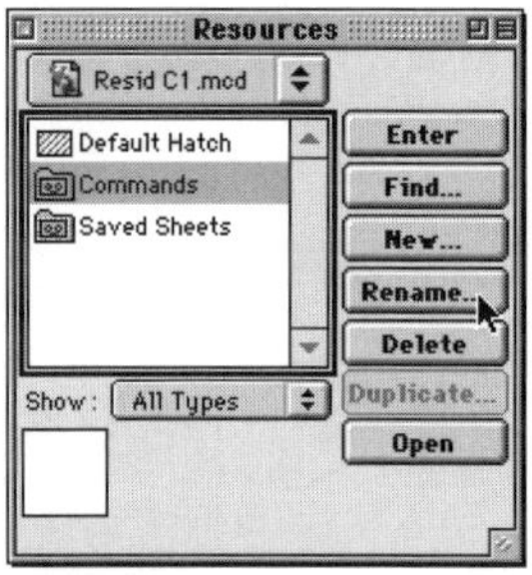

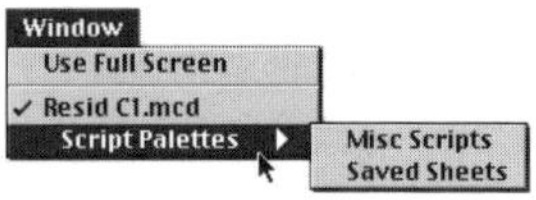

the *ASSIGN NAME* dialog box opens, type in a name, in this case *misc scripts*. All of the scripts are listed in the floating palette. If you close the palette, it can always be reopened by selecting its name in the *RESOURCES* palette and clicking the *OPEN* button or you can go to *WINDOW>RESID C1.MCD>SCRIPT PALETTES* and select the desired palette. All of the open VectorWorks files will be listed here along with their various resource windows.

You can have many script palettes and locate the scripts as they are created. First, select the *NEW* button in the *RESOURCES* palette. When the *CREATE RESOURCE* dialog box opens, select the *SCRIPT PALETTE* button and then *CREATE*. When the *ASSIGN NAME* dialog box opens, enter the desired name and click *OK*. More than one palette can be opened at a time. When creating scripts, the new script will be placed in the active palette - just click a palette to make it active. Unfortunately you can not easily move existing scripts from one palette to another.

active

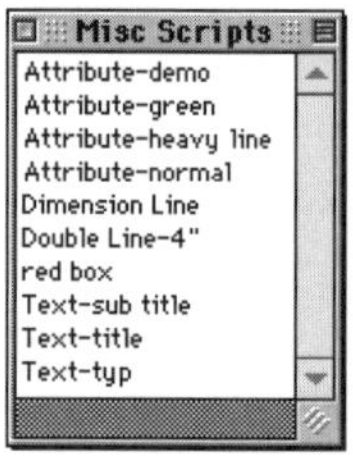

inactive

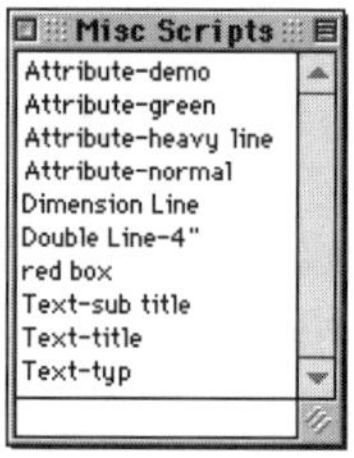

ADDING DEFAULT INFORMATION

Once all of the information is entered for drawing organization, you can start entering the typical default information such as title blocks, beginning text for keys, legends, project information, and guides. Remember that it is easier to enter the information once, so that the formatting is in place, and to revise it for each project.

Title Block And Borders

At this point you can create your own title block or use the one created in one of the earlier chapters. Basically, you will create the graphic elements and enter just the office information. Anything specific for a project will get entered later in the specific project document.

Step 1 - creating the title block

Use the *title sheet* script to make *title* and *title block* active and create your own title block. Since we are creating a template, do not enter any specific project information. If you are using any surfaced objects in the graphic, change the fill to *NONE* in the *ATTRIBUTES* palette. Also, grouped objects automatically move to the *none* class, so if you group the block use the *OBJECT INFO* palette to move it back to the *title block* class. Add a border keeping in mind the margin your plotter requires.

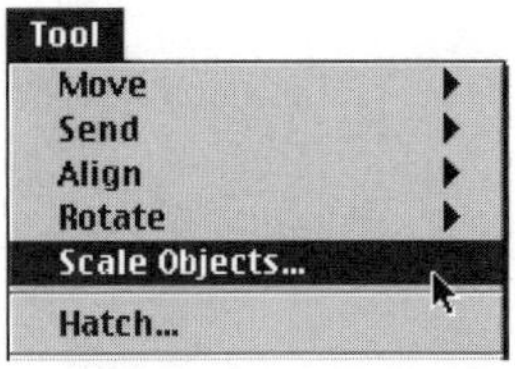

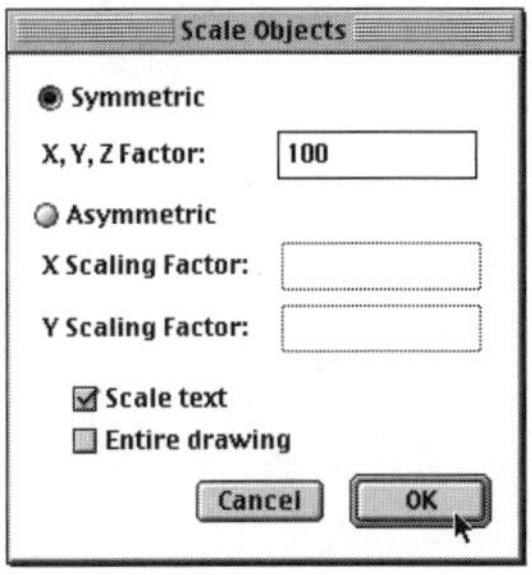

If you are doing a *COPY* and *PASTE* of the previous title block, navigate with the *RESOURCES* palette to open the *chapt 3.mcd [chapt 3.sta]* template. Make *title* the active layer and *none* the active class. Do a *SELECT ALL* and *COPY*. Make the document, *Resid C1 [Resid C1.mcd]*, and *title* layer and *title block* class active, then *PASTE*. With the block still selected, select the *TOOL>SCALE OBJECTS* command to open the *SCALE OBJECTS* dialog box. Select *SYMMETRIC* and enter 100 for the *X,Y,Z FACTOR* and check the *SCALE TEXT* box, then *OK*. Position the block as necessary. Use *EDIT GROUP* to revise the text information and change the fill for everything to *NONE*. You might need to select the graphic element and use *EDIT GROUP* again in order to change the fill. Go to *WINDOW*, select the untitled document, and click the *close* box without saving.

When you actually use this template, enter the project information in the *title* layer and *title block* class. Information that is page specific, such as the scale, sheet name, and sheet number, will be entered in the corresponding layer and in the corresponding class. So for example, for the *partition plan*, the *first floor* layer and *wall-info* class should have the appropriate sheet number, title, and scale. Notice that this layer and class also have the **✘** in the visibility matrix signifying they are visible and active.

It would be appropriate to place some of the text blocks designating the sheet name and scale now. Notice that we are entering the information for each sheet on the active layer and active class as designated with the ✘ in the matrix. Not all layers get information added and some have the information added more than once. There are thirteen sheets needing titles. Use the new sheet scripts to make the appropriate layers and classes active by double-clicking a script or press/dragging to select in the *sheets pop-up shortcut menu*. Use the *text-title* script for the sheet name and the *text-sub title* script for the scale.

SHEET NAME	ACTIVE LAYER	ACTIVE CLASS	*SCALE*
Title Sheet	*Title*	*title-info*	NA
Site Plan	*LL Grade*	*landscape-info*	1/16"=1'-0"
Demolition Plan	*First Flr*	*demolition-info*	1/8"=1'-0"
Partition Plan	*First Flr*	*walls-info*	1/8"=1'-0"
Roof Plan	*Roof*	*roof-info*	1/8"=1'-0"
Refl Ceiling Plan	*First Flr Clg*	*lighting-info*	1/8"=1'-0"
Tele & Elec Plan	*First Flr*	*electrical-info*	1/8"=1'-0"
Flr Finish Plan	*Foundation Flr*	*floor-info*	1/8"=1'-0"
Furniture Plan	*First Flr*	*furniture-info*	1/8"=1'-0"
Cabinetry Plan	*First Flr*	*cabinetry-info*	1/8"=1'-0"
Exterior Elev	*LL Front*	*elevation-info*	1/4"=1'-0"
Details	*Details 1-1/2*	*details-info*	*as noted*
3D View	*LL Grade*	*3D info*	NA

If using metric, it should read as follows;

SHEET NAME	ACTIVE LAYER	ACTIVE CLASS	SCALE
Title Sheet	*Title*	*title-info*	NA
Site Plan	*LL Grade*	*landscape-info*	*1:200*
Demolition Plan	*First Flr*	*demolition-info*	*1:100*
Partition Plan	*First Flr*	*walls-info*	*1:100*
Roof Plan	*Roof*	*roof-info*	*1:100*
Refl Ceiling Plan	*First Flr Clg*	*lighting-info*	*1:100*
Tele & Elec Plan	*First Flr*	*electrical-info*	*1:100*
Flr Finish Plan	*Foundation Flr*	*floor-info*	*1:100*
Furniture Plan	*First Flr*	*furniture-info*	*1:100*
Cabinetry Plan	*First Flr*	*cabinetry-info*	*1:100*
Exterior Elev	*LL Front*	*elevation-info*	*1:50*
Details	*Details 1:10*	*details-info*	*as noted*
3D View	*LL Grade*	*3D info*	NA

Step 2 - adding a date stamp

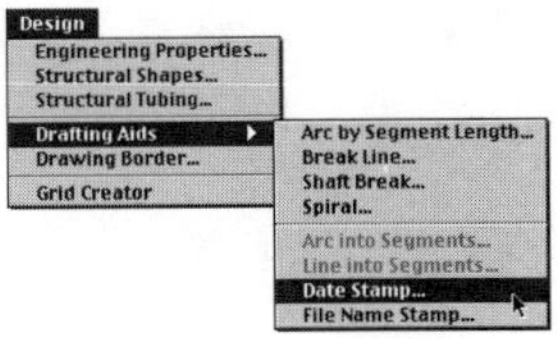

Use the *title sheet* script to make *title* and *title block* active again. Select the *DESIGN>DRAFTING AIDS>DATE STAMP* command. The *DATE STAMP* dialog box opens.

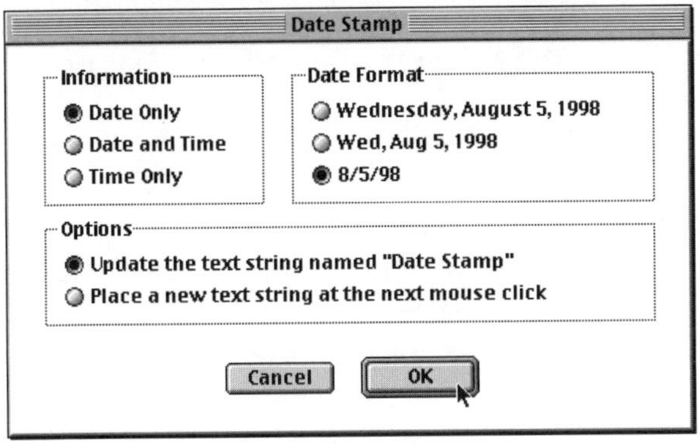

Make your selections under *INFORMATION* and *DATE FORMAT* then select the first button under *OPTIONS, UPDATE THE TEXT STRING NAMED "DATE STAMP."*

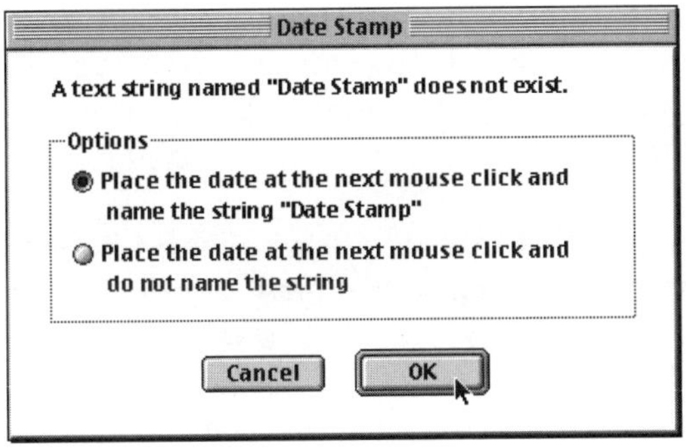

Another *DATE STAMP* dialog box opens stating that *A TEXT STRING NAMED DATE STAMP DOES NOT EXIST*. Select the first button which will place the date and name the string. This command uses the text defaults. The next time you use this command, only the first dialog box will open because you now have a text string for it to update. Select the text object and move it in place on the title block. Also notice in the *OBJECT INFO* palette on the *DATA* pane that the object is named *date stamp*.

Legends, Keys, Etc.

Typical legends, keys, indexes, general notes, etc can be set up within the template. These can always be modified later for a specific project, but at least you can have the format and a starting point already created. Typically, these would be placed on the correct layer and class as previously outlined for adding the scale. Again, do make use of the *text* scripts and the *saved sheet* scripts for placing information.

Step 1 - creating an index

Select the *title sheet* script to make *title info* the active class and *title* the active layer. As a habit, I usually use two text blocks, one for the title and another for the information itself. This just makes formatting a little easier and you can avoid the *Tab* key for indenting - you would just move the text block.

Typically it is easier to *GROUP* the two text blocks, but note, when one or several objects are grouped, even if in the same class, the grouped object automatically moves to the *none* class. So, you would need to move it back to the desired class, by selecting the grouped object and changing the class in the *OBJECT INFO* palette.

DRAWING INDEX

A-1 Title Sheet
A-2 Site Plan
A-3 Demolition Plan
A-4 Partition Plan
A-5 Roof Plan
A-6 Reflected Ceiling Plan
A-7 Telephone & Electric Plan
A-8 Floor Finish Plan
A-9 Furniture Plan
A-10 Cabinetry Plan
A-11 Exterior Elevations
A-12 Details
A-13 3D View

Select the *TEXT INSERTION* tool and double-click the *text-title* script, then click and type, *drawing index*. Now double-click *text-sub title,* click, and type; *A-1 Title Sheet, A-2 Site Plan, A-3...,* using the *Return [Enter]* key to place a hard return after each number. Use the *saved sheet* scripts and place the sheet number on the appropriate layers and classes. You may want to make the *TEXT>SIZE* quite large.

Step 2 - creating general notes

Assuming the general notes are located on the *title sheet*, the *title info* class and the *title* layer should then be active. Since VectorWorks does not have the word processing options of indent or hanging indent, I typically double-space between each note and give a bold style to the number.

If you really want the hanging indent, where the number sticks out beyond the text, you would need to place the number as a separate text object. Needless to say, this can get quite cumbersome, so sometimes it is best to just change the office standards until the word processing capabilities in VectorWorks improve.

Step 3 - creating the wall legend

Select the *partition plan* script to make the *first flr* layer active. If the wall legend goes on all plan sheets except the *site* and *roof plans,* place the legend on the *walls-existg* class. If it only appears on the *demolition* and *partition plans,* you will need to place it in the *demolition info* and a duplicate on the *walls-info* classes.

Select the appropriate *AEC Objects>Wall Style* tools and draw a small segment for each partition type. *S*elect each segment and with the *Object Info* palette move them to the appropriate class and change *caps* to *both*. If you had set the attributes for *walls to be demolished* in the *Edit Class* dialog box to *fill>default,* it will use the *class style* of *demolition info*. Notice when that wall segment is moved to a different class, it looses its *pen* style and *fill pattern*. Just select segment and use the *Attributes* palette to again apply the dash style and pattern. And finally, create two text blocks, one for the title, *wall legend*, and one for the description of each individual wall type. Again, *Group* the objects and change the class to the correct class.

Step 4 - other legends and stuff

At this point, you might want to organize and decide on other legends or keys to add, remembering to place them on an appropriate layer with the corresponding class. You might consider a lighting or electrical key, a list of commonly used abbreviations, a typical finish key for the elevations, and typical specifications. Just remember, it is easier to create each of these items once in the template and use it as is, modify it as necessary, or just delete it, rather than starting from scratch each time.

Borders And Guides

For the *detail* layers, it is easier to create a template with borders and/or guide lines that divide up the sheet. The lines can be placed to exactly divide the drawing area, excluding the title block itself. You can have it divide the sheet into 2 rows and 3 columns, or 3 rows and 4 columns, or whatever. You can also place guides for locating titles for each detail.

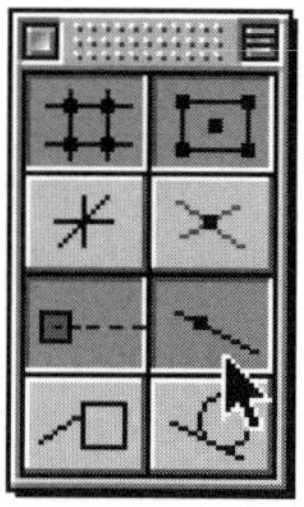

Step 1 - locating the lines

Select *details* sheet so details 1-1/2 and *details info* are active. The first thing to do is to draw the lines which will be used as the borders or guides. Using the *Constrained Single Line* tool, draw as many lines as necessary. Make use of the *Snap To Distance* constraint to divide a line into equal segments in order to exactly locate the remaining lines. Just double-click the icon to open the *Snap Distance* dialog box and enter the appropriate *fraction* or *percent*. The *smartcursor cue, along line,* will appear when within snapping distance.

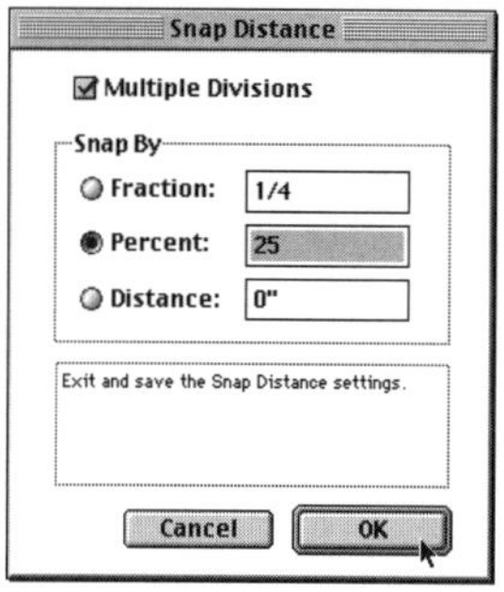

Step 2 - creating borders

If you want the sheet to always have the same divisions for details, then change the lines to the heaviest weight. Select all of the lines and use the *EDIT>Lock* command. This way the lines will not be inadvertently moved.

Step 3 - creating the guides

If you want the borders to be flexible, then it makes sense to create guide lines that you can snap to. A single sheet can be divided up into thirds and quarters at the same time so that in the future you would just draw the borders with the *Line* tool snapping to the desired divisions on the guides. It is handy to use the *Snap To Intersection* constraint when adding the actual borders.

Select all of the lines just created and select *EDIT>Guides> Make Guide*. The lines will change to a colored line. Line thickness is irrelevant to guide lines. Notice that a new class has automatically been created called *guides*. In our *saved sheet* scripts the *guides* class visibility is automatically remembered as *invisible*. Use the *Hide Guides* or *Show Guides* commands to set the visibility. When you need to print just select *Hide Guides*. Notice that the *guides* class is then made *invisible*. On the *sheets pop-up* shortcut menu, you can go to *edit sheet* and select the *details* sheet to change the default of the *guides* class to be *visible*.

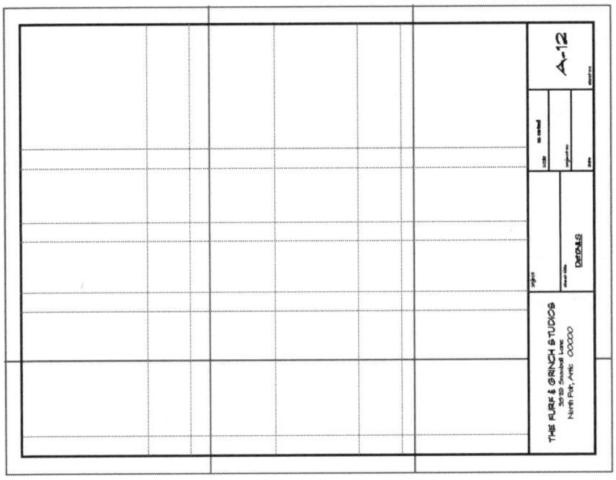

Symbols

VectorWorks comes with quite a number of symbols. Unfortunately, not all of them will look, be labeled, or have an insertion point located exactly as you would wish. It would be appropriate to import the most commonly used symbols. Once they are imported, it is easy enough to edit, rename, or even delete them without affecting the symbol in the original document.

Step 1 - importing symbols of interest

There are bunches of symbols you can import and at one point you should probably take the time to see what is in the *toolkit*. Once you have navigated all the way through to a symbol, click it in the scrolling list to select, then click the *import* button. Notice that a thumbnail diagram shows in the lower right box. Also notice that the icon in the *Resources* scrolling list looks like the icon for the *2d Symbol Insertion* tool with a 2 and/or a 3 above the icon.

This tells you if it is a 2D symbol, a 3D symbol or a hybrid symbol which has both a 2D and a 3D component. Do not import tons of symbols, since this will add to the document size, but rather import those which you think will be of use on a typical project type.

Step 2 - modifying symbols

Be aware that some symbols have several classes that also get imported. Do delete these new classes from the *Classes* dialog box and then go in and edit each imported symbol. Place the 2D and 3D components in the appropriate class for the template you are creating.

Some of the insertion points for these imported symbols are centered on the object, others are on a back corner or centered on a side - so you may want to revise the insertion point. Remember that modifying the symbol only changes the symbol in the file it was modified in and not the original symbol in the *toolkit* folder. If you do edit the symbols, remember to modify both the 2D and the 3D component in the same manner.

Step 3 - organizing symbols

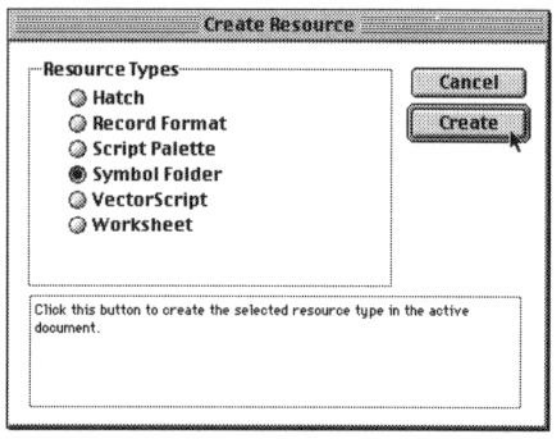

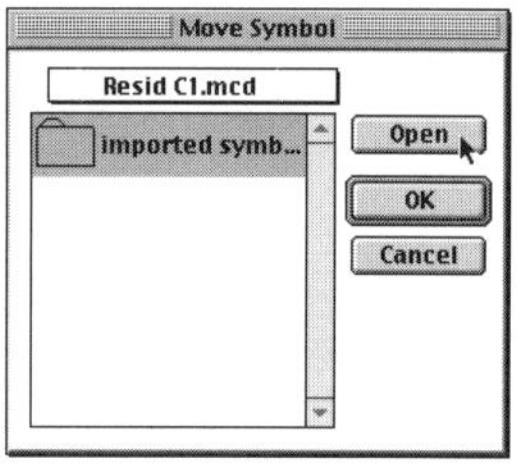

You can create folders to organize the symbols. In the *Resources* palette, click the *New* button and when the *Create Resource* dialog box opens, select *Symbol Folder*. Give it a name in the *Assign Name* dialog box. The folder will now be located in the *Resources* palette for the active file. Select an appropriate symbol to be placed in the folder and then the *Move* button. You can *Shift*-click to select several consecutive symbols to be relocated or *Command*-click [*Control*-click] for out of order multiple symbols. All symbol folders in this file will be listed in the *Move Symbol* dialog box that opens. Use the pop-out menu on top to navigate, select a folder, and then click *Open*. When you select *OK*, the symbol is placed in the folder.

Schedules

There are several schedules you might typically use in a residential project such as doors, windows, plumbing fixtures, cabinetry, and appliances. You can create the initial schedules with the headers, appropriate number of columns, and a typical number of rows. There are a variety of methods for created schedules, each with a different amount of flexibility.

Step 1 - creating a simple window schedule

If you imported a window symbol, a window record will have automatically been imported as well in the *Resources* palette. If not, to automatically create a record, select *AEC>Create Record* command. When the *Create Record* dialog box opens, select *window record* in the pop out list and *ok*.

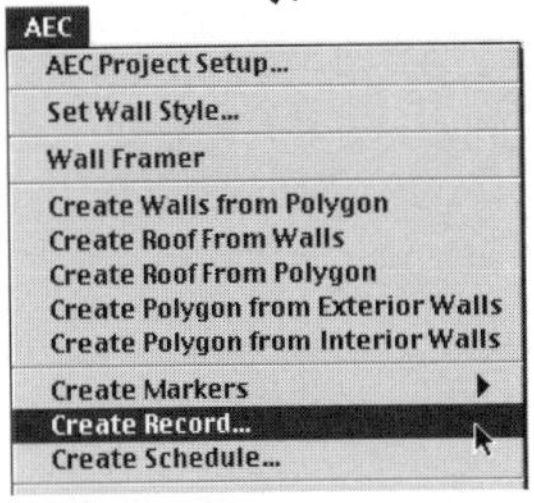

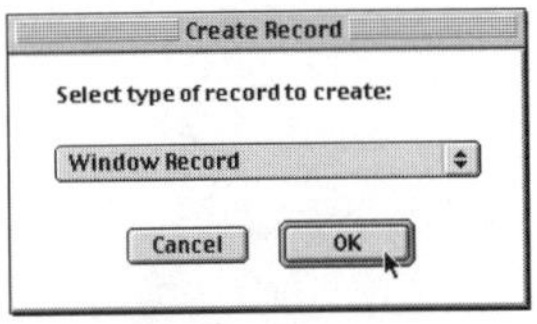

Now select *AEC>Create Schedule* and when the dialog box opens select *window schedule* from the pop up menu. The schedule will use the fields in the record we created and automatically set up the work sheet in the default font.

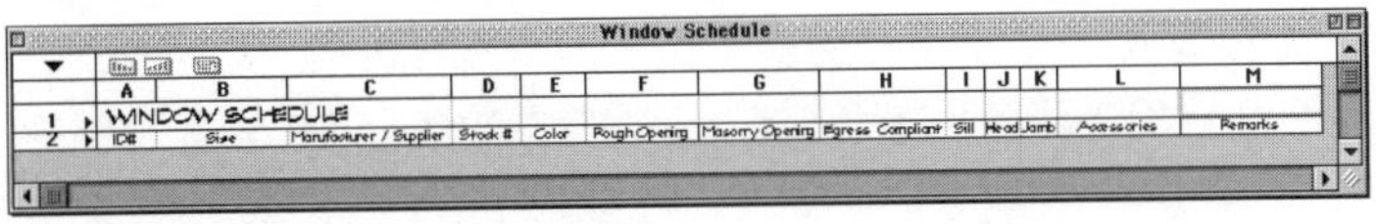

Now every time you use a symbol with this record attached, it will be listed in the *window schedule*. The imported symbols already have the record attached. If you created your own, you would need to select the symbol in the *Resources* palette and then the attach button. When the *Attach Record* dialog box opens, select the appropriate record and then the *attached* box.

Step 2 - creating a custom door schedule

If you did not want to use all of the fields in the record format, you would select the *ORGANIZE>Create Report* command. The *Create Report* dialog box opens, with a list of all of the records in the file.

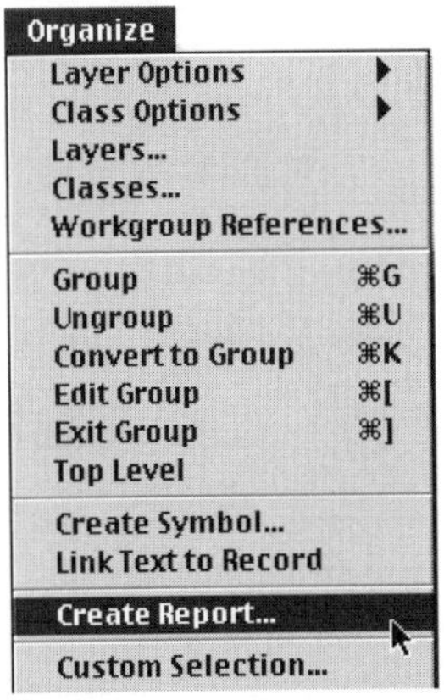

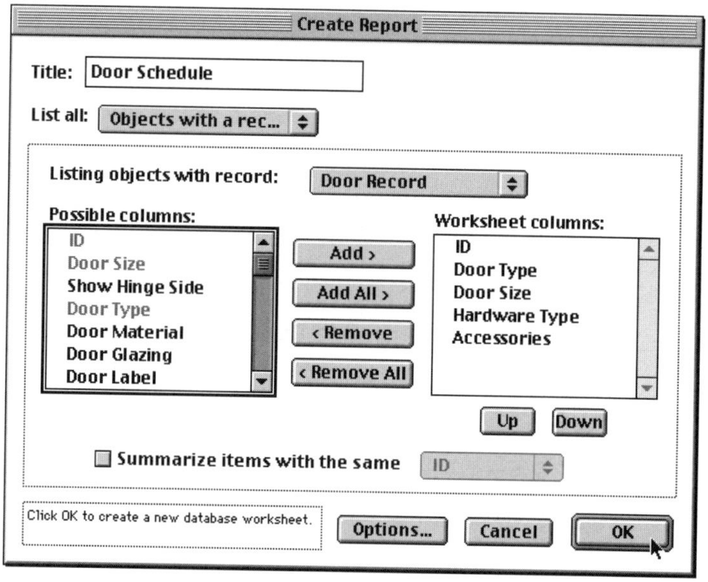

Enter the name for the report and select the desired record. Use the buttons in the center to move the desired fields from the *POSSIBLE COLUMNS* over to the *WORKSHEET COLUMNS* side. The order that the fields are listed in will be the order in the worksheet itself, so use the *UP* and *DOWN* buttons if necessary. When you click *OK*, a database worksheet will be created listing off all of the symbols or objects with the designated *door record* attached. This method does not use the default text so you will need to edit it.

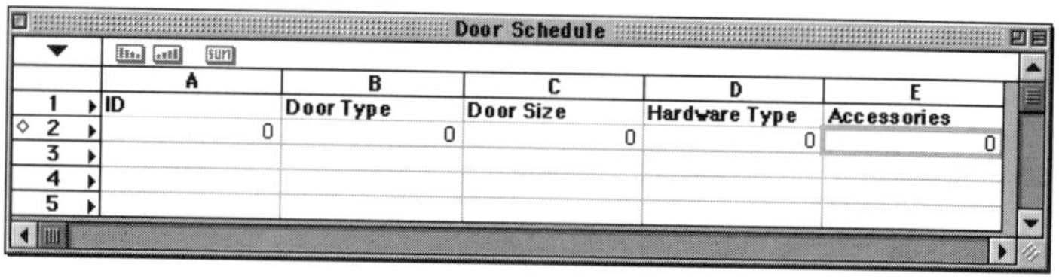

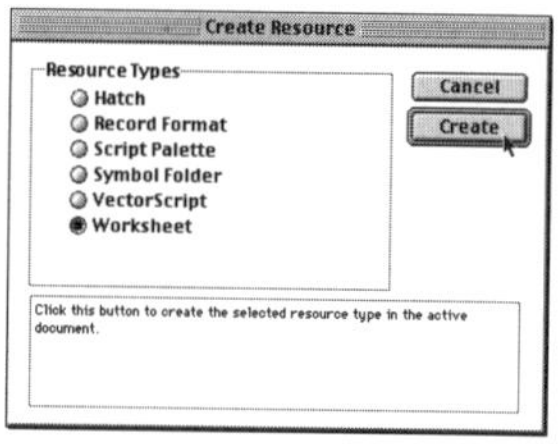

Step 3 - creating a worksheet

You may want to create a worksheet where you manually enter information into the cells. First select the *NEW* button in the *RESOURCES* palette. The *CREATE RESOURCE* dialog box opens. This time select *WORKSHEET* and click the *CREATE*

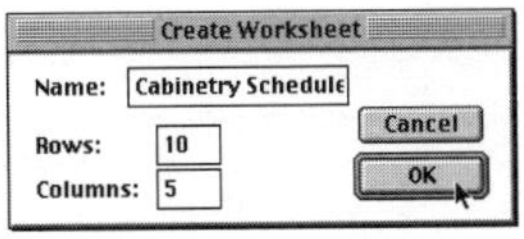

button. A *Create Worksheet* dialog box opens. Under *name*, type *cabinetry schedule*, under *rows* enter 10, and under *columns* enter 5, then click *ok*.

Step 4 - placing information in a worksheet

The new worksheet automatically opens as a floating window. If not, double-click the worksheet name in the *Resources* list. The *Worksheet Entry* window also opens with the first cell for column A, row 1 selected, allowing you to enter information in the edit box. When the worksheet is active this dialog box automatically opens. If it does not appear just click in the appropriate cell on the worksheet to make it active and have the window open.

Type the name *cabinetry schedule*. Notice the text appears in the edit box in the *Worksheet Entry* box and does not yet appear in the worksheet itself. This allows you to view the text before it gets entered. If it looks fine just hit the *Return [Enter]* key or click the ✔ box, otherwise edit it in the bar like a normal text object. This method also does not use the default text.

Click in cell A2 to select and type *ID#* and hit the *Tab* key. The text is placed in the cell and the cursor automatically moves to the right. In *B2, type size (w x ht), C2, # doors/ drwrs, D2, hardware, E2, comments.*

Hitting the *Return [Enter]* key automatically places the text in the worksheet and moves the cursor to the cell just below. Hitting the *Tab* key places the text and moves to the cell directly to the right. Clicking the ✔ places the text, but does not move the cursor to another cell. Clicking the ✘ cancels the text without any action.

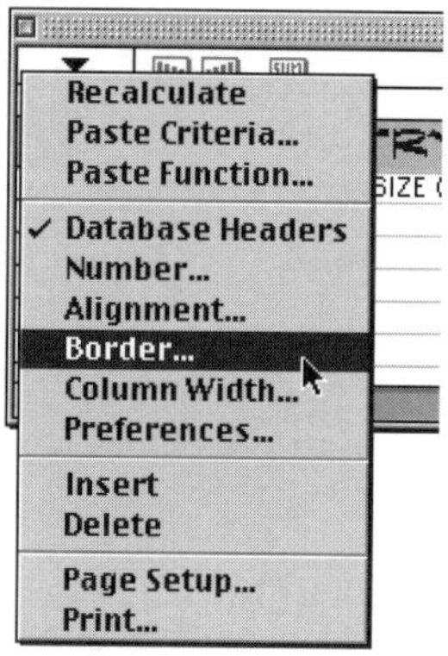

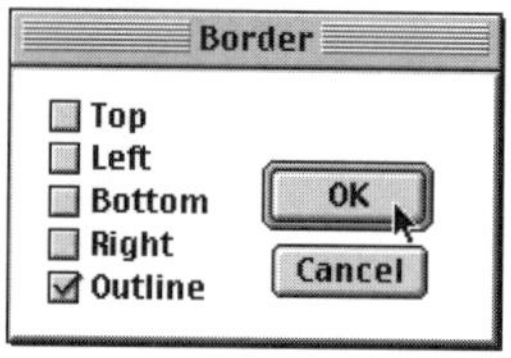

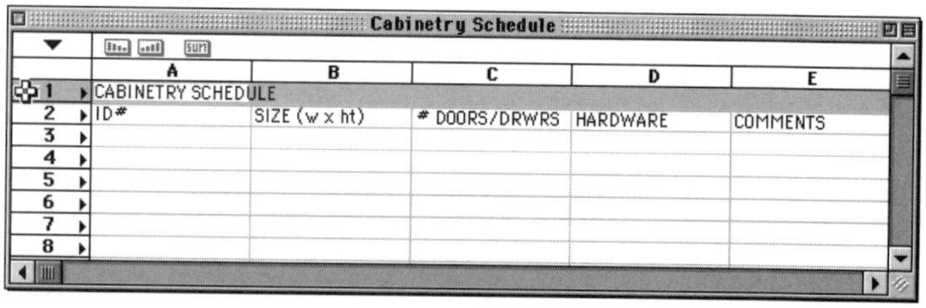

Step 5 - fine-tuning the appearance

Click the 1 to highlight the whole row and change the *Font* to the desired font, the *Size* to 18 point, and the *Style* to *Bold* all under the *TEXT* command menu title. With it still highlighted, press the arrow on the left in the worksheet and go down to *Borders*. Select *outline* and *ok*.

Click the 2 and change to the desired font, the *Size* to 14 point, and the *Style* to *Bold*. Also give it an *outline* border. Press/drag the 3 through 10 numbers to highlight these rows. Change the *Font* and the *Size* to 12 point.

Now under column A press-drag rows 2 through 10 and select *Alignment* under the left arrow giving it a *Center* alignment. Finally, click in the blank box to the left of A and above the 1 to select the whole worksheet and give it a border with an *outline*.

If the worksheet is closed by clicking the *close* box, then the *worksheet object* will appear on the drawing if *on drawing* is selected for this worksheet in the *Resources* palette. Make sure it is placed on the *first floor* layer and the *cabinetry-info* class. The worksheet can be treated like any other object and given a pen weight and color as well as a fill color and pattern. The pen just changes the outline. Select all of the *worksheet objects* and change the fill to *none* and the pen to the fourth heaviest line weight.

Some of the columns may need to be wider or narrower. Since the worksheet can not be edited directly on the drawing, the worksheet window would need to be opened by either selecting it in the *Resources* palette and clicking the OPEN button or going to *WINDOW>RESID C1.MCD> WORKSHEETS>CABINETRY SCHEDULE*. Once opened press/drag on the column separators between the letters to resize the column widths.

USING A TEMPLATE

Now that we have gone through all of these steps, the question comes up of how do we use all of the information we just created. One thing to be aware of are the classes that automatically get created with imported symbols and *plug-in* tools. Because we are using the *saved sheet* scripts, these new classes will not have appropriate visibility settings for each script. You can either edit each script or just delete these classes in the *CLASSES* dialog box. Any objects in the deleted class will automatically get moved to the *none* class.

Many times it is easier to modify an existing template in order to create a new one. The one we just created can easily be turned into a viable template for a two story residence. All you would need to do is add two layers, *second floor* and *second floor ceiling*, and then modify the Δz ($\pm z$) for the *first floor ceiling*. You would also need to adjust the visibility settings for the *saved sheets* and create new ones for this new floor.

Creating The Template

After the file is created to your satisfaction select the *title sheet* script so that the classes and layers have the correct visibility settings for the first sheet, then select the *FILE>SAVE AS TEMPLATE* command. Under *NEW FILE NAME*, enter the same name the document has been saved under. Make sure you have navigated to the appropriate folder where the document should be saved and select the *SAVE* button. A new dialog box opens and asks you if you wish to replace the existing document. Click the *REPLACE* button. Now every time this file is double-clicked to open, a new untitled document opens.

As a note, if you should wish to change anything in the original template, just open this file as a new untitled document. Make the changes to the document and do a *Save As Template* using the same name as the existing template file, same as above. Note that Windows files need *.sta* appended to the end of the file name to be saved as a template file. Also, on the Windows side, you will need to delete the original file, since the template will not automatically replace it.

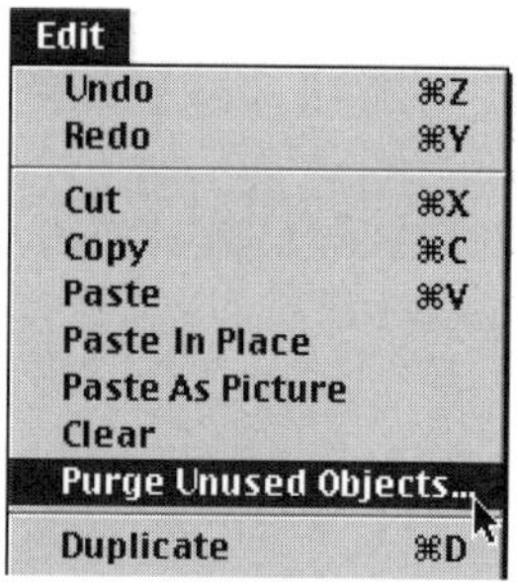

Deleting Items

After the template is all set up and being used for a project, you will find that many of the items are not necessary on a specific project. In order to make the file smaller you would get rid of those items not being used. Select the *EDIT>Purge Unused Objects* command.

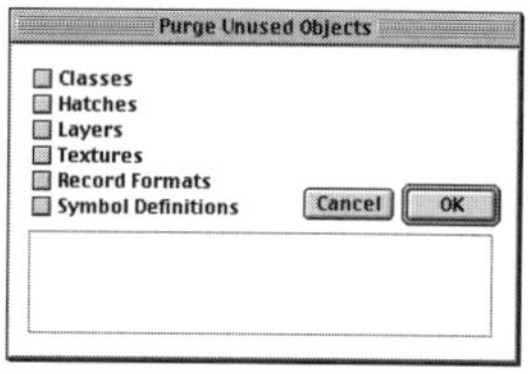

When the dialog box opens, check *symbol definitions, hatches,* and *record formats*, then *ok*. If you also choose *layers* and *classes*, you might need to adjust the *saved sheet* scripts by selecting *edit sheet* in the *sheets pop-up* shortcut menu. The unused objects will disappear from the file.

USING VECTORWORKS IN SUMMATION

As you can see by all of the topics covered in this chapter, many items can be placed within a template. The organizational art becomes just what items do you typically need, so as not to overload the document.

Basically what needs to be determined is – what are the time saving elements, whether it is easier to make another type of template, or whether it is easier to just import or create an item for a specific project. You can always place a ton of items and just use the *Purge Unused Objects* command, although there is a point when too many items make the template file unwieldy. And of course, the more you use the program the more fine-tuning can be done on the template to suit your projects and your method of working.

So, now that we have hopped into the program and skipped around many topics, you are ready to jump into VectorWorks on your own. You might want to consider the companion book, *THE WORKSMANUAL - AN INTRODUCTION AND BEYOND TO VECTORWORKS* for a more comprehensive overview and in-depth explanations. Otherwise...good luck with drawing!

INDEX

Symbols

A

B

C

D

E

F

M

N

S

T

U

V

W

Z

Order Form

Quan	Amount	
______	________	$49.00 **the WorksTutorial** - A hop, skip, and jump into VectorWorks v8
______	________	$68.00 **the WorksManual** - An introduction and beyond to VectorWorks v8 (available March 2000)
______	________	$68.00 **the WorksBook Teacher's Companion** - An instructor's guide for the WorksTutorial v8
	________	Sales tax: add 8.25% sales tax for California shipping address only
	________	Shipping:

Shipping:

US: $7.50 per book + $3.50 for each additional book
$16.00 per book + $5.00 for each additional book - 2nd day UPS
Canada: $9.00 per book
Europe/South & Central America: $11.00 per book
Asia/Africa: $22.00 per book
Pacific Rim: $13.50 per book

$ ________ **TOTAL ENCLOSED**

SHIP TO: Name ________________________

Firm ________________________

Address ________________________

____

____

PAYMENT: Check or bank draft in US currency
Credit Card: MasterCard or VISA or AmEx (circle one)

Card #: ________________________

Expiration date: ________________________

Card holder's name: ________________________

Phone number: ________________________

Signature: ________________________

Mail check orders to:

improbability press
369 South Doheny Drive Ste 189
Beverly Hills, CA 90211

Fax credit card orders to:
310-279-3705

30 day money-back guarantee

Quantity discounts available for orders of 10 books or more